Oliver Cromwell

BOOKS BY JOHN BUCHAN

OLIVER CROMWELL

By JOHN BUCHAN

'What if a man should take upon him to be king?'

With Illustrations

BOSTON

Printed by *The Riverside Press* for HOUGHTON MIFFLIN
COMPANY in PARK STREET near the COMMON

The Riverside Press
CAMBRIDGE · MASSACHUSETTS
PRINTED IN THE U.S.A.

S. C. B.

CONJUGI DILECTISSIMAE

LABORUM STUDIORUM GAUDIORUM

CONSORTI

Preface

EVERY student of the seventeenth century in England must desire sooner or later to have his say about its greatest figure. I have yielded to the temptation, partly because I wished to add to my portrait of Montrose a companion piece; partly because Oliver Cromwell has lately been made the subject of various disquisitions, especially on the Continent, which seem to me to be remote from the truth.

I can claim no novelty for my reading of him, which in substance is that of Mr. Gardiner and Sir Charles Firth; but I have examined certain aspects of his life in greater detail than these historians. My aim has been, in the words of Edmund Gosse, to give 'a faithful portrait of a soul in its adventures through life.' I hope I may claim that at any rate I have not attempted to constrain a great man in a formula.

The authorities are familiar and have for the most part been printed. To earlier scholars I owe a debt which is too obvious to need specifying, but which I most gratefully acknowledge. What new manuscript material I have had access to has been useful chiefly for elaborating the background. I have been sparing in my notes, confining my documentation to points which are still dubious, or on which my view differs from that generally held; but I have been careful to give full references for all Oliver's own written and spoken words.

J. B.

ELSFIELD MANOR, OXON.
June, 1934

Abbreviations

A. P. S.	*Acts of the Parliaments of Scotland.* **12 vols.** 1834–75.
Anc. & Loth. Corr.	*Correspondence of Sir Robert Kerr, first Earl of Ancram, and his son William, third Earl of Lothian.* 2 vols. 1875.
Baillie	*Letters and Journals of the Rev. Robert Baillie.* 3 vols. 1841.
Balfour	*Historical Works (Annales) of Sir James Balfour.* 4 vols. 1824–25.
Burnet, *Mem. of the Hamiltons*	*The Memoirs of James and William, Dukes of Hamilton,* by Gilbert Burnet, 1677.
Burnet, *Own Time*	*History of His Own Time,* by Gilbert Burnet. 2 vols. 1724.
C. J.	*Journals of the House of Commons,* 1547–1714. 17 vols.
C. P.	*The Clarke Papers* (ed. Firth). Camden Soc. 4 vols. 1891–1901.
Cal. S. P. Dom.	*Calendar of State Papers, Domestic.*
Clarendon, *Hist.*	*History of the Rebellion,* by Edward, Earl of Clarendon (ed. Macray). 6 vols. 1888.
Clarendon, *Life*	*The Life of Edward, Earl of Clarendon.* 2 vols. 1857.
Clarendon S. P.	*State Papers Collected by Edward, Earl of Clarendon.* 3 vols. 1767–86.
E. H. R.	*English Historical Review.*
Firth, *C. A.*	*Cromwell's Army,* by Sir C. H. Firth. 1902.
Firth, *H. of L.*	*The House of Lords during the Civil War,* by Sir C. H. Firth. 1910.
Firth, *Last Years*	*The Last Years of the Protectorate,* by Sir C. H. Firth. 2 vols. 1909.
Fortescue	*The History of the British Army,* vol. I, by Hon. Sir John Fortescue. 1899.
Gardiner, *Civil War*	*History of the Great Civil War,* by S. R. Gardiner. 4 vols. 1893.
Gardiner, *Comm. & Prot.*	*History of the Commonwealth and Protectorate,* by S. R. Gardiner. 4 vols. 1903.
Gardiner, *Const. Docs.*	*The Constitutional Documents of the Puritan Revolution.* Ed. by S. R. Gardiner. 1906.
Gardiner, *Hist.*	*History of England,* by S. R. Gardiner. 10 vols. 1886.
Hist. MSS. Comm.	*Reports of the Royal Commission on Historical Manuscripts.*

Hodgson	*Autobiography of Captain John Hodgson.* 1882.
Hutchinson	*Memoirs of the Life of Col. John Hutchinson,* by his widow (ed. Firth). 2 vols. 1885.
L. J.	*Journals of the House of Lords,* 1528–1714. 18 vols.
L. & S.	*Cromwell's Letters and Speeches,* by Thomas Carlyle (ed. Lomas). 3 vols. 1904.
Lans. MSS.	*Lansdowne Manuscripts.* (British Museum).
Ludlow	*Memoirs of Edmund Ludlow* (ed. Firth). 2 vols. 1894.
Noble	*Memoirs of the Protectorate House of Cromwell,* by Mark Noble. Ed. 1787.
North MSS.	*Papers of the North Family* (Bodleian).
O. P. H.	*The Parliamentary... History of England... to the Restoration of Charles II.* (*The Old Parliamentary History.*) 24 vols. 1751–62.
Prayer Coll.	*Corrispondenza dei rappresentanti genovesi a Londra* (ed. Carlo Prayer). Genoa. 1882.
Rel. Baxt.	*Reliquiae Baxterianae,* 1696
Rushworth	*Historical Collections of Private Papers of State, etc.,* by John Rushworth. 8 vols. 1721.
S. H. S.	Scottish History Society.
Sandwich MSS.	*Papers of the first Earl of Sandwich.* (Hinchingbrooke.)
Sprigge	*Anglia Rediviva... being the history of the... Army under Sir Thomas Fairfax,* by J. Sprigge, 1647.
Thurloe	*A Collection of the State Papers of John Thurloe, etc.* (ed. Birch). 7 vols. 1742.
Trans. of R. H. S.	*Transactions of the Royal Historical Society.*
Walker	*Historical Discourses upon several Occasions,* by Sir Edward Walker. 1705.
Warwick	*Memoirs of the Reign of King Charles I., etc.,* by Sir Philip Warwick. 1702 and 1813.
Whitelocke	*Memorials of the English Affairs, etc.,* by Bulstrode Whitelocke. 1682.

(Th.) refers to the Thomason collection of tracts in the British Museum. The press numbers will be found in Mr. G. K. Fortescue's *Catalogue.* 2 vols. 1908.

Contents

BOOK V. THE PRINCE

Illustrations and Maps

Book One
THE COUNTRYMAN

Chapter I

THE STAGE

(1599–1642)

The sun's o'ercast with blood: fair day, adieu!
Which is the side that I must go withal?
I am with both: each army hath a hand;
And in their rage, I having hold of both,
They whirl asunder and dismember me.

King John.

A GREAT man lays upon posterity the duty of understanding him. The task is not easy even with those well-defined, four-square personalities, who belong to a recognizable type, whose purpose was single and whose career was the product of obvious causes; for we have still in our interpretation to recover an atmosphere which is not our own. It is harder when the man in question falls under no accepted category, and in each feature demands a new analysis. It is hardest of all with one who sets classification at defiance, and seems to unite in himself every contrary, who dominates his generation like some portent of nature, a mystery to his contemporaries and an enigma to his successors. In such a case his interpreter must search not only among the arcana of his age, its hidden forces and imponderable elements, but among the profundities of the human spirit.

Oliver Cromwell has long passed beyond the mists of calumny. He is no longer Hyde's 'brave bad man'; still less is he the hypocrite, the vulgar usurper, the bandit of genius, of Hume and Hallam. By common consent he stands in the first rank of greatness, but there is little agreement on the specific character of that greatness. He is admired by disciples of the most divergent faiths. Some see in him the apostle of liberty, the patron of all free communions, forgetting his attempts to found an established church and his staunch belief in a national discipline. Constitutionalists claim him as one of the pioneers of the parliamentary system, though he had little patience with government by debate, and played havoc with many parliaments. He has been hailed as a soldier-saint, in spite of notable blots on his scutcheon. He has been called a religious genius, but on his religion it is not easy to be dogmatic; like

Bunyan's Much-Afraid, when he went through the River none could understand what he said. Modern devotees of force have seen in him the superman who marches steadfastly to his goal amid the crash of ancient fabrics, but they have forgotten his torturing hours of indecision. He has been described as tramping with his heavy boots relentlessly through his age, but his steps were mainly slow and hesitating, and he often stumbled.

Paradox is in the fibre of his character and career. Like Pompey, he was *suarum legum auctor ac subversor;* a devotee of law, he was forced to be often lawless; a civilian to the core, he had to maintain himself by the sword; with a passion to construct, his task was chiefly to destroy; the most scrupulous of men, he had to ride roughshod over his own scruples and those of others; the tenderest, he had continually to harden his heart; the most English of our greater figures, he spent his life in opposition to the majority of Englishmen; a realist, he was condemned to build that which could not last. Even at his death the dream-fabric was dissolving, so that Cowley, after watching the splendid funeral, could write: 'I know not how, the whole was so managed that, methought, it somewhat expressed the life of him for whom it was made — much noise, much tumult, much expense, much magnificence, much vainglory, briefly a great show, and yet, after all this, but an ill sight.' 'The joyfullest funeral I ever saw,' wrote Evelyn, 'for there were none that cried but dogs.'

He who studies Cromwell must be prepared for many conundrums. Behind him, largely explanatory of both the man and his work, lies the conundrum of his time. He lived in an era of transition, when the world was moving away from the securities of the Middle Ages and labouring to find new sanctions for the conduct of life. The seventeenth century saw the end of the wars of religion and the beginning of the wars of economic nationalism, and Cromwell stood at the point of change. It was an era of dilapidation and disintegration; dilapidation which is the breakdown of shape and line; disintegration which means the dissolving of things into minute elements. Iconoclasts there had always been, and there were iconoclasts then who would have replaced one idol by another; but more dangerous were the analysts and the atomisers under whose hand belief crumbled altogether. In politics, in thought, in religion, in art there was everywhere a dissolution of accepted things. In 1611 Bacon drew for James the picture of a happy England: 'Your People military and obedient; fit for war, used to peace. Your church enlightened with good preachers, a heaven with stars. Your judges learned and learning from you; just, and just by your example. Your nobility at a right distance between Crown and People; no oppressors of the People, no overshadowers of the Crown. Your servants in awe of your wisdom, in hope of your goodness; the fields growing from desert to garden; the City growing from wood to brick. Your merchants embracing the whole compass of the earth.' [1] It was a dreamer who spoke, and almost every detail was false. The story of the epoch is one of disillusion and disbelief, and at the same time of a furious endeavour to reach a new stability. The age of faith made one last effort to perpetuate itself before yielding to the age of reason.

Idealisms, contradictory, inept, perverted, ran riot; one man strove to preserve what was best in them and bring out of confusion a settled order; he failed, and the fervour died. The noble obscurity of the opening of the Shorter Catechism, 'Man's chief end is to glorify God and to enjoy Him for ever,' and Winstanley's vision of a commonwealth where the Scriptures were 'really and materially to be fulfilled,' [2] were exchanged for the prose of John Locke: 'The great and chief end of men uniting into commonwealths and putting themselves under government is the preservation of their property'; [3] and Milton had to seek Paradise regained within his own soul. England, never favourable to revolution, returned, with certain differences, to the old ways, and Hyde could once again eat cherries at Deptford.

I

The curtain rises upon a shaggy England. The gardenland with which we are familiar was not yet, for there was little enclosure, except in the deer-parks of the gentry, though in the richer tracts around the more thriving villages hedges had begun to define the meadows and ploughlands. There were great spaces of heath and down which were common pasture, and the farms were like those of Picardy today, with fields un-

[1] *Works*, VI, 452.
[2] *A New-Year's Gift for the Parliament and Armie*, 1650 (Th.).
[3] *Two Treatises of Government*, II, ix, § 124.

marked except by the outline of the crops. The roads, even the main highways, were rudimentary, and over large areas impassable in snow or flood. Around the habitable places flowed the wilds of an older England, the remnant of those forests which had once lain like a fur over the country, and in their recesses still lurked an ancient vagabondage. A man could walk in primeval woodland from the Channel to the Tees, and on heather from the Peak to the Forth.

But, since the land had had a century of peace, the England of the Tudors had slowly changed. The villages, with their greens, churches and manor houses, had now more stone and brick than oak and plaster. The new security had made houses which were once forts expand into pleasaunces and gardens. The towns were stretching beyond their mediæval limits into modest suburbs, and London was spreading fast into her northern and western fields. The nation was still a rural people; a town-dweller had open country within view, and was as familiar as the villager with rustic sounds and sights, and even in London the Fleet Street linen-draper could cross Tottenham hill on a May morning for a day's fishing. There was as yet no harsh barrier between city and country.

This uniformity was varied by two strong forces in the national life, the distinctions of locality and of class. The cities had still the mediæval particularism; they were tenacious of their liberties, jealous of their burgher rights, not to be dictated to by king or parliament, and they had their own militia for defence. Only London, Bristol and Norwich had more than 10,000 inhabitants, but every township under its ancient charter was to itself a little kingdom. In landward parts each district had its special customs and its vigorous local patriotism, so that a man from Yorkshire was almost a foreigner to a man from Somerset, and in any dispute the first loyalty would be owed to the tradition of a man's own countryside. These traditions were curiously varied, so that it is not easy to define a temper as common to the whole nation. Party attachments in their ordinary sense had not begun, but provincial ties were never so binding. The plain man, gentle or simple, who was used to following the fashion, was certain in the eastern counties, in Buckinghamshire, and in Northamptonshire to be something of a radical and a puritan, while in Kent and in Cornwall and in the north he could be counted upon to be staunch for church and king. This localism, bequeathed from the Middle

Ages, led to a snug and idiomatic life, grounded deep in the soil and tenacious of its heritage. Herrick's lore

> of may-poles, hock carts, wassails, wakes,
> Of bridegrooms, brides, and of their bridal cakes

would be cherished the more because the dwellers fifty miles off told the same tale with a difference. The vigour of this local life meant that it would be long before a public matter became an intimate concern of the whole land, and that in any such dispute half the nation would take sides at the start because of fantastic and irrational loyalties.

The other force which broke the uniformity of English life, that of class distinction, was still in the making. The scale ascended from the vagabond and broken man to the labourer and the small craftsman; to the tenant-farmer and the yeoman in the country and the merchants and artificers in the towns; then in the cities to the merchant-adventurer, and in the country through the lesser gentry to the great landowners. Of these grades two had come to special prominence. The city merchant on the grand scale, with a holding in companies that traded in the ends of the earth, had now so many points of contact with public affairs that he had perforce to become something of a politician. The yeoman, owning his own land, was a pioneer in new methods of agriculture, an independent figure with a vote for parliament, one who was inclined to think his own thoughts and ask no man's leave. He was the link between the peasantry and the gentry, the most solid thing in England, wearing russet clothes, in Fuller's words, but making golden payment. As for the gentry, there was as yet no sharp cleavage by vocation. A younger son did not lose rank through adopting a trade. A Poyntz of Midgham did not feel his Norman blood degraded by the fact that his father was a London upholsterer and that he had been born over the shop in Cornhill. Something of this liberality was due to the fact that the nobility had been comprehensively leavened by the new Tudor creations. The Bohuns and Mortimers and Mowbrays had gone, and the new grandees were nearer to the commonalty. They had been largely made by the Crown, but they were for the Crown only so long as the Crown did not tamper with their privileges and fortunes. The Whig oligarchy of a later age was already in the making. They were a ruling class, not a caste, and therefore they were realist and not romantic; they might oppose the king, but it would not be for the sake of the people, for they had little concern with whimsies about popular rights. When the clash came the great houses were largely neutral or against the Throne; for loyalty on the old pattern we must look to the smaller gentry who had more ancient strains in their blood and less to lose.

Such was the face of England to a superficial observer in the opening seventeenth century. A foreign traveller with an eye in his head would have reported that the long peace had made the country prosperous and the people content. The new poor law preserved a semblance of order, and there was far less ostensible misery than in other lands. He would have noted a great middle class, running from the yeoman up to a point short of the higher nobility, which had the same kind of education and which mixed freely. Above all he would have recorded a vigorous provincial feeling, which it would be hard, short of a great foreign menace, to unify for any national purpose. Much of the government of England was done locally by the justices in the country and the corporations in the towns, and to the ordinary citizen the Throne was a faraway thing. He would have added that the great nobles, secure in their vast estates, had less need to be courtiers than elsewhere.

But the face of England was not the heart of it. A shrewd observer might have detected some perilous yeast at work in men's souls.

II

The era of the economist had not yet dawned, but social conditions were preparing for him. In the Middle Ages English industry and trade had been largely regulated by religious discipline. The sixteenth century saw the breakdown of all the old relationships; mediæval rural society collapsed with the weakening of feudal ties and the secularizing of church lands; the gilds lost their power, and the private capitalist emerged; commerce organized itself on an international basis; landowners regarded their estates not as a nursery of men-at-arms but as a source of financial profit. The old church had frowned upon usury, and therefore upon capitalism, but that tabu was beginning to fade out of the intellectual air. Luther, indeed — at heart a monk and a peasant — had small sympathy with this consequence of the Reformation,[1] but Calvin, the middle-class

---

[1] See Schapiro, *Social Reform and the Reformation* (1909), and the quotations from Luther in Troeltsch, *Die Soziallehren der Christlichen Kirchen* (1912).

lawyer, provided, perhaps unwittingly, its theoretic justification. Calvinism began in the towns, its protagonists were craftsmen, attorneys, and traders, its creed was largely built upon Roman law and the Jewish Old Testament. It made commercial practice respectable by making the virtues which led to success in it virtues acceptable to God — thrift, austerity, an adamantine discipline. It made the middle classes a self-conscious and self-confident order, revolutionaries as against the elder society, but stout upholders of their new-won privileges. 'The bourgeoisie,' Karl Marx has written, 'whenever it got the upper hand, put an end to all feudal, patriarchal, idyllic relations, pitilessly tore asunder the motley feudal ties that bound man to his "natural superiors," and left remaining no other bond between man and man than naked self-interest and callous cash payment.' [1]

The seventeenth century opened in economic disequilibrium. Currency problems had been acute during Elizabeth's reign, due partly to the depreciation of the lighter and smaller coinage and partly to the vast influx of precious metals into Europe from the Spanish colonies. When Charles I came to the throne rents and prices were calculated to have risen during the previous century by between three and four hundred per cent. This meant a fall in real wages and much suffering for the poor, a problem with which the new poor law was intended to cope; it meant, too, an increasing stringency in the finances of the Crown, with fateful results in the near future. But high prices brought prosperity to many classes; the capitalists, great and small, the nobles with their square miles of territory, the yeoman and the tenant-farmer who got a better return for their labours, and, being self-supporting, did not feel the increase in the cost of their modest purchases. An age of social dislocation is usually an age of social speculation, and at first there had been many who dreamed of a Reformation which would not only purge the church but recast society. Bucer, the tutor of Edward VI, had advocated a kind of Christian socialism under which prices should be fixed and profits limited, and the State

[1] In *Das Kommunistische Manifest* quoted by Tawney, *Religion and the Rise of Capitalism*, 269. 'It is not wholly fanciful to say that, on a narrower stage, but with not less formidable weapons, Calvin did for the *bourgeoisie* of the sixteenth century what Marx did for the proletariate of the nineteenth, or that the doctrine of predestination satisfied the same hunger for an assurance that the forces of the universe are on the side of the elect as was to be assuaged in a different age by the doctrine of historic materialism.' *Ibid.*, 111–112.

should supervise the methods of industry and agriculture;[1] while Latimer with his fiery eloquence had taught the social responsibilities of wealth and the title of the poor man to the rich man's surplus.[2] But by the second decade of the seventeenth century such dreams had vanished from high places, and had gone underground to be brooded over by the humble. The antithesis that remained was between the paternalism which the Stuarts had inherited from the Tudors, and the self-confident individualism of the new age. A remnant of the mediæval economy, with the Crown behind it, was arrayed against the rudimentary first economics of the modern world.

The Tudors had had no doubts about their course. Their business was to make the central government all-powerful, and economic individualism seemed to them as much a peril as the jurisdictions and privileges of turbulent nobles. They were determined upon securing a united people, with separate functions allotted to each class, and a watchful paternal government over all. They attempted to regulate wages and prices and rates of interest, to curb the oppressive landlord and trader, to ordain methods in industry, commerce and farming. By the grant of patents and monopolies they desired to give the Crown as representing the nation a direct interest in private enterprise.[3] The spirit was the spirit of Laud — on his better side; its philosophy was eloquently laid down by Hooker; perverted as was its practice, there was greatness in a creed which held that the State was no mere arrangement to meet the convenience of the citizens, but an organic and mystic brotherhood, the temporal pattern of the kingdom of God. On this point at any rate the extremists of royalism and of revolution were at one.

But such a faith was out of tune with an age of which individualism had become the keynote. The disintegration had gone too far for much of the old cement to hold. Already in the first years of the century a different gospel was being preached. 'All free subjects are born inheritable, as to their land, so also to the free exercise of their industry, in those trades whereto they apply themselves and whereby they are to live. Merchandise being the chief and richest of all others, and of greater extent and importance than all the rest, it is against the natural right and liberty of the subjects of England to re-

[1] *De Regno Christi.*   [2] *The Fifth Sermon on the Lord's Prayer.*
[3] See the authorities quoted by Tawney, *op. cit.*, 323-24.

strain it into the hands of some few.'¹ Here were new notions and fateful words — 'natural right,' 'liberty of the subject.' The ordinary man was beginning to deny to the State any title to interfere with his way of earning his bread and butter. What had begun under the Tudors with a dislike of the meddling ecclesiastical courts in lay matters was fast becoming a repugnance to all State interference with private business. *Laissez-faire*, the thing if not the phrase, had come into England.

This intolerance of restraint in one particular sphere drew strength from the religious faith of an important section of the people. The presbyterian, who would have coerced the whole nation into agreement with his views on the next world, would permit no man to dictate to him on the affairs of this one. It is right to emphasize the link in puritanism between business and godliness, for it was to mean much in the coming strife. The typical puritan was the small master, who owned his land or his tools, and who to keep his footing had to spend laborious days. His religion taught him to detest the vices of idleness and extravagance and to shun common pleasures, and the same abnegation was forced on him by his worldly interests. A rigid self-discipline was the necessity as well as the ideal of his life. 'All that crossed the views of the needy courtiers, the proud encroaching priests, the thievish projectors, the lewd nobility and gentry — whoever was jealous for God's glory and worship, could not endure blasphemous oaths, ribald conversation, profane scoffs, Sabbath breaking, derision of the word of God, or the like — whoever could endure a serious, modest habit or conversation, or anything good — all these were Puritans.'² Such a catalogue had an economic as well as a spiritual significance. The way of salvation was also, in most cases, the way of prosperity, for the meek would inherit the earth, as well as the kingdom of Heaven. The love of money, not money itself, was the root of all evil; it was deadly sin to forget the interests of the soul in the task of getting wealth, but if these were assured other things would be added unto them. 'Be wholly taken up in diligent business of your lawful callings,' Richard Baxter enjoined, 'when you are not exercised in the immediate service of God.'³ 'Godliness,' said another preacher, 'hath the promises of this life as well as of the life to come.'⁴

¹ *Declaration of a Committee of the House of Commons*, May 21, 1604.
² Hutchinson, I, 114–15.   ³ *Christian Directory*.
⁴ Younge, *The Poores Advocate* 1655 (Th.).

From this it was a short step to seeing material success as in some degree a proof of spiritual health, since the two sprang from cognate disciplines. The poor were no longer 'God's poor,' and poverty so far from being the state suited to a Christian was more likely to be the consequence of sin. The intense individualism of the puritan and his sense of a direct responsibility to his Maker weakened inevitably his sense of social responsibility. The way to the Celestial City lay through Vanity Fair — 'he that will go to the City, and not go through this town, must needs go out of the world'; but the pilgrim, while fleeing the vanities, might reasonably do a little lawful merchantry. Bunyan, a saint and a peasant, has an eye only on spiritual values, but the general temper of puritanism was less hostile to Mr. Save-All than to Mr. Linger-after-lust, and many notable professors had been to school with Mr. Gripeman 'in Love Gain, which is a market town in the county of Coveting, in the north.'

The English economy was moving therefore away from the ordered mediæval society towards a system where capital demanded a looser rein, an atomic society impatient of the old restraints, laying the emphasis on personal rights and individual duties. Upon this, confusing the issues and blurring the distinctions, fell the blast of theory from the laboratories of many thinkers. We must consider in greater detail the intellectual background.

III

To attempt a survey of the thought of the era is to enter a tangled world, where the shape of the wood is hard to discover and even the tall trees are choked by undergrowth. The seventeenth century had a simple cosmic philosophy, that of the old Ptolemaic universe, but inside this rudimentary framework it spun an intricate web. No age has been more deeply moved by ideas, but these ideas are not to be hastily identified with modern notions which they may at first sight resemble, since they derive from a mood and an outlook far different from our own.

Religion, as in the Middle Ages, was still interwoven with the texture of men's minds. The Council of Trent, by formulating certain dogmas which had hitherto been vague, had made final the barrier between protestant and catholic, but protestantism itself dwelt in a divided house. The spirit of the Reformation, which was on the side of freedom and simplicity and the return of Christianity to its source, had in England soon been diverted by political needs, and presently schisms were revealed in both doctrine and church government of which the origin was as much secular as religious. Moreover there was still the mediæval hankering after an absolute creed and a universal church, so that each divergence was apt to claim to be the only truth, and to admit no compromise. We shall not understand the epoch unless we realize that, though the germinating ground of many of our modern beliefs, it is also to be regarded as the closing scene of the Middle Ages. Religion coloured the whole of life, secular and sacred were indissolubly mingled, a public act was regarded not as a matter of expediency, but as linked somehow or other with the soul's salvation. God and the Devil were never absent from the political stage, and their presence led to the quickening of passion as well as to the obscuring of reason.

Let us first consider this pervading religion as exhibited in ecclesiastical bodies. The Elizabethan settlement had explicitly laid down what the Church should believe, how it should be governed, and how its services should be conducted. If protestantism chose to quarrel within itself, it was essential that England at any rate should be undivided. The royal jurisdiction was made supreme, and there was one obligatory rule of worship. The Thirty-Nine Articles crystallized theology, a prayer book regulated ritual, and around both there soon began to gather that conservative sentiment which in England quickly sanctifies innovations. Church and Throne seemed in the eyes of many to be indissolubly united, and the support of the second to be the surest defence of the first.

But the settlement contained within itself much matter of strife. Uniformity meant a strict enforcement of discipline, and the powers which Elizabeth gave to her ecclesiastical commissioners were far greater than those exercised by the courts of the old Church. The layman found his daily life harassed by new legalities. Again, anglicanism had separated itself from continental protestantism, and was admittedly a *via media* between the old and the new, and earnest iconoclasts found interwoven in the new formulas much stuff derived from that which they had been taught to reprobate. There was also a supineness and laxity in the new clerical civil-service, disquieting to serious folk. Milton saw them in their youth at college 'writhing and unboning their clergy limbs to all the antic and dishonest gestures of Trinculoes, buffoons, and bawds,' [1] and in *Lycidas* they are the 'blind mouths,' who know nothing of the craft of the shepherd: and Richard Baxter, a kindlier witness, has a vivid picture of the ecclesiastical squalor of the Shropshire of his youth.[2] But the fundamental trouble was due to the natural reaction against the absoluteness of the first Reformers. High-churchism in its modern meaning, which is the claim of a church to an overriding authority over, and complete independence in, sacred things, was unknown to the anglican of the seventeenth century; the true high-churchman in that sense was the presbyterian. The seventeenth-century anglican highchurchman is to be defined by his appeal to other authority than the bare letter of the Scriptures; by his insistence that the Reformation had involved no breach of continuity with the past, and that his church was catholic in Hooker's sense, following 'universality, antiquity and consent'; and finally, since he believed in a uniform national church, by his clinging to the authority of the Crown. He was an Arminian in doctrine, since the Calvinistic predestination led inevitably to an atomic individualism; and, though he had little sympathy with the extravagant royalism of men like Sibthorpe and Manwaring, he looked in practice to the king as the court of ultimate appeal.

Within the Church there were elements like Falkland and his friends that stood for liberty before authority, championed the right of private judgment, and desired a church of 'volunteers and not of pressed men,' and there were those that followed Laud and sought one rigid pattern of thought and worship under the aegis of the Throne. Between these extremes lay the great mass of plain citizens who had acquired a sentimental attachment to an institution not a century old, who valued decency and order above prophetic fervours, and preferred to think of their church as holding an honest, comprehensible, royal warrant. They were Erastians in the ordinary sense of that disputed term, for they asserted the omnipotence of the secular State as against the clericalism of Rome and Geneva. Theology was not a branch of politics — the State in its ecclesiastical policy must obviously take counsel with the experts — but assuredly politics were not a branch of theology.

Such moderation as existed in the early seventeenth century

[1] *Apology for Smectymnuus.*   [2] *Rel. Baxt.*, 13.

is in the main to be looked for in the Church. But it was a mood rather than a faith, based on apathy and mental indolence as much as on conviction, and therefore it could not have the compelling power of the extremer creeds. The dynamic force in anglicanism lay rather in the rigidity of a man like Laud, who was rational in doctrine and the patron of Hales and Chillingworth, but in ritual and government was a fanatic apostle of uniformity. Those on every side who believed in their creeds were agreed on one thing, that toleration was deadly sin, and that they must spend themselves to enforce compliance with that in which they believed. In the last resort only the State could ensure this enforcement, and therefore the State must be brought to their way of thinking. The Civil War in one aspect may be regarded as the struggle of various communions for the control of the secular arm.

As against the moderates and the *politiques* stood the school of thought, inside and outside the Church, which may be called in the largest sense puritan. It represented the last wave of the impulse which made the Reformation, coming as a new surge when the first great tidal movement had become slack water. To begin with, it was a stirring within the Church itself, due to a special conception of what that Church's character should be. Under Elizabeth there were puritans in high places — Burleigh and Leicester, Jewel and Grindal; the Elizabethan adventurers had a puritan tincture, like Sir William Smyth, the first governor of the East India Company; Hakluyt and Purchas and John Walker, the friend of Drake, were puritans. At first the bond of connection was merely a desire to purge the usages of the Church from all taint of romanism. In 1603 the aim of puritans, as shown by the Millenary Petition, was only that their preference for simplicity should be legalized. But the harsh treatment of the protesting divines hardened and enlarged their dissidence. They became first indifferent and then hostile to episcopal government. Forced back upon themselves, they developed ever increasing points of divergence from the conforming majority. They ceased to ask merely for toleration, and became a reforming and a disruptive force both in Church and State. To a belief in simplicity of worship they added a passion for simplicity of life. Doctrinally they tended to emphasize what was harshest in Calvinism as against the lax Arminianism of their opponents. They found in the Scriptures a stern moral code, and became rigid censors of conduct.

The term puritan began to be defined popularly by its extreme sense, and with justice, for the extremist was the essential puritan. A measure of puritanism was indeed almost universal in a fear of romanizing influence, of high-flying clergy, and of government by ecclesiastics, so that in 1625 Pym could complain with truth that Laud under the name of puritans 'collecteth the greatest part of the king's true subjects.'[1] But the dynamic power was in the few who, with the Bible as their base, were prepared to admit no impediment of tradition to the liberty of their interpretation, and waited hourly on a new revelation. No more significant words were spoken than those of John Robinson, the pastor of the Pilgrim Fathers, on the eve of their departure. 'The Lord has more truth yet to bring forth out of His Holy Word.... I beseech you to remember it — 'tis an article of your church covenant — that you be ready to receive whatever truth shall be made known to you.'[2] In such a mood of utter confidence and tense expectation lay the certainty of revolution.

Outside the Church puritan dissent manifested itself in two main groups. The first was presbyterianism, which drew its inspiration from the Genevan and French churches; its central doctrines were the priesthood of all believers and parity among ministers; and on these fundamentals there was based a system of government by lay elders, a system in essence unclerical and democratic. At first it was the creed of a party inside the Church; 'almost all those who were later called Presbyterians,' wrote Richard Baxter, 'were before conformists';[3] and such antecedents saved English presbyterianism from the supreme intransigence of the Scottish Kirk. It was the creed of a considerable part of the nobility, of a great mass of country gentry, and of the solid merchants of London, and it was adopted by many because it seemed to represent a middle way. But, even in its English form, it involved certain perilous extensions. It asserted the separate kingdoms of Church and State, but it was always in danger of blurring the outlines, and demanding for the first the powers and functions of the second. Moreover it claimed to be the only church, since it was based on *jus divinum*, and, as defined by men like Cartwright and Goodman, it required that the State should compel the nation into its fold. Its creed led logically to a theocracy, and its apparent

---

[1] *Pym's Report*, 1625 (Camden Society), 179.
[2] Neal, *Hist. of the Puritans*, II, 110, etc.   [3] *Rel. Baxt.*, 33.

anti-clericalism to a clericalism as strict as Rome's. There was justice in the words of a later critic that presbyterianism in its seventeenth century form was 'inconsistent with all government except its own oligarchic spiritual tyranny, and even with that adored Democracy which it pretends to hug and embrace with so much tenderness and affection.' [1]

Presbytery believed in an organic church, with a graded hierarchy of government, but the other group, the independents, stood for the sovereignty of the smaller unit, the congregation. There is no such disruptive force as a common creed held with a difference, and the hostility between presbyterians and independents was mainly due to their different conceptions of popular rule. Descending through devious ways from outlawed continental sects, the latter asserted not the liberty of the individual but the liberty and authority of the worshipping unit, and since they admitted no higher ecclesiastical constraint their views involved a measure of toleration. They had not the jealousy of the civil magistrate which their opponents displayed, for he might be their only buckler against an intolerant universal church; if they were left at peace within their own little communion they had no desire to interfere with others. To Laud they were schismatics, a blot on the fair pattern he had designed, and, to the presbyterian, Laodiceans and heretics in the fundamentals. 'The Independents,' wrote the exasperated Robert Baillie, 'have the least zeal to the truth of God of any men we know.' [2]

Behind all ecclesiastical parties in England, shaping them without the knowledge of the partisans, lay a profound dread of Rome. The Tudors had defied the Pope with ease, but they had weaned with difficulty the people of England from the ceremonies of the ancient Church. Yet by the close of the sixteenth century the fissure had become a chasm. The danger from Spain had identified protestantism with patriotism; events on the Continent — the massacre of St. Bartholomew, the success of the Counter-Reformation, the circumstances which gave rise to the Thirty Years War — impressed the ordinary Englishman with the power and malignance of the Church which he had forsaken; and the Marian persecutions at home became a legendary horror as presented by popular writers. The Reformation in the eyes of many was still in jeopardy. Moreover England contained, in spite of the penal laws, a great multitude

---

[1] Nalson, *Common Interest of King and People*, ch. IX.   [2] Baillie, II, 361.

of Romanists, and, since an exact computation was impossible, their numbers were exaggerated by suspicion. Lancashire, Cheshire and North Wales were catholic strongholds, and, except in the east, every shire could show a catholic nucleus. The typical English catholic, who desired only to be allowed to follow his worship in peace, was obscured by the missionary activity of the Jesuits, whose purpose was avowedly to win back England to their faith. Their method was the assertion of popular rights as against the monarchy, and the doctrines of Bellarmine and Suarez, which were given an English version by writers like Doleman,[1] seemed to have perilous affinities with the politics of the ultra-protestants. The consequence was a wide distrust and a profound hatred of Rome. To the puritan she was the mother of idolatry, a splendid edifice which, like an Egyptian temple, had in its inner shrine a cat or a crocodile; to the royalist she was the foe of kings and of all secular government, the more to be feared because his English opponents seemed to be tainted with her poison;[2] while to the ordinary man she was the 'wolf with privy paw,' an enduring menace to England's ways and English freedom. To most men, as to Thomas Hobbes, she was the 'kingdom of darkness'; therefore one section sought to purge from their church whatever savoured of her in creed and worship, while another, with more political foresight, strove to set up against the power of the Keys the sacrosanctity of the Crown.

The ecclesiastical unrest was determined mainly by historical causes and by economic and political pressures. Pure theory played but a minor part, and there was little of the mediæval heresy-hunting. Even the dispute about church government was at first conducted on practical rather than on academic grounds, the purpose with most men being not so much the discovery of an absolute revelation as the fashioning of something orderly and enduring — in the spirit of Bruno's apophthegm, 'If the first button of a man's coat be wrong buttoned, then the whole will be crooked.' In matters of doctrine there was to begin with little argumentative fervour, except over the eucharist. Calvinism in England was more a communion and a way of life than a body of dogma, Arminianism a tendency

[1] See his *Conference about the Next Succession to the Crown of England*, 1593.
[2] 'These men cry out against Popery, and yet profess what all good Protestants esteem the most malignant part of Jesuitism.' Dudley Digges, *The Unlawfulness of Subjects taking up Arms*, 64 (Th.).

rather than a tenet. As in all such epochs, there were minds that sought the kernel and not the shell of truth. The rationalism of *All's Well That Ends Well* — 'They say miracles are past; and we have our philosophical persons to make modern and familiar things supernatural and causeless' — had its modest disciples, but its spirit was still almost wholly Christian. Platonism, at once devout and sceptical, combined a passion for the unseen and the eternal with joy in the seen and temporal; it heard, with George Herbert, 'churchbells beyond the stars' and not less, with Thomas Traherne, exulted in the richness of the visible world.[1] But as the years passed the struggle became more bitter and the antagonisms sharper, dogmas which had been only vague inclinations took definite shape when they were contraverted, and the most tolerant were forced into a confession of faith. The overriding controversies, which in the last resort shaped all the sectarian and party wrangles, were narrowed to two; what was the true relation between a church and a civil society, and to what degree was a man to be permitted to find his religion for himself.

IV

'I had as lief be a Brownist as a politician,' said Sir Andrew Aguecheek, but the happy aloofness of Shakespeare's age was gone, and politics had become the nation's daily bread. The practical problem was how the State was to take over the direction of that side of human life which had been the province of the old Church, and how the intricacies of feudalism could be superseded by a simpler and more unified system. It was a problem for all Europe, and on the Continent it was solved in the main by an increase in monarchical absolutism. The State everywhere had to take cognizance of more and more social interests and not confine itself to public order and national defence. But England was not prepared for any such summary answer, having in her bones an old tradition of law and popular consent. Protestantism, as we have seen, was a dissolvent on the political as well as on the religious side, for, like a new chemical added to a compound, it left no element unchanged. There were those who sought an answer in a restoration of what they believed to be the ancient custom of the land — which is the reason why, in the first year of the Long Parlia-

[1] See Traherne's *Serious and Pathetical Contemplation of the Mercies of God.*

ment, conservative royalists like Falkland and Hyde, Capel
and Hopton, worked harmoniously with Pym and Hampden.
There were others who sought not restoration but revolution,
and on this issue the ultimate battle was joined. It became a
matter of the interpretation of 'law,' and the theorists on all
sides were forced to a growing abstractness, so that political
thought tended more and more to adopt the categories of dogmatic theology. The nascent physical science provided a few
conceptions; the notion of a constitutional balance or equilibrium, for example, was common to both Harrington and
Cromwell.[1] But even the secular thinker was forced by the prevailing atmosphere to give his conclusions a semi-religious sanction.[2] Let us glance briefly at the main ideas which formed the
intellectual background to the political strife.

The first is the famous dogma of the divine right of kings.
James I, lacking the wisdom of his Tudor predecessors, chose to
theorize about the prerogative instead of contenting himself
with using it. His crude assumptions met with a not less crude
rejoinder, and the excess of his claim was equalled by the
exaggerations of the counter-claim; if Bacon, for example,
would have made the judiciary a slave of the Crown, Coke
would have exalted it above Crown and parliament. But the
doctrine of divine right, rationally stated, had a sound historical
warrant. It was at least as respectable as the opposite notion
of some original social compact. When extreme theories of
popular rights were promulgated, it took on a corresponding
extravagance, but in its essence it had a real justification. It
was based upon two deep popular instincts; the need for continuity in national institutions, and the need of a sanction for
the secular power not less august than had been claimed for the
mediæval church. It was the first step in the emancipation of
politics from clerical interference and in the development of
the organic view of the State. It was in substance anti-clerical.
'The only way to escape from the fetters imposed by traditional methods was to assert from the old standpoint of a Scriptural basis and to argue by the accustomed fashion of Biblical
quotations, that politics must be forced from theology and
that the Church must give up all attempts to control the State.

[1] *L. and S.*, III, 420.

[2] 'If the name of God is taken broadly as meaning a moral order of the universe, an
idea which was, in the seventeenth century, seldom expressed by any other word, then
all positive and optimistic theories of the state are theories of divine right.' G. N. Clark,
The Seventeenth Century, 223.

The work of the Reformation was to set men free in all departments of thought and enquiry from subjection to a single method and a single subject. In the case of politics the achievement of this result was possible only through claiming at first theological sanction for the non-theological view of politics. Only when this result is achieved will politics be free to develop theories which shall be purely philosophical and historical.'[1]

The instinct which gave the doctrine birth may have been utilitarian, but it soon acquired a mystical element. Men may be faithful to institutions, but their passionate loyalty is reserved for persons, and in an unfaltering fidelity to a king many found a firm lodgment among the quicksands. The Throne attracted to itself an imaginative glamour which was the last sunset glow of the Middle Ages. Its occupant, bearing divine authority, was priest as well as king. When Charles before his execution was denied his chaplains, he could say — and his words found an echo in many hearts — that it was no matter, since the regal and sacerdotal offices were one.

The second class of germinal idea was connected with sovereignty and law. Where lay the ultimate authority — in the people at large, in parliament as representing the people, in a divinely ordained king, or in some mystical body of custom and ordinance which bore the name of Law? Some answer must be found if government was to be carried on. There must be some final power which could make laws, and therefore was above the Law. Men were feeling their way to the Austinian conception of sovereignty, and the novelty of the idea made the different sides state their conclusions with a stark absoluteness. A clear thinker like Montrose might seek the solution in an equilibrium of rights and functions, but most minds hankered after one single, ultimate, and unquestionable fount of power. 'There is a necessity that somebody must be trusted.' The fanatics of divine right found an easy answer, but many royalists who were not of that school agreed in principle with Strafford's practical view that in the last resort there must be a power in the executive above the law, since the highest law is the safety of the people: it was Charles's blundering which discredited what today is a maxim of all government, for he acted so as to make the extreme medicine of the constitution its daily bread.

[1] J. N. Figgis, *The Divine Right of Kings*, 260.

The doctrine of a balance of powers was not acceptable in an epoch which both on practical and theoretical grounds craved for a simple dogma, and those who turned from it, as well as from the extreme view of the royal prerogative, endeavoured to find solid ground either in the rule of law or in the plenary power of parliament. The first mode of thought included many besides the lawyers like Coke whose doctrines really involved the sovereignty of the judiciary.[1] Ancient precedents looked many ways, and to give the judges the right to determine a rapidly changing constitution was to lay on them an impossible burden. The strict legalist confused the whole question, for he was in the habit of construing political principles as legal rights. But there was a profounder instinct among men of all parties in favour of a 'law fundamental' to which king and people alike were subject. This was the true sovereign, the 'law of the land'; it was cited by Charles and Montrose at their deaths, and it was the heart of Pym's attack on Strafford. Parliament men like Prynne and St. John and Selden made it their foundation and Lilburne appealed to it at his trial; but so did a royalist like Judge Jenkins, who wrote in 1647: 'The Law of this Land hath three grounds: First, Custome; Second, Judiciall Records; Thirdly, Acts of Parliament. The two latter are but declarations of the Common Law and Custome of the Realme touching Royall Government, and this law of Royall Government is the Law Fundamentall.'[2] Englishmen could not violate it if England was to remain England. The doctrine remains valid today, for there must be internal and external limits to all sovereignty.[3] But this idealization of the common law, of traditional reason and the wisdom of the ancients, provided no instrument of governance: the law fundamental might be an ultimate court of appeal and a guide in policy, but it could not control the administration of the State without putting the prerogative into the hands of the judges; moreover it had no means of change and of adaptation to new conditions. A sup-

[1] 'All things to be measured by the golden and straight metewand of the Law, and not by the uncertain and crooked cord of discretion.' 4 *Inst.*, 41.

[2] *Works* (1648), 5. In 1604 the doctrine was thus stated by the Speaker of the House of Commons. 'The Laws are of three kinds: the 1st, the Common Law, grounded and drawn from the Law of God, the Law of Nature, and the Law of Reason, not mutable; the 2nd, the positive Law, founded, changed and altered by and through the occasions and policies of times; the 3rd, Customs and Usages, practised and allowed with time's approbation, without known beginnings.'

[3] See Dicey, *Law of the Constitution*, ch. I.

pler mechanism was needed, and this was found by general consent in parliament. No royalist, it should be remembered, was hostile to parliamentary institutions as such; he opposed only what he regarded as their maleficent extension.

A great authority has called the Civil War a struggle of the common law against the king; [1] but it was also a struggle of parliament against the common law as then interpreted. Could that law be altered or added to, and, if so, by whom? This was the true question, and a lawyer of the old school was as little inclined to concede this power to parliament as to the Throne. Look on a parliament, Bacon had told James I, as not only a necessity, but as a precious means of uniting the Crown with the nation, and he advised him to have a store of 'good matters to set the Parliament on work, that an empty stomach do not feed on humour.' But James not only checked the natural development of parliament's functions in a new age, but opposed its ancient and indubitable rights. Yet no body at the start offered a more fruitful alliance, since the House of Commons represented all that was most vigorous in the nation. The growing expenses of the Crown, which were mainly the needs of the government of England, would have not found it niggardly had it been honestly taken into the royal confidence, for the Englishman, in Fuller's words, cared not how much his purse was let bleed, so it was done by the advice of the physician of the State. [2] The members were neither courtiers nor office-seekers: those long-descended squires represented in the main 'a type of character that has never reappeared in our history — directness of intention and simplicity of mind, the inheritance of modest generations of active and hearty rural life; now at last informed by Elizabethan culture; and now at last spiritualized by a Puritan religion.' [3] But parliament had to learn its business as much as the king. The House of Commons of 1621 numbered among its members men like Wentworth and Pym, Hampden and Coke and the elder Fairfax; but its conduct in the cases of Sheppard and Lloyd showed how much it lacked in decency and common sense. [4]

The first duty of the House of Commons was to safeguard its privileges which the king denied — the right of free debate

[1] Maitland, *Const. History of England*, 271.
[2] *The Holy State*, II, ch. xviii.
[3] Trevelyan, *England under the Stuarts*, 103.
[4] *Proceedings and Debates of Parliament of 1621*, I, 51, etc.

and the control of taxation, and this was the special task of Sir John Eliot, the purest and most logical of them all. It knew that it represented what was best and sanest in England, and that especially it represented England's wealth, for, as an observer said of the 1628 Parliament, it could have bought out the upper House thrice over.[1] In its defence of its privileges it had the support of the black-letter lawyers, but presently it parted company with them, for it was forced by the pressure of circumstances to demand an authority which seemed to the antiquary as alien to the constitution as the extravagant claims of the king. Step by step, since the country must be governed, it was driven to demand a legal sovereignty. The change began in 1629 after Buckingham's murder, when it attempted to lay down an ecclesiastical policy in the first of the historic resolutions which Denzil Holles put to the House. The boldness of the innovation was recognized, and at first, while divesting the king of certain prerogatives, parliament did not assume them for itself. 'We cannot,' said Pym of Charles, 'leave to him sovereign power.... We were never possessed of it.'[2] But the practical conundrum had somehow to be solved, and, conscious of popular support, it entered upon what in the eyes of the jurists was nothing short of a revolution. Its view was that of Hobbes: 'it is not wisdom but authority that makes the law.' Against it were now arrayed not only those who held the mystic view of the royal prerogative, but the sticklers for the ancient usages, the lawyers who had been the first to oppose the king, so that Milton, zealous for parliamentary omnipotence, could write of 'that old entanglement of iniquity, their gibberish laws.'[3]

What we loosely call 'democratic' ideals had scarcely come to birth in the political world, though, as we have seen, there was a certain emotional socialism and egalitarianism implicit in the Reformation. When Milton speaks of the sovereign people he only expresses his belief in the right of rebellion against political or religious oppressors. The elementary rights of the poor were better championed by the Crown than by middle-class puritans or aristocratic parliamentarians. There were strange ferments in the under-world of England, but they only revealed themselves by an occasional jet of steam from some crack in the volcanic crust. But one issue in the strife lay at the root of all democracy — the right to personal liberty,

---

[1] *Court and Times of Charles I*, I, 331.   [2] Rushworth, I, 562.
[3] *Tenure of Kings and Magistrates.*

the denial of any power to dispense with that law which normally protected a subject's life and property, the hostility to special tribunals which usurped the duties of the common courts of justice. A settled law and the equality of all men before it were claims which survived the wreckage, for they had behind them the essential spirit of England.

From such a tangle of political dogma there was little chance of escape except by violence. A nation, which is only by slow degrees becoming politically self-conscious, is apt to pin its faith to abstractions, and with abstract thinkers there can be no settlement, since each takes his stand on what he holds to be eternal truth. Puritan and Laudian clashed in a final antagonism; absolutist lawyer and absolutist revolutionary had between them no common ground. Charles's bleak abstraction of kingly honour was faced with an abstraction scarcely less bleak of a sovereign Commons. The cool Erastian had his jibe at the theological dervishes, and then, if he were a wise man, held his tongue. The political realist was forced in the end to choose the side which repelled him least, and often to die for a cause in which he only half believed.... One man alone shook himself clear of the mellay, and tried out of the chaos to build up a new England.

V

In all revolutions there is some such background of intellectual ferment as I have sketched. But the creeds of the thinkers do not make impact directly upon the national mind. Popularly there is what Joseph Glanvill called a 'climate of opinion,' which is created partly by forces from the intellectual laboratory, forces often strangely perverted, but largely by moods and notions of which the thinkers take little cognizance. To many royalists the people on the eve of the Civil War seemed to be surfeited with happiness, and the rebellion to be the crazy and perverse impulse of a nation which, in Izaak Walton's phrase, was 'sick of being well.' The truth is far otherwise. The early seventeenth century was full of maladies.

In the first place the minds of men were oppressed by a haunting insecurity. Most of the old certainties had vanished; religion was no longer an intelligible discipline directed by an infallible church, the English economy was changing fast, and government had lost the firm Tudor touch. The craving was for a new authority, a fresh assurance, some fixed point among the shifting sands, and the new sanction must be nothing short of the highest. So Omnipotence was claimed as the author of every creed brought to birth by confused mortals: there was a divine right of kings, and a divine right of presbytery; *jus divinum* in episcopal orders, in the old fabric of the laws, and in the new authority of parliament; presently there were to be whispers of heaven-bestowed rights in the common man. It was an age when everything, however crude, claimed a celestial warrant, and implicit belief in one or the other was held to be the first duty. Of Mr. Incredulity in the *Holy War* Bunyan writes that 'none was truer to Diabolus than he.'

Side by side with this passionate longing for faith went a profound sense of disillusion. There was morbidity in the air, for the mind turned back upon itself and got weary answers. The spring and summer of the world had passed and autumn was come.[1] A great mass of the commonalty was unaffected, just as a great mass of the commonalty was wholly neutral in the war; but the mood was shared by most who in whatever degree felt the compulsion of thought. In some the consequence was a cynical obeisance to what seemed the winning side, often with comical results; in others of a stouter mettle a sceptical and mocking aloofness, like that of Selden, who visited the Westminster Assembly, he said, to enjoy the Persian pastime of seeing wild asses fight. But if disillusionment resulted in some cases in worldly wisdom and in others in a politic scepticism, its effect on many was to create a disbelief in all venerated things and a predisposition to violent novelties. The strong underground current of antinomianism in religion and politics was fed as much by a melancholy satiety with the old things as by a fierce partiality for the new.

But, deeper still, lay the private concern of men with their souls and the world beyond the grave. Everywhere there was an awakening of conscience and a quickened sense of sin. This mood had indeed been widespread ever since the dawn of Christianity, but under the old church with its discipline and sacraments men had been corporately assisted to make their peace with the Almighty. Now each was left to fight out the battle

[1] For this aspect of the age see the present writer's *Montrose*, 15–19. The opposite view was urged by a few enthusiasts for the Reformation; cf. Milton's undergraduate poem *Naturam non pati Senium*, and George Hakewill's *An Apologie or Declaration of the Power and Providence of God in the Government of the World* (1627).

alone in his soul, and no help could be looked for from Mr. Two-Tongues, the parson of the parish. There might be disputes about terrestrial sovereignty, but there could be none about the awful sovereignty of God. He demanded perfect purity and exact obedience, and every human deed and thought was impure and rebellious. Grace alone could give salvation, grace through the mediation of Christ,[1] and the dogmas of theology suddenly became terribly alive, for on them hung the issues of life and death. There was an Enchanted Land, as in the *Pilgrim's Progress*, where the soul could be drugged into apathy, and all distinctions blurred; but that way lay damnation, and the only hope was to fight out the battle. The conscience had become morbidly sensitive, and the brain crazily subtle, and many went through months and years of mental agony. Those who emerged triumphant knew themselves as the children of the promise; God and Christ, in Bunyan's words, were continually before their face; their mood was one of absolute submission and passionate devotion; they marched steadfastly through the world, having passed beyond temporal fears. Such men might be apathetic about questions of civil right, having their gaze so constantly fixed upon the things beyond time; but once let these civil rights be linked in any way with moral and religious issues and they would uphold them to the death. As in the days of the Crusades, a power had been engendered which was outside politics but might well play havoc with policy, for its source lay in a sphere where ordinary political canons had no meaning.

No aerial viewpoint is high enough to bring into our vision the whole confused manifold of the epoch, and the most searching eye will scarcely find a pattern in its complexity. Creeds and moods shade into each other; the wheel repeatedly comes full circle, and extremes rub shoulders with their opposites. But, as we gaze, it would seem that the intricacy sorts itself into two great masses of light and shade. There is the main body of Englishmen, pursuing their callings and pleasures, deep rooted in the soil, and perplexed only at odd moments by con-

---

[1] The doctrine of the imputed righteousness of Christ was interpreted according to the nature of the individual: to many it was a legal bargain which relieved them from the fear of Hell and the consequences of sin, but to those of a higher spiritual development it was a redemption from sin itself and the making possible of a Christ-like life. Ralph Cudworth protested against the materialism of the merely legal conception in his famous sermon before the House of Commons preached on March 31, 1646.

troversy. With them are the old ways of the land and the homely loyalties. Some have no religion, but 'fleet the time carelessly as they did in the golden world'; some have the religion of the household gods; but some too, like Traherne and Vaughan and George Herbert, are Christians after the ageless pattern of the saints. Many are grossly sunk in matter, but many can kindle to unselfish causes, and all are realists, with a firm hold upon the things of sense and time. Opposite to such, eternally opposite, are those whose eyes are always turning inward to their souls, who believe that they themselves and their England are in the valley of decision and that momentous issues hang upon their lightest deeds. To them Herrick's maypole is a 'great stinking idol,' and Robin Goodfellow a satyr of the Pit. Such men are puritans, in the strict sense of a word which since their day has been grievously debased. They are indifferent Christians, for there is more in them of the Roman Stoic and the stern Israelite than of the meek gospel of Christ. Milton's charge against Laud is strictly true of his own party — that they bedecked and deformed the conception of God with 'palls and mitres, gold and gewgaws fetched from Aaron's old wardrobe or the flamen's vestry.'

Puritanism has long been degraded to mean the pedantries of comfortable folk who can afford to cosset their consciences, but let that not blind us to the magnificence of its beginnings. It was a faith for iron souls who, having made it their own, were ready to force the world to bow to it. It was self-centred, but the self was a majestic thing. It was a creed for the few —

> Such as thou hast solemnly elected,
> With gifts and graces eminently adorned,
> To some great work, thy glory,
> And people's safety.

Could this spiritual aristocracy mould England to its pattern? Could it, perhaps abating its rigour, inspire the community with something of its high purpose? Could the phœnix, the 'secular bird' — in the famous imagery of *Samson Agonistes* — ever mate with the 'tame villatic fowl'? That, more than any niceties of political or ecclesiastical structure, was the riddle to which Oliver Cromwell sought an answer.

Chapter II

THREE HOUSEHOLDS: PUTNEY, HINCHING-BROOKE, HUNTINGDON

(1495–1599)

I would relate
How vanquished Mithridates northward passed,
And, hidden in a cloud of years, became
Odin, the Father of a race by whom
Perished the Roman Empire.

WORDSWORTH. *The Prelude.*

I

IN THE early years of the sixteenth century the village of Putney on the Thames was a thriving place. It was part of the great manor of Wimbledon, an estate of the see of Canterbury, and consisted of a cluster of houses round a church by the riverside, and a street which straggled southward towards a breezy common. It possessed a fishery dating from Saxon times, and a not less ancient ferry to Fulham on the northern shore. Travellers and merchandise bound for west Surrey from the capital were landed there to continue the journey by road, so the place had the prosperous bustle of a little port.

In those years, as in all England, its population was changing its character. New industries were beginning and new folk were arriving. Two households especially had settled there and given the older inhabitants much food for talk. A family of Ap William, small squires in Glamorgan, had done some service to Henry VII in his bid for the throne, and like many of their countrymen they followed the Tudor to court and were rewarded with copyhold grants in the neighbourhood of London. They were people of a modest substance and had a right to coat armour, though we may dismiss the fanciful descent from Caradoc and the lords of Powis provided for them by later genealogists. They seem to have retained their Welsh property for a considerable time after their settlement by the Thames. The first of the name known to us was a responsible person, who was steward of the manor of Wimbledon and to trade a land agent and accountant. His two sons, Morgan and Richard, took Williams as their surname, and continued by

Thames side. Richard was given copyholds at Mortlake, entered the Church, and his descendants in high places perpetuated the Williams name. Morgan inherited the Putney copyholds, and had a small post at court in connection with the Welsh guard. He had other avocations, being a brewer and a seller of beer on a large scale, for he had breweries also at Mortlake and Greenwich. Now and then he fell foul of the manor authorities for cutting more fuel on the common than he was entitled to, but in general he seems to have been a person of means and repute.

Sometime about 1495 Morgan Williams married Katherine Cromwell, the elder daughter of a neighbour who had a house in Wandsworth Lane. This neighbour, Walter Cromwell, was also prosperous after a fashion. He followed the trades of brewer, blacksmith and fuller, and owned or leased a good deal of land in the vicinity. The Cromwells had migrated from Norwell in Nottinghamshire about the time the Williams family arrived from Wales; they were of good yeoman stock, but did not carry arms, and could prove no connection with the noble house of Tattershall which gave England a Lord Treasurer.[1] Walter proved a difficult father-in-law for the respectable Morgan Williams. He was constantly drunk and for ever brawling; the records of the manor-court show many fines for exceeding his commoner's rights and for evading the assize of beer; on one occasion he was convicted of wounding to the danger of life. In the end his offences grew so rank that he, who had once been constable of Putney, took to forgery and thereby forfeited his lands. After 1514 the manor knew him no more.

He had one son who made a great stir in England. Thomas Cromwell was born about 1485 and in his early years must have owed much to his brother-in-law, a debt which he was to repay to Morgan Williams's son. He soon quarrelled with his drunken father, and took himself off abroad. For several years he wandered about Italy and Flanders, learning much about the wool trade and international banking, and acquiring a strong distaste for the ways of Rome. Ultimately he settled in London as a merchant and money-lender, and Cardinal Wolsey noted his abilities and made use of them. In 1523 he was in parliament, and presently he was Wolsey's confidential agent,

---

[1] Fuller tells us that Thomas Cromwell refused to take the arms of Cromwell of Tattershall and insisted on a new grant: 'he would not weare another man's coat for fear the owner thereof should pluck it off his ears.'

busy dissolving the lesser monasteries to provide funds for the Cardinal's grandiose schemes at Oxford and Ipswich. He stood by his master to the end, but did not fall with him, transferring his services to the king. The rest of his career as *malleus mona-chorum* is part of the history of England. He was Henry's chief agent in the destruction of the monasteries, and as such became among other things Master of the Rolls, chancellor of Cambridge, Lord Privy Seal, Vicar-General, Lord Chamberlain, a knight, a baron, and at last Earl of Essex. But the marriage which he arranged for the king with Anne of Cleves was his undoing, and on July 28, 1540 he lost his head on Tower Hill, to the general satisfaction of the nation. 'Putney saw his cradle in a cottage, and England saw his coffin in a ditch.'

It is a story which makes fairy-tales seem prosaic. No stranger figure ever laid its spell on England than this short square man, with the porcine face and the litter of shaven chins, the small wicked mouth, the long upper lip and the close-set eyes. Yet we know that that leaden countenance could kindle to humour and supreme intelligence, and that when he chose he could be a delectable companion. He had no principles in the moral sense, but he had one or two vigorous intellectual convictions, which were not without wisdom. He would have had the king forego foreign adventures, and bend himself to the single task of unifying Britain. He was determined to make the monarchy supreme, and to ensure that Henry had all the powers which had been wrested from the Pope. He was zealous for the publication of the Bible in English, seeing in that the best way of making final the breach with Rome. He cared nothing for religion, though he is one of John Foxe's 'martyrs,' and at his death he renounced all protestant heresies, yet he must rank as one of the chief instruments of the English Reformation, for his administrative gifts were of the highest, and were equalled only by his greed and corruption. The best that can be said for him is that he had perhaps somewhere in his gross soul a belief that his road to wealth and power was also the road to national greatness.

He had one other slender merit; he did not forget his own kin, for he made the fortunes of his nephew Richard Williams. Richard was born on the family property of Llanishen in Wales.[1] In 1529 we find him in the service of Lord Dorset, and presently he is on his uncle's staff, and busy suppressing religious

[1] So says Leland in his *Itinerary*, but he may be confusing father and son.

houses. He took his uncle's name, without the leave of Chancery, in order to advertise his kinship with the rising sun; but in serious matters like legal documents he wrote himself 'Williams (alias Cromwell)' as his great-grandson Oliver did in his marriage settlement. He was active against the Pilgrimage of Grace, and he soon won the king's favour by his skill and courage in the tilting-yard. Knighthood followed, and lands and estates flowed in upon him from the ruined church, mainly by way of purchases made at a nominal price — the nunnery of Hinchingbrooke, the great abbey of Ramsey, which was worth half the foundation of Westminster, other lands in the midlands and the eastern shires. His master's fall did not shake him (though he courageously mourned in public for his benefactor), for he was too secure in the royal favour. He fought in the French war of 1541, and went on amassing manors and constableships till his death in 1546. He married the daughter of a lord mayor of London, and left prodigious wealth, for from his landed estates alone he must have had in revenues the better part of a quarter of a million. The nimbleness of Wales and the rough power of the midlands had combined in Sir Richard to produce something glittering and adventurous and yet shrewdly cognizant of the main chance. He had made his way into the inner circle of the aristocracy, and had created not only a fortune but a family.[1]

II

Of Sir Richard we know nothing intimate; but for Sir Henry, his successor, we have the great house which he built at Hinchingbrooke about 1560 and which may be taken as a mirror of his tastes. What had been a nunnery since the days of the Conqueror was transformed by him into one of the stateliest of Elizabethan dwellings. It stands on the left bank of the Ouse half a mile west of the town of Huntingdon; the river, dark with

[1] Carlyle says truly (*L. and S.*, I, 29) that Richard Cromwell appears on a 'background of heraldic darkness,' and some of the details I have given above are not perfectly established. The local antiquary and the fanciful genealogist have run riot in the matter of the Cromwell pedigree. The authorities, such as they are, are the court-rolls of the manor of Wimbledon: the information collected by Leland, Holinshed, Stow, Fuller and Dugdale: odds and ends in the State Papers: Mark Noble's gossipy and confused *Memoirs of the Protectoral House of Cromwell*, and John Phillips in *The Antiquary*, II, 164–69. The Cromwell side of the pedigree is fully discussed by R. B. Merriman in his *Life and Letters of Thomas Cromwell* (1902). The descendants of Oliver are dealt with in Waylen's *House of Cromwell* (1880).

the clays of Bedfordshire, flows pleasantly past its bounds, and with its wide park and noble timber it is still a haunt of ancient peace — a symbol of the adoption of the Williams and Cromwell adventurers into the secure aristocracy of England. In those days the town of Huntingdon was a prosperous place with no less than four churches. It was the outpost of the solid cultivable midlands, with their green pastures and smoothly undulating hills, for all to the east was the Fens, still largely unreclaimed, a waste of quaking bogs and reedy watercourses.

Sir Henry had another seat at Ramsey, where he had made a mansion out of the old gate-house, but his usual residence was Hinchingbrooke. He would appear to have had more Williams than Cromwell in him, for his life was decorous, he made no enemies, and, being freehanded with his great fortune, he was much loved in the countryside. The ancestral smithy and brewhouse of Putney had become very distant things for this resplendent gentleman, who lived as expansively as any Howard or Neville. His house was on the great north road, and it was never empty of guests. In 1563 he was knighted, and in August of the following year he entertained Queen Elizabeth on her return from a visit to Cambridge. He was a strict protestant — naturally, considering the origin of his wealth, and a strong queen's man; he marshalled his county at the time of the Spanish Armada, furnished a troop of horse at his own charge, and delivered patriotic harangues to the trained bands. He took his full share of other public duties, sitting in parliament as one of the knights of the shire for Huntingdon, being four times sheriff of Huntingdon and Cambridge shires, and serving on a royal commission to enquire into the draining of the Fens. But his chief repute was for splendour and generosity. He scattered largesse among the poor wherever he moved between Hinchingbrooke and Ramsey, and the scale of his entertainments was a marvel to the county, so that he won the name of the Golden Knight. Like his father he married the daughter of a lord mayor of London, by whom he had six sons and five daughters. No misfortune broke the even tenor of his life, except the loss of his two wives. The second was supposed to have been done to death by necromancy, and three reputed witches were burned for it; their goods were forfeited to Sir Henry, and he spent the proceeds in providing for annual sermons in Huntingdon, by alumni of Queen's College, Cambridge, against the sin of witchcraft — sermons which were being preached as late as 1785.[1] The Golden Knight died at a ripe age shortly before his royal mistress, and the countryside had never seen a costlier funeral.

Sir Henry had not greatly depleted the fortune which he had inherited. His well-dowered daughters married substantial squires, including a Whalley in Notts and a Hampden in Bucks. His four surviving younger sons had each an estate worth the equivalent of £1500 a year. But Oliver his heir had not the Cromwell gift of getting and holding. He began magnificently by entertaining King James on his first journey from the north and opening that monarch's eyes to the riches of England. Since he left Edinburgh, said the king, he had not received such hospitality. Sir Oliver spared no cost, and built a new window to the banqueting-hall for the occasion. The whole neighbourhood was made welcome, and the dignitaries of Cambridge arrived in their robes to congratulate the new king. James departed with a deluge of gifts — a massive gold cup, horses and hounds and hawks, and a shower of gold for his suite. The host, who had been knighted five years before by Elizabeth, was duly made a knight of the Bath at the coronation.

Sir Oliver continued as he had begun. Besides his father's wealth he had married money and inherited an estate from an uncle, but — apart from the change in economic conditions — no fortune could long support his genial ways. Most of his life he sat in parliament, where he served diligently on committees, and he busied himself with many enterprises, including schemes for draining the Fens and for colonizing Virginia. Several times he entertained the king at Hinchingbrooke, and with James in all likelihood came his son Charles, but his extravagance seems to have lain less in occasions of magnificence than in a steady profusion and ill management. Fuller's character of him reveals the type of man who is much loved by his neighbours and by the commonalty, but whose seed is not long in the land.[2] In 1627 he was compelled to dispose of Hinchingbrooke to Sir Sidney Montague, uncle of the Manchester of the Civil War, and the Cromwells ceased to be the chief family of the shire. When war broke out he and his sons stood valiantly by Charles, and new debts were incurred by his raising of men and by gifts to the king's chest. Only his nephew's repute saved him from sequestration and beggary. He lived on at Ramsey till 1655,

[1] Noble, I, 26 *n*.   [2] *Worthies* (ed. 1811), I, 474.

dying in his ninety-third year through tumbling into the fire, the 'oldest knight in England.' Within three generations the alien Williams and the kinless Cromwells had produced the very pattern of a long-descended, chivalrous and unworldly English gentleman.

III

With Sir Oliver's brother, the second son of the Golden Knight, we enter a different world. Robert Cromwell chose the *fallentis semita vitæ*, as if in revolt from the splendour of Hinchingbrooke; he did not go to Oxford, like his brothers Henry and Philip, but on the lands which fell to him at Huntingdon devoted himself to farming and trade. He was comfortably off, for between his inheritance and his marriage portion he had the equivalent of £2000 a year today, and he kept well within his income's limits. He had pastures in which he grazed cattle, and fields of grain from which he got the malt that he used in his supplementary business of brewing. He sat in one of Elizabeth's parliaments as member for the town of Huntingdon, was bailiff of the borough, and on the commission of the peace for the county. For the rest his only public activity was that matter of draining the Fens which lay near the heart of every dweller in the eastern midlands.

Tradition makes Robert Cromwell a serious, quiet man, careful in the things both of this world and the next, and a portrait of him which hangs at Hinchingbrooke bears out this character. The face is long, lean and composed, the features regular and delicate, with a hooked nose, a sensitive mouth, a high forehead, and grave eyes well set under deep brows. The refinement with which we may credit the Williams stock has ousted the coarse bluntness of the Cromwells. It is the face of a man who is no leader, whose instinct is not for action but for peace and self-examination. Such strength as it reveals is for endurance rather than for the world's coercion.

He married a widow, Elizabeth Lyon, daughter of William Steward of Ely, and fantastic biographers have assumed that she was a Stewart and allied to the royal house of Scotland.[1] But the piquant notion is untenable; she was of the ancient Norfolk house of Styward, and a kinsman had been the last prior of Ely and had had high words with her husband's grand-

[1] *e.g.* Noble, I, 84.

father Sir Richard, when he was out against the religious
houses.[1] Sir Richard had thought him 'froward,' but the prior
proved accessible to reason, became the first protestant dean of
Ely, and did well for himself out of his change of creed. Her
brother, Thomas, was well-to-do; he farmed the cathedral
tithes, and had been knighted by James. The miniature of her
at Windsor is of some interest, for it shows the influence which
shaped the features of her son. The face has many points of
resemblance to his — the heavy lower part combined with the
well-formed mouth, the long nose, the prominent troubled eyes,
the forehead very full above the brows. Oliver's was a heavy and
blunt face, but it had not the porcine bluntness of Thomas
Cromwell's.

To this small country gentleman and his wife, in their modest
home just off the High Street of Huntingdon, were born ten
children, of whom six daughters grew to maturity and one son.
This son, baptized Oliver after his uncle, entered the world at
three o'clock in the morning on the 25th day of April in the
year 1599. 'I was by birth a gentleman' he was to tell one of
his parliaments, 'living neither in any considerable height nor
yet in obscurity.' [2] He might have put the claim higher, for his
ancestry was at least as distinguished as that of many of the
new peerage, the wool-staplers and courtiers and merchant-
adventurers who had risen on the ruins of the ancient nobility.
Much nonsense has been written about the publicans and
blacksmiths of Putney and the brewers of Huntingdon, for old
England had no petty snobbishness about vocations. Oliver
was sprung of races long rooted in the soil, varied races deduc-
ing from many quarters. He had the potent Cromwell stock
with its hard instinct for success, the blood of prosperous
London merchants, and the Styward inheritance of the stubborn Saxondom of the Fens. And to leaven it he had the rarer
strain of the Welsh gentlefolk from Glamorgan, which could
flower into the fantastic gentility of the Golden Knight and
the quixotic Sir Oliver. His ancestry was a medley, like that of
the English people, and most of the creative forces in England
had gone to the making of him.

[1] *L. and S.*, I, 26.   [2] *L. and S.*, II, 367.

Chapter III

THE FENLAND SQUIRE
(1599–1640)

To every good and peaceable man it must in nature be a hateful thing to be a displeaser and molester of thousands; much better would it like him, doubtless, to be a messenger of gladness and contentment.... But when God commands to take the trumpet and blow a dolorous or jarring blast, it lies not in man's will what he shall say, or what he shall conceal.

MILTON, *Reason of Church Government.*

'I myself am like the miller of Granchester, that was wont to pray for peace amongst the willows.'

BACON.

I

LITTLE has come down to us about the childhood and youth of Oliver. If the Chequers portrait is authentic, he appears at the age of two as a composed child with solemn dark eyes. There are the usual tales of portents and marvels and vaticinations of future greatness, and — from the royalist side — of youthful delinquencies. Though there was little in common between the grave livers of Huntingdon and the glittering household of Hinchingbrooke, the Cromwell family was clannish, and the young Oliver must have been often at his uncle's house and seen something of its gaieties. It is a pleasant, and by no means fantastic, thought that there he may have met and played with the delicate little boy who was Prince Charles, and who was his junior by a year. He grew up into a strong ruddy lad, long in the trunk and a little short in the legs, with heavy features, auburn hair, blue-grey eyes and a great mole beneath his lower lip. His temper was quick but easily pacified, he was inclined to fits of moodiness, and now and then to bouts of wild merriment.

His country upbringing made him an adept at field sports, an expert rider, and one who loved a good horse, a good hawk and a good hound. For the rest he had his education at the town grammar school, a twelfth century building founded by that David Earl of Huntingdon who was afterwards king of Scotland. There he learned his Latin rudiments and something more, for the master was one Thomas Beard, a puritan who had written Latin plays, a tract to prove that the Pope was

Antichrist, and a work of some repute in its day, *The Theatre of God's Judgments*, the argument of which was that even in this life the wicked were punished and that every event was a direct manifestation of the divine justice. The pupil often felt the weight of the master's rod, but he seems to have liked and respected him, and to have been influenced by his teaching, for Beard must have implanted in him his sense of God's intimate governance of the world and the instinct always to look for judgments and providences and signs from on high. This puritan bias was intensified by what he heard at home. Thither in his childhood came news of the Gunpowder Plot, of Prince Henry's death which saddened all loyal protestants, and of the devious ways of the king. When the boy had a moment to spare from his games and sports, he may have reflected upon the family talk of the outer world, and pictured it as a perpetual battle-field between the awful Jehovah who filled the thoughts of his parents and his schoolmaster, and a being called Mammon, in whose train his uncle Oliver was a noted pursuivant.

On the 23rd of April, 1616, two days before his seventeenth birthday, he journeyed the fifteen miles from Huntingdon to Cambridge and was entered at Sidney Sussex college. It was the day of Shakespeare's death, a milestone in England's road from Elizabethan sunlight into the new shadows. Sidney Sussex was a foundation which Laud denounced as a nursery of puritanism, and its master, Samuel Ward, was a stern disciplinarian who had been one of the translators of King James' Bible. Oliver's tutor was a certain Richard Howlet, a discreet and moderate man who twenty-two years later appears in Ireland as dean of Cashel, and who won the approval of Archbishop Ussher.[1]

Cambridge in 1616 was not a place to stir the intellect of a sluggish young squire from the Fenlands. The new learning of the Baconians was still in its infancy, and the fare of the ordinary commoner was still the husks of the Quadrivium. To Milton ten years later the studies were an 'asinine feast of sowthistles and brambles,' and the undergraduates were 'mocked and deluded with ragged notions and babblements while they expected worthy and delightful knowledge,'[2] and his third academic 'prolusion,' *Contra Philosophiam Scholasticam*, was a

[1] *Cal. S. P. Dom (Ireland)*, cclvi, 107; *L. and S.*, I, 36 *n.*
[2] *Tractate on Education.*

bitter attack upon the whole system. We may be certain that Oliver made no such complaint; nor was he drawn into the little circle of those whom Milton called the 'fantasticks,' men like George Herbert, who was now a young fellow of Trinity and was soon to be public orator. He had a certain taste for music which never left him; he knew a little Latin, enough to enable him in later life to make shift to converse with foreign envoys, though according to Bishop Burnet he spoke it 'very viciously'; and he appears to have been a fair mathematician according to the easy standards of the time. He was also interested in geography, for his family had had their share in merchant-adventures, and he seems to have read a good deal of history, ancient and modern. In particular, with him as with Montrose, Raleigh's *History of the World* was a favourite book, and in 1650 we find him bidding his son Richard recreate himself with it — 'it's a body of History, and will add much more to your understanding than fragments of story.' [1]

Poetry, art and philosophy meant nothing to him, though later he was to develop a taste for pictures, and as for theology he was content with the home product. Clearly he was always an infrequent reader; a proof is that in his letters and speeches he avoids the contemporary habit of quotation, citing only the Scriptures. During his short time at Cambridge he was more concerned with sport and company than with studies, and the royalist biographer may be trusted who describes him as 'one of the chief matchmakers and players of football, cudgels, or any other boisterous sport or game.' The discipline was strict, but it was often defied, and we may assume that Oliver was not slow in breaking bounds. He had a heavy, vigorous body to exercise, and his mind was still in a happy stagnation. He was of the type against which Milton protested in his *Vacation Exercise* of 1628.

> Some people have lately nicknamed me the Lady. But why do I seem to them too little of a man? I suppose because I have never had the strength to drink off a bottle like a prizefighter; or because my hand has never grown horny with holding a plough-handle; or because I was not a farm hand at seven, and so never took a midday nap in the sun — last perhaps because I never showed my virility the way those brothellers do. But I wish they could leave playing the ass as readily as I the woman.'

[1] *L. and S.*, II, 54

II

Oliver's university life did not last more than a year, and he took no degree. In June 1617 the elder Cromwell died, and, as the only son of the house, he returned to Huntingdon to wind up his father's estate and manage the property. Two thirds of the income was left to the widow for twenty-one years to provide for the upbringing of the host of daughters, but Oliver had expectations from his uncles, and could look forward to a reasonable fortune as a country squire. So, the immediate business being completed, he followed what was the common practice of the time and went to London to acquire a smattering of law, for in those days a landed proprietor was his own man of business. His name does not appear upon the books of any of the inns of court, and Lincoln's Inn and Gray's Inn have competed for the honour of his membership.

Of his life in London we know little except the episode which concluded it. One would fain believe that, like Eliot, he was present in Palace Yard on that misty morning in October 1618, and saw Walter Raleigh, the last Elizabethan and the author of his favourite book, lay his comely head on the block. Royalist gossip has filled his London years with wantonness, and it may well be that one who had been at Cambridge a boon companion was not averse to hearing the chimes at midnight. But his revelries must have been modest or well concealed, for through his Hampden connections he became a visitor at the home on Tower Hill of a most reputable city merchant, Sir John Bourchier, who had bought himself an estate at Felsted in Essex, but was no kin to the noble Bourchiers of that shire. On August 20th, 1620, a few months after he had come of age, he married the daughter Elizabeth, who was a year his senior. She brought him a substantial dowry, but it would appear to have been a love match, and the affection between the two burned strongly till the end. 'Truly, if I love thee not too well,' he wrote to her after thirty years of wedlock, 'I think I err not on the other hand much. Thou art dearer to me than any creature.' [1] Her portrait shows her comely and full-faced, with arched eyebrows and a strong nose, a countenance at once homely and dignified. She was an excellent housewife and a devoted mother, but she never intermeddled with her husband's political, and still less with his religious, life.

[1] *L. and S.*, II, 114.

An early marriage with such a woman does not suggest the rake. When Oliver brought his bride to Huntingdon, the whole family, mother, sisters and wife, lived in the same house. The young husband found much business on his hands. Since prices for farm produce had fallen heavily,[1] it was no easy task to get a profit out of the land. According to royalist pamphleteers Oliver's early years of marriage were years of extreme profligacy, when he committed every sin in the calendar, and his career of vice did not close till he fell suddenly into religious mania.[2] Later writers have based the same charge on his own confession. In October 1638 he wrote to his cousin, the wife of Oliver St. John: 'You know what my manner of life hath been. Oh, I lived in and loved darkness, and hated the light; I was a chief, the chief of sinners. This is true: I hated godliness, yet God had mercy on me.'[3] Richard Baxter, who was no royalist tattle-bearer, calls him 'a prodigal in his youth, and afterwards changed to zealous righteousness.'[4] The courtier Sir Philip Warwick, who lived for a time in Huntingdon, says that 'the first years of his manhood were spent in a dissolute course of life, in good fellowship and gaming, which afterwards he seemed very sensible of and sorrowful for, and, as if it had been a good spirit that had guided him therein, he used a good method upon his conversion, for he declared that he was ready to make restitution unto any man who would accuse him or whom he could accuse himself to have wronged.'[5] And there is Dugdale's story, which may have something in it, of his attempt to have his uncle Sir Thomas Steward certified as a lunatic,[6] and those entries in the Huntingdon parish register, probably forgeries, which suggest that in 1621 and again in 1628 he submitted to some kind of church censure.[7]

Oliver's own confession need not be taken too seriously. It has been the fashion of the saint from Augustine downwards to paint in dark colours his life before he entered the state of grace, since every action was coloured by the then corruption of his heart. Innocent recreations are seen as 'the lusts and fruits of the flesh' now that the old man has been put off.

[1] D'Ewes, *Autobiography*, I, 180.
[2] The charges as summarized in Noble, I, 97-100.
[3] *L. and S.*, I, 90.   [4] *Rel. Baxt.*, 98.
[5] Warwick, 276.   [6] Noble, I, 100.
[7] Mr. Gardiner (*Oliver Cromwell*, 5-6) thinks that the forgeries may represent an authentic local tradition.

'From a child,' Bunyan wrote, 'I had but few equals, both for cursing, swearing, lying and blaspheming the holy name of God'; [1] and we do not believe him. But though Oliver's self-depreciation was common form in his day, there may be a spice of fact behind the hyperboles. Of certain sins of the flesh we may reasonably acquit him, but he had a wild humour and loved horseplay, and it may well be that at one time he was a riotous companion. He may also have been a gamester, for Doctor Beard's predestination was a gambler's creed. He had almost certainly his moments of passion when he could be guilty of acts of violence and injustice. Sir Philip Warwick's tale of his offers of restitution may be believed, for they are characteristic of the man.

Two facts are certain about his early years of married life. The first is that he was ill. Warwick knew his Huntingdon physician, Dr. Simcott, who told him that Oliver was a 'most splenetic' man, and had fancies about the town cross, and used to summon him at midnight and other unseasonable hours under the belief that he was dying. [2] We know, too, that as late as September 1628 he consulted a fashionable London physician, Sir Thomas Mayerne, who set him down in his case-book as 'valde melancholicus.' The balance of his temperament was maladjusted and he was subject to moods of depression and to nightmarish dreams. The condition was no doubt partly physical, some glandular affection which the body would outgrow, but it was largely the consequence of the second fact — that in those years he was passing through a profound spiritual crisis.

The teaching of his parents and his schoolmaster, the puritan background to the pleasant life of Cambridge, talks maybe with his cousin Hampden and Hampden's friends, the atmosphere of the age, stray words remembered from sermons, texts recollected from the Bible, and his own fundamental gravity of mind had produced their fruit at last. Oliver had to face a grim communion with his soul. Of this struggle we have no record, and can judge of its nature only by the character of the man thus re-created. We may believe that it was bitter and protracted, for his mind was always tortuous, and clearness came only after desperate strivings and confusions. We know something of the spiritual development of two other great puritans, Milton

---

[1] *Grace Abounding.* Cf. the confession of the younger Vane in Sikes, *Life and Death of Sir Henry Vane, Knight.*

[2] Warwick, 249.

and Bunyan, but it is not likely that Oliver's crisis was of the same type as theirs. He had none of Milton's intellectual elasticity or his steady confidence in the power and value of the human reason; and, starting with a wider education than Bunyan, he must have escaped many of the more fantastic doubts which are described in *Grace Abounding*. But in effect he had to face Bunyan's problem, the awful conundrums of election and predestination, and his vivid imagination, his scrupulous candour with himself, and his strong and stiff-necked spirit made the Slough of Despond and the Valley of Humiliation no easier for him than for Bunyan's Pilgrim. He had to struggle with a literal interpretation of the most terrible words of Scripture, groping among vast and half-understood conceptions with no guide but his own honesty, goaded all the while by the knowledge that the quest was a matter of life and death, that for him, as for Bunyan, 'above Elstow Green was heaven, and beneath was hell.' He had to go through all the items of the grim Calvinistic schedule — conviction of sin, repentance, hope of election, assurance of salvation — the experience which theology calls 'conversion,' and which, in some form or other, is the destiny of every thinking man. 'Wilt thou join with the dragons; wilt thou join with the Gods?'

The end was peace, for, in the language of his faith, he 'found Christ' — not by any process of reasoning, but by an intense personal experience in which his whole being was caught up into an ecstasy of adoration and love. We shall not understand Oliver unless we realize that he was in essence a mystic, and that the core of his religion was a mystical experience continually renewed. Much of his life was spent in a communion outside the world of sense and time. 'You cannot find nor behold the face of God but in Christ,' he wrote to his son; 'therefore labour to know God in Christ, which the Scriptures make to be the sum of all, even life eternal. Because the true knowledge is not literal or speculative but inward, transforming the mind to it.' [1]

Two further things may be said of Oliver's conversion. The religion based on it was not that narrow legal compact with the Almighty, tinctured with emotion, which belongs to a shallow later evangelicalism; nor was it, as with so many puritans, a creed based on prudential fears. It had more in common with Ralph Cudworth's famous sermon,[2] or the Calvinism of the

[1] *L. and S.*, II, 53-54.   [2] See p. 47 *n., supra*.

Cambridge Platonists. His view was that of Whichcote, that 'he is the best Christian whose heart beats with the truest pulse towards heaven, not he whose head spinneth out the finest cobwebs.' It made him impatient of minor dogmatic differences among Christians, since his own faith was based on personal experience, and no man could look into another man's heart. Isaac Pennington's words, startling words for the seventeenth century, might have been his, had he been capable of so precise a statement: 'All truth is shadow except the last truth. But all truth is substance in its own place, though it be but a shadow in another place. And the shadow is a true shadow, as the substance is a true substance.'

Again, with this toleration went a strange tenderness. Oliver was a man of a profound emotional nature who demanded food for his affections. His religion, being based not on fear but on love,[1] for fear had little place in his heart, made him infinitely compassionate towards others. A sudden anger might drive him into harshness, but he repented instantly of his fault. Tears were never far from his eyes. I can find no parallel in history to this man of action who had so strong an instinct for mercy and kindness, even for what in any other would have been womanish sentiment, and it sprang directly from his religion. He writes to a friend on the loss of a son in language which has still power to move us: 'There is your precious child full of glory, to know sin nor sorrow any more. He was a gallant young man, exceeding gracious. God give you his comfort.'[2] His own agony at the death of his eldest son was remembered even on his death-bed. His letters to his family are full of a wistful affection. Of his favourite daughter Elizabeth he writes: 'She seeks after (as I hope also) that which will satisfy. And thus to be a seeker is to be of the best sect next to a finder, and such an one shall every faithful humble seeker be at the end.'[3] And he could appeal thus to the Barebone Parliament on behalf of all honesty and simplicity: 'We should be pitiful... and tender towards all though of different judgments. ... Love all, tender all, cherish and countenance all, in all things that are good.... And if the poorest Christian, the most mistaken Christian, shall desire to live peaceably and quietly under you — I say, if any shall desire but to lead a life of godliness and honesty, let him be protected.'[4] That is a height to which

[1] See. *L. and S.*, II, 259.   [2] *Ibid.*, I, 177.
[3] *L. and S.*, I, 246.   [4] *Ibid.*, II, 293–94.

even the charity of Bunyan scarcely attained, and to the common puritan it must have seemed no better than a blasphemous and slacklipped folly.

III

He had found the way of peace, since he knew that he was a vessel decreed for honour and not for wrath; but with him peace was never a constant mood. For some ten years he seems to have suffered from dark interludes of doubt, and to the end there were times when a cloud would descend upon his spirit and he had to examine himself with a trembling heart to make sure of his calling and election. Yet there were bright seasons even in the deepest gloom when he looked upon life with happy eyes, and found a new glory in a world in whose every detail he saw the love of his Creator. 'I live,' he wrote, 'in Meshech, which they say signifies *Prolonging*, in Kedar which signifies *Blackness*; yet the Lord forsaketh me not. Though he do prolong, yet he will (I trust) bring me to his tabernacle, to his resting-place. My soul is with the congregation of the firstborn, my body rests in hope, and if here I may honour my God either by doing or suffering, I shall be most glad.' [1]

Oliver had now come to his full strength of body. He stood about five feet ten in height, his shoulders were massive, and he had a noble head thatched with thick brown hair which fell below his collar. There was vitality, and passion, too, in the long thick nose with the wide nostrils, and determination in the large, full-lipped mouth; yet it was an attractive face, for it left a dominant impression of kindly sagacity. In his rough country clothes he must have looked at first sight like any other substantial grazier from the shires, unless the observer had time to mark his brooding, commanding eyes. He was good company, for, though he ate sparingly and drank little but small beer, he could be very merry and join heartily in catches and glees that took his fancy. Indeed in his relaxed moments his mirth was apt to be obstreperous; for he loved horseplay and on occasion could play the buffoon, he was a great laugher, and had a taste for broad country jests and frank country speech. He rode heartily to hounds, whether the quarry were fox or buck, and his hawks were his pride; one of his earliest extant letters is about a falcon that had gone astray, with his

[1] *L and S.*, I, 89.

name on its varvell.[1] His manners were simple and his taste unfastidious, for he had never mixed in fine society, or in such lettered circles as Falkland drew around him at Great Tew or Hyde frequented on his first coming to town.

But such an one could not be incurious about the doings of the great world beyond the Ouse or insensitive to social duties. His religion was no fugitive and cloistered thing but the faith of a man-at-arms. Many puritans looked at the light and were dazzled; Oliver looked also at the objects which it lit. He passed from the problem of the relation of man to his Maker, to the problem of the relation of man to the world. He desired to see the earth made an easier place for Christian people, and even in those days he may have dreamed of an England in which might be built Jerusalem. He was to write later: 'If any whosoever think the interests of Christians and the interest of the nation inconsistent, I wish my soul may never enter into their secrets.' News came late and slow to Huntingdon, but when it came it was startling enough, and was anxiously discussed in the taverns and by the firesides. In those days England was by no means insular, for many Englishmen saw their own battles being fought in foreign fields. Oliver must have followed anxiously the doings on the Continent, the ups and downs of Mansfeld and Christian of Brunswick and the King of Denmark, the victories of Tilly's Army of the League, and the misfortunes of the Elector of the Palatine and the 'Queen of Hearts.' He must have puzzled like other people over James's blundering foreign policy, and shrunk from his coquettings with Spain, grieved over the misfortunes of the French Huguenots and England's feeble attempts to protect them, and grown impatient with the follies of Buckingham. Presently the old king died, and the stammering child he remembered long ago at Hinchingbrooke sat on the throne. Two years later the splendid Sir Oliver sold his estate and disappeared from the life of Huntingdon — an event which can have had little bearing on Oliver's life, since in his new mood he must have seen little of his uncle's family.

The news from London itself was growing graver. It looked as if the new king were a Rehoboam and not a Solomon. He had got himself a bride — not, to the relief of England, the threatened Infanta of Spain, but a vivacious girl of fifteen with wonderful dark eyes, the king of France's sister and the daughter

[1] *L. and S.*, III, 313-14.

of Henry of Navarre. But if her father was Henry her mother had been a Medici, a house on which English eyes looked darkly. She was a catholic, too, and had brought over many papists in her train, and mass was now said regularly in the royal palace. To Huntingdon came only stray gossip but it was disquieting, and Oliver's distate was increased, as a serious countryman, for courts and kings. What were these gaudy folk to whom power had been given, and but little wisdom in the use of it? Elizabeth to be sure was 'of famous memory,' for she had stood for the freedom of religion and of England. But his recollection of James at Hinchingbrooke was only of a man with thin shanks and padded clothes, a tongue too large for his mouth and a scraggy beard, who gobbled in his talk and had less dignity than his meanest lackey.[1] Clearly there was no inherent virtue in the regal office.

And the new king, the thin little boy with a Scots accent whom he had played with, promised no better. Rumour said that he was cold and hard, that he gave his confidence to the dangerous madcap Buckingham, and that he leaned away from godliness to the side of those who would corrupt the church with mummery. He had called two parliaments and had quarrelled with them. It seemed that he was improvident and always short of money, and, since he had flouted parliament, he was raising supplies by forced loans in each shire. Echoes of speeches in the Commons reached the banks of the Ouse; attacks like Eliot's on Buckingham and the whole mismanagement overseas — 'Our honour is ruined, our ships are sunk, our men perished, not by the enemy, not by chance, but by those we trust'; refusals to vote supplies without assurance of reform; exposures of false doctrine and lying priests. Parliament was the sole defence of the plain man, but it looked as if its very existence were in danger. 'Remember' the king had told its members, 'that parliaments are altogether in my power for their calling, sitting and dissolution; therefore, as I find the fruits of them good or evil, they are to continue or not to be.' As Oliver discussed public affairs with his graver neighbours, the notion grew in his mind that it was his duty as a Christian and a lover of England to take a hand in this conflict of light and darkness.

Meantime he went on soberly with his farming. Prices were rising, wheat was no longer half a crown a bushel, and he was

[1] Sir Anthony Weldon, *The Court and Character of King James* (1650), 177.

getting a better return from his land. Religion was his main concern, and one of his duties was to assist the fund for buying in
impropriations so as to ensure the appointment of godly ministers, and paying itinerant 'lecturers' to preach in neglected
parishes. His family was growing fast, for by 1628 he had five
children: Robert, whose death at Felsted in 1638 nearly broke
his father's heart; Oliver, who died in the war; Bridget, who
was to marry first Ireton and then Fleetwood; Richard, who was
to be his father's successor as Protector; and Henry, who was
to be Lord Deputy in Ireland. He still attended church, his
children were duly baptized there, and Richard's godfather
was Henry Downhall who was later on parson of St. Ives,
but more and more his taste inclined to a different kind of
communion. Three days after Henry's baptism, on January
23rd, 1628, Oliver's fellow-townsmen of Huntingdon returned
him to parliament for the borough, his colleague being another
old member of Sidney Sussex, James Montague, the third son
of the Earl of Manchester.

IV

When parliament met on March 17, 1628, it was in a troubled
atmosphere. Abroad, Wallenstein had occupied Holstein,
Schleswig and Jutland, and was sitting down before Stralsund;
England was at war with France, and Buckingham had miserably bungled the expedition to relieve La Rochelle; the king
was clamouring for a new fleet, and various worthy gentlemen
had gone to prison for refusing to subscribe to his forced loans.
The House was in a dangerous temper. Buckingham must be
called to account; security must be found against illegal imprisonment and arbitrary levies; certain rights of parliament
must be fixed beyond a peradventure; most important of all,
the high-flying wings of Laud, now bishop of London, must be
clipped. The king thought only of subsidies, but his faithful
Commons asked further questions. If money was needed for
the service of the State, was it to be raised by the king at will
or by the estates of the realm? Were the men who administered
the government to be responsible to the said estates or to the
king alone? Was the national church to be guided by the king
in defiance of the desires of the representatives of the people?
Was a member to be allowed to speak his mind in parliament
without fear of punishment? Were the law and the justiciary to

be free from arbitrary royal interference? These were searching questions, new, many of them, in substance as well as in form.

When Oliver entered parliament he found a body which fairly represented the wealth, rank and talent of England. In earlier days the knights of the shire had been usually men of distinction, but the borough members had been nonentities; but with the Tudors the prestige of the House had grown, and now the ordinary borough member was also *armiger* and *generosus*. The standard of debate had risen, and scriveners found a ready demand for copies of speeches. Long-descended squires sat on the benches beside noted lawyers from the inns of court, blackletter scholars, and city merchants whose names were known over half the world. When he looked round him he saw Sir Edward Coke bent with the burden of eighty years; Glanvil and Maynard and Denzil Holles; young Ralph Hopton fresh from the German wars; the mocking gaze of Selden; his cousin John Hampden with his long thoughtful face, thin lips, and bright melancholy eyes; Pym, burly and shaggy and vigilant as a watchdog; and the dark saturnine brows of Wentworth. Not often has destiny brought under one roof at one time so many of her children.

Oliver played but a small part in that parliament, so its tale may be briefly told. In its first session the Commons embodied their grievances in the famous Petition of Right,[1] which after a struggle passed both Houses and was accepted by the king. This second Magna Charta laid down that henceforth no man should be compelled to pay monies to the State without consent of parliament, that the commissions for executing martial law should be cancelled, and that an end should be put to the billeting of soldiers and sailors. It dealt only with immediate grievances, and did not touch the deeper questions at issue. Wentworth would have had it in the form of a bill which would have become statute law in the ordinary way, but, though supported by Pym, he was overruled by the lawyers, with the result that all that was won was a declaratory statement of the existing law assented to by the king in a highly ambiguous form. The House went on to remonstrances about popery and Arminianism, till it was prorogued on June 26th. In August Buckingham died under Felton's dagger at Portsmouth, so one main rock of offence was removed. In the second session the House devoted itself to religious questions and to the alleged illegality of ton-

[1] The text is in Gardiner, *Const. Docs.*, 66–70.

nage and poundage — a futile session which ended on March 2nd, 1629, in a brawl. The Speaker, Sir John Finch, announcing that the king had decreed an adjournment, tried to stop the debate by leaving the House. Holles and Valentine held him by force in his chair and the door was locked, while Eliot read a comprehensive statement of grievances which was passed by acclamation. Then Black Rod was permitted to enter, and for eleven years parliament ceased to be.

On the 11th day of February 1629 in the second session of this farcical parliament Oliver made his maiden speech. The House then sat from seven in the morning till noon and the afternoon was given up to committees. It was scarcely a speech; rather an anecdote told in the committee for religion with Pym in the chair. The discussion turned on the doings of Dr. Neile, the bishop of Winchester, and Oliver intervened to support the charge of romish inclinations with a story of a certain Dr. Alablaster who had preached black popery at Paul's Cross, to which Dr. Beard, his old Huntingdon schoolmaster, proposed to reply when his turn came for the sermon. But Neile had sent for him and forbidden him to refute Alablaster, and when Beard disobeyed him had him reprimanded.[1] Thereupon it was ordered that the Speaker should invite Dr. Beard to come up and testify against the bishop. The matter has no interest except as Oliver's first utterance in an assembly which he was in time to dominate and ultimately to destroy. It was probably an ill-delivered and halting affair, for his voice was poor, and he had no fluency. Only after he had become sure of himself did he acquire a vigour and an idiom of his own. 'When he delivered his mind in the House,' wrote Winstanley of his maturer days, 'it was with a strong and masculine eloquence, more able to persuade than to be persuaded. His expressions were hardy, opinions resolute, asseverations grave and vehement; always intermixt (Andronicus-like) with sentences of Scripture, to give them the greater weight, and the better to insinuate themselves into the affections of the people. He expressed himself with some kind of passion; but with such a commanding, wise deportment, that at his pleasure he governed and swayed the House, as he had most times the leading voice. Those who find no such wisdom in his speeches may find it in the effect of them.'[2] That style of oratory is not learned in a day.

[1] L. and S., I, 57-58. Gardiner, Hist., VII, 55-56.
[2] England's Worthies (1660), 528-29.

Oliver returned to Huntingdon with much to think about. He had sat in the great council of the nation and watched the wheels of government. He had observed and listened to the king — heard him speak the insolent sentence that he did not threaten the House, since he would scorn to threaten any but his equals; he had been present at the wild scene at the session's close when the king was defied. His opinion of royalty had not risen. He had heard the convictions to which he had been feeling his way expounded with eloquence and precision. Eliot's neurotic fervour was perhaps little to his taste. As his writings show, Eliot was in some ways the most far-sighted and logical political thinker of his generation, but in practical life he was not fitted for leadership, but only for martyrdom. He was always in a fever of rhetoric, trembling with emotion, ruining his case by vain extravagance, without sense of atmosphere, and beyond belief tactless. The result was that in all but a few intimates he roused little affection, and in his opponents the most strenuous dislike. But Pym was another matter, and Pym's speeches in that parliament were one of the germinal influences in Oliver's career.

For Pym then was at his best. He had not yet shown himself one of the adroitest party managers in our political history, but he had given proof, as never before or after, of a broad statesmanship. Even his weakest side, his papist-baiting and his heresy-hunting, Oliver would not find antipathetic, for some earlier words of Pym's on the catholics were his own creed. 'If they should once obtain a connivance, they will press for a toleration, from thence to an equality, from an equality to a superiority, from a superiority to an extirpation of all contrary religions.'[1] Unlike the lawyers he did not lose himself in antique precedents.[2] He was a reformer, but not as yet a revolutionary, a puritan but no fanatic; above all he had an English robustness and hard good sense, and a supreme competence in business. To Oliver, Pym's expositions must have come as a welcome change from Coke's subtleties and Eliot's rhapsodies. We can still feel the power of those earlier speeches. 'If, instead of concord and interchange of support, one part seeks to uphold an old form of government, and the other part introduces a new, they will miserably consume one another. Histories are

---

[1] *Proceedings and Debates of* 1621 *Parliament*, II, 234.

[2] Pym was never called to the bar, though he studied law. By profession he was, in modern parlance, first a treasury clerk and then a company promoter.

full of the calamities of entire states and nations in such cases. It is, nevertheless, equally true that time must needs bring about some alterations.... Therefore have these commonwealths been ever the most durable and perpetual which have often reformed and recomposed themselves according to their first institution and ordinance. By this means they repair the breaches, and counterwork the ordinary and natural effects of time.'[1] It is the high constitutional wisdom of Edmund Burke.

Among parties at that moment, even between the stoutest antagonists, there seemed to be a curious agreement on ultimate principles; the difference was rather in interpretation and application. Eliot, for example, could declare: 'Where there is division in religion, as it doth wrong divinity, so it makes distraction among men.... For the unity I wish posterity might say we had preserved for them that which was left for us' — which were almost the words of Laud on the scaffold. Both sides flattered themselves that they sought the preservation of ancient rights and ancestral liberties. Yet the House of Commons in 1628 was in very truth a revolutionary assembly, a far more daring innovator than the king, though it innocently believed itself conservative. Only Wentworth saw whither the current was bearing it. In some of its demands it had history behind it. Freedom of speech, for instance, had long been claimed formally at the beginning of each session, and even Elizabeth, though she dealt faithfully with too candid critics, nominally recognized it. The Commons indeed had no very high motive in the matter, and cared little for free speech as such: they asked to be themselves protected from the king's vengeance, but in 1621 at Pym's instigation they had dealt summarily with one of their own members who had annoyed them by some badinage about Sunday sports. The control of the purse strings had also a good, if somewhat patchy, historical warrant. But to ask that the executive should be responsible to parliament, and that Church and State should be directly governed by the desires of the people's representatives and not by the will of the king was a demand for the transfer of sovereignty and an act of revolution.[2]

[1] Gardiner, *Hist.*, VI, 313.

[2] It cannot be too forcibly stated that parliament was the chief innovator. The shrinkage in value of the ordinary revenue of the Crown, which paid for the governance

Parliament's case did not rest on any antiquarian precedents but on the changed mood of the nation. The Tudor autocracy, as typified by Charles, simply did not represent the religious and political desires of the English people; of these desires parliament was the only mouthpiece; if parliament was overridden the people were impotent. That on the broadest lines was Pym's case, as it was also the case of Wentworth and Hyde and Falkland. The old constitution had broken down and must be put together again. The solution by means of an adjustment of powers and a balance of functions was made difficult by the current unitary habit of thought, which sought a single fount of authority. Yet something like this was the original policy of the reformers. It seems to have been Pym's; it was certainly Wentworth's — 'To the joint well-being of sovereignty and subjection do I here vow all my care and diligence.'

Three facts rendered compromise impossible and made it certain that parliament would in the long run claim an absolute and overriding authority. The first was that it had already won so much. In the days of Elizabeth privy councillors arranged and controlled the business of the Commons. They sat on every committee. They promoted all the legislation. Parliament might pass laws, but the Crown in council made them. Had James in his later years had managers like Burleigh and Cecil the system might have been bequeathed to his son. But in the first decade of the seventeenth century the Crown grew slack in this business of management and the House produced its own leaders. We see this in the 1621 parliament when the privy councillors were elbowed aside by men like Coke and Sandys and Phelips, and each succeeding parliament made it clearer. The new system of committees aided the development, and the privy council, so far as the House was concerned, was no longer an effective cabinet. A new and powerful machine had come into being, the working of which the king and his advisers did not understand. The Commons had snatched the initiative in lawmaking, and from that it was but a short step to the claim that the king should act only through parliament.[1] The second

of England, made it necessary for the Crown to apply regularly for what had hitherto been exceptional grants, and parliament exacted as the price of these a complete revolution in its constitutional status.

[1] This subject has been fully treated by Prof. W. Notestein in *The Winning of the Initiative by the House of Commons*. (Proc. of Brit. Academy, 1918.)

fact was the religious aspect of the strife. The king as head of the Church claimed to direct belief and worship, and he had so used this power as to quicken the popular fear of Rome and of romanizing practices. Against these, if he retained his prerogative, there was no bulwark, and there is nothing on which men are so little ready to compromise as on religion. The third fact was the character of Charles. Buckingham's death had left him face to face with his people; his policy now was his own and could not be blamed on any favourite. If a residual authority was vested in him, could he be trusted to use it wisely? Men might assent to the abstract ideal of monarchy, but it was a different thing to agree to leaving large prerogative powers in the hands of this particular monarch, who, it was already plain, was in his way as stubborn as Prynne or Leighton, and who was not likely to abide by any bargain.

All these considerations were present to a cool observer like Sir Thomas Wentworth, and he was slow to make up his mind. One motive for decision he did not possess, for he was a Laodicean about the religious strife. He could not understand why the lesser matters of belief and discipline should be allowed to bulk so large; to him much of the quarrel was about things 'purely and simply indifferent.' He looked at the problem with a shrewd secular eye, a practical eye, for he was in no way interested in theories. The delicate adjustment for which some of his friends argued seemed to him unworkable, for it would end in stagnation; it was necessary to emphasize the power of one part of the machine in order to make the wheels go round. That part he decided must be the monarchy. Clearly parliament could not take over the executive, for it had simply not the means; these the Crown alone possessed, an inheritance from a long past, and a substitute could not be easily improvised. He did not rank high the practical sagacity of the tearful House which had carried the Petition of Right. Moreover the safety of the nation in a crisis might depend upon an executive power above and beyond the ordinary law. He hated inefficiency, corruption and oppression, and when it came to fighting these there must be an authority to act swiftly in emergencies. 'Let us make what law we can,' he told the Commons; 'there must be — nay, there will be — a Trust left in the Crown.'[1] Charles might

[1] Gardiner, *Hist.*, VI, 266–67.

have his faults, but could not ministers be found who would counteract them, for nations had often been prosperous under feeble kings? The Tudors by aggrandizing monarchical power had saved the land from anarchy; there was a risk of a new anarchy, and where else lay salvation? Therefore he placed the emphasis on the Crown, though he gave it no autocracy. It was the central point of national unity, and, if it failed, the land would be delivered up to the strife of sects and factions. There was a sound democratic instinct in him, for he was much concerned for the welfare of the 'meaner people' — Montrose's very phrase: and he would have assented to Montrose's appeal to the commonalty:

> Do you not know, when the monarchical government is shaken, the great ones strive for the garlands with *your* blood and *your* fortune? Whereby you gain nothing... but shall purchase to yourselves vultures and tigers to reign over you.[1]

So, the Petition of Right having been accepted, and Buckingham being out of the way, he turned from the House of Commons to a different task, entered the royal service, and set out to contend with indisputable vultures and tigers. His decision is memorable, for the day was to come when Oliver, who now thought him an apostate from the cause of God and country, had to face the same problem and reach, unwillingly, a like conclusion.

V

In the forty-five years of Elizabeth's reign there had been only thirteen parliamentary sessions, and no one had complained; but times had changed, and the eleven years during which Charles governed without summoning the House saw a growing anxiety and discontent. As it chanced, they were years of material prosperity for England, prices were good, commerce expanded, and the only sufferers were the very poor, who were not vocal. They were peaceful years, too, for the war with France ended in 1629, and that with Spain in 1630. But among thoughtful people they were years of ferment.

Abroad, the parliamentary interregnum saw the ruin of the Palatine family, the brilliant campaign of Gustavus Adolphus which ended with his death at Lützen in 1632, the assassina-

[1] Napier, *Memorials of Montrose*, II, 52.

tion of Wallenstein and the treaty of Prague, and the degenera-
tion of the war into a dynastic quarrel. But English eyes were
no longer turning overseas, for the critical events were befalling
on English soil. Charles was giving his people an example of
autocracy in action. The scene at the close of the last session of
parliament was not forgiven. Nine members were sent to the
Tower for sedition; the judges would give no clear ruling about
parliamentary privilege, but in the subsequent trial on a writ of
habeas corpus the verdict of the court was for fine and imprisonment; six made their peace with the king, but Strode and Valentine remained in captivity for ten years, and Eliot died in
durance — the first, indeed the only true, martyr in the cause
of parliament.

For the rest Charles governed the land by means of the
competent Tudor machine. Some of its work was admirable.
High-placed law-breakers got as short a shift as humble malefactors, and the Elizabethan poor law was wisely and efficiently
administered.[1] The difficulty was money, and, parliamentary
subsidies being unavailable, much ingenuity was shown in the
matter of ways and means. Charles found government, with
prices rising, a costly business, and since he would not accept
parliament's terms, he set himself to scrape together funds from
every quarter. Tonnage and poundage were levied without
parliamentary grant to the disgust of the merchant community,
and many old impositions were resurrected and new ones devised. Persons of standing were compelled to accept knighthood
or pay a fine in composition; ancient forest laws were revived,
and neighbouring landlords, whose great-grandfathers had en-
croached on the forest bounds, had to pay heavily for ancestral
enterprise;[2] monopolies, forbidden by the act of 1624 to private
persons, were granted to corporations, and were extended to
the commonest articles of domestic life.[3] These imposts were
an irritation, but, except the monopolies, they were scarcely
felt as a burden, for taxation as a whole was not high.

[1] See E. M. Leonard, *The Early History of English Poor Relief* (1900) and R. R. Reid,
The King's Council of the North (1921).

[2] Rockingham forest, *e.g.*, was enlarged from six square miles to sixty, and Lord Salisbury had to pay £20,000 and Lord Westmoreland £19,000 for their encroachments.

[3] Colepeper told the Long Parliament that monopolies were 'a swarm of vermin
which have overcropt the law. Like the frogs of Egypt, they have gotten possession
in our dwellings, and we have scarce a room free from them; they sup in our cup, they
dip in our dish, they sit by our fire; we find them in the dye-vat, wash-bowl and pow-
dering tub; they share with the butler in his box; they have marked and sealed us from
head to foot.' Rushworth, IV, 33.

But one experiment set all men talking, for a great figure chose to test its legality. In 1628 when the land was at war, ship money was levied on the coast towns, and with much grumbling it was levied again in 1634, a time of peace, the excuse being the need to suppress piracy. Next year it was extended to inland towns, and in 1636 it had become a permanent tax. A test was provided by Lord Saye and John Hampden, who refused to pay, and in 1637 Hampden's case was selected for trial, when seven judges out of a bench of twelve decided for the Crown.... The result had been expected, but Hampden had brought to a clear issue the debate between king and parliament, for the reasons given by the majority of the judges left no doubt about the implications of the royal prerogative. They laid it down that no statute could impair that prerogative, that a statute was void which weakened the king's power to defend the country, and that in a case of necessity, of which he alone was the judge, he could dispense with any law.

Two men in these years bulked large in the public view. The first was Wentworth who, having steered the Petition of Right to port, had now entered the royal service. Few characters have been so travestied by legend, for he was far from being the melodramatic devotee of blood and iron of the old history books. He was a simple man, with strong affections, and he wrote the most endearing letters to his children. He would have been happy as a plain country gentleman, busy about his gardens and stables and kennels, for he had a great love of nature and wild sport. In Ireland, whenever he could escape from his duties, he was off to fish for trout, or to hawk — he complains of the absence of partridges around Dublin which compelled him to fly his falcons only at blackbirds — or to oversee the erection of his little shooting-lodge.

His first task was, as president of the Council of the North, to see that the king's law was enforced beyond Trent, to protect every man in his belongings, and to raise money for the Crown — that is to say, for the services of the State. As a privy councillor he was a member of what was the equivalent of the cabinet. He had to administer the poor law, supervise the draining of the Yorkshire fens, keep the militia up to strength, and wrestle with obstructive nobles and stupid gentry. His methods often lacked tact, for he did not suffer fools gladly, and his fiery honesty made him intolerant of rogues. He could be hasty and harsh, but he put the north into some kind of order, and his many enemies in those parts could substantiate no single charge against him at his trial.

Then came his appointment in 1632 as lord deputy of Ireland, in succession to the incompetent elder Falkland. If England was disturbed, Ireland was ancient chaos; the land was poverty-stricken, and the 'great' Earl of Cork was making a fortune out of money-lending; the coasts were harried by pirates, the plantation system was breaking down, and the rule of the lord justices in Dublin was a farce. A more seemingly hopeless task never confronted a man with a passion for order. It is on his eight years of Irish government that his chief title to fame must rest, and it may fairly be said that no British pro-consul ever undertook a severer labour or in a short time produced more miraculous results. He raised the status of the alien protestant church and the character of its divines. He did not attempt to press the Laudian policy of conformity, and he disbelieved in penal measures; 'it is most certain,' he wrote to Laud, 'that the to-be-wished Reformation must first work from ourselves,' so he made war on simony and corruption, and told refractory bishops that he would have their rochets pulled over their ears. He refused to bear hardly on the catholics, postponing any attempt at their conversion till he had provided a church worth being converted to, while Pym across the water was declaring that he 'would have all Papists used like madmen.' In Ulster he tried mild measures to bring the high-fliers to reason, though he detested 'the vanity and lightness of their fantastic doctrine,' and it was only in the interests of public peace that he was compelled in the end to make the life of men like Robert Blair so uncomfortable that they retired to Scotland. His method with the ministers had much of the initial patience and ultimate firmness of Cromwell's. He believed that for the sake of peace Ireland should be economically dependent upon England, but he did not interpret this maxim harshly, and in many respects his economic views were ahead of his time. He succeeded to a revenue which fell far short of the expenditure, and to a heavy debt, and he left the country solvent, largely by checking peculation. He had to struggle against the vested interests of monopolists and land-grabbers and corrupt officials, who had great purchase in England both at court and in parliament, and, like most servants of the Stuarts, he had to fight with his flank turned and his rear threatened. He was determined that Ireland should not be the milch cow of 'that nation of people or rather vermin, which are never to be found at the courts of great princes.'

He toiled with resolution, energy and invincible courage, and his successes far outbalanced his failures. He ended with a surplus instead of a deficit, and a large reserve fund. He put the plantations in order, and, though he had no military experience, provided an efficient defence force, much of which he trained himself; he cleansed the foul stables of officialdom, set the church on a sound basis of temporalities, and vastly improved its quality; he so enlarged the export trade that it was nearly double the value of the imports; above all, he put into the land a new spirit of ease and hopefulness. Ireland, as he told the king, was now 'a growing people in their first Spring.' He did all this by a prodigal expenditure of mind and body. He had never been strong, and all his life he was plagued with gout and the stone. Ireland made him an old man in his early forties. 'I grow extremely old and full of grey hairs since I came into this kingdom,' he wrote, 'and should wax exceeding melancholy, were it not for two little girls that come now and then to play by me. Remember, I tell you, I am of no long life.' He was always oppressed by the thought that his time on earth would be too short for the work he had to do. But he consoled himself with the reflection that 'he lives more that virtuously and generously spends one month, than some other that may chance to dream out some years and bury himself alive all the while.' [1]

There was no doubt felt in England of the success of Wentworth's work, for every post and every traveller out of Ireland told the tale of it. He had few illusions about how his old parliamentary comrades would now look on him. 'I am not ignorant,' he wrote to Laud in 1634, 'that my stirring herein will be strangely reported and censured on that side, and how I shall be able to sustain myself against your Prynnes, Pims and Bens, with the rest of that generation of odd names and natures, the Lord knows.' By his former colleagues he was regarded with mingled admiration, hatred and fear, but principally fear. They felt towards him as an extreme Marxist might feel towards an enlightened, humane and successful capitalist. He was making

[1] Strafford should be studied in his letters. The great collection is Knowler's *The Earl of Strafford's Letters and Despatches* (1739) with Sir George Radcliffe's memoir. Lady Burghclere (*Strafford*, 2 vols., 1931) has printed many new ones from the archives of Lord Fitzwilliam and Lord Mostyn. Dr. Hugh O'Grady's *Strafford and Ireland* (1923) is an admirable study of the Irish administration.

autocracy efficient and therefore respectable, breaking cheerfully all their pet laws to the profit of the lieges, and thereby
buttressing that very fabric which they sought to demolish.

The other dominant figure was William Laud, first known to
Oliver as archdeacon of Huntingdon, and since then in succession bishop of St. David's, of Bath and Wells, and of London,
and now archbishop of Canterbury and the occupant of high
civil posts which it was not wise for a churchman to hold. The
character of Laud has waited long for a fair assessment, for till
the other day Macaulay's coarse abuse was apparently the
verdict of history. But this little man,[1] with his horseshoe brows
and prim mouth and sharp restless eyes, is too subtle a figure
for an easy verdict. It is clear that he had great natural gifts of
head and heart, and that there was honesty in his dreams and
much valuable matter in his work. He had a spacious conception of the Church as the guardian of sane progress not in England only but throughout the globe, a missionary church, the
spiritual counterpart of a great terrestrial empire. Only
through such a church, he believed, could the perilous encroachments of Rome be stayed.[2] He was tolerant in matters
of dogma. The disciple of Lancelot Andrewes and the friend
and counsellor of George Herbert and Nicholas Ferrar had a
sincere personal religion. He had always an honourable tenderness towards poverty. He had a passion for sound learning and
as chancellor he set Oxford upon a new and better road.

Even on the more dubious side of his career, his work in the
Star Chamber and the High Commission, there is something
to be set to his credit. These courts, on the testimony of Sir
Matthew Hale, filled a gap in the legal system, and could reach
offenders who laughed at the ordinary tribunals. Laud knew
neither fear nor favour, and his normal administration was not

---

[1] It is curious how many notable royalists were small men: Falkland, Hales, Chillingworth and Sidney Godolphin were all tiny; as were also Charles and Henrietta Maria.

[2] 'Perhaps a great clamour there is, that I would have brought in Popery. You know
what the Pharisees said against Christ himself, in the eleventh of *John*. "If we let him
alone all men will believe in him, *Et Venient Romani*, and the Romans will come and
take away both our place and our nation." Here was a causeless cry against Christ that
the Romans would come, and see how just the Judgment of God was; they crucified
Christ for fear lest the Romans should come, and his death was that which brought in
the Romans upon them, God punishing them with that which they most feared. And
I pray God this clamour of *Venient Romani* (of which I have given to my knowledge no
just cause) help not to bring him in; for the Pope never had a harvest in England since
the Reformation as he hath now upon the sects and divisions that are amongst us.'
*The Archbishop of Canterbury's Speech or his Funerall Sermon, Preached by himself on the
Scaffold*, 10th *Jan.* 1647 (Th.).

harsh, for he put no man to death, and the fines imposed were beyond all comparison less than those imposed by parliament. He had to administer a cruel law — of which he did not recognize the cruelty, for there was a cold donnish insensitiveness about him — and we are shocked at the barbarous punishments inflicted upon Prynne and Leighton, Bastwick and John Lilburne; but it may be questioned if they really shocked the moral sense of the community, though they gave superb material to his enemies. These men had been guilty of libels which in earlier times would have been construed as treasonable and for which they would have suffered death, and it is better to lose your ears than to lose your head.

Laud's tragedy, and that of his country, was that he was an able and honest man set in a place where his ability and honesty were the undoing of himself and his master. 'A busy logical faculty, operating entirely on chimerical element of obsolete delusions, a vehement, shrill-voice character, confident in its own rectitude as the narrowest character may the soonest be. A man not without affections, though bred as a College Monk, with little room to develop them; of shrill, tremulous, partly feminine nature, capable of spasms, of much hysterical obstinacy, as female natures are.' So Carlyle,[1] and his verdict does not greatly differ from that of James I: 'He hath a restless spirit, and cannot see when things are well, but loves to bring matters to a pitch of reformation floating in his own brain.' Laud forgot Bacon's profound sentence: 'It were good that men in their Innovations would follow the example of Time itself, which, indeed, innovateth greatly, but quietly, and by degrees scarce to be parceived.' He applied the brain of a college pedant to the spacious life of England.

We cannot deny vigour to a mind to which Wentworth turned for advice, but it was vigour without perspective. He had Wentworth's love of order, but he insisted on it in the one sphere which was not ripe for it, and, unlike Wentworth, he could not distinguish between essentials and things 'purely and simply indifferent.' Laud was at utter variance with the great mass of the English people. He put the emphasis upon uniformity of worship when the serious minds of his age were absorbed in spiritual struggles which had nothing to do with ceremonial. He preached the doctrine of one great, unified, comprehensive church, when the popular tendency was towards

[1] *Historical Sketches*, 282.

minute schisms. He was a devotee of ritual, and most of the usages he would have made compulsory seemed to the plain man to be what Oliver called 'poisonous popish ceremonies.' His church courts were so active and meddlesome that the ordinary man's life was made a burden.[1] If Wentworth's doings filled the parliamentarians with fears because he seemed to be making a success of autocracy, Laud's were a blessing to them because they made the Church, and the king the Church's protector, hated and despised. The small, untiring, resolute, courageous archbishop is a tragic figure, for he had no inconsiderable faith to preach but not the gifts to make it acceptable. He was a devoted priest and a great ecclesiastic, but what the world sought was a prophet.[2]

VI

In those fateful years Oliver was back among his pastures and ploughlands. He busied himself in the management of his Huntingdon farm, and as one of the borough's members of parliament was forced to take a hand in local affairs. He refused to accept knighthood, and had consequently to pay the fine of ten pounds, but there is no evidence that he stood out against the ship-money tax. A daughter Elizabeth, his favourite child, was born in 1629. In 1630 he was the centre of a controversy which shook the little town. Hitherto Huntingdon had had a constitution of the mediæval type, two bailiffs and a common council annually chosen; but that year a new charter was granted conferring the government upon a mayor, a recorder, and twelve aldermen elected for life. This was probably the doing of a certain Robert Barnard, a barrister and a newcomer who had bought an estate hard by. Oliver accepted the change, and took office, along with Barnard and Dr. Beard, as a justice of the peace for the borough. But presently he discovered that the burgesses were alarmed about their rights to the common land under the new constitution, he thought that there was reason in their case, and he spoke his mind vigorously

[1] 'In the twelve months ending at the date of the assembly of the long Parliament, in the Archdeacon's court in London no fewer than two thousand persons were brought up for tippling, sabbath-breaking and incontinence.' Morley, *Oliver Cromwell*, 59.

[2] There is a large Laudian literature, much of it extremely partisan. His works in nine vols. are collected in the Oxford edition, 1847–60. A useful series of studies is the 1895 Commemoration volume, *Lectures on Laud*, which contains an estimate by Mandell Creighton and a full bibliography.

to Barnard the new mayor. The corporation complained to the privy council, and Oliver and another were summoned before it and committed to custody. The case was referred to the arbitration of the Earl of Manchester, who had the charter amended to meet the grievance, but censured Oliver for the violence of his speech. The quarrel was patched up, and the opponents were formally reconciled.

But the thing rankled, for Oliver could not away with the intriguing Barnard, and it may have been one of the reasons which induced him to leave Huntingdon. Another was his sense of the unsettlement of the times, and his desire to be free from the burden of owning land and to have his fortune in a more compact and portable form. In May 1631, with the consent of his mother's trustees, he sold out his landed property in Huntingdon for the sum of £1500,[1] and leased and stocked a grazing farm at St. Ives, five miles down the Ouse. The lands were at the east end of the town, some marshy fields beside the river, fairly good pasture for dairy cows and with the advantage of an ancient cattle-market in the town behind them. There for five years he led the life of a grazier, striving with wet winters when the Ouse came down in flood, and summer droughts when the heavy clay soil cracked and gaped, and perplexed by the vagaries of live-stock prices. His mother apparently went on living at Huntingdon and the daughter born to him in the new house — Mary, afterwards Lady Fauconberg — was baptized in Huntingdon church. He attended the church at St. Ives and was on good terms with the vicar; on a winter Sunday he would wear a strip of red flannel round his neck, for his throat was weak.[2]

We have little record of those years. In 1633 Laud had his will, and the society for buying up impropriations and providing for lecturers was suppressed, the patronage reverting to the Crown. Oliver, as we have seen, had a strong interest in these lectureships, and we find him in January 1635, reminding one Mr. Storie 'at the sign of the Dog, in the Royal Exchange, London,' that if he failed to send his subscription the lectures in Huntingdon must come to an end:

> To build material temples is judged a work of piety; but they that procure spiritual food, they that build up spiritual temples, they are the most truly charitable, truly pious.... It were a piteous thing to see a lecture fall, in the hands of so many able and godly

men as I am persuaded the founders of this are; in these times, wherein we see they are suppressed, with too much haste and violence, by the enemies of God his truth. Far be it that so much guilt should stick to your hands, who live in a city so renowned for the clear shining light of the Gospel.[1]

He was in low spirits, for the sky was dark in both Church and State, and it would seem, too, that he found his life as a grazier hard and unprofitable. It may well be that the legend is true that he contemplated leaving England for a freer country. It was the high tide of puritan emigration, largely from the eastern shires, and the news came weekly that this man or the other — among them young Henry Vane, the son of the comptroller of the king's household — had sailed for Massachusetts. Pym, whom Oliver had followed in parliament, had now given up politics, and was a busy official in Lord Warwick's company of the adventurers for the plantation of the Bahamas. With him were grouped such men as Lord Saye, Lord Brooke, Lord Holland, Sir William Waller and Oliver St. John, and John Hampden was associated with a venture in Connecticut.[2] These were the inner circle of puritan leaders, and the tale of their enterprises and hopes must have come through Hampden to the farm by the Ouse.

The project, if it was ever entertained, was dropped, for in 1636 Oliver had an accession of fortune. His uncle, Sir Thomas Steward, died, and he succeeded him as farmer of the cathedral tithes at Ely. He removed thither, his mother joining him from Huntingdon, and for the next eleven years made his home in a house, still standing, close to St. Mary's church. There was born Frances, his last child and youngest daughter. He would appear to have given up the farm at St. Ives, and to have had now more leisure for local affairs. The great cathedral with its starry tower meant nothing to him, and he was soon at variance with its clergy about the conduct of the services; his own religious experience made him intolerant of ceremonial and of all that came between the human soul and its Maker. But he was developing a wholesome interest in secular matters, being a man who hated mismanagement and petty injustice.

We have seen him interfering intemperately at Huntingdon to defend the rights of the humbler commoners, and now he

[1] L. and S., I, 79.

[2] The details are in the Cal. S. P. Colonial, 1574–1660, and are summarized by C. E. Wade, John Pym, 150–164.

was drawn into the long controversy about the draining of the Fens — the same trouble that Wentworth had had to face a few years before with Cornelius Vermuyden in connection with the Yorkshire Don. In 1634, a company of adventurers, headed by the Earl of Bedford, secured the right to drain the fens around Ely and carry the Ouse direct to the sea. An immense acreage of the reclaimed land was to go to the company, a proportion to the Crown, and the rest to provide a fund for the upkeep of the drainage works. In 1637 the syndicate announced that its task was completed and claimed its reward. Thereupon a great clamour arose; some of the shareholders complained that Bedford was getting too much; the neighbouring landowners resented their loss of commonage, and a multitude of small folk, squatters, fishermen, thatchers, fowlers, and willow-cutters, protested that their occupation was gone. Oliver took up the cause of the petty commoners, and undertook to guarantee them against legal process for five years, they paying him a groat for every cow they pastured on the disputed common-land. In 1638 the king intervened, declaring that the drainage work was incomplete and that the Crown would finish it, and decreeing that every man should in the meantime remain in possession of his customary rights. In this business Oliver won a wide local repute as a popular champion, a repute which was in the future to serve him well. Four years later, in 1641, he again took the field on behalf of his old neighbours of St. Ives. Some lands at Somersham had been enclosed without the commoners' consent and sold to Lord Manchester. The commoners petitioned parliament, the House of Lords upheld Manchester, and there was rioting and breaking of boundaries at Somersham. Oliver induced the Commons to appoint a committee of inquiry, and Hyde, its chairman, was deeply shocked by the proceedings. Oliver lost his temper, argued passionately the commoners' case, impugned the chairman's ruling, and dealt faithfully with the Manchester family, so that Hyde 'found himself obliged to reprehend him, and to tell him that, if he proceeded in the same manner, he would presently adjourn the committee and complain to the House of him.'[1]

Oliver was happier in Ely, not only because he was interesting himself in a plain forthright business like the defence of the poor man's rights, but because he had come to despair less of the State. For strange and exciting news was coming out of

[1] Clarendon, *Life*, I, 78.

Scotland. Hitherto Scotland had been as little known to him as Cathay; he had heard of it as a land full of zeal for a pure gospel; he may have met one or two Scots ministers, and as a grazier he may have bought store cattle from Scots drovers. But suddenly it became a place tremulous with a new dawn. It seemed that the king and Laud had been at their old game there of trying to dictate men's religion, and had introduced a new service-book which had been flung back in their faces. All Scotland had pledged itself in a national covenant to have nothing to do with Rome or with any innovation not sanctioned by parliament and the general assembly of its own Kirk. More, that Kirk had held an assembly in November 1638, and had utterly cast out bishops. Every week brought more heartening news. The king was proposing to coerce the Scots by arms, and had gone north with what forces he could raise, but the Scots had themselves armed, and the king had listened to reason and promised them everything — free assemblies and free parliaments. These hyperboreans were fighting England's battle, and had now won what honest Englishmen sought.

But presently came news that the peace was hollow, that the king had gone back on his word, and was summoning an army to take order with the Scots. He had no money and must inevitably have recourse to parliament, and sure enough the writs went out early in 1640 for a new House of Commons. Like a war horse Oliver sniffed the coming battle, for now at last great matters would come to trial. Presently he begged a friend in London to send him 'the reasons of the Scots to enforce their desire of uniformity in Religion' [1] — that seemed to him the only weak point in the policy of an admirable people. Huntingdon was now a thing of the past, but the town of Cambridge, grateful for his championing of the fen-men, returned him as its member.

As Oliver rode south in April to the meeting of the Short Parliament — perhaps making a circuit to pick up his cousin Hampden in the Chilterns — he must have been conscious that he had reached the turning point in his career. He had no impulse to plan out his life by the rules of worldly ambition, but he had strange premonitions, and his instinct must have told him that he was done with the tithes of Ely as with the cowpastures of St. Ives. He was now forty-one years of age, which was then regarded as far on in middle life. He was a different

[1] *L. and S.*, I, 96.

man from the ruddy young squire who took his bride to Hunt-ingdon — even from him who, eleven years before, had had his first taste of parliament. There were lines on his brow, streaks of grey in his hair, and his features were leaner and harsher, for his spirit had been through deep waters. An uncouth but an unforgettable face. 'Look in those strange, deep, troubled eyes of his, with their wild, murky sorrow and depth — on the whole wild face of him; a kind of murky chaos: almost a fright to weak nerves; at which, nevertheless, you look a second time, and sundry other times, and find it to be a thing in the highest de-gree worth looking at.' [1] He was careless in his dress even for a countryman, and fine gentlemen would laugh at him, but the laugh would die on their lips, for there was more in his appear-ance for awe than for ridicule. There is a tale that one of them, on first seeing him in parliament, asked John Hampden who he was. 'That sloven,' said Hampden, 'whom you see before you, hath no ornament in his speech; that sloven, I say, if we should ever come to a breach with the king (which God forbid), in such a case, I say, that sloven will be the greatest man in England.' [2]

Oliver had not found himself — that he was never to do in this world — but after much striving he had learned a rule of life. He had a profound and passionate, if undogmatic, religious faith. In politics, except inasmuch as they touched upon his religion, he was less decided; indeed so far he had been curiously unpartisan. His only speech in parliament had been a plea not for coercion but for fair dealing to all sides, and in his local quarrels he had actually been on the side of the king, and had opposed the Russells and Montagues and other puritan gran-dees. He had somewhat of a cross-bench mind, not easily brigaded with sect or party. His supreme convictions were the worth of what Lincoln called the 'plain people,' and the re-sponsibility of a man to his fellows as well as to his God.

In the eleven years of country life he had come slowly to maturity. They had not been years of idyllic retreat, as Andrew Marvell sang, in private gardens:

> where
> He lived reservèd and austere,
> As if his highest plot
> To plant the bergamot.

---

[1] Carlyle, *Historical Sketches*, 346.   [2] Noble, I, 268.

They had been years of active social life, where he had come to
know the hearts of the Fenland people and something of the
heart of England. They had been years of strenuous self-
examination and much lonely pondering — dejection, too, till
the doings in Scotland gave him hope. He had watched the
course of events at home and abroad with anxious eyes, fretted
at Laud's doings, trembled over Wentworth's success, gloried
in Hampden's defiance, shuddered at Tilly's sack of Magde-
burg, exulted in the victories of the King of Sweden and sor-
rowed for his death. He had no experience of war, but when in a
year or two he took the field he showed himself already a master
of its first principles, and it is reasonable to believe that a close
study of works like *The Swedish Intelligencer* had opened to him
the mind of Gustavus.

But the formative power of those years lay most, perhaps,
in the magical environment of the fens, with their infinite spaces
of water and sky. Out of them from immemorial time grew one
of the stubbornest of English stocks. 'A gross, unpicturesque
land, of reed-grass, weedy verdure, of mud and marsh, where
the scattered hills, each crowned with its church and hamlet,
rise like islands over the continent of peat-bog; and indeed so
mostly still bear the name of Ey, which in the ancient dialect
of all Deutschmen, Angles, Norse, or whatever they are means
Island.'[1] Like the desert it is a land inhospitable to man, where
humanity must toil hard to keep its feet and each vantage has
to be grimly won from nature. Like the desert, too, it holds life
close to its elements, leading to monotheism in religion and a
certain stark virility in conduct and manners, for nature there
has no delicate cosmetics with which to flatter the soul. Out of
such places have come mystics and prophets, iron autocrats
and iron levellers — all of them simple men.

[1] Carlyle, *Historical Sketches*, 58.

Chapter IV

THE APPROACH OF WAR
(1640–1642)

Forasmuch as we do find that hardly within the memory of all times can be shewed forth a fit example of precedent of the work we have in hand, we thought ourselves so much the more bound to resort to the infallible and original ground of nature and common reason, and, freeing ourselves from the leading or misleading of examples, to insist and fix our considerations upon the individual business in hand, without wandering or discourse.

BACON, *Preface to the Articles of Union of England and Scotland.*

THE tale of the Short Parliament is soon told. Most of the members were new, and they accepted at once the leadership of Pym. Charles had hoped that his evidence of Scottish intrigues with France would rouse the nationalism of Englishmen, but the House refused to be interested, and turned resolutely to the grievances which had been maturing during the long recess. It was a grave and businesslike and still a moderate assembly, and its proceedings gave Lord Falkland, a new member, 'such a reverence for parliaments that he thought it really impossible that they could ever produce mischief or inconvenience to the kingdom, or that the kingdom could be tolerably happy in the intermission of them.' [1] Pym's speech on April 17th, the greatest he ever delivered, expounded soberly the case for reform — the offences against the liberty and privilege of parliament and the liberty and the property of the citizens, and the doings of Laud and his ecclesiastical courts.[2] The king demanded subsidies before he would consider grievances, not unnaturally perhaps, considering that he was on the verge of war. Finding the House resolute, he dissolved it suddenly on May 5 after a three weeks' session. The irritation of the members was not allayed by the fact that Convocation went on sitting and granting subsidies from the clergy. 'It must be worse before it can be better,' St. John grimly told Hyde. 'They must now be of another temper; they must not only sweep the house clean below, but must pull down all the cobwebs which hang in the top and corners.'

Charles turned to the malcontents in the north. The parliament held in June in Edinburgh openly decreed revolution, a

[1] Clarendon, *Hist.*, VII, 222.   [2] Rushworth, II (2), 1131–63.

committee of public safety was appointed, and in July Leslie
was on the march. Wentworth, summoned from Ireland and
made Earl of Strafford, found the tools breaking in his hand.
'Pity me,' he wrote to a friend, 'for never came any man to so
bad a business.' On August 28th Leslie defeated the kings'
army at Newburn on the Tyne and next day received the town
of Newcastle's surrender. The rejoicings in London after this
English defeat warned Charles of the unpopularity of the war,
against which twelve peers had already petitioned.[1] He adopted
the ancient device of summoning a great council of peers to
meet at York, but the general sense of the council was with the
petitioners, while Pym and his followers were known to be deep
in the confidence of the Scots. His exchequer was empty, his
army was a rabble, and he was compelled to bow to the inevitable. The treaty of Ripon patched up a temporary peace, and
writs were issued for a new parliament.

I

The new parliament, to be known in history as the Long,
which met on November 3rd, was the most fateful assembly
that has ever sat in the old chapel of St. Stephen. It was not
like the 'great, warm and ruffling parliament' which had passed
the Petition of Right, a declaratory body to give voice to opinions, or like the Short Parliament, a gathering of perplexed and
moderate reformers. The events of the summer months had
wrought a portentous change in many minds. Pym's April
speech was his last as a reformer, and now he and his group
were moving fast towards revolution. Nevertheless the assembly contained all varieties of view and all that was most
weighty in English life.

In it sat the leading gentry of every shire; it was an aristocratic body and it contained a greater proportion of ancient
blood than the House of Lords today. Most of the famous
figures of the Civil War were there, so that it was like a parade
of troops before the day of battle. Formal government and
opposition parties were not yet in being, but members of a like
mind sat together. Charles did not lack friends in the House,
some of them office-holders, some of them already vehement
royalists, some still doubting. For Wilton sat Sir Henry Vane,
the secretary of state, who as an official had made a great

[1] Gardiner, *Cons. Docs.*, 134.

fortune and become the owner of wide lands in the north; his character stares at us from Van Dyck's canvas, the *faux bonhomme*, the supple courtier, with sly, shifty eyes and a greedy mouth. John Ashburnham, the king's confidential secretary, sat for Hastings, and Henry Wilmot for Tamworth, and from Bury St. Edmunds came Henry Jermyn, the queen's master of the horse, who already bore an ill repute. Wells sent the soldierly person of Sir Ralph Hopton, and Dorset the younger Digby, Lord Bristol's son, soon to be Charles's most intimate adviser, but at present, owing to family grievances, a little estranged from the court. From Hertfordshire came the noble figure of Arthur Capel, 'a man in whom the malice of his enemies could discover very few faults.'[1] There was a little group, too, whose ultimate policy was still undecided. One was John Colepeper from Kent, who had soldiered abroad and knew much about the arts of both agriculture and war. Another was Edmund Waller from St. Ives, the poet of Sacharissa, a quaint singing-bird among falcons. There were the lawyers, Edward Hyde from Saltash and John Selden from Oxford university, both on the popular side, yet with reservations which made them suspect by the hot-heads. And for Newport in the Isle of Wight sat the young Lord Falkland, a small man with an ugly voice and a somewhat vacant countenance, who was nevertheless reported by his friends to be a miracle of wit and wisdom, and who more than any other of his time was born to a heritage of unfulfilled renown.

There were as yet no clear party divisions, and Pym still cast his spell over the whole House, except a few rakes like Wilmot and Jermyn and young exquisites like Sir Philip Warwick. But he had his own special following, on the fringes of which were the elder Fairfax, the holder of a Scottish peerage, who represented the great shire of York; Sir William Waller from Andover, and Sir John Hotham from Beverley, a dull irritable man with a grievance. Deeper in the group were the lawyers, the dry Oliver St. John, Strode made implacable by his sufferings, Strafford's brother-in-law Denzil Holles, and old Rudyerd, the friend of Ben Jonson, who had already sat in six parliaments. There were also the avowed revolutionaries, disreputable cynics like Henry Marten from Berkshire, and slender-witted but stubborn theorists like Sir Arthur Haselrig, and hot foes of episcopacy like Nathaniel Fiennes from Banbury and the

[1] Clarendon, *Hist.*, XI, 266.

young Henry Vane from Hull, just appointed treasurer of the
navy. Vane's religion had carried him to America and his politics had brought him home, and now he filled among the groups
of the left something of the position of Falkland with the centre
and the right. He was a man of mystery, of undoubted parts,
not generally liked, but by a few worshipped. Clarendon tells
us that he 'had an unusual aspect which... made men think
that there was somewhat in him of extraordinary.'[1] What that
was we may judge from the Lely portrait. The long Hapsburg
chin, the prominent lustrous eyes, the loose talking lips reveal
the intense spiritual egoist.

Pym was the undisputed leader of the House and the auto-
crat of his own group, Pym shaggy as ever and now grown very
fat, so that the court ladies called him the Ox. He had definitely become a party manager, and at meetings in the country, at Lord Saye's castle of Broughton in Oxfordshire, and at
Sir Richard Knightley's house of Fawsley, or in town in his
lodgings behind Westminster hall, he held frequent conclaves of
his supporters. His chief lieutenant was John Hampden, one
of the richest men in England, to whom the ship money case
had given a nation-wide fame. Hampden was a poor speaker,
but, like Falkland, he cast a spell over his contemporaries.
Clarendon calls him a 'very wise man, and of great parts, and
possessed with the most absolute spirit of popularity, that is
the most absolute faculties to govern the people, of any man I
every knew.'[2] His power lay in two things, his single-minded-
ness, for he knew precisely what he wanted, and his subtlety
and tact, for like many of the single-hearted he was an adroit
diplomatist. He was eminently persuasive, for he was never
dogmatic, and so gently insinuated his views into other men's
minds that they believed them to be their own unaided creation. He was that rare combination, an idealist with an acute
judgment of ways and means, perhaps at the moment the wisest
head in England; but Pym had the greater daimonic force, and
he remained the leader till the civilians were ousted by the
soldiers.

Known to few as yet, but in the inner circle of Pym's followers, stood the member for Cambridge. Oliver was still new
to the business, but he was eager to learn, and he had in the

---

[1] *Hist.*, III, 34. The royalist diarists were always on the look-out for this *aliquid insigne.* Sir Philip Warwick found it with some justice in Hamilton.

[2] *Hist.*, VII, 83.

House a powerful family backing. John Hampden, Oliver St. John and Edmund Waller were his first cousins, Valentine Wauton, the knight of the shire for Huntingdon, was his brother-in-law, and Sir Richard Knightley had married Hampden's daughter. At the beginning of the Long Parliament he had seventeen kinsmen or connections in the House, and later he had twenty-one.[1] He was at once placed upon many committees, and in the first days of the session he intervened in debate — not on a matter of high policy, for that he had scarcely yet mastered, but on a question of an individual wrong, John Lilburne's imprisonment in the Fleet. Let Sir Philip Warwick introduce the new member.

> The first time I ever took notice of him was in the beginning of the Parliament, held in 1640, when I vainly thought myself a courtly young gentleman, for we courtiers valued ourselves much on our good clothes. I came into the House one morning, well clad, and perceived a gentleman speaking whom I knew not, very ordinarily apparelled; for it was a plain cloth suit that seemed to have been made by an ill country tailor; his linen was plain, and not very clean, and I remember a speck or two of blood upon his little band which was not much larger than his collar; his hat was without a hatband; his stature was of a good size; his sword stuck close to his side; his countenance swollen and reddish; his voice sharp and untunable, and his eloquence full of fervour. For the subject matter would not bear much of reason, it being in behalf of a servant of Mr. Prynne's, who had dispensed libels against the Queen for her dancing, and such like innocent and courtly sports; and he aggravated the imprisonment of this man by the Council table into that height that one would have believed the very government itself had been in danger by it. I sincerely profess it much lessened my reverence unto that great council, for he was very much hearkened unto.[2]

II

Pym till his death was the dominating figure in parliament, the first civilian party leader in England. He had all the equipment — a caucus which met in secret, a machine outside the House in the shape of his company of adventurers, and a party chest provided by the wealth of the city of London. He had an elaborate intelligence system, and his agents were in every

[1] Weyman, 'Oliver Cromwell's Kinsfolk.' *E. H. R.*, Jan., 1891.
[2] Warwick, 247.

tavern and in the court itself. He was partisan now, not statesman, for his mind was closed to the arguments of his opponents,
and dominated by a single, narrow, inflexible purpose. He had
not thought out the consequences of his policy, and he emerged
badly from the later controversy with Hyde on abstract matters of government. His was a destructive rather than a creative
mind, but on his main purpose he had not a shadow of doubt.
Parliament, not the king, must have the final word on every
matter which touched the interest of England.

Few in the House desired that final breach which meant
war, but there was no man with the authority and statesmanship to prevent it. But had a Richelieu been the leader of the
majority it is likely that he would have failed, the king being
what he was. The nicest and wisest delimitation of monarchical
powers, which would have satisfied Falkland as well as Pym,
Hampden as well as Wentworth, would have shipwrecked upon
the character of Charles. He had no gift of reading the temper
of his people or of recognizing harsh realities. His principles
were blind, irrational devotions. How could an equipoise of
rights be established if one side to the bargain was determined
to take the first opportunity to upset it? There was a dangerous
logic in Pym's view that there was no half-way house for England at that moment between an enslaved and a supreme parliament, an impotent and an autocratic monarch. Moreover
Charles was left to his own devices, for he was soon to have no
advisers. Presently Mr. Secretary Windebank and Lord Keeper
Finch fled the country, and Strafford went to the Tower.
Bristol was out of favour, Endymion Porter was only a courtier,
and Nicholas no more than a clerk. He turned to the worst of
all counsellors, his audacious, light-headed queen.

The first work of parliament was to remedy proven abuses
and to this the king offered small opposition. Tonnage and
poundage, ship-money, and all levies made without parliamentary authority went by the board, and with them the special courts, the Star Chamber and the High Commission, the
Council of the North and the Council of Wales and the Marches.
Men illegally imprisoned were released. The meeting of parliament was set above the royal caprice, and in February 1641
there was passed a triennial act which bound the king to call a
parliament every third year — a measure with the passing of
which Oliver had much to do. More, on May 11, the king assented to a further bill under which, without its consent, he

could not dissolve or prorogue the present parliament — a strange concession, for it made that parliament independent not only of the Throne but of its own constituents. Here reform passed clearly into revolution. The vital ecclesiastical question, too, came soon to the forefront. There was a powerful section in the House, including Fiennes, the younger Vane, Hampden and Oliver, who desired the abolition of episcopacy root and branch. A petition on these lines was arranged for from the city, and Oliver in February 1641, and again in May, argued vehemently in its favour. This was an attack less upon the Church than upon the Laudian bishops, and indirectly upon the royal prerogative. On the scandal of the present system almost the whole House was agreed, but some, like Hyde and Falkland, would have had a controlled episcopacy as the best barrier against the kind of ecclesiastical tyranny which flourished in Scotland. Oliver on the other hand preferred to make a clean sweep of clerical dignitaries and to entrust their jurisdiction to parliamentary commissioners. He was still at the stage when the infallible wisdom of parliament seemed to him axiomatic and a cure for all mischiefs.

But the first months of the new House were overshadowed by one urgent question — what was to be done with the man who had threatened the very existence of parliamentaryism by making autocracy efficient? It was a race between the two factions. Strafford tried to induce the king to strike first, and to charge Pym and his friends with treason because of their intrigues with the Scots. But Charles hesitated, and Pym, informed by his agents of all that was happening at court, was the first to get in his blow. Strafford was impeached before the House of Lords, and on November 11, 1640, was arrested and committed to the Tower. A month later Laud followed him.

The trial which followed is no part of our story, for Oliver's share in it was small. But, since it raised certain major issues in an acute form, it deserves a brief consideration.

The first point to note is the tribunal by which Strafford was tried. The House of Lords, flooded with new creations, had lost much of its prestige in the country and its authority over the House of Commons. Its members represented wealth and court influence rather than popular prestige and experience in affairs. The ancient families were apt to be contemptuous of the upstarts. Arundel, 'in his plain stuff and trunk hose and his beard in his teeth,' could tell Lord Spencer that his own

ancestors had suffered in the king's service 'in such a time as
when perhaps the lord's ancestors that spoke last kept sheep.' [1]
Hence, though the majority were likely to take the king's side,
there was a considerable critical opposition inclined to the reformers, and for the most part representing the more ancient
nobility. In the discussion of the Petition of Right the Lords
stood by the Commons, and after Buckingham's death the desire of the majority was undoubtedly to work in harmony with
the lower House. There were peers, like Saye and Brooke and
Warwick, who saw eye to eye with Pym, and there were many,
like Bristol, who were prepared to go far in concessions to preserve the unity of the nation. The latter's words to Charles at
York in September 1640 represented the general feeling of his
order. 'You see, sir, you have lost your kingdom's heart by
your taxes and impositions, and that till you are united to
them, by giving them just satisfaction in all their grievances,
you are no great king, for without the love and hearts of his
people, what can a king do?' [2] When the Long Parliament began, the king could probably count on a majority on most
questions among the one hundred and fifty peers, but it was a
leaderless majority and it was subject to violent fluctuations of
opinion. It desired to live at peace with the Commons and it
held no extreme views on the royal prerogative. To Strafford
and his ways the great bulk were hostile on public and private
grounds. They would give him justice but no sympathy, but
they regarded themselves as a court of law, whose verdict was
to be determined by legal evidence.

This was not the view of Pym and his following. They were
determined on Strafford's death, for it was the only alternative
to their own destruction. They paid him the tribute of extreme
fear. 'Stone-dead hath no fellow' was the counsel even of the
just and gentle Essex. If the law of treason would not cover his
case, a new law must be made. They would permit no juridical
etiquette, no rules of fair dealing, to stand in their way. For
them the question was not legal but political. 'He had endeavoured to subvert the fundamental laws of England and
Ireland, and instead thereof to introduce an arbitrary and
tyrannical government against law'; 'he had laboured to subvert the rights of parliaments and the ancient course of parliamentary proceedings.' Pym's speeches were all a deification of
law and a demand for its reign, but in the stages of the trial it

[1] Gardiner, *Hist.*, IV, 114. Walker, 221. [2] Firth, *H. of L.*, 71.

was made clear that the law he glorified was not the standing law of the realm but a political dogma favoured by the single estate of the Commons.

The trial began on March 22, 1641, and by dawn each morning the great hall of Westminster was packed. Mr. Robert Baillie, the emissary of the Scottish Covenanters, looked on at the spectacle with wondering provincial eyes and has left us a vivid picture; — the tall bowed figure of the accused in deep black wearing the George, the Lords in their robes and the Commons members within and without the rails, the vacant throne, the king in his box breaking the trellis with his own hands that he might hear better, the other boxes to the roof crowded with ladies and foreign notables, the chattering and laughter and guzzling while the grim drama was played out.[1] From the first Strafford had no shadow of a chance. He had made enemies of the most powerful forces in the land: the implacable place-hunters whom he had foiled, the parliamentary theorists, the grim Scots whom he had known and disliked in Ulster, and who made a god of things 'purely and simply indifferent.' He faced his enemies with unflinching courage, though his body had become very frail. 'My heart is good,' he wrote, 'and I find nothing cold within me.'

Of the details of the trial this is not the place to write, or of the conduct of the two Vanes which largely determined his fate.[2] Strafford defended himself with a patient reasonableness, though he was tortured by pain, and it was soon clear that he could not be convicted of treason as the law then stood. After fourteen sittings this became patent to the Commons leaders and they resorted to other means. There was a general alarm as to what the king might do — march up the army from Yorkshire or seize the Tower to overawe parliament — and on this wave of fear, assisted by organized London mobs, they carried to success a simpler plan. It was Strafford's head or theirs. All pretence of judicial proceedings was relinquished. A bill of attainder was passed by the Commons and defended in the

[1] Baillie, I, 314, etc. The trial is fully described in Rushworth, *Trial of Strafford* (1680) and in the *Brief and Perfect Relation of the Answers of the Earl of Strafford* (1647). The popular feeling is shown by the number of pamphlets issued after his death; yet even the most hostile show some recognition of his greatness. See the most curious of them all, entitled *A Description of the Passage of Thomas, late Earle of Strafford, over the River of Styx, with the conference betwixt him, Charon, and William Noy.*

[2] See Gardiner, *Hist.*, IX, 229, 319, etc. Ireland, *Sir Henry Vane the Younger*, 149, etc. Lady Burghclere, *Strafford*, II, 233, etc.

Lords by Oliver St. John with arguments alien to any civilized
code. 'Why should he have law himself who would not that
others should have any? We indeed give law to hares and deer
because they are beasts of chase; but we give none to wolves or
foxes, wherever they are found, because they are beasts of
prey.'[1] The Lords passed the bill on May 8th; Strafford urged
the king to assent to it in the interests of peace, and Charles,
renouncing his plighted word, accepted the sacrifice. The
doomed man met death with calm eyes; it was all one to him
whether he laid his head on the block or was torn to pieces by
the mob; his race was accomplished.[2] Ussher, who accompanied
him to Tower Hill, said that he 'had never known a whiter
soul' — the verdict, let it be remembered, of one who differed
widely from him in temperament and doctrine.

Another judgment was that of Richelieu — 'the English
were so foolish that they killed their wisest man.'[3] A great
man beyond doubt, perhaps the greatest English man of action
in two centuries except that member for Cambridge whose
harsh face was to be seen among the jostling Commons at the
bar. But wise in Richelieu's sense he was not, for he misread
his times, and he lacked that *tact des choses possibles* which is
of the essence of statesmanship. He had a theory of government much of which was eternal truth, and which applied by a
man like him might have insured prosperity and peace. But
there was no second Strafford, and above him was Charles.
One man could not direct every detail of a country's administration, and in the hands of Charles and his ordinary advisers
the Strafford plan would have been only a more potent weapon
of misgovernment. It is no answer to say that the House of
Commons proved little less tyrannous and far more inefficient;

[1] Rushworth, *Trial of Strafford*.

[2] 'Do we not mistake indeed the temper of great minds all along, when we imagine
that because they devote themselves to the business of life, they are therefore devoted
to life? Rather should we not say that they adopt that means of getting through it.
Some trial awaits all men, adversity the pampered, neglect the proud, occupation the
indolent, and life itself the great. The big ardent mind must be doing something, or it
pines and dies, must be filling up the awkward void, storing time with acts, and making
life substantial. But take away life, and the worldly principle is over; they are no longer
bound to it than they exist in it, they do not regret the loss of that which they only
spent because they had, or love the rude unsightly material which their labour moulded.
Life, the simple animal or passive, they never knew, or felt, or had.' J. B. Mozley,
Essays Historical and Theological, 95–96.

[3] This was also the view of John Evelyn. 'On the 12th of May I beheld on Tower-
hill the fatal stroke which severed the wisest head in England from the shoulders of the
Earl of Strafford.'

the House of Commons was the English people's own creation, and the nation could only learn wisdom by the old method of trial and error. That Pym, for all the violence of his methods, represented a deep-seated and universal feeling is clear from the passage of the attainder. Selden, indeed, outraged as a lawyer in his innermost sanctities, voted against it, but men like Falkland and Hyde and Capel did not oppose it.

Yet beyond question it was an act of revolution, a challenge which, when men began to reflect, was to cause a deep and final division in English minds. The choice was now between two forms of arbitrary rule. Digby in his courageous speech in the Commons put the point clearly. 'I do not say but the rest may represent him as a man worthy to die, and perhaps worthier than many a traitor. I do not say but they may justly direct us to enact that such things shall be treason for the future. But God keep me from giving judgment of death on any man and of ruin to his innocent posterity upon a law made *a posteriori*.' [1] The House of Commons in the name of law had begun to defy the law; in the name of free speech to persecute those who, like Strafford's few friends, had the temerity to differ from it; in the name of liberty to behave like a more intolerant court of High Commission. The hounds of revolution had been unleashed and in Strafford they had pulled down the one man who might have controlled them. 'Sure I am,' wrote Sir Philip Warwick, 'that his station was like those turfs of earth or seabanks, which, by the storm swept away, left all the inland to be drowned by popular tumult.' [2]

III

With Strafford in his grave and the chief political demands conceded by the king, parliament turned to those ecclesiastical questions which to many of its members were the major issue. The Root-and-Branch Bill had been becalmed in committee, and in June the bill passed by the Commons to exclude bishops from parliament was rejected by the House of Lords. All the summer bickering continued on this matter between a persistent lower House and a reluctant upper. The latter refused to accept a protestant test, which would have excluded catholics from their numbers; the Commons impeached thirteen bishops,

[1] Rushworth, III, (i.), 225–28.
[2] Warwick, 113.

decreed the abolition of all Laud's innovations in ritual, and attacked the prayer-book. Meantime there were ominous demands from Scotland for the establishment of presbytery in England, and on the Scots the parliament leaders were largely dependent. A House which had been nearly unanimous over the reform of civil abuses and the safeguarding of its privileges, and had shown a great majority against Strafford — which, moreover, in these matters had had popular opinion behind it — now began to show a deep cleavage within itself. It was well enough to get rid of Laud's extravagances, but the attack was now being pushed against things dear and ancient, the familiar service of the Church. Hyde and Selden and Falkland drew away from their former allies, and a party of constitutional royalism began to form itself in the House, and to win acceptance in the country. Conscious of this loss of support, Pym and his section became bolder and more desperate. They began to contemplate an appeal to force as an inevitable step, and they raised the vital question of the control of the military forces. They had reason to fear an armed *coup d'état*, and were resolved to forestall it. Before the session ended on September 9th, the Commons had virtually assumed military authority by ordering Lord Holland to secure the key seaport of Hull, and by making provision for guarding the Tower of London.

Meantime on August 10 Charles set out for Scotland. Misled by the Marquis of Hamilton, he believed that in that country, where religious separatism was rampant, but a traditional royalism seemed nevertheless to be universal, he might secure a makeweight against his enemies of the Commons. Dislike was growing between Scots and English, dislike which it was to please heaven to increase on better acquaintance. He hoped especially for the support of Leslie's army. The first days in Edinburgh disillusioned him.[1] Leslie's army was disbanded, and Charles was forced to grant to the Scottish parliament a firmer control over the executive and the judiciary than anything claimed at Westminster. He was compelled to put the Covenanting leaders in high office, and the bogus plot known as the 'Incident' was used to strengthen the position of Hamilton and Argyll. Meantime he had written in October a letter

---

[1] Goldwin Smith (*Three English Statesmen*, 41) says that the king on his Scottish visit was 'inflamed by contact with the fiery spirit of Montrose.' But Montrose never had speech with Charles, and during the whole of his visit was in prison in Edinburgh castle. His letter to the king several months before had counselled a policy of moderation and compromise.

to be circulated among the peers, in which he announced his intention of preserving the established doctrine and worship of the Church, and his resolve to die in the maintenance of it. Likewise he took occasion to promote two of the bishops whom the Commons had impeached. Pym, realizing that he was losing ground in the country, as he had already lost ground in the House, and believing that at any moment the king might appeal to force, decided that his position could only be sustained by some dramatic deed. He would appeal to the people at large with a statement of his case and a remonstrance on the disorders of the kingdom.

Suddenly out of Ireland came a thunderbolt. Charles had word of it on October 28 on the links at Leith, and by November 1, the day when Pym's remonstrance was to be discussed, the news reached parliament and ran like wildfire over London. The peace which Strafford had imposed had ended in blood and fire. The native Irish had risen in Ulster, and the Anglo-Irish gentry of the Pale were about to join them. Women and children had been brutally murdered; fifty thousand — a hundred thousand — a hundred and fifty thousand Englishmen were already dead. The rumours were largely untrue, for it is probable that in the first few months not more than four thousand colonists died by violence and perhaps an equal number from hardships and starvation; but the total was soon to be terribly swollen by retaliatory slaughterings, and the cautious Sir William Petty was of opinion that in ten years from 1641 more than half a million perished. This is not the place to trace the causes of the Irish rebellion. Ultimately they are to be found in centuries of misgovernment and misunderstanding, and notably in the barbarities and confiscations of the Elizabethan settlement. But a potent proximate cause was the removal of Strafford, and the disbandment of his army. He had given Ireland impartial justice and an equal law, but his regime had not yet rooted itself, and when his strong hand was withdrawn lawlessness leaped forth the more violently because of its suppression. He had treated the catholic faith with fairness and moderation, and to catholics the rule of those who had done him to death meant only persecution. They had not forgotten Pym's declaration that he would have all papists treated like madmen.

To Englishmen of both parties the rebellion seemed an ebullition of hellish wickedness, which it was their first duty to suppress with a fierce hand. But to the majority in parliament the thing had a still darker look. Most of them were of the class which had speculated in Irish land, who, as Oliver said eight years later 'had good inheritances which many of them had purchased with their money.' They saw in the natural rising of the oppressed and disinherited a deep-laid popish plot, and they suspected the connivance of Charles. Had not Sir Phelim O'Neill, the Ulster rebel leader, declared that he held a commission from the king? [1] Charles had always been tender to Rome, his queen was a bigoted catholic, and the ecclesiastical policy which he favoured meant coquetting with the mammon of un-righteousness. Even Falkland in the summer had said that the aim of the Laudian bishops was 'to try how much of a papist might be brought in without popery, and to destroy as much as they could of the Gospel without bringing themselves into danger of being destroyed by the law.' Their dread of Rome was intensified a thousand times, and with it their suspicion of the king. He had already threatened to raise an army to coerce parliament; if he were trusted with new forces to deal with Ireland might not he apply them to the same end?

The logic of such arguments can scarcely be denied, and it determined parliament's conduct. In the first week of November Pym moved as an additional instruction that, unless the king should accept only such councillors as parliament approved, parliament should take the matter of establishing security in Ireland into its own hand. Edmund Waller to his credit protested against this subordination of the interests of protestantism and England to a party cause, but the House was proponderatingly on Pym's side. He had in effect demanded the control of the executive power in Ireland. Oliver went further. This was a matter in which his feelings were deeply moved, and he would have no half measures. On November 6 he carried a motion that the Houses should confer upon the Earl of Essex the command of all the trained bands south of Trent, such command to continue at their pleasure — a claim for executive control in England. Parliament went on to pour oil on the Irish conflagration. In December it resolved that there should be no toleration of popery in Ireland or anywhere else under the Crown, and that funds for the Irish war should be got by further confiscations of Irish land, such land to be a security for the loans to be raised. In this matter Oliver played a leading part. A public subscription was levied in the House

[1] Rushworth, IV, 402. The commission was a forgery. See Gardiner, *Hist.*, X, 92 *n.*

and in the city, and he put down his name for £500. He was not a rich man, but his little fortune was quickly realizable, and he could contribute in cash a year's income.

Meantime Pym, who was not to be beguiled from the larger issues, pressed on the Grand Remonstrance, which was his appeal to the nation. Its two hundred and six clauses reviewed the long list of grievances against the king in language which was often exaggerated and always dull, and set forth the good work done already by parliament. So far it was an ordinary political manifesto, but at the end it laid down a drastic policy on the delicate matter of church reform. 'It is far from our purpose or desire,' it ran, 'to let loose the golden reins of discipline and government in the Church... for we hold it requisite that there should be throughout the whole realm a conformity to that order which the laws enjoin according to the Word of God.' But — bishops must be excluded from the House of Lords, the universities must be purged, 'unmeaning ceremonies' must be discarded, and in fact there must be a new Reformation. To achieve this end a synod of divines should be summoned, and in future the king must call to his council only such persons as were pleasing to parliament.[1]

This declaration showed men where they stood. It was a defiance, a war-cry, intended, with what Clarendon calls its 'sharp reflections,' to force a decision. Strangely enough its promoters believed that it would pass with little opposition, since, unlike the Root-and-Branch Bill, it did not abolish episcopacy. So Oliver seems to have thought, for he poohpoohed Falkland's proposal that there should be ampler time for debate, on the ground that few would oppose it.[2] But Pym knew better. He saw no hope of compromise and was resolved to push matters to a crisis — absolute parliament in place of absolute king; and he was aware that the new party of constitutional royalists saw the implications of his policy. The debate began at 9 A.M. on November 22, and was conducted all day with passion. Night fell, candles were brought in, but still the controversy raged, and it was not till two o'clock the following morning that the Remonstrance was finally carried by eleven votes. There rose a great hubbub about the printing of it and the right of members to record their protests, and the hands cf angry men stole to their scabbards. 'I thought,' wrote Philip Warwick, 'we had all sat in the valley of the shadow of

[1] Gardiner, *Const. Docs.*, 202–32.   [2] Clarendon, *Hist.*, IV, 51.

death; for we, like Joab's and Abner's young men, had catched at each other's locks and sheathed our swords in each other's bowels.' Going out of the House, Falkland reminded Oliver of their previous talk. 'Was I right about the debate?' Oliver's answer was, 'Another time, I will take your word for it.' He added, in a whisper which showed his own mind and the height to which intransigence had grown: 'Had the Remonstrance been rejected I would have sold all I possess next morning and never seen England more, and I know that there were many other honest men of the same resolution.' [1]

Two days later Charles returned to London. For the moment there was a curious reaction in his favour even in that stronghold of puritanism, perhaps because on his Scottish visit he had conceded so much to presbyterianism, perhaps, since he was still the protestant king of England, because the populace had to set up some figure-head against the hated Irish. Substantial men were beginning to think that enough had been done to safeguard the rights of parliament, and to be alarmed at the growth of sectarian anarchy. He was received in the city by welcoming crowds and a royalist lord mayor, and may well have believed that he still retained the affections of his people. He had returned from Scotland with one clear conviction: there was no help to be got from beyond the Tweed, and he must look for support to the loyalty of Englishmen; but for this purpose he must act firmly and take order with Pym and his friends, if they would not listen to reason. His aimless drifting had led to the tragedy of Strafford; he was king, with the machine of government at his disposal, and he must be ready to use his power. So, when the Grand Remonstrance was presented to him by a deputation which included Sir Ralph Hopton, he received it with good-humoured indifference, and pointed out some of the many weaknesses in that portentous document.

The royalist reaction was short-lived. An election in the city gave the parliament party a majority in the common council, and Charles's ill-judged dismissal of the parliament guard revived all the old suspicion. Worse still, he appointed as lieutenant of the Tower one Lunsford, a dissolute bravo who might be trusted to stick at nothing. The fury of the city compelled him presently to cancel this appointment, and put in Lunsford's place Sir John Byron, who at any rate was a man of honour. But the mischief had been done. Mobs, drawn largely from the

slums outside the walls called the 'liberties,' beleaguered Westminster, and bishops and peers were roughly handled. Pym approved of this rowdiness: 'God forbid,' he said, 'the House of
Commons should dishearten people to obtain their just desires
in such a way.' [1] Out of these tumults sprang two familiar
names, given in contempt by the factions to each other —
roundheads for the cropped apprentices, and cavaliers for the
king's men.

For one moment it would appear that Charles dallied with a
policy of serious conciliation. Even now war might have been
averted if he had succeeded in bringing the parliament leaders
into the executive. The principle of ministerial responsibility to
parliament was too violent an innovation to be readily conceded, but the thing might slowly have come into being had the
leaders of the Commons been included in the government.
Oliver St. John had been for months solicitor-general, but that
was then a post of small importance. Early in 1641 several of
the opposition peers — Bedford, Essex, Saye and Kimbolton
— had been brought into the privy council, but they were not
of the inner circle and had no weight in policy. He had also
thought of giving office to Pym, Hampden, and Holles, but the
scheme fell through. Now it was revived, and on the first day
of January Pym was offered the chancellorship of the exchequer. The matter is obscure, but Pym either ignored the
king's summons to an audience or declined the post. Next day
it was given to Colepeper, and Falkland received the vacant
secretaryship of state, while Hyde, who believed that he would
be more useful out of office, sat in the House as a minister
without portfolio. That day vanished the last hope of orderly
constitutional progress.

In January the situation rapidly worsened. The Commons
worked themselves into a state of hysteria, for which there was
some warrant. Rumour had long been rife of plots for armed
intervention on the king's side, organized for the most part by
trivial people like Suckling and Wilmot and Jermyn, and such
army as was in being was believed to be highly malcontent with
parliament. Pym's intelligence service and the younger Goring's treachery had provided irrefragable evidence. The queen
was known to be intriguing for foreign help, from France, Holland, Denmark, the Pope, even from Scotland, and when the
proofs came to the knowledge of the parliament leaders they

[1] Clarendon, *Hist.*, IV, 114.

resolved to impeach her. She knew well what a damning case could be made against her, and she listened to the advice of Digby, who stood himself in the same danger. Strafford had fallen because Pym had been allowed to strike first; now the king must get in the first blow and impeach the Commons leaders of treason. Charles, deeply moved by his wife's peril, was persuaded, and, on January 3, the attorney-general appeared before the House of Lords with a charge against Lord Kimbolton, and five members of the lower House, Pym, Hampden, Holles, Haselrig and Strode, while the Commons received a demand for their arrest.

Then came folly upon folly. Charles desired to proceed by law and not by violence, and, as the law stood, the accused, notably because of their Scottish intrigues, were as much guilty of treason as Strafford. But his impatience sent him crashing through all constitutional laws and customs. Next afternoon he went down to 'the House in a coach, with an armed retinue of three or four hundred men behind him. News of his intention had long before been sent to Pym by Will Murray and by one of the queen's women, Lady Carlisle,[1] and the five members had discreetly withdrawn. Charles strode into the chamber to find the birds flown, and to receive from Speaker Lenthall the classic answer that 'he had neither eyes to see, nor tongue to speak, in this place but as the House is pleased to direct me.' Next day he sought for the culprits in the city with no better success.

It was for the king the Rubicon which could not be recrossed. By his action he had exasperated the Commons to fury, and alienated the Lords. He had lowered his royal dignity, and convinced the ordinary man that neither his honour nor his judgment was to be trusted. He had attempted violence and failed, and had closed every avenue of reconciliation. On January 10 he left Whitehall — not to return to it till he returned to die.

The inevitable result was that the question of army control revived in an acute form. The militia became suddenly a matter of desperate importance. If the king had a purpose of violence, could he be allowed to retain his sword? Pym set his machine to work, the city trained bands were marshalled under Skippon,

---

[1] For Will Murray, who afterwards became Earl of Dysart, see Buchan, *Montrose*, 134, and Burnet, *Own Time*, I, 244. Lady Carlisle was Lucy, daughter of Henry, Earl of Northumberland, and widow of the first Earl of Carlisle. She was a vain, avaricious *intrigante*, but, though she was a close friend of Strafford, there is no evidence for the statement in the *Complete Peerage* that she had been his mistress, and it is highly improbable that she was ever Pym's.

the river was guarded, the mobs were out, and Hampden's Buckinghamshire constituents were pouring in with minatory petitions. The Commons decided, and the Lords concurred, that the fortresses, and the militia of the kingdom should be placed in hands which parliament approved. It was a violent innovation, since by all law and precedent the control of the military forces, though the Commons paid for them, lay with the Crown, but in the circumstances it had some justification. The Lords passed the Bishops' Exclusion Bill, which the king accepted; he temporized on the Militia Ordinance, till on February 23 the queen, carrying with her the crown jewels, had safely left the country. Then he accepted it with qualifications which would have defeated its purpose. On March 2 he set out for the north. It was the casting of the die. Oliver's motion, which had been dismissed as premature on January 14th, was now adopted, and both Houses resolved that the kingdom should be put in a posture of defence. On March 5th they appointed new parliamentary lords-lieutenants and gave them command of the militia.

For six months negotiations dragged on, but the minds of both sides were prepared for war, and the events were like the ranging shots of the guns before a battle. Pym reigned supreme at Westminster, and the few royalists in the Commons had an uneasy life. Falkland could do nothing, for his calm reason was out of place in this carnival of half-truths. Hyde, a watch-dog with every hackle erect, replied with effect to Pym's declamations, but Hyde with his mediocre legal conservatism was, as Bacon said of Salisbury, 'fit to keep things from growing worse, but not fit to redeem things to be much better.' He was no man to ride a storm which had left conservatism far behind. Both sides were outside the ancient law, and both sides had a strong *prima facie* case. The constitution had clearly broken down and must be reconstructed; the question was how. By giving sovereignty to parliament, said Pym, which represented the nation. But that, said Hyde, would only be to replace an old tyranny by a new. What warrant was there for maintaining that the people of England approved of parliament's recent deeds? Changes there must be, but in any change there must be a rational division of functions, which would ensure not only the liberties of the people but efficient government, and parliament was not a body which could itself administer. The land was in anarchy, and it was trying to save it by barren dogmas. And he might have added, in the words which Sir John Evelyn used three years later in the House of Commons: 'If there be any that do dream it necessary to reduce all things to their first principles, and know no way to perfection but by confusion, may their thoughts perish with them.' [1]

Further there was the primary question of religion. The bishops were a lesser matter, for the true issue was the very foundations of the Church. The decorous compromise of anglicanism was threatened by violent men who would replace it by presbytery, or would break all bonds of discipline and establish a multitude of sects. Whatever side controlled the Church had the power of moulding the thought of the nation — what would be represented today by the control of the schools and of the press. Toleration was still to most men deadly sin, and failure to carry their full policy meant the loss of that which they held most dear. It was true that attachment to a creed was more passionate on one side than on the other; 'they who hated the bishops,' said Falkland, 'hated them worse than the devil; they who loved them did not love them so well as their dinner';[2] but as controversy advanced men found that what had been a flickering affection was soon fanned into a blaze. 'No king, said one party, shall rob us of our religion. No parliamentary majority, said the other party, shall rob us of our religion. It was this and this only, which gave to the great struggle its supreme importance.' [3]

Yet some compromise might have been reached between Pym and Hampden, Falkland and Hyde, but for one disastrous fact. In arguing on the rights of parliament, royalists thought of the present parliament, and in arguing on the rights of the king their opponents thought of Charles. The Long Parliament had so far not given its opponents much cause to trust or admire it; it had been arbitrary, neurotic, tyrannical, intolerant of criticism. Had there been fresh elections, it is likely that Pym would have found himself in a minority. But Charles had managed to diffuse an atmosphere of lively distrust. His gentleness and charm might attach his friends to him, but his public conduct had been in the highest degree fantastic, disingenuous and uncertain.

[1] *O. P. H.*, XIII, 428.   [2] Clarendon, *Hist.*, III, 241.
[3] Gardiner, *Hist.*, X, 29.

He had no gift of resolute purpose or single-hearted action; the prominent velvet eyes under the heavy lids were the eyes of an emotional intriguer. They were the eyes, too, of a fanatic, who would find in the last resort some curious knuckle of principle on which he would hear no argument. 'He loved not the sight of a soldier, nor of any valiant man,' it had been written of his father, and Charles had no single gift of the man-at-arms except personal bravery. The old monarchy could only survive if its representative had those qualities of plain dealing and sturdy resolution which were dear to Englishmen; and it was the irony of fate that this king should be part woman, part priest, and part the bewildered delicate boy who had never quite grown up. A freakish spirit had been unloosed, as a shrewd observer [1] noted: 'such an unhappy genius ruled these times (for historians have observed a genius of times as well as of climates or men) that no endeavour proved successful, nor did any actions produce the right though probable effects.'

For six months the two sides manœuvred for position. The political trimmings and tacking were meaningless and intended only as propaganda. The king, having got the Prince of Wales into his keeping, was not inclined to be complaisant, and the House of Commons showed the hardening of its temper by committing to prison certain Kentish gentlemen who presented a petition on behalf of episcopacy. The House of Lords sank so low in attendance that it passed out of the picture. Pembroke, who brought a message to the king at Newmarket begging him to return, and suggesting that the Militia Ordinance might be accepted for a time, was told, 'By God, not for an hour!' On June 2 the king received from the House the Nineteen Propositions, which represented Pym's ultimatum, and which claimed on every vital point sovereignty for parliament. It demanded the selection of ministers and judges, the control of the militia and the fortresses, and liberty to reform the Church as it pleased — the direct exercise of functions which no large deliberative body could hope to perform efficiently.[2] The propositions were refused, and the issue was joined. Lyttelton, the lord keeper, fled to York with the great

[1] Thomas May.

[2] Pym's policy had much in common with the scheme of 'limitations' to the Prerogative, which Fletcher of Saltoun introduced in the Union debate in the Scots Parliament. See Fletcher's *Speeches*, 1703, and G. M. Trevelyan, *England under Queen Anne*, II, 236-37. In essence it was republican, and inconsistent with any form of monarchy.

seal, and Hyde by devious ways through Cotswold and the Peak succeeded in joining his master.

More important were the military events. Hull contained the stores collected for the Scottish campaign, the greatest armoury in the kingdom, and it was also the chief port by which help could be received from the Continent. Sir John Hotham had been sent by parliament to occupy the place, and when on April 23 Charles attempted to enter Hull the gates were shut in his face. It was the first overt act of war. Meantime at York he was collecting money and plate and drawing his supporters to his side. On June 16 commissions of array were issued and the royalist muster began, and next day Newcastle was occupied for the king. His opponents, meanwhile, were busy applying the militia ordinance in every shire where their influence prevailed, and Warwick, in command in the Downs, carried the fleet to the side of parliament. On July 4 a committee of public safety was appointed.[1]

On July 12 Essex was nominated commander-in-chief of the parliament forces, and the remnants of the two Houses swore to live and die with him, 'for the preservation of the true religion, laws, liberties and peace of the kingdom.' Already there had been blood shed at Manchester, and in early August there was more at Coventry. On August 22 at Nottingham — chosen as being nearer London than York and within hail of the west — the king, accompanied by the Prince of Wales, the Duke of York and the two younger Palatin princes, set up his standard. It was the evening of a wet and windy day, and only a little concourse had gathered. Every detail of the ceremony was emblematic of the man and the confusion of his cause. Charles himself in the rain emended the wording of the proclamation, for he was a precisian in style, and the herald had difficulty with his corrections and read it haltingly, so pedantry and bravado went hand in hand. Presently the gale blew the standard down, and for some days it lay prone on the ground.

IV

England had entered upon a civil war of which it may be written, more than of most historic controversies, that neither

[1] The fifteen members were Northumberland, Essex, Pembroke, Holland, Saye, Pym, Hampden, Fiennes, Holles, Pierpoint, Glyn, Henry Marten, Sir P. Stapleton, Sir J. Meyrick, and Sir W. Waller. *L. J.*, V, 128; *C. J.*, II, 651.

side had a monopoly of justice. An effective rejoinder could be made to every plea advanced, and men in the end chose their cause for other reasons than cold logic. An argument was sharpened into a formula, and a formula into a war-cry, and the extremest statement of each case became the accepted creed. Most Englishmen refrained from any decision, and, since the issue did not move them, abode in a puzzled neutrality. 'They care not what government they live under,' as Haselrig complained, 'so as they may plough and go to market.' There were many who sought only a quiet life, like young Mr. Evelyn, fresh from Balliol, who, after amusing himself with constructing a fish-pond and a solitude at Wootton, thought England likely to be an uncomfortable dwelling-place and betook himself abroad. There were some like Salisbury and Pembroke who, thinking only of their parks and chases, swung shamelessly with the tide. Even the serious and patriotic found themselves in confusion. 'Both sides promises so fair,' wrote Lady Sussex, 'that I cannot see what it is they shoulde fight for.' 'I am in such a great rage with the parliament as nothing will passify me,' wrote another country gentlewoman, 'for they promised us all should be won if my Lord Strafford's hed were off, and since then there is nothing beter.' [1] But even on the most perplexed a decision was forced. Richard Baxter in his ripe age might write: 'I confess for my part I have not such censorious thoughts of those that were neuter as formerly I had, for he that either thinketh both sides raised an unlawful war, or that could not tell which (if either) was in the right might well be excused if he defended neither'; [2] and Andrew Marvell might consider that 'the cause was too good to have been fought for,' and that men should have trusted God and the king; [3] but such detachment was for the ordinary thoughtful man strictly impossible. The trumpets had spoken and he must range himself.

Some had no doubts. The extremists on both sides were secure and happy. The young men of pleasure naturally followed the king's banner, for on the other side was the detested puritanism. Simple and loyal souls answered to the call of a personal allegiance. For men like Hopton and Capel, Sir Marmaduke Langdale and Sir Jacob Astley, there could be no hesitation, since their sworn fealty was involved. So also the king's

[1] *Verney Memoirs*, I, 255.   [2] *Rel. Baxt.*, 39.
[3] *The Rehearsal Transpros'd.*

standard-bearer Sir Edmund Verney, though on the merits of
the case he was with parliament. 'I have eaten his bread and
served him near thirty years and will not do so base a thing as
to forsake him.' [1] This forthright and unquestioning loyalty
was well expressed by Lord Paget, the parliament's own nominee
as lord-lieutenant of Buckinghamshire. 'It may seem strange
that I, who with all zeal and earnestness have prosecuted, in
the beginning of this parliament, the reformation of all disorders in church and commonwealth, should now in a time of
such great distractions desert the cause. Most true it is that
my ends were the common good; and whilst that was prosecuted, I was ready to lay down both my life and fortune; but
when I found a preparation of arms against the king under the
shadow of loyalty, I rather resolved to obey a good conscience
than particular ends, and am now on my way to his Majesty,
where I will throw myself down at his feet, and die a loyal
subject.' [2] Grandees like Newcastle were natural royalists because they were themselves semi-royal, and there were younger
men, some of them soon to die, who found in the summons a call
to manhood and a nobler path. Such was Carnarvon, who was
transformed from a virtuoso and sportsman into a most gallant
soldier. Such was Northampton, whose luxurious life was exchanged for one of simple hardihood. 'All distresses he bore
like a common man, and all wants and hardnesses as if he had
never known plenty.' These men the war revealed to themselves and to their fellows, so that, in Clarendon's beautiful
words, they were 'not well known till their evening.'

But even among the royalists who had no doubts there was
little zeal for the conflict. They understood the horrors of a civil
war where families, like Verneys and Feildings, Arundells and
Godolphins, were divided against themselves, and, like Defoe's
cavalier, they dreaded to hear men cry for quarter in the English
tongue. Among the more reflecting there was a deeper perplexity, and cheerfulness was in inverse proportion to a man's
intellectual stature. Hyde, indeed, had a stalwart argumentative faith in his own special creed, and he believed that, to
secure its triumph, it was necessary first of all that the king
should read parliament a stiff lesson. He stood for what he
regarded as the traditional English constitution, a mixed or
limited monarchy. Hobbes with his dialectic has made sport
of the doctrine,[3] but Hyde read rightly the instinct of his coun-

[1] *Verney Memoirs*, I, 277.   [2] *L. J.*, V, 152.   [3] In *Behemoth*.

trymen and in the long-run his view prevailed. Yet he only
held his faith by shutting his eyes to one damning fact, the
character of Charles. He must have known in his heart that
the victory of the king would not mean the kind of monarchy
he desired: like Montrose, he had to choose between two perils,
and he decided for what seemed to him the lesser. Let monarchy
be preserved and by the grace of God it might be mended; if it
fell, then the foundations would be removed, and the whole
fabric would crumble.

Falkland, a subtler and abler mind, asked more searching questions. He had not, like many, the passion of personal fealty,
and in his philosophic detachment he had as little love for one
side as for the other. He thought of the rival creeds as Bacon
thought of the Grecians and the Alchemists — 'That of the
Grecians hath the foundations in words, in ostentation, in
confutation, in sects, in schools, in disputations; that of the
Alchemists hath the foundation in impostures, in auricular traditions and obscurity.' He saw no hope of a fortunate issue, for
the triumph of either side would mean the triumph of an extreme, and therefore of unreason; and he feared that Englishmen would presently be divided by an unbridgeable river of
blood. Therefore 'from the entrance into this unnatural war
his natural cheerfulness and vivacity grew clouded, and a kind
of sadness and dejection of spirit stole upon him.' He was of a
temper and composition, Clarendon adds, 'fitter to live *in re-
publica Platonis* than *in faece Romuli.*'

On the parliament side there were also the doubters and the
half-hearted. To many, especially the plain soldiers like Sir
Thomas Fairfax and Sir William Waller, it was a cruel necessity, in which they could only pray that they might comport
themselves like Englishmen and Christians. Waller's letter to
Hopton is an expression of this sad chivalry.

> My affections to you are so unchangeable that hostility itself
> cannot violate my friendship to your person, but I must be true
> to the cause wherein I serve.... The great God, who is the searcher
> of my heart, knows with what reluctance I go upon this service,
> and with what perfect hatred I look upon a war without an enemy.
> ... The God of peace in his good time send us peace, and in the
> meantime fit us to receive it. We are both upon the stage and we
> must act the parts that are assigned us in this tragedy. Let us
> do it in a way of honour, and without personal animosities.[1]

Clarendon, S. P., II, 155.

Sir Simonds D'Ewes, stout parliament man as he was, had no heart to write his diary. Hampden, too, must have had heavy thoughts. He was clear on the immediate issue, but beyond that he saw only darkness, and his long face became graver and the deep eyes more melancholy, though the mouth was firmer set.

But to some it seemed to be the dawn of a new world. Milton, rapt from academic visions, was filled with illimitable hopes which were soon to shape themselves in splendid prose. It was a time of 'jubilee and resurrection' and 'age of ages wherein God is manifestly come down among us, to do some remarkable good to our church and state.'[1] It seemed 'as if some divine commission from heaven were descended to take into hearing and commiseration the long and remediless afflictions of this kingdom.'[2] His heart swells with admiration for his country-men, and his eyes glow with ecstatic visions of his country's destiny. 'Let not England forget her precedence of teaching the nations how to live.' He abounds in a lover's hyperboles — 'a right pious, right honest, and right hardy nation'[3] — 'an eagle mewing her mighty youth' — 'a nation not slow and dull, but of a quick, ingenious, and piercing spirit; acute to invent, subtle and sinewy in discourse, not beneath the reach of any point the highest that human capacity can soar to.'[4] Soon he was to be disillusioned and to find the bulk of Englishmen 'imbastardized from the ancient nobleness of their ancestors';[5] but for the moment he was in a honeymoon rapture. Yet the thought to which he gave utterance three years later was always in his mind. There could be no freedom without discipline, and if old bonds were cast off new ones must be forged by the enlightened spirit. Pearls must not be cast before swine,

> That bawle for freedom in their senseless mood,
> And still revolt when truth would set them free.
> License they mean when they cry libertie;
> For who loves that, must first be wise and good.

Something of this rapture was shared by certain of the parliamentary leaders, by men like the younger Vane, the fanatics of puritanism, the seekers after a republic. But not by Pym, the most confident of all. He had suffered the fate of many

---

[1] *Animadversions upon the Remonstrant's Defence.*
[2] *Apology for Smectymnuus.*   [3] *Ibid.*
[4] *Areopagitica.*   [5] *Eikonoklastes.*

great partisans, and had allowed a fighting cause so to obsess him that it shut out the rest of the world. He thought only of the immediate purpose and the instant need, not of what lay beyond — which is proper for a subordinate commander, but not for a general-in-chief, and still less for a statesman. As much as Strafford he had lost the *tact des choses possibles*, and, if Browning's vision be true, and in some better world he 'walks once more with Wentworth,' the two rivals may have discovered in the same lack the reason of their ultimate failure.

As for Oliver he had the fewest doubts of any. Half the strife in parliament had been about questions which he scarcely understood and had little interest in, and on these he dutifully followed his leader. Clearly he was all the time in a state of high excitement, finding his temper hard to control, and impatient of the rules of procedure. But on three matters he had his resolution fixed. Fourteen years later, as the undisputed ruler of England, he was to tell a parliament, 'our business is to speak Things,'[1] and now his views were a plain deduction from facts as he saw them. In the first place parliament must be predominant, for it alone represented the 'plain people.' The other two principles were negative, for his thoughts were not yet in a constructive phase: 'I can tell you, sir, what I would not have,' he told certain questioners; 'though I cannot, what I would.'[2] Episcopacy must be abolished, since it was the bishops, as he knew from his own experience, who were foremost in starving the nation of the Gospel and in coquetting with Rome. This was his deepest conviction, for religion was his major interest. Lastly Charles could not be trusted, and some way must be found of making him impotent for evil. That way could only be war. Already Oliver had shown that he had the courage of his opinions, for he had somewhat embarrassed his colleagues by moving to demand the dismissal of Bristol from the king's council, and he had been the first to propose to put the land in a state of defence. He cared nothing for the republican theories in which Vane dabbled, but, looking at facts, he saw that if parliament did not beat the king, the king would assuredly destroy parliament, and indeed might at any moment achieve a *coup d'état*. Therefore he was for war — war at once — war to a finish.

As soon as he was permitted he acted, for here was something which he understood. In July he spent £100 of his own money

[1] *L. and S.*, II, 509.   [2] Warwick, 177.

in sending down arms to Cambridgeshire, and he obtained a vote permitting the town of Cambridge to raise two companies of volunteers. With his brothers-in-law, Valentine Wauton and John Disbrowe, he prevented the University from sending £20,000 worth of plate to the king, and seized the local magazine. When the Bishop of Ely tried to put into force the royal commission of array, he fell upon him with a hastily raised levy, surrounded the colleges during service in chapel, and packed off three heads of houses as prisoners to London.[1] The member for the borough had taken command of the shire. By the end of August he was back in town, having raised a troop of sixty light horse, with Disbrowe as their quartermaster, for the army of Essex. At forty-three he had found his proper calling, and a force of incalculable velocity had been unloosed on the world.

[1] *L. and S.*, I, 112 *n*.

Book Two
THE CAVALRY COMMANDER

Chapter I

THE RIVAL FORCES

(1642–1646)

England now is left
To tug and scamble and to part by the teeth
The unow'd interest of proud-swelling state.
Now for the bare-pick'd bone of majesty
Doth dogged war bristle his angry crest,
And snarleth in the gentle eyes of peace.

King John.

I

THE marshalling of the rival forces revealed how little the dispute had as yet become an issue for all England. Even in the later stages of the war the total number of soldiers in the field was scarcely one-fortieth of the population. The ordinary citizen was apathetic and desired only to be left in peace; his sympathies may have inclined slightly to the side of king or of parliament, but he was not prepared to bestir himself for either. At first not even half the gentry were in arms, and to the end the labourer only fought when he was constrained by his betters. The struggle from first to last was waged by two small but resolute minorities. It was not a war of classes, for the dividing line ran through every rank of society, and it was not exclusively a war of regions. In essence it was a conflict of ideas, but a local leader — Derby in Lancashire, Oliver in the eastern shires — who was passionate in his cause, could swing his neighbourhood to his side. Nor was it in the common sense a war of religion, for the antagonists were alike Christians and protestants, emphasizing different aspects of their creeds, so that the campaigns had none of the horrors of those of Alva and Wallenstein. Moreover, the edge was taken off the controversy at the start by the unexpected wisdom of the king. He declined to use his power in Yorkshire to arrest Fairfax and other parliamentarians, and through Colepeper and Falkland he made reasonable overtures to the House of Commons — overtures which were brusquely rejected, so that to many doubting moderates throughout the land, who had been inclined to the cause of parliament, the campaign seemed to open with Charles as the peacemaker and Pym as the irreconcilable.

Yet on broad lines it is possible to compute the rival strengths mainly on a geographical and social basis, a fact which had a direct bearing on strategy. Parliament's power lay in the towns, for it was there that puritanism especially flourished. London was overwhelmingly in its favour, and London contained one-third of the urban population of England. In royalist Lancashire Manchester was for the parliament, as were the woollen towns of west Yorkshire, and the same was true of the little clothing boroughs of Gloucester and Somerset. Only the university and cathedral cities were definitely for the king. Again, it may be said that the royal strength lay chiefly in the north and west, and the parliamentary in the south and east, the richest districts of England.[1] In the less cultivated regions, the moors and the sheep-walks, and among the Celtic stocks of Wales and Cornwall, royalism was the accepted faith, for there the peasants docilely followed the gentry, and there was no middle-class to raise questions. Most important of all, parliament held the dockyards and the chief ports (except Newcastle and Chester), and the fleet — sixteen ships of war in the Downs and two in Irish waters, as well as twenty-four merchantmen — was on its side. This meant that it could move supplies easily, and hinder the king's communications with the Continent; also that the overseas commerce, which provided its sinews of war, could go on unchecked.

The situation of England in 1642 is curiously paralleled by that of the United States at the opening of the Civil War. The American North, like the English parliament, had behind it the more populous regions and by far the greater wealth. It had the fleet and could command the seas. It had the largest cities and the chief industries. The South had a smaller population, but it had a society of country-dwellers who could ride and shoot, and were consequently better adapted at the start for the business of war. The war was made by idealists who swung great masses of pacific and uninstructed citizens. Both sides stood for principles in which they passionately believed, and neither stained its hands with barbarities. Again, the rival forces seemed to be brought blindly to a clash; there was no immediate military objective before either side; it was a trial of physical strength, a submission of two irreconcilable faiths to ordeal by battle.[2]

[1] In the ship money assessment of 1636 three-fourths fell upon the counties south-east of a line drawn from Bristol to Hull.

[2] Sir Charles Firth has drawn further interesting parallels in his Rede Lecture, 1910.

There was another point common to the two struggles — neither side had an army in being, each had to create one. With a people mainly apathetic this must be largely a question of finance. Hobbes considered that had the king had the money he might have had all the soldiers he wanted, 'for there were very few of the common people that cared much for either of the causes, but would have taken any side for pay or plunder.' Parliament had the supreme advantage that it could raise loans from the merchant community, could collect customs duties at the ports, and could levy new taxes on the area it controlled, taxes which roused the less opposition since most Englishmen looked on it as the rightful taxing authority.[1] Charles had no such regular sources to draw upon, and for the most part lived from hand to mouth, mortgaging crown lands, pawning crown jewels, and receiving gifts in plate, and cash, and kind from his supporters. The catholic gentry put their fortunes at his disposal, and great nobles like Newcastle and Richmond raised regiments from their own estates, and equipped and maintained them.[2] Money was urgently needed, because neither king nor parliament had any means of compelling the citizens to serve as of right. Neither had a true legal warrant, whether by commission of array or by ordinance of militia, and, though men might at first submit, they were certain, as Hopton was to find in Cornwall, sooner or later to make difficulties. But, more important, there was no proper machinery of recruitment. The defensive power of England by land had been suffered to decline till it had almost vanished.

There had been no real army in England since the days of Henry VIII. Expeditionary forces had gone abroad under James and Charles to fight in foreign quarrels, mercenaries and pressed men and for the most part wretched stuff, 'a rabble of raw and poor rascals.' For home defence there was a nominal militia, since it was the legal duty of every man to serve against invasion, and Elizabeth had established the trained bands, selected groups in every county, calculated in 1623 to reach the number of 160,000. But the training was to the last degree casual and perfunctory — one day a month during the summer — and, though under Charles the arms were better, only the

[1] *e.g.* The New Assessment, which developed into the later Property and Land Tax. and the Excise.

[2] The Earl of Worcester, who had a rent-roll of £24,000, gave the king £120,000 during the first half of 1642.

London regiments learned to shoot. This was the material out of which the armies were made which Charles led against the Scots in 1639 and 1640, and of which Sir Edmund Verney wrote, 'I daresay there was never so raw, so unskilful, and so unwilling an army brought to fight.' King and parliament contended as to which should control the militia; the matter was vital to constitutional theory, but in practice it meant little, for the militia as it stood was of no more value than the ragged regiment that Falstaff marched through Coventry, 'cankers of a calm world and a long peace.'

But there was some soldierly training among the higher ranks. Scions of the gentry had long been in the habit of going abroad to the wars, though to a less degree than among the Scots. When it came to raising new forces an expert could generally be got as major or colonel of a foot battalion or lieutenant of a troop of horse. Some had fought under Prince Maurice of Nassau in the Dutch service, and some in the Swedish service under Gustavus. Just as the leaders on both sides in the American Civil War were graduates of West Point, so the chief figures of the royal and parliament armies were veterans of the continental wars. On the one side among those who had had such field experience were Essex, Warwick, Skippon, Sir William Waller, and Scots like Balfour, Crawford and Ramsay: on the other, Astley and Hopton, the elder Goring, Gage, Lindsey, the Scots Ruthven and King, the young Palatine princes Rupert and Maurice, and a certain Captain George Monk out of Devon who was one day to be a resounding name. Such men had learned new lessons in army organization, in gunnery and in minor tactics, and, if it came to creating armies, would be useful in shaping the raw material.

Each side began by attempting to use the antique skeleton organization that existed, and neither did much with it. Parliament could lay its hands on the greater number of men and a better equipment, but the discipline was all to make. Each side laboured to seize the county magazines where the arms of the trained bands were stored, but the bands themselves were for the most part a rabble.[1] Hence the arms were mainly used to

[1] 'The trained bands, accounted the main support of the realm, and its bulwark against unexpected invasion, were effeminate in courage and incapable of discipline, because their whole course of life was alienated from warlike employment, insomuch that young and active spirits were more perfect by the experiences of two days. Wherefore these men might easily repine at oppression, and have the will to preserve themselves, yet a small body of desperate Cavaliers might overcome and ruin them at pleasure.' *Bibliotheca Gloucestrensis*, quoted by Firth, *C. A.*, 17.

equip volunteers. At first the staple was voluntary enlistment, officers being commissioned to raise regiments. On the king's side the young courtiers entered the king's guards; on the parliament side the gentlemen of the inns of court enlisted in Essex's bodyguard, and the London apprentices flocked to the regiments of Brooke and Holles. But presently both sides had to resort to compulsion, and in the second year of the war impressment ordinances were issued by both king and parliament for the districts which they controlled. When the New Model was introduced more than half its infantry were pressed men. One result of the initial lack of enthusiasm in the rank and file was that only a small proportion of the men on the rolls could be expected to turn up at any given moment in the field.[1]

Two other difficulties faced the commanders on both sides. One was the intense localism which made it hard to get men to serve out of their own districts, and which consequently led to the multiplication of weak local units. 'When the enemy had left their own particular quarter they thanked God that they were rid of him and returned to their usual avocations.'[2] Parliament was the chief sufferer; in 1643 and 1644 it had four more or less independent armies, under Manchester, Fairfax, Waller and Denbigh, and the raising of each new one depleted the ranks of the old. This localism also gave undue weight to the local magnates. In Yorkshire the royal cause suffered because the Earl of Cumberland was supine, and in Wales because the Herberts were at feud with many of the gentry, while in Leicestershire the other side was compromised by the quarrels between the houses of Huntingdon and Stamford.[3] On one point parliament was wiser than the king, for when a parliamentary regiment fell below strength it was usually merged in another; whereas, on the royal side, losses were supplied by the raising of new regiments and the lavish granting of commissions, so that the army was full of colonels commanding handfuls.[4]

[1] In the summer of 1642 Essex was supposed to have 24,000 foot and 5000 horse, but at Edgehill he numbered only some 13,000. In April 1643 he started nominally with 16,000 foot and 3000 horse; in July he had actually only 6000 foot and 2500 horse. The position was just as bad with the royalists. Firth, *C. A.*, 22–23.

[2] Fortescue, I, 201.

[3] Clarendon, *Hist.*, V, 443, 445; VI, 275, 287.

[4] See Warwick, 236. In September 1644 Lord Cleveland's infantry brigade in Cornwall had six regiments but only 800 men; at Naseby Howard's cavalry brigade had seven regiments and 880 men. Firth, *C. A.*, 26. The same thing happened in the American Civil War, where only the Wisconsin regiments were kept up to strength.

The other difficulty was the snare of fortresses, and this largely contributed to the ruin of the king's cause. The castles and manors of his supporters were fortified and garrisoned as they had been in the old wars of England, and thereby hopelessly crippled the main purposes of the campaign. There was a financial reason for the practice. Since there was little money, troops were left in garrison at free quarters with a district assigned for their support. This was disastrous for the countryside, and not less disastrous for strategy. It was an unhappy following of the practice of the Thirty Years War, and kept a field army from ever being at its maximum strength. It would have been better for Charles to have dismantled and evacuated every fortress, and to have held only certain vital seaports, for the garrison custom weakened his striking power and gravely prejudiced him in popular esteem.[1]

II

The art of war has remained in its essentials the same in all ages, but the science of war has in the last two centuries moved far from the beggarly elements which we must now consider. To understand the practice of seventeenth century armies we must accustom our minds to a primitive and rudimentary technique.

The infantry had advanced in prestige since the fifteenth century, but since it had no bayonet and only an indifferent gun it had not yet become the 'queen of battles,' and was usually ranked at about one-fifth of the fighting value of cavalry. Its weapons were the pike and the musket, and in 1642 the proportion of musketeers to pikemen was about two to one. The pike was regarded as the more honourable weapon, and when a gentleman served in the ranks he usually trailed a pike; the pikeman too was the bigger and finer fellow and wore the heavier defensive armour. His pike was eighteen feet long, and he also carried a sword which was rarely much use to him. His value was in close hand-to-hand fighting, and the issue was often decided by 'push of pike.' The musketeer had no de-

[1] On the fatal lure of fortresses see the testimony of the parliament general Sir John Meldrum, *Cal. S. P. Dom.* (1644–45), 91, and the royalist Sir Richard Willis, *Diary of Richard Symonds* (Camden Soc.), 270. The situation in a county like Oxfordshire is amusingly portrayed in John Lacy's play, *The Old Troop* (1672). Lacy was an actor who fought for the king, but the royalists Flay-flint and Ferret-farm are as trenchantly satirized as the roundheads Holdforth and Tubtext.

fensive armour, and no defensive arms against cavalry except the clumsy 'Swedish feathers,' five-foot stakes which he stuck in the ground before him. His weapon was still mainly the matchlock, which fired a bullet weighing a little over an ounce; his powder was made up in little cartouches of tin or leather, which he carried in a bandolier worn over his left shoulder. Everything about his equipment was cumbrous — the heavy weapon, the coils of match which he had often to carry lighted, and which were at the mercy of ill weather. Presently the matchlock was replaced by the snaphance or flintlock, for the cavalry, and for the foot companies which guarded the artillery and ammunition. The musket was effective at about 400 yards, but owing to the patchy training there was little real markmanship, except among the royalist verderers and game-keepers.

The drill was complicated, and badly learned. At first the battle formation was ten deep, each rank firing and then falling back to the rear to reload; but Gustavus had taught quicker loading, and had made the files six deep, and this was now the formation generally adopted in England; three deep was even used when it was necessary to prevent outflanking. Also the Swedish custom of the 'salvee' was coming in, by which the six ranks fired at once,[1] a use adopted by Montrose in Scotland and followed by the New Model. The usual handling of infantry was that a 'forlorn hope' skirmished ahead, fired, and fell back; the musketeers then delivered their volleys and retired to the shelter of the pikemen, who charged home. The pikemen were usually in the centre. If cavalry attacked and the foot had no hedges or ditches to shelter them, the only chance was to do as the London trained bands did at Newbury — form square, with the musketeers under the cover of the pikes. The marching power of the foot was poor, for even the light-armed musketeer must have carried at least double the modern weight, and at the best they may have done twelve miles a day. Nevertheless for all its handicaps the infantry was a vital arm, for without it sieges and occupations and campaigns in broken country were impossible. The destruction of the king's foot at Marston Moor lost him the north, and the same disaster at Naseby meant the loss of England.

The cavalry was usually one-half the strength of the foot,

---

[1] This was done by 'doubling' the six ranks into three, which delivered their fire respectively kneeling, stooping and standing.

and was regarded as the superior arm, the pay of the trooper being three times that of an infantryman. It was especially a gentleman's service, since every man of reasonable estate was at home in the saddle.[1] The old heavy cavalry was going out of fashion, and was being replaced by the harquebusiers, who carried pistols, carbine and sword, and by the more lightly armed dragoons, who were the equivalent of the modern mounted infantry, and wore a light helmet, a light cuirass, or even an ordinary padded buff coat. The light horse did all the reconnoitring, outpost, and covering work of an army. Gustavus's practice in the handling of cavalry was slowly coming in: that is, three deep instead of the old five, fire reserved, and a charge home; Rupert and Montrose were pioneers in the change and Oliver soon followed. The king had at the start a notable advantage on this side. He was indeed more short of armour and arms than the parliament, for it was long before he got 'backs and breasts' for all troopers and a sufficiency of carbines, but he had more and better horses, better horsemasters, and in the gentry accustomed to hawk and hunt far better horsemen.

The other services may be briefly summarized. Artillery, which was to play an important part in the war, was only just emerging from the Middle Ages.[2] The field gun ranged from the culverin, which fired a ball of nearly twenty pounds, had an extreme range of about 2000 paces, and required eight horses to move it, to the little three-pounder called the 'drake.' It was no light task to load a heavy piece, for the powder was carried loose in a barrel. Explosions were frequent, and this was why the guard for the guns had to be men with flintlocks and not matchlocks.... Pay on both sides was small and irregular, and habitually in arrears. The commissariat was provided either by quartering soldiers on the country or by requisitioning supplies at scheduled prices. Dress was at first anything that a commanding officer fancied, and it was necessary to have distinguishing badges; red coats came in with the New Model. Tents were little used by either side, troops being billeted in villages or

---

[1] A curious instance is an advertisement for mounted recruits for Flanders which asked for 'any that are old soldiers or *gentlemen.*' *Mercurius Politicus*, 15–22 July 1658 (Th.). Since the horse was the chief form of transport gentlemen were inured to immense journeys; *e.g.* in 1639, Sir Edmund Verney rode with the king from Berwick 339 miles in four days. *Verney Memoirs*, I, 67.

[2] At the siege of Corfe Castle and of Canon Frome the mediæval 'sow' was used, and at the siege of Gloucester Chillingworth constructed 'engines after the manner of the Roman Testudines.' Firth, *C. A.*, 165.

bivouacking in the open air.... There was a multitude of flags, every company of foot and troop of horse having its standard. When battle was joined there was cheering and shouting, unlike the Swedes and Scots who fought in silence.... The intelligence department was in the hands of the scoutmaster-general, but intelligence methods were rudimentary. Nothing is more curious in the war than the ignorance of both sides about the doings of the other, so that Essex stumbled on the king, and Hopton on Waller, and battle seemed to be joined by the merest accident.

At first there was little discipline on either side. Nehemiah Wharton, sergeant in Brooke's regiment in the parliament army, has left us a description of the march of the Londoners westward in the first month of the war,[1] and it reveals a state of chaos among those troops who might have been expected to be the most orderly. 'Our soldiers generally manifested their dislike to our lieutenant-colonel, who is a goddam blade and doubtless hatched in hell, and we all desire that either the Parliament would depose him, or God convert him, or the devil fetch him away quick.' Slowly things improved, as both sides issued 'articles of war,' the disciplinary ordinances which they proposed to administer. The Englishman is naturally insubordinate and even at the best discipline was lax; both sides, for example, were arrant poachers, and carried along with them a collection of hounds. Each accused the other of vices, of which Sir Philip Warwick perhaps gives a fair summary in his quotation from a royalist soldier: 'In our army we have the sins of men, drinking and wenching, but in yours you have those of devils, spiritual pride and rebellion.' Both sides had chaplains and observed the ordinances of religion. Rupert had a service before Marston Moor, while on the parliament side there was an almost continuous preachment. But after Edgehill most of the puritan ministers went home, and their place was taken by volunteers, those sectaries who were soon to control the army and rule the destinies of England.

III

The sword to which the disputants appealed was a cumbrous weapon, but it was wielded in an unencumbered land, a country

[1] It is reprinted in full in *Archaeologia*, XXXV, (1853), and abridged in *Cal. S. P. Dom.*, 1641–43.

mainly of marsh and moor and open pastures, with ample freedom to manœuvre. But for manœuvring power a supple machine is needed and a directing brain, and at first on both sides
there was small sign of either.

The main difficulty lay in the high command, and this was
naturally greater on the parliament side, where the protagonist
was a large deliberative body. The two Houses, as we have
seen, appointed a committee of safety in July 1642, and, when
the Scots army came into the field, this was extended into a
Committee of Both Kingdoms. But such committees were
strictly subordinate to parliament, and had to take its orders,
and the impossible situation was created of a campaign conducted by a debating society. Only disaster convinced parliament of the folly of this plan. Essex was confused by instructions constantly changed and often contradictory, and it needed
the storming of Leicester by Charles and a panic in London to
give a commander freedom of action, 'without attending commands and directions from remote councils.' [1] By June 1645
Fairfax was empowered to do what he liked after consulting his
council of war, and later Oliver had the amplest liberty. A
general's council of war was no serious handicap to him; it consisted of his staff and the regimental commanders, but he was
not obliged to take its advice. 'I have observed him at councils
of war,' Whitelocke wrote of Fairfax, 'that he hath said little,
but hath ordered things expressly contrary to the judgment of
all his council.'

The royalists suffered from the opposite fault. From the
start their command was concentrated, but in feeble hands.
The king's authority as commander-in-chief was absolute. He
had his privy council, eleven peers and five commoners, with
Falkland as secretary of state, but it was not an expert body,
and it was generally at variance with the generals. The chief
military adviser was whoever had Charles's confidence at the
moment, whether it was a soldier like Rupert, or a civilian like
Digby, and behind all there was the steady and most potent
influence of the queen. Had Charles had any genius for war, or
had there been a great soldier who possessed his undivided
trust, the dice at the start would have been heavily weighted
against the cumbrous parliamentary machine.

Both armies had the traditional hierarchy; — the commander-in-chief; the second in command, the lieutenant-

[1] See the petition of the city of London in *O. P. H.*, III, 228.

general, who had also the command of the cavalry; the major-
general, who was in charge of the foot, and drew up the order
of battle; and the lieutenant-general of the ordinance. There
was no chief of staff, in the modern sense, but in the parliamentary army the secretary to the commander performed
some of his functions.[1] This lack of any true staff system as
headquarters would have gravely interfered with the carrying
out of any large strategical scheme, had one existed, but, at
the start at any rate, there was no such plan on either side.
Each underrated the other; most people thought, like Richard
Baxter,[2] that the war would be over in a month or two, and that
the first battle would decide it; only those who, like Cromwell,
demanded a complete and final victory foresaw a long campaign. On the parliament side the general aim was the capture
of the king — Essex's commission was 'to rescue his Majesty's
person, and the persons of the Prince and the Duke of York,
out of the hands of those desperate persons who were then about
him'; on the royalist side it was the recovery of London. That
is to say, the first had the vaguer objective, and inevitably during the early months it lost the initiative and fell back upon the
defensive.

There were no formed military reputations of the first class
to which either side could confidently turn. Parliament was free
to choose its leader in the field, and, as commonly happens in a
civil war, it selected him largely on political grounds. The son
of Elizabeth's tragically fated favourite, the third Earl of Essex
had little reason to love courts or kings, and had long lived in
a retirement solaced by never-ending pipes of tobacco. His
gentleness and homeliness made him widely popular, especially
in London, but he had only the scantiest military experience,
the slenderest military talent, and no power to restrain the
turbulent forces behind him — a poor equipment wherewith to
launch out upon seas, where, in Clarendon's words, 'he met
with nothing but rocks and shelves, and from whence he could
never discover any safe port to harbour in.' Sir Thomas Fairfax
was a far abler man, competent if uninspired, a soldier born for
such a war, for, says Richard Baxter, 'he was acceptable to
sober men, because he was religious, faithful, valiant, and of a
grave, sober, resolved disposition, very fit for execution and

[1] This post was held by Rushworth under the New Model, and by William Clarke
under Monk, and out of it developed the modern Secretaryship of State for War.

[2] *Rel. Baxt.*, 43.

neither too great nor too cunning to be commanded by the Parliament.' Sir William Waller was another such both in character and attainments, and there were many veterans of the foreign wars who were soon to prove their competence. On the king's side the first commander, the Earl of Lindsey, had long experience, but he was an old and tired man, and was little more than a figure-head to balance Essex. The royalist strength lay in its subordinate leaders, like Hopton and Astley, who were trained soldiers, and in the natural fighting stuff of the country gentry which in the process of time produced many capable brigadiers. It lay also in the commander of the horse, Prince Rupert, who in spite of his youth had served in more than one campaign, and who had that type of mind, both scientific and imaginative, which turns happily to the military art.

But the war began with neither armies nor generals. Both were still to make. Victory, in a contest so evenly matched and so divorced from the interest of the bulk of the nation, would go to that side which first created an efficient fighting machine, or rather — since men are more important than machines — which first produced a great soldier. The race, though none could then foresee it, lay between the young Palatine prince of twenty-three, and the grizzled Cambridge parliamentarian of forty-three, now captain of the 67th troop of Essex's horse, and laboriously beginning to instruct himself in the craft of war.

Chapter II

EDGEHILL

(1642)

For the conduct of the war: at the first men rested extremely upon number; they did put the wars likewise upon main force and valour; pointing days for pitched fields, and so trying it out upon an even match; and they were more ignorant in ranging and arraying their battles. After they grew to rest upon number rather competent than vast; they grew to advantages of place, cunning diversions, and the like; and they grew more skilful in the ordering of their battles.

BACON.

EARLY in September the parliament army lay around Coventry and Northampton, and its strength was daily increased by reinforcements from London. It was well equipped, for it had the arms brought from Hull which had been collected for the Scottish campaign, and presently it was to have the munitions sent from Holland by the queen, which were intercepted at sea. Pym's chief anxiety was money. Already the war was costing £30,000 a week, and soon the charge would be doubled, but he had the consolation that he was in a better position for raising funds than the king. Essex was in no hurry to join his command. He had a difference with parliament over his title, desiring to be lord high constable, with full power to negotiate peace. This the Houses refused, for they trusted his loyalty but not his policy, since he had already shown himself too much of a moderate. His leave-taking was cold, and on the afternoon of September 9th he left London, carrying with him his coffin and winding-sheet and the hatchment for his funeral, as tokens that he would be faithful unto death even to his ungracious masters. But neither Essex nor parliament had any doubt of the result. His army of twenty thousand would make short work of Charles's impoverished rabble. Their hope was for the speedy capture of the king in his quarters and a triumphant return to the capital. Meanwhile, east and south-east England were in their hands, for Portsmouth had surrendered two days before to Sir William Waller, and in all that area only Sherborne castle, precariously held by Hertford, stood out for the king. Sir John Byron and his troopers had evacuated Oxford, and Lord Saye was busy disarming the colleges.

Charles could not linger at Nottingham. He was not yet

strong enough to meet Essex in the field, and he had reinforcements to collect on the Welsh marches. So on the 13th he
turned west, and on the 20th was in Shrewsbury. His proclamation that, if God gave him victory, he would maintain the
reformed religion established in the church of England, support
the just privileges and freedom of parliament, and govern according to the laws, brought him many recruits from among
sober men whose views had been changed by the recent truculence of Westminster. Volunteers flocked to his standard from
the gentry of Shropshire and Cheshire, and he was joined by
5000 levies from Wales. His main lack was arms, for he had
only what he could borrow from the trained bands or collect
from private houses. No single pikeman had a corselet, and
few of the musketeers had swords, while many, especially
among the Welsh, had nothing but pitchforks or cudgels.[1]
There was also the difficulty about money, which could only
be raised by the sale of an occasional peerage or by freewill gifts
from adherents, notably the catholic gentry. In such circumstances he must look for a base which would be to him what
London was to Essex, and his thoughts naturally turned to
Oxford.

Sir John Byron, having left Oxford, made for Worcester to
join his master, and the news sent Essex hurrying westward
from Northampton, on a route parallel to the king's. At Worcester Rupert joined Byron, and the two decided that the city
with its walls in ruins was no place for defence. Nathaniel
Fiennes with Essex's advance guard had arrived on the 23rd
and was reconnoitring west of the Severn, while the main parliament army was only four miles off. Rupert, while covering
the retreat of Byron's convoy with the Oxford contributions in
cash and plate, was also busy on reconnaissance, and at Powick
bridge on the river Teme he fell in with Fiennes. Catching the
latter at a disadvantage in a narrow lane, he charged him
furiously and routed his horse so utterly that they fled nine
miles, with no pursuer behind them, swam the Severn, and at
Pershore swept off with them in panic a hundred picked men
of Essex's bodyguard; 'which,' wrote Nehemiah Wharton, 'is
such a blot on them as nothing but some desperate exploit
will wipe off.'[2]

Next day Essex occupied Worcester. He had missed his

[1] Clarendon, *Hist.*, VI, 74. Bulstrode, *Memoirs*, 75, 85–86.
[2] *Cal. S. P. Dom.*, 1641–43, 393. Cf. Ludlow, I, 41. Clarendon, *Hist.*, VI, 44–46.

chance of destroying the king while he was weak, and every day was now adding to his enemy's strength. Moreover he had permitted him to gain confidence from a small but indisputable triumph. The affair at Powick bridge convinced the royalists that their foes were, in Falkland's words, but 'tailors or embroiderers or the like,' and that they had no stomach for battle. At Shrewsbury Charles had his communications open with Wales, and, by way of the Mersey, with Ireland, and he was in a loyal countryside, so he waited till he got his forces up to strength. Essex at Worcester was in the kind of strategic position beloved by the generals of the continental wars, for he was nearer to London than the king, and could also prevent him from marching down Severn to Gloucester or Bristol. But his intelligence system was poor, and Bedford, who commanded his horse, was a wretched scoutmaster. His chief news came from London: how Hertford had abandoned Sherborne and was now in South Wales: how Sir Ralph Hopton was trying to raise Cornwall; how the Fairfaxes and the Hothams were quarrelling in Yorkshire. Presently came graver tidings — that Cornwall had declared for the king, that help was coming to him from Denmark, that the Earl of Newcastle had 8000 men in the north. Parliament was ill at ease, and was showing its nervousness by forced levies and confiscations, and by raising under the command of Lord Warwick a new army of 16,000 men. Then came word that Charles was marching on London, and that the city royalists were brazenly wearing red ribbons in their caps. The king left Shrewsbury on October 12, and, moving by way of Bridgenorth, Wolverhampton and Birmingham, was at Kenilworth on the 19th. Only on that day did Essex move.

He had forfeited the advantage of his greater proximity to the capital, and Charles was now ahead of him. Parliament had many strongholds on the road, like Coventry and Warwick, but these the king was avoiding: soon only Banbury would stand between him and London. Essex put forth his best speed, but it was no great thing, and his troops got well ahead of his artillery train. The two opponents had launched forth into the mist, and for ten days knew nothing of each other. Yet when they started they were only twenty miles apart, and they were moving through a country largely open and unforested. It was emblematic of the fog of uncertainty which lay over all England. Near Southam Mr. Richard Shuckburgh, a Warwickshire squire, was starting out with his hounds for a Saturday's hunt, when he was amazed to find himself faced by an army, and presently by the king himself. When he asked what the trouble was he learned for the first time of the war; took his hounds back to kennels and gathered his tenants; fought all the next day, and won knighthood on the battlefield.

On the evening of the 22nd Charles arrived at Edgecote on the infant Cherwell, the stream which thirty miles to the south circled the walls of Oxford. Next day he meant to send out a detachment to summon Banbury, and to give the rest of his weary army a day of leisure. But that night came word from Rupert that the enemy was at his heels. Essex had reached the little town of Kineton some nine miles off. Clearly the king must stop and fight; he could not afford the appearance of being chased by the enemy, and now was the chance for that decisive battle, of the issue of which Powick bridge had made every royalist confident. Moreover between the two armies lay the scarp of Edgehill, where the Cotswold uplands dropped steeply to the midland plain. Let that strong position be occupied, and Essex would fight at a disadvantage. There was little rest that night for the royal army, as the sleepy troopers, many of them supperless,[1] were beaten up from their quarters in the neighbouring hamlets. At dawn Rupert and his horse were on Edgehill, and Essex at Kineton saw him and realized that the hour of battle had come.

Beyond question Rupert erred, for he forfeited the chance of surprise. The hill was too steep to fight on the upper slopes. It was a superb defensive position could the enemy be forced to attack, but a poor place from which to launch a battle. A few hours later this was realized, and the royal army descended into the plain. The right course was to have taken Essex unawares, for his position was highly insecure. He had outmarched many of his guns, and John Hampden with two regiments had been left behind to bring them on. His horse and foot were in scattered quarters in a dozen villages. Till he saw Rupert on the hill he had no notion where the king was. If we can judge from Ludlow's experience, the rations were short, and the internal staff work was wretched. A surprise attack at dawn by way of Avon Dassett and the skirts of the uplands might have annihilated the parliament army. But there had been trouble

[1] 'There were very many companies of the common soldiers who had scarce eaten bread in eight and forty hours before.' Clarendon, *Hist.*, VI, 83.

in the royal councils. Charles had excepted Rupert, his general of the horse, from the control of Lindsey, the general-in-chief, and the latter had not unnaturally begged to be relieved of his command and to be allowed to return to his regiment. So old Patrick Ruthven, a veteran of the Swedish and Scottish wars, stone deaf and much addicted to the bottle, was given the truncated command. Rupert, having quarrelled both with Lindsey and Falkland, was in one of his headstrong moods when he became swashbuckler rather than soldier.

Though the royal cavalry were promenading on the scarp at dawn it took all the forenoon to get the rest of the army there. About one o'clock the descent began. First went the horse, and then the foot and cannon, and the slope was so steep that the gun-teams had to be unhooked.[1] Essex had taken up position the better part of a mile from the summit of the hill in what was known as Red Horse Vale, across the highroad between Kineton and Banbury. It was broken ground, with a certain amount of fresh plough, a few ditches and hedges in the vicinity of the hamlet of Radway, and for the rest wild pasture with many patches of thorn. The royal army was in much the same kind of terrain but at a slightly higher elevation, with at its back the abrupt lift of the hill, part open and part covered with scrub. The weather was windless and dry, the distances a little dim with autumn haze, and the air, as the afternoon went on, sharpening to frost.

Essex made no attempt to interfere with the royal deployment, for he had too many troubles with his own. He had twelve infantry regiments and forty-two troops of cavalry — a total of some 11,000 foot, something over 2000 horse, and something under 1000 dragoons. He had a great superiority in artillery, but only half his guns had arrived. His first line was drawn up in flat meadows beneath the glacis of the hill, though on the left the ground rose somewhat; on that flank there were some ditches and hedges, and on the right flank a few small thickets north of Radway. On the left in the first line musketeers and dragoons lined the hedges. Then came the main body of cavalry, twenty-four troops under Sir James Ramsay. On their right was the infantry brigade of Charles Essex, and beyond it the brigade of Sir John Meldrum, which included the best of the parliament foot. On the right wing were the two cavalry regiments of Sir William Balfour, who was the parliamentary

[1] Bulstrode, *op. cit.*, 77.

lieutenant-general of the horse, and Sir Philip Stapleton; with Stapleton were Ireton and Ludlow, and with Balfour, Nathaniel Fiennes; Cromwell's troop seem not to have been in action at the start, but arrived before the decisive moment of the battle.[1] On the extreme right, among the Radway thickets were more musketeers and dragoons. In the second line, on the left behind Ramsay's cavalry was a body of horse on a little hill, and on their right Ballard's infantry brigade, which contained the London regiment of Holles, the lord general's regiment from the shire of Essex, and Sir William Fairfax's regiment lent from Charles Essex's brigade. On the extreme right was Lord Feilding's[2] regiment of horse, echeloned on the right rear of Stapleton. Musketeers were interspersed among the cavalry on the left flank. The guns in shallow entrenchments were placed in the gaps between the infantry brigades, with the greater strength on the wings. The whole force wore orange scarves as a distinguishing badge, but otherwise there was little uniformity in accoutrement; the men of Holles' regiment were in red, of Lord Brooke's in purple, of Lord Saye's in blue, of Ballard's in grey, while John Hampden's men, now tramping along the road from Warwick, were in forester's green. Among the ranks flitted the puritan ministers, urging the troops to stand fast for religion and the laws.

On the king's side the foot numbered 9000, the cavalry 2500, and the dragoons a little less than 1500. Rupert had had his way, and the battle order was not that of the Dutch wars in which Lindsey believed, but the Swedish fashion of Leipsic and Lützen, the foot six deep and the horse three deep. Ruthven, the nominal commander, drew up the army in a single line, though he had two small reserves of horse, one under Sir John Byron on his right wing, and one under either Carnarvon or Digby on the left. On the extreme right was a handful of dragoons, and then the main cavalry under Rupert, which included the royal horse guards and the Prince of Wales's regiment; with him rode Bulstrode and Philip Warwick and Lord Bernard Stuart. Then came the infantry under Sir Jacob Astley, the major-general of the foot;[3] first the brigade of John

---

[1] Such is the natural deduction from Fiennes's narrative, and it may explain the rumour that Oliver was not at Edgehill. Holles, *Memoirs*, 17.

[2] This was Basil Feilding, afterwards the 2nd Earl of Denbigh, who had been Montrose's companion in Italy when he made the grand tour.

[3] His prayer before the battle is famous: 'O Lord, thou knowest how busy I must be this day. If I forget thee, do not thou forget me.' Warwick, 229.

Belasyse; in the centre the brigade of Sir Nicholas Byron, which contained the king's foot guards, called the Red Regiment, under Lindsey's son Lord Willoughby, and Lindsey's own regiment led by the veteran himself; then the brigade of Richard Feilding. The left wing was held by Henry Wilmot's cavalry, with whom Falkland served since his quarrel with Rupert. On the extreme flank lay Sir Arthur Aston's dragoons. The guns were placed as in the parliament line, between the infantry brigades. In front was the usual 'forlorn hope,' a small skirmishing force of musketeers.

The battle began shortly after two o'clock in the afternoon with a royalist advance. The dragoons under Colonel Washington on the right and Sir Arthur Aston on the left cleared the flanks, the 'forlorn hope' fired and fell back, and on both sides the cannonade opened. It did not last long, but the parliament guns did more damage than the king's, for the latter's pieces, being on higher ground, were apt to shoot over the enemy, and bury the balls harmlessly in ploughland. Thus Rupert ordered the charge. His weakness in firearms made him invent new tactics, for he bade his men reserve their fire till they were among the enemy. The royal horse guards had the king's permission to charge with him, and as the whole body swung round at the gallop the reserve under Sir John Byron could not restrain themselves and followed. As Rupert moved, one of Ramsay's troops under Sir Faithfull Fortescue (they had been raised for service in Ireland and had no love for the parliament) fired their pistols into the ground and rode forward to join him. Shaken by this defection the parliament horse could not meet the royalist whirlwind. They broke and fled, driving through their own second line, and scattering Ballard's four regiments of foot. The reserve of horse with which Cromwell's son Oliver served, stationed behind on rising ground, was also caught in the rout. On to Kineton swept the pursuit, where in the streets were found Essex's transport and much booty; on still along the Warwick road, till the royalist van fell in with John Hampden's two regiments and were checked by their vollies. The parliament left wing had become a mob.

At the same moment Wilmot charged on the king's left. He had more difficult ground before him, all hummocks and pockets and hawthorn clumps, and for some reason he missed the main parliament cavalry of Balfour and Stapleton. What he struck was Feilding's regiment in the second line, and Sir

William Fairfax's foot, and he scattered them as Rupert had scattered Ramsay. He drove on towards Kineton with Carnarvon's reserve troop galloping behind him. The parliament wings had been broken, and the flanks of the centre exposed. Well might Essex despair of the day and seize a pike to die in the ranks.

But the easy success of Rupert and Wilmot was to deprive the king of an otherwise certain victory. There was not a single royalist horseman left on the field, but there were the cavalry of Stapleton and Balfour which Wilmot had unaccountably missed. As the royalist infantry advanced to what seemed an assured triumph, upon their left flank fell Stapleton and upon their left rear fell Balfour. The result was that Richard Feilding's left brigade never came into action at all; it was broken and routed, and the parliament horse were among the guns and pressing hard upon the flank of Nicholas Byron's brigade, while Meldrum assaulted it in front. Then began a grim struggle of foot against foot. Nicholas Byron formed front to flank, and, with Belasyse's brigade on the right, stood stubbornly around the royal standard. He flung off Stapleton's horse, and the king's guards and Lindsey's regiment came to push off pike with the regiment of Brooke and the flower of the parliament infantry. Neither side would yield, and so desperate was the struggle that, according to the account in the memoirs of James II, 'each as if by mutual consent retired some few paces, and then struck down their colours, continuing to fire at one another even till night.' But Lindsey's regiment was cut to pieces and Lindsey mortally wounded; the guards, too, paid a desperate toll, for the royal standard was taken, Sir Edmund Verney killed, and Willoughby made prisoner. Belasyse suffered little less heavily, but two of his regiments stood so gallantly that he was able to patch up some sort of front with the help of Feilding's re-formed brigade.

The tide had turned, and victory now appeared to lie with the parliament. To Hyde, who was on the crest of the hill with the young princes, it must have seemed that all was lost. But no more than the king had Essex any reserves with which to strike the decisive blow. As the dusk fell the battle lost all semblance of order and became a blind struggle of oddments of horse and foot. The cavalry of Rupert and Wilmot straggled back to the field, too disorganized and weary to affect the issue, but their presence saved the remnants of the heroic royalist infantry. The king's standard was rescued by a catholic officer, Captain John Smith — whether by stratagem or by a feat of arms is uncertain — and slowly the weary combatants drew apart. Falkland pressed Wilmot to make a fresh attack, as Hampden was to press Essex on the following morning, but Wilmot replied that they had got the day and should live to enjoy the fruits thereof. But indeed the day was no man's. Two forces, meeting by accident, had flown at each other's throats, wrestled blindly, and then drifted apart from sheer fatigue. Clarendon's words are the best comment: 'In this doubt of all sides, the night (the common friend to weary and dismayed armies) parted them.' Neither side has shown any generalship; the most that can be said is that the rank and file of each had revealed certain special aptitudes which might mean something for the future. The heavier losses, especially in officers, were with the king.[1]

As the commander of the 67th troop in Essex's horse sat by his fire of thorns that night, when the frost was too sharp to permit of sleep, his mind was heavy with thought. That day, and in the past weeks, Oliver had been learning fast. He had had his first experience of that business of war on which he had long pondered. The opening battle had been fought, and, though his own side had had the superiority in men and guns and behind them the cause of freedom and religion, they had won no victory; indeed but for the glaring folly of their opponents the stalemate might have been a tragic defeat. The parliament foot had fought stoutly when opposed to other foot, but against cavalry Ballard and Sir William Fairfax had made no stand. That was to be looked for; more serious was the plain

[1] The authorities for Edgehill are full and reasonably clear, for we have personal narratives from almost every arm on both sides. Besides the official reports, there are, on the royalist side, the accounts of Clarendon, Bulstrode, Philip Warwick, Lord Bernard Stuart, James II, and Lord Belasyse, and, for the Parliament, Fiennes, Wharton, Ludlow, and Keightley. All these were eye-witnesses. There is also an extensive pamphlet literature. The authorities have been discussed by Colonel Ross (*E. H. R.*, II, 533–43), and, more recently and most adequately, by Mr. Godfrey Davies (*E. H. R.* XXXVI, 30–44). My one difficulty about the action is the conduct of Wilmot in missing Stapleton and Balfour. It is hard to believe that this was an accident, for the royalists were on slightly higher ground and could scarcely have completely lost sight of two large regiments. It seems to me more likely that Wilmot deliberately bore to his left so that he might have the easier task. He was not much of a soldier, and Philip Warwick in his account of the battle observes that all who had followed his career knew his fondness for peace. The battlefield is not changed today in any notable feature, and in going over the ground I cannot see where six hundred men could have been concealed. The only authority which accepts the charitable interpretation of Wilmot's conduct is the royalist narrative in Carte, *Ormonde Papers*, I.

inferiority of the parliament horse to the enemy's. His own ploughboys and prentices from Cambridgeshire, men whom he had himself picked and trained, had done bravely, but they had had the *beau rôle*, attacking the naked royalist flank; else- where no parliament mounted unit had stood for a moment against the enemy's charge. Feilding had gone down before Wilmot, and Ramsay's twenty-four troops with their reserves had been scattered like chaff by Rupert, and his own son in Lord St. John's regiment had been among the routed.

Certain tactical lessons stood out with burning clearness. It was not the fire of cavalry that signified but the shock of their charge; the horse, not the sword or musket, was their true weapon. A study of the *Swedish Intelligencer* and of Gustavus's methods had given him an inkling of this, and now Rupert had inscribed the lesson with a sharp pen and bloody ink. Attack — swift and resolute attack — was the true way; assault was the only defence. But that attack must be disciplined and regulated, for Rupert had flung away the battle by pushing it beyond its tactical purpose. Also heavy armour was of little use; Ludlow, shelled like a lobster, had found his cuirass a grave encumbrance.[1] But the chief thought which filled Oliver's mind was of that mysterious thing, fighting spirit. Piety was not enough, unless it was of the militant brand, a spirit as tough and daring as that of the king's gallant, adventurous and long-descended youth. A moral fervour must be matched against the chivalry of England. After Powick bridge he had talked with his cousin Hampden. 'Your troopers,' he said, 'are most of them old decayed serving-men and tapsters and such kind of fellows, and their troopers are gentlemen's sons, younger sons, and persons of quality. Do you think that the spirit of such base and mean fellows will be ever able to en- counter gentlemen who have honour and courage and resolu- tion in them? You must get men of a spirit that is likely to go on as far as gentlemen will go, or else I am sure you will be beaten still.'[2] Hampden had agreed, but thought the hope im- practicable. Edgehill convinced Oliver that the thing must be done unless all were to be lost, and as he rode London-wards with Essex he decided that his immediate duty was a new kind of recruitment, to raise 'such men as had the fear of God be- fore them, and made some conscience of what they did.'

---

[1] Ludlow, I, 44.   [2] *L. and S.*, III, 65.

Chapter III

IRONSIDES IN THE MAKING
(1642–1643)

I am not in the roll of common men.
Where is he living, clipp'd in with the sea
What chides the banks of England, Scotland, Wales,
Which calls me pupil, or hath read to me?
First Part of King Henry IV.

I

FROM Edgehill Essex made all haste to a distracted London.
Charles, too weak to risk pursuit, received the surrender of
Banbury, and on October 29 entered Oxford, which was henceforth to be his headquarters. Parliament, shaken out of its
first confidence, was ready to open negotiations with him, but,
when the news came that he was marching on London, it flung
up rough field fortifications and raised new levies, since it was
clear that Charles at the moment had no mind to treat. Rupert
swept down the Thames valley, failed in an attempt on Windsor
castle, and on November 13th cut up the regiments of Brooke
and Holles in Brentford. Next day Essex had 24,000 men
drawn up at Turnham Green and the city was saved. Ramsay
with 3000 men held the bridge at Kingston on the king's right
rear, and Hampden, who was now the Rupert of the parliament
side, urged in vain a turning movement. Essex was not sufficiently confident of the quality and discipline of his troops to
have any liberty of manœuvre. Yet Turnham Green has been
rightly called the Valmy of the Civil War. It checked the king's
advance and gave his opponents leisure to make an army.
Charles retraced his steps and established himself in Oxford.
There he created a fortified zone, with the city as the keep, and
a defensive ring of posts at Banbury, Brill, Reading, Abingdon,
Wallingford and Marlborough — a ring soon to be completed
by the capture of Cirencester. He had his outposts within thirty
miles of London.

Elsewhere in England before the close of the year things
went well for the royal cause. Hertford was bringing to Oxford
the foot he had raised in South Wales. Sir Ralph Hopton drove
the parliament troops out of Cornwall, and, since the Cornish

trained bands would not fight beyond their own borders, he entered Devonshire with a force of volunteers. The arrival of the Earl of Stamford forced him back across the Tamar, but in Cornwall he was safe, and on January 19 at Bradock Down near Liskeard he utterly routed Stamford and began to threaten Plymouth. Up in the far north the Earl of Newcastle crossed the Tees with 8000 men, including the famous Whitecoats (so called from their clothes of rough undyed wool), the best infantry on the royalist side. He defeated Hotham in the North Riding, made York secure, and hemmed in the Fairfaxes in the south-east of the shire. Though he failed to reduce the clothing towns of the West Riding, he took Pontefract castle, and placed a garrison in Newark-on-Trent. To Newcastle had fallen the best chance of the opening stage of the campaign. He had immense wealth, and in the shires of the extreme north a recruiting ground for stalwart royalists. He stood between the parliament and its potential allies of Scotland. Had he been a man of another mould he would have had the issues of the war in his hands. But for all his gallantry and loyalty he was little of a soldier. His sumptuous and scholarly soul was too fine and too sluggish for the rough work before him. He was the eternal dilettante, and, in Sir Philip Warwick's phrase, 'had the misfortune to have somewhat of the poet in him,' and that poetry not of the stiff heroic kind.[1]

To Charles and his advisers, sitting that midwinter in Christ Church, it seemed that the occasion was ripe for a large strategic plan. Whose was the plan? Mr. Gardiner thinks that it may have come through the queen from the Prince of Orange: it may have been Rupert's; it may have been the work of civilian brains like Hyde's or Falkland's; it certainly did not spring from the confused head of old Ruthven, now Earl of Forth and nominal commander-in-chief. Charles had a secure base at Oxford with communications open to the west. The plan was for Hopton to move east through the southern counties into Kent, while Newcastle marched south to the Thames. They would join hands on the river below London and cut off all sea-

[1] Cf. Clarendon's account: 'He liked the pomp and absolute authority of a general well.... But the substantial part and fatigue of a general he did not in any degree understand (being utterly unacquainted with war) nor could submit to.... In all actions of the field he was still present, and never absent in any battle, in all which he gave instance of an invincible courage and fearlessness in danger.... Such articles of action were no sooner over than he returned to his delightful company, Music, or his softer pleasures.' *Hist.*, VIII, 85.

borne commerce, while the king, moving from Oxford, would account for Essex. The scheme was excellent, but its success depended upon exact timing and skilled leadership, upon the willingness of the separate armies to fight far away from their own countrysides, and upon no one of them being defeated in detail. Hopton must be able to sweep Stamford and Waller from his road. Newcastle must have taken order with the Fairfaxes in Yorkshire and have no fear of a flank attack from Cheshire; moreover he must be able to break through the parliament cordon in the eastern midlands. The king must be in a position at least to immobilize Essex. There was one further condition which to men in that age seemed essential, and which no royalist general was wise enough to disregard. The ports held by parliament must be taken — Plymouth and Bristol in the west, Hull in the north-east; they could not be left as a menace to the flank or rear of an advancing army; also Gloucester must be secured, since it commanded the road to Wales. It was this fatal nervousness about strong places which largely contributed to the ruin of the great plan. Hull in particular was to be for parliament in the north what the lines of Torres Vedras were to Wellington.

Newcastle was the chief menace, for at Newark he was only a hundred miles from London and the mind of parliament turned to Scotland for an ally who could distract him. In the meantime the northward road must be guarded, and mere county organizations would not suffice. Before the end of the year an association of the midland shires was formed under Lord Grey of Groby — Leicester, Derby, Nottingham, Rutland, Northampton, Bedford, Buckingham and Huntingdon, and Warwickshire and Staffordshire were joined together under Lord Brooke. An eastern association comprised Essex, Suffolk, Norfolk, Hertfordshire and Cambridgeshire, and to it Huntingdon and Lincoln were added in the following year. This last association was the strategic heart of the parliament position. It contained the area where puritanism was strongest, was defended by London and the Thames on the south and by the sea to east and north, and it lay on the flank of Newcastle's threatened invasion. In the beginning of 1643 Oliver Cromwell, who was a member of the Huntingdon and Cambridge committees, left London to look into matters in the eastern shires.

II

Oliver went first to Hertford, where he seized the high sheriff in the market-place of St. Albans as he was proclaiming the king's commission of array, and despatched him to London. Then he went to Huntingdon, where he had some candid words to say to his old antagonist Robert Barnard, who had the repute of a cryptic royalist.[1] Early in February 1643 he was in Cambridge, and his first task was to raise a volunteer force to defend the place against Lord Capel. That danger past, he set about fortifying the town. He pulled down houses, and made havoc of the walks and new gates at King's and the bridges at St. John's and Trinity; mounted four guns, and used the timber collected for the rebuilding of Clare Hall to erect barracks for his men. By January 26 he was a colonel, having probably received his commission not from Essex but from Lord Grey of Wark. For the following months he moved about the eastern shires like a flame, checking royalist intrigues, learning the art of war, as we shall see, in many little battles, collecting money, and above all collecting men. Cambridge became his wash-pot, and over all East Anglia he cast his shoe. Let us see the methods by which he turned his command into a regiment, which was soon to be the model for an army.

In October 1642 he had a troop of sixty men, and three officers. In December he had under him eighty men. At Cambridge the single troop was increased to a regiment, which in March 1643 numbered five troops, and in September ten. In the end it became a double regiment of fourteen troops, eleven hundred strong, with for each troop four commissioned officers, three corporals and two trumpeters.[2]

The quality of this regiment was a new thing in England. Oliver's summons to arms took high ground. He sought, he said, 'not theirs, but them and their welfare, and to stand with them for the liberty of the gospel and the laws of the land.' What he aimed at was a body like Gideon's Three Hundred, inspired by a common zeal, welded together by a common discipline, sensitive like an instrument of music to the spirit of its commander. Naturally his first thought was to have men of his own passionate religious creed. Richard Baxter has well stated this purpose. 'These men were of greater understanding than common soldiers, and therefore

[1] *L. and S.*, I, 115–16, 130.   [2] *Exchequer MSS.: Rel. Baxt.*, 96

were more apprehensive of the importance and consequence
of the war; and, making not money, but that which they took
for the public felicity to be their end, they were the more
engaged to be valiant; for he that maketh money his end doth
esteem his life above his pay, and therefore is like enough to
save it by flight when danger comes, if possibly he can; but
he that maketh the felicity of Church and State the end,
esteemeth it above his life, and therefore will the sooner lay
down his life for it. And men of parts and understanding
know how to manage this business, and know that flying is
the surest way to death, and that standing to it is the likeliest
way to escape; there being many usually that fall in flight
for one that falls in valiant fight.' So Oliver must have reasoned. He valued two things, character and brains. His
enemies declared that he cared only for piety, and selected
his officers anyhow, provided they were 'godly precious men.' [1]
The charge was untrue. Oliver's first demand was for fighting
quality, but he believed rightly that that sprang not from
mere bellicosity but from a strong and rational purpose. In
his own words, 'a few honest men are better than numbers,'
and with him honesty meant conscience. There were misfits
in his ranks, devout men who were no soldiers and stout
fighting men who were rogues, but the average quality was
very high. This principle of selection was no new thing, for
Essex and Hampden proclaimed it; [2] the difference with Oliver
was that he made it a reality.

Inevitably his ranks were full of independents, separatists,
antinomians, baptists bearing the stigma of continental ana-
baptism, and all the wild sects that spring up in a time of
religious stress. One troop, Christopher Bethell's, was believed to be packed with heretics. [3] These men had in them
the spirit that wins battles, and Oliver, who never belonged
to any religious body after he drifted away from the church,
had a natural kindness for those who refused to let priest or
layman come between them and their Maker. This prepos-

---

[1] *Manchester's Quarrel with Cromwell* (Camden Soc.), 72.   A royalist pamphleteer of
1644 wrote: 'Now begins an Hosanna to Cromwell, one that hath beate up his Drummes
cleane through the Old Testament; you may learne the Genealogy of our Saviour by
the names in his Regiment; the Muster-master uses no other list than the first chapter
of *Matthew*. With what face can they object to the King the bringing in of Forreigners,
when themselves intertaine such an Army of *Hebrews*?' *The Character of a London
Diurnall*.

[2] Gardiner, *Civil War*, I, 153 *n*.   [3] *Rel. Baxt.*, 53.

session was due partly to temperament and creed, but largely to his practical instinct. 'How to get the best soldiers was the problem which made Cromwell tolerant, and tolerance built upon so material a foundation would to the end have in it something narrower than Chillingworth's craving for the full light of truth. Cromwell, with all his massive strength remained always a practical man, asking not so much what the thing is, as how it can be done." [1] A year later he came on this point hard against the narrow Scots creed, and was compelled to speak his mind to Major-General Lawrence Crawford. 'Sir, the State, in choosing men to serve them, takes no notice of their opinions; if they be willing faithfully to serve them, that satisfies." [2] In this he was not quite candid, for he himself took eager note of a man's opinions; he wanted utter conviction and a furious zeal like his own.

There was also the question of social standing. Oliver's troopers represented a far higher social class than the average cavalry regiment on either side. To begin with they were men whom he knew, the youth of Cambridge and Huntingdon, young yeoman farmers, freeholders and freeholders' sons.[3] Later he cast his net all over the east and the east midlands: picking up likely fellows, an incomparable recruiting sergeant with his homely humour, his rustic cajoleries and his sudden prophetic raptures. But in his selection of officers he scandalized the genteel, for, as he wrote in September: 'I had rather have a plain russet-coated captain that knows what he fights for, and loves what he knows, than that which you call a gentleman and is nothing else. I honour a gentleman that is so indeed.' [4] Some of his troop commanders were gently born. The 2nd troop was under Edward Whalley, his cousin who was also lieutenant-colonel of the regiment; the 3rd under his brother-in-law John Disbrowe; the 4th under his son Oliver, a lad of twenty; the 4th under young Valentine Wauton, his nephew; the 14th under Henry Ireton, a scion of an ancient Nottinghamshire house. But the captain of the 1st troop was James Berry, a friend of Richard Baxter, who had been a clerk in an ironworks in Shropshire; Robert Swallow of the 11th, the 'maiden troop' armed by subscription among the girls of Norwich, was looked askance at by the well-born; and Ralph Margery of the 13th was so very

---

[1] Gardiner, *Civil War*, I, 312.
[3] Whitelocke, 68.
[2] *L. and S.*, I, 171.
[4] *L. and S.*, I, 154.

plain and russet-coated that the gentility of Suffolk would have none of him.[1]

The regiment was governed by a rigid discipline. With so many religious men in its ranks it was necessary to have a strict code of behaviour so that tender consciences should not be grieved. In May Oliver could write of his men: 'No man swears but he pays his twelve pence; if he is in drink he is set in the stocks or worse; if one calls the other "Roundhead" he is cashiered; in so much that the countries where they come leap for joy of them.'[2] Offences against property and person were sternly punished, for it was not a war against Englishmen, though royalists had their belongings sequestrated. The actual military discipline was severe. In April Oliver had two troopers who had deserted whipped in the market-place of Huntingdon and then 'turned off as renegadoes.' More notable still were the constant drills and exercises. He and they had their job to learn, and in so high a cause no labour could be too great. He strove to give his command so strict a unity that in no crisis should it crack; he would learn not only how to lead, but how to handle cavalry. The result has been described by Clarendon: 'That difference was observed shortly from the beginning of the war: that though the king's troops prevailed in the charge and routed those they charged, they never rallied themselves again in order, nor could be brought to make a second charge the same day; whereas Cromwell's troops if they prevailed, or though they were beaten and routed, presently rallied again and stood in good order till they received new orders.'

In the matter of arms Oliver made no great innovation. His men were not cuirassiers but harquebusiers, though they dispensed with the harquebus. They wore iron pots and 'backs and breasts,' and their only weapons were sword and pistol. But he had realized the true part of cavalry in war, and paid very special attention to the horses. Horse-flesh he had always loved, and he knew more about it than most royalist squires. Mounting a regiment was assumed to cost £10 per trooper, and the price of a horse ran from £5 upward; since money was short he had to get his mounts as cheaply as possible, and in this his old experience made him an adept. He

---

[1] For details of the troops see Sir Charles Firth, 'The Raising of the Ironsides.' *E. H. R.* (1899), 17-73.

[2] *Cromwelliana*, 5.

had to put up for the most part with the heavy animals of the Fenlands, but he liked to have them crossed with a lighter strain, and he had a quick eye for good blood. He bought horses at fairs and markets, requisitioned them, begged and borrowed them, and when necessary stole them. He and his officers became the most shameless horse-thieves in England. Whalley of the 2nd troop got into a scrape at Newmarket for commandeering a horse belonging to the Earl of Carlisle.[1] Margery of the 13th was constantly in similar trouble, and Oliver himself was not exempt from criticism.[2] He was a wonderful horse-master, and taught his men scrupulously to feed and dress their animals, and 'when it was needful, to lie together on the ground.' He knew how much the value of cavalry lay in the condition of the horses, especially if the charge was to be pressed home.[3]

He nursed his men too. He saw that they were well fed and well clad, and he laboured to have them regularly paid. During the first half of 1643 the pay was often in arrears — it was better after Manchester's army was formed in August — and Oliver's letters during this time are filled with appeals to give the labourer his hire.... 'Make them able to live and subsist that are willing to spend their blood for you. I say no more.' — 'Lay not too much upon the back of a poor gentleman, who desires, without much noise, to lay down his life and bleed the last drop to secure the Cause and you. I ask not your money for myself.... I desire to deny myself; but others will not be satisfied.' — 'You have had my money; I hope in God I desire to venture my share. So do mine. Lay weight upon their patience, but break it not.'[4] His regiment was his family, their prowess was his, his honour was theirs, he had no interest beyond their welfare. With such a spirit in their commander small wonder that a new type of fighting force was born in England.

This was perhaps the happiest stage in Oliver's life. 'My troops increase,' he wrote lyrically to St. John in September. 'I have a lovely company; you would respect them, did you know them. They are no Anabaptists, they are honest, sober Christians; they expect to be used as men.' He was doing work

---

[1] *L. J.*, V, 656.   [2] *L. and S.*, I, 160–62.

[3] He would never allow his horses to be driven too hard. Cf. before Winceby (Vicars, *God's Ark*, 45), and after the 2nd battle of Newbury (Ashe, *Relation of Newbury*, 6).

[4] *L. and S.*, I, 138, 149, 156.

for which by his early training he was supremely fitted, marrying the precision of a man of affairs with what he now felt to be a natural genius for war. He was shaping human material which he loved to what he believed to be the purposes of God.

III

In the year 1643 the king had the initiative and the tale of the war is the tale of his efforts to carry out his main strategical plan, and march the armies of the north, the west, and the south-west upon London. They had to beat their local opponents and clear their flanks from the menace of hostile forts and fortresses, while the king widened his hold on the south midlands. The main danger to parliament and that with which Oliver was chiefly concerned was Newcastle's threat from the north. But first let us see how the royal arms fared elsewhere in England. Futile negotiations were attempted during the early months of the year, but neither side had a serious purpose: the real issue must be decided in the field, and in August both the antagonists took to impressing men.

Hopton in the west was the most successful of the royalist generals, for in his Cornishmen he had a nucleus of stalwart troops on which he could rely. His victory of Bradock Down in January was followed in May by the annihilation of Stamford's army at Stratton, and the instant overrunning of Devon. Waller, who had cleared Hampshire and Wiltshire, and secured, as he believed, the key-points of Bristol and Gloucester, hastened to check this eastward march; but meantime Hertford and Prince Maurice had joined Hopton from Oxford, and after much brilliant manœuvring round Bath, a drawn battle was fought on July 5 on Lansdown Heath. Hopton moved to Devizes with Waller at his heels, and on the 15th on Roundway Down the latter was decisively beaten. Prince Maurice overran Dorset, on the 26th Bristol after four days' siege fell to Rupert, and, but for Plymouth and Gloucester, all the west was in the king's hands.

Meantime there had been much fighting on the flanks of the main movements. Sir William Brereton's victory at Nantwich in January did not prevent the royalists of the west midlands from joining hands with their friends in Newark, and Lord Byron's successes in Cheshire removed the danger of an attack on Newcastle's flank. Essex bestirred himself in April and took

Reading, the eastern point of Oxford's defensive periphery, but a sick and mutinous army prevented his doing more, and his attempt to invest Oxford in June was of the feeblest. He could not prevent Maurice from reinforcing Hopton, or the arrival in the city of the queen's convoy, and later of the queen herself. In September he was faced with an urgent duty. Gloucester, the bridge-head for Wales, was held by parliament, and Charles, after Hopton's victories and the fall of Bristol, felt himself free to reduce it. Waller had been given a new army to oppose Hopton, and the relief of Gloucester fell to Essex. With an army reinforced by the London trained bands he marched across Cotswold,[1] in spite of Rupert's attacks, and on September 5 the royalists were forced to raise the siege. There followed a situation like that before Edgehill, for Essex had to march his men home, and there was a race for a start on the road to London. On the downs southwest of Newbury on September 20th the royal army barred the way and the first great battle of the war was fought. The valour of the London prentices repelled Rupert's charge, and, though Essex failed to break through, the royalists had suffered so heavily that they fell back to Newbury and left the way free to Reading and the capital.

Yet it was only a qualified success, for in October Reading fell again to the king, and in November Waller's new army failed at Basing house and Arundel surrendered to Hopton. Except for Plymouth and Gloucester and a few small Dorset ports all the west and south-west was the king's. Moreover news came in September that a truce had been made with the Irish rebels, which would release a great body of troops as reinforcements for the royal cause. The negotiations of parliament with the Scots, which had been in progress since the spring, were brought in August to a notable conclusion. Charles remained blind to the danger, rejected Montrose's warnings, and chose to accept Hamilton's easy optimism about Scottish loyalty. On August 7 the suppliant English commissioners arrived at Leith. They asked for a civil alliance, but the Scots, who had the master hand in the bargain, made the price of it a religious covenant. Leven was to carry a Scots army to parliament's assistance, parliament paying the bill, and the two nations were to unite in abolishing episcopacy and establishing a uniform presbyterian church. The younger Vane, indeed, who

[1] It was by no means a brilliant feat of marching — only about ten miles a day.

was himself an independent, succeeded in leaving a loophole for toleration by his amendment that the church of England should be reformed 'according to the Word of God.' The ratifying document, the Solemn League and Covenant, having been adopted by the Scottish Estates, was solemnly subscribed by what was left of the House of Commons in St. Margaret's church on September 25. This act may well be regarded as one of the most fateful of the war. It assured the ultimate triumph of parliament, for it is as certain as such things can be that without the support of the Scots even the genius of Oliver must have failed. But it also made peace impossible, for it laid upon England an obligation to accept an unpopular church, it made final the breach with the king, and it was later to set an insurmountable barrier between parliament and army. Charles's scaffold and Oliver's principate were among its fantastic fruits.

The architect of the bargain did not long survive its completion, for on November 8 John Pym died of cancer, becoming, in Richard Baxter's words, 'a member of a more knowing, unerring, well-ordered, right-aiming, self-denying, unanimous, honourable, triumphant Senate than that from whence he was taken.' It had been a year of significant deaths. The flower of the younger royalists had fallen in the field: Sidney Godolphin at Chagford, Northampton at Hopton Heath, Sir Bevil Grenville on Lansdown Heath, Falkland himself at Newbury, courting death like a lover. Lord Brooke, who was regarded by many as Essex's successor, had died at Lichfield, and John Hampden on Chalgrove Field had got his mortal wound from Rupert's horse — Rupert in honour of whose mother's wedding he had written verses at Magdalen.[1] But with Pym passed the true pilot of the storm, and his death left no strong hand on the rudder. He alone had made compromise impossible. He must rank as one of the foremost of all parliamentarians, for he had not only saved for parliament its ancient liberties but had made a new thing out of it, since he had given it sovereignty. He was a great revolutionary, whom von Ranke has compared to Mirabeau: 'Characters like his stand midway between the present, which they shatter for ever, and the future, which however generally develops itself on principles different from those which they have laid down.'[2] He had many things in common with Oliver. Like him he did not know the road he was travelling; he had no consistent policy; he had no long vision; but

---

[1] *Lusus Palatini* (1613).   [2] *Hist. of England* (Eng. trans.), II, 394.

within a narrow range he had the same infallible instinct for facts. As with him, too, religion was the mainstay of his being, and he would have enforced his own beliefs against the will of all England. The two men were the slaves of masterful dreams, and if the one far transcends in greatness the other it is because the dream which moved him was richer in its human quality, lit by a more spacious imagination, and warmed by diviner fires.

IV

We return to that alley-way between London and the north, where at the far end Newcastle was grappling with the Fairfaxes and in the centre Oliver was creating a zone of defence. The latter's first task was to clear the territory of the eastern association of royalist nuclei, of which there were many. Lowestoft, Lynn and Crowland successively felt his heavy hand, and promising royalist risings were crushed at the start. This work completed, he turned his mind to greater matters. He had his own area under control, but Lincolnshire was at the mercy of the royalists in Newark, and in Yorkshire the Fairfaxes were daily becoming harder pressed. He saw that the true strategy was to take Newark and then move north to relieve Yorkshire, and these in fact were Essex's orders. But for such a movement a union of forces was needed, and this was hard to compass. Sir John Gell in Nottingham and Derby was willing, but Hotham in Lincolnshire was already intriguing with the queen, and in Leicestershire Lord Grey of Groby, Stamford's son, thought more of protecting his father's house of Broadgates than of beating the enemy. 'Believe it,' Oliver wrote bitterly to the committee of Lincoln, 'it were better in my poor opinion Leicester were not, than that there should not be an immediate taking of the field by your forces to accomplish the common end, wherein I shall deal as freely with him when I meet him as you could desire.' [1] Meantime he was cheered by his first victory in a field action. On May 13 he was at Grantham, awaiting allies who never came. But he found something else, a royalist force from Newark, two miles from the town. He had twelve troops of horse, 'some so poor and broken that you shall seldom see worse,' and the enemy had twice his number. For half an hour the two bodies exchanged

[1] *L. and S.*, I, 133.

shots, and then Oliver charged his opponents at a trot and scattered them like chaff. In that fight in the late spring dusk lay the germ of all his future cavalry successes.[1]

By the end of May he was at Nottingham, where he was joined by Hotham, Gell and Grey of Groby. But he could not infuse his own spirit into his colleagues. Sir Thomas Fairfax had done well at Wakefield, but he was hourly in danger of being cut off by Newcastle from the midland and eastern associations. More, if Fairfax were once immobilized, Newcastle would soon be at Newark, and far on the road to London. But local jealousies, personal quarrels, and, in Hotham's case, treachery kept the Nottingham concentration idle. Hotham escaped to join his father in Hull, and presently the treason of the two was revealed, and the vital seaport was only saved by a miracle for parliament. The Fairfaxes were left to their fate, and on June 30th at Adwalton Moor near Bradford were heavily defeated by Newcastle. They fled to Hull, and all of Yorkshire save the south-eastern corner was in the king's hands.

Oliver in impotent wrath watched the bungling of the parliament leaders. Had his own force, and those of Gell, Grey and Hotham, been joined to Fairfax, there would have been eleven thousand men to hold Newcastle, and the Grantham skirmish had given him confidence in himself and in the quality of his troops. Sir John Meldrum, sent down by Essex to take the general command, had let the queen slip through to Oxford. Newcastle had now the initiative, but happily he did not seem inclined to make any speedy use of it, for he still dallied in south Yorkshire. Yet the royalist successes had given fresh heart to the enemy, and half the countryside was in revolt. Oliver had his hands full. He beat off a raid from Newark upon Peterborough, and stormed Burleigh house by Stamford. And then came news which sent him galloping northwards. On July 20th Lord Willoughby of Parham had taken Gainsborough, which was an important bridge-head on the Trent. The royalist commander in Lincolnshire, Charles Cavendish, the Earl of Devonshire's son, had promptly laid siege to it. To relieve Willoughby Oliver joined Meldrum at Grantham, and on July 28 they were within sight of the beleaguered town.

There followed some crowded and fateful hours. Cavendish, aware of the coming of the relief force, had posted his horse on the edge of a little tableland, the sides of which were a rabbit-

[1] See his own account in *L. and S.*, I, 134-35.

warren. Oliver's troops had to pick their way up the difficult slopes, and then, disordered by the ascent, to face an enemy drawn up in battle formation. But, disordered as they were, Oliver commanded an instant charge. 'We came up horse to horse, when we disputed it with our swords and pistols a pretty time, all keeping close order, so that one could not break the other. At last, they a little shrinking, our men, perceiving it, pressed in upon them and immediately routed the whole body.' The bulk of the parliament horse pursued the rout for five or six miles, but Oliver, remembering Rupert's blunder at Edgehill, kept back three of his troops. It was well he did so, for Cavendish had a regiment in reserve, with which he was crumpling the parliament's second line, when Oliver fell upon his rear. The reserves were scattered, and Cavendish was slain by Captain James Berry, formerly of the Shropshire ironworks. A little food and ammunition was got into the town, and then, at the news of a royalist thrust from the north, the relieving force marched out to reconnoitre. To their amazement they found themselves in the presence of Newcastle's main army. Most of the parliament foot fled in confusion, but the horse brilliantly covered the retreat, falling back slowly by alternate squadrons.[1] That day Oliver had achieved two of the most difficult feats of a cavalry commander, to attack an enemy in formation with troops disordered by difficult ground, and to withdraw weary men in the face of a fresh foe in overwhelming numbers. Gainsborough had clinched the lesson of Grantham.

But it was a fruitless success. The place soon fell to Newcastle, Lord Willoughby had to abandon Lincoln and retire to Boston, Oliver could not hold Stamford but must return to Peterborough. His appeals for reinforcements grew more clamant. 'If something be not done in this, you will see Newcastle's army march up into your bowels, being now, as it is, on this side Trent.' In August parliament was sufficiently convinced of the gravity of the situation to authorize the formation of an army in the associated counties under the Earl of Manchester, with an infantry strength of 10,000. This was the force detailed to face Newcastle, and in it Oliver was one of the four colonels of horse. He was virtually the second-in-command.

[1] The evidence for the fight is Oliver's own letter (*L. and S.*, I, 140–43), and the letters of Meldrum and Willoughby from the *Tanner MS.* in *Trans. of R. H. S.* (1899), xiii.

Newcastle had the king's orders to press on to London at any cost, but his army refused to move till Hull was taken. He broke up his camp at Nottingham and returned to Yorkshire to set about the siege. But the Fairfaxes defended it stubbornly, and on the sea and river side their communications could not be cut. They sent their horses across the Humber, and Oliver went north to receive them, crossing to Hull on September 26, and there having his first meeting with Sir Thomas Fairfax. The latter joined him on the Lincolnshire shore, and the mounted troops under Oliver, Fairfax and Willoughby now numbered some 3000. The three found Manchester at Boston in the beginning of October, and the combined forces bent themselves to clearing Lincolnshire of royalists and protecting it against the raids from Newark. Hull would absorb Newcastle's attention, and it was their business to reconstitute the southern zone of defence, for the royalists held Lincoln and Gainsborough and were threatening to run a line of fortified forts from the Trent to the sea.

The fighting took place on and around the ridge of downs which run the length of Lincolnshire from the Humber to the fens of Holland. Twelve miles north of Boston lay the castle of Bolingbroke, against which Manchester advanced his foot on October 9th. To its relief came Sir John Henderson, the governor of Newark, with a strong body of cavalry, who cut up the scattered parliament outposts. On the 11th a battle became inevitable, though Oliver would fain have avoided it, since his horses were in poor condition, and he was far from certain of the quality of some of his new levies. The mounted forces met near the hamlet of Winceby, which lies on the crest of the watershed. It was open ground for cavalry, and the two sides were of about equal strength. Oliver charged at the head of his men; his horse was shot and rolled over on him; when he attempted to rise a royalist trooper knocked him down: never in his career was he nearer death. Eventually he found another mount, and was able to take part in that half-hour's struggle, when the royalists' first line was forced back on its reserves, and then the whole army driven from the field.[1] That night Manchester occupied Horncastle. Next day the garrison of Hull smote the invaders so lustily that the following morning Newcastle raised the siege. A little later Manchester re-took

[1] Accounts of Winceby are in *Fairfax Correspondence*, I, 62, etc.; Vicars, *God's Ark*, 45; Rushworth, V, 281; the various *True Relations* (Th.); and *L. J.*, VI, 255.

Lincoln and Gainsborough, and the immediate threat from the north was averted. The king might still hold two-thirds of the land, but it looked as if the tide were turning. Newcastle would soon be enclosed between two fires, for Leven with 18,000 foot and 3000 horse, was making ready to cross the Tweed.

The year 1643 saw the making of the Ironsides and also the making of Oliver the soldier. He began it as a simple captain of horse, and he ended it as the most successful of the parliament's cavalry commanders. He had been made governor of the isle of Ely, and as such had given the dignitaries of Ely cathedral a rough handling. He had been acting as second-in-command of Manchester's army since its formation, and on January 21, 1644, received his commission as lieutenant-general. A month later he became a member of the war cabinet, the Committee of Both Kingdoms [1] — a clumsy piece of mechanism, but more representative than the original committee of public safety and better than the whole parliament. Alone of the parliamentary generals he had no failure to his name. Waller and Brereton and the Fairfaxes had all lost battles, and Essex had only escaped defeat because he had avoided field actions. But Oliver whenever he appeared had been like the deadly stoop of a peregrine.

He was forming himself, and his colleagues were learning that when he saw his way clear he brooked no opposition. He talked plainly to the local committees and was far from respectful to the grandees. He had already expressed his views about Lord Grey of Groby, and when he found Lord Willoughby unsatisfactory he posted to London to tell the House of Commons what he thought of him, and forced his resignation. He had quietly ousted Lord North, the parliament's lord-lieutenant, from any say in Cambridgeshire or the isle of Ely.[2] Manchester, that 'sweet, meek man' was clay in his hands. If he was unpopular with the notables he was also coming to be distrusted by the presbyterians, who were so powerful in civil politics. They disliked his carelessness of formalism in his troopers, provided they had the root of the matter in them, and they were aware that he loved the Solemn League and Covenant little

[1] Besides Cromwell it embraced Essex, Manchester, Warwick, Northumberland, the two Vanes, Sir W. Waller, St. John, and Haselrig, and, as Scottish members, Loudon, Maitland, Barclay and Johnston of Wariston.

[2] *North MSS.*

more than he loved the church service at Ely, and had postponed signing it till his position as Manchester's lieutenant-
general compelled him. Many a decorous parliament man
shook his head as news came out of the eastern counties of the
triumph of this intractable Boanerges.

But discerning men were aware that a new thing had appeared in England. Here was one who had no doubts, who believed wholly in the righteousness of his cause and was resolved
that that cause should prevail in the field, who dismissed con-
temptuously all half-measures and faint-hearted overtures for
peace, and who turned his eyes fearlessly to instant needs.
He was welding gentility and rusticity, ruffianism and fanaticism into a novel and most formidable army. More, he was
devising a new art of war. Old soldiers of the foreign campaigns,
conning the news of Gainsborough and Winceby, saw the
methods of Gustavus carried to a new pitch of speed and
subtlety — witness that retreat by detachments which had
baffled all Newcastle's army. Here was something worlds removed from the plodding mediocrity of Waller and Fairfax —
that touch of genius possessed at the moment only by Rupert,
and by another whose fame was still to make, the young Montrose who in a month or two was to set out from Oxford to re-
conquer Scotland.

Chapter IV

MARSTON MOOR

(1644)

He stopp'd the fliers;
And by his rare example made the coward
Turn terror into sport; as weeds before
A vessel under sail, so men obey'd
And fell below his stern.

Coriolanus.

At the opening of the year 1644 the first enthusiasm of royalism was ebbing, and the formidable fighting spirit which comes from desperation was not yet born. The king's strategic plan had made little progress. Hopton's victories had led nowhere, Hull and Gloucester were still in the parliament's hands, and the troops from Ireland were at the best half-hearted, and, having hitherto been fighting catholics, not greatly inclined to do battle with fellow protestants. In the beginning of the year there were various small royalist defeats, and it was an ominous fact that so many of the prisoners were ready to take the Covenant and enter the parliament's service, including a certain George Monk, who, after the second fight at Nantwich on January 25, transferred his allegiance to the side which he was one day to dominate. Meantime there was creeping slowly from the north the shadow of Leven and his Scots.

But if the situation seemed gloomy to Charles's headquarters at Oxford, it seemed little more cheerful to Oliver. His command was now in a better position as to regular supplies of money, but there was no sign that the parliament generals meant to make good use of it, Newark was still a thorn in the side of the eastern shires, and at Sleaford three of his best troops had been beaten up in their quarters by a sally of its garrison. He was given isolated tasks which he performed efficiently, like the sack of Hilsden house in Buckinghamshire in March, his raid on Banbury, and his driving off cattle from under the very walls of Oxford. But the settlement of the major issue was as remote as ever. When Newark seemed likely to fall to Meldrum, Rupert had made a brilliant dash from Shrewsbury and compelled Meldrum's ignominious capitulation. Moreover Manchester, who had hitherto listened to him,

was now paying more heed to Crawford, his major-general of
foot, whose sympathies lay with the presbyterian moderates,
and who seemed to Oliver to have but meagre military talents.
Newcastle, it was true, had had his fangs drawn, having been
pushed into York by Fairfax and Leven, and there was no
danger of his moving south of Trent. But at this rate the war
might last till doomsday, and Oliver knew how slender a hold
he and his like had upon the affection of the people at large. A
field victory, a crushing field victory, was the one thing needful.

Presently it appeared that Essex had a plan. Newcastle was
to be left to Fairfax and the Scots, and he and Manchester were
to combine their armies in a general assault upon the king
from a base at Aylesbury, while Waller should deal with Hopton
in the west, and Brereton with Byron in Cheshire. On March
29 Waller had a success at Cheriton in Hampshire, which put
Hopton on the defensive and checked any hope of his advance
into Surrey and Kent. But he could not follow it up, since his
trained bands went home, and meantime Prince Maurice was
besieging Lyme Regis in Dorset — the defender of which was
one Robert Blake, soon to be a famous name — and Lincoln
fell again into the royalists' hands. At a council held in Oxford
in April it had been decided that Rupert must go north to relieve Newcastle, while the king's army under Lord Brentford
(who was formerly Lord Forth) should cover the road to the
west and keep Essex and Manchester busy. Accordingly the
Oxford zone was narrowed by the evacuation of Reading and
Abingdon.

At the end of May came Essex's first attempt on Oxford.
On the 29th he was at Islip on the north, while Waller operated
on the Berkshire side. The attack was feebly pushed, but the
king could not afford to be invested and starved out, so he
altered his plans, and resolved to leave only a small force in
Oxford, and to keep his main army free, like Rupert's, for field
operations. On June 3 he slipped out between Essex and Waller,
and in two days was in Worcestershire.[1] He was followed by the
parliament generals, and Essex proceeded to the worst blunder
of his career. He was of opinion that his first duty was to relieve Lyme, in spite of the remonstrances of the House of
Commons, so he went south with his army, leaving to Waller
the task of pursuing Charles. The king easily outraced Waller,

[1] See Vaughan-Thomas, *Night March of Charles I* (1853), for the details of this brilliant little enterprise.

but Brentford was not Rupert, and Cropredy bridge, which might have been a decisive royalist victory, was so bungled as to be an inconclusive skirmish. Yet Waller was in grave danger, and if Waller failed London lay open, while Essex was marching westward to disaster. The only hope for parliament lay in the north.

Manchester had bestirred himself and on May 6 he recaptured Lincoln. Oliver had some fighting with Goring's men from Newark, but the campaigning in that area was for the moment at an end. It had become clear that Rupert meant to relieve Newcastle in York, and that all of Manchester's horse and foot would be wanted north of Trent. Oliver, who had been joined by David Leslie with a detachment of Scottish horse, was the first to move, and by the middle of May his cavalry screen was in the Doncaster district, with Manchester slowly advancing behind it. York was reached by the foot on June 3, when Oliver had his horse in line from Wakefield to Knaresborough, between the Calder and the Nidd, awaiting the coming of the enemy from the west.

He had some weeks to wait, for Rupert had much to do in Lancashire. He relieved Lathom house, which Lady Derby had gallantly defended, plundered Stockport, and stormed Bolton and Liverpool. Then news from York, where Newcastle was in grave peril, hurried him across the Pennines. A letter from Charles, written before leaving Worcestershire, gave ambiguous orders, but Rupert interpreted them as instructions, if he felt himself strong enough, to relieve York and fight the parliament armies. 'Before God!' was Colepeper's comment, when Charles gave him the letter to read, 'you are undone, for upon this peremptory order he will fight whatever comes on't.' On the 28th he was in touch with Oliver's outposts, and on the 30th he was at Knaresborough, sixteen miles from York. The parliament generals, fearful of being trapped between him and the York garrison, drew off their forces on the morning of July 1st to Marston Moor on the road to Knaresborough. But Rupert was never prone to do what his opponents expected. He turned to his left, crossed the Ure and the Swale, came down the east bank of the Ouse, seized the bridge at Poppleton, and on the evening of the 1st rode into York. There was consternation in the parliament camp. It was feared that he would cut off their retreat to the south, and their hope of support from Denbigh and Meldrum. So on the morning of the

2nd they decided to anticipate him by falling back on Tad-caster.

Rupert himself was determined to force a battle, though Newcastle would have preferred to wait for Clavering and his reinforcements from the north, for he realized that the royalist strength was but little more than half the enemy's. But Rupert as usual had his way. During the night of the 1st and on the morning of the 2nd his army was busy crossing the bridge of boats at Poppleton. By 9 A.M. his advanced horse was on the moor at Long Marston which the parliament armies had just quitted, and in sight of the parliament rearguard of horse on the low slopes to the south. Urgent messages were sent by Sir Thomas Fairfax, which did not reach Leven till he was almost at Tadcaster. The parliament forces turned back, and by two o'clock in the afternoon were marshalled in the wet rye looking down upon Rupert's army on Marston Moor. Since the Wars of the Roses no armies of such size had fronted each other on English soil.

Marston Moor lay seven miles west of York city between the roads to Boroughbridge and Wetherby. In length it was about a mile and a half, much overgrown in its western parts with furze and broom, and sloping gently northward to Wilstrop wood, a point some fifty feet above the sea. Along its southern rim lay a ditch with a hedge on the far side, boggy and difficult at the centre and western ends, but in the middle largely filled up. South of the ditch the ground rose to what in those parts was a considerable hill, reaching a height of one hundred and fifty feet at the tree clump a mile to the south. All this slope was under cultivation, fields of rye and wheat, without any separating walls or hedges. At each end of the slope lay a village, the hamlet of Tockwith on the west, and the more considerable straggling village of Long Marston on the east. A few other features must be noted. At the Tockwith end of the ditch there was a piece of marshland with a rabbit-warren to the south of it. In the centre of the Moor itself, about half a mile from the ditch, was a cattlefold, known as White Syke Close. At the Long Marston end a lane called Moor Lane crossed the ditch at right angles; here the furze was very thick, and the ground was made more difficult by being seamed by many runnels. At five o'clock on the afternoon of July 2 the parliament army lay along the slope south of the ditch, while

Rupert had marshalled his forces north of it on the open moor.

The parliament front, since it contained far the larger number of men, slightly overlapped that of its opponents. Its strength was close on 27,000, some 20,000 infantry and the rest cavalry. Of this force Leven's Scots formed the largest contingent; they had no longer the strength with which they crossed the Tweed in January, mainly owing to the privations of that inclement spring; but they still mustered about 12,000 foot, and 2000 horse. Manchester had some 5000 foot, and 3000 horse; Lord Fairfax had 3000 of the first, and 2000 of the second. The royalist army at the most did not exceed 18,000. Rupert had brought 8000 with him into Lancashire, where his strength had been increased by local levies; Goring had joined him with 5000, and Newcastle added some 3000 more. We may give him a maximum of 11,000 foot, and 7000 horse.[1]

Rupert drew up his men in an odd position for a great cavalry commander. He placed them at the very edge of the ditch — 'their foot were close to our noses,' wrote Oliver's scoutmaster. He had of course his 'forlorn hope' in the ditch itself, but why did he adopt for much of his army a plan which put him at a disadvantage with the enemy's superior artillery, and would cramp his movements in a cavalry charge. Lord Eythin, Newcastle's second-in-command, was severely critical, and Rupert's reply showed that he meant to draw further back, if the battle were deferred to the following morning. The answer seems to be that he expected an immediate attack in the afternoon by only a portion of the parliament force, the cavalry, and that his position was meant to be defensive; he wished the enemy to break his teeth on his resistance, before he used his splendid horse in the counter-attack. He had learned much since Edgehill, and it is clear that he had given a good deal of thought to the ordering of a battle on which hung the fortunes of his cause.

He followed the customary plan of infantry in the centre and cavalry on the flanks. His right wing was in two lines, the first, of three regiments, under Lord Byron, with Sir John Urry [2] as second-in-command, the second, also of three regiments, under Lord Molineux. Urry, following the continental prac-

---

[1] I have followed on this point Colonel Ross, *E. H. R.*, April 1890, whose figures are accepted by Sir Charles Firth, *Trans. of R. H. S.*, 1898.

[2] Urry or Hurry was an old soldier of the foreign wars, who changed his side several times, and was finally with Montrose. He was executed in Edinburgh after Carbisdale.

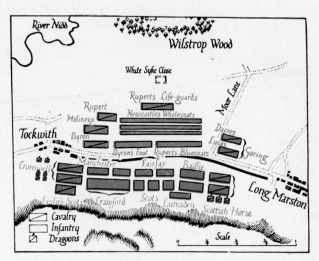

Position at 7 P.M.

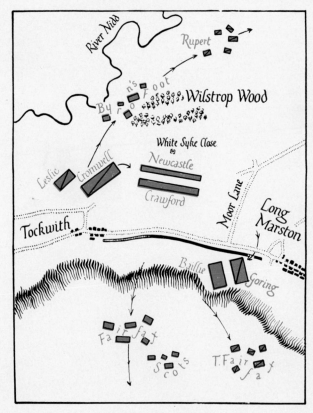

Position about 8.30 P.M.

BATTLE OF MARSTON MOOR

tice, placed companies of musketeers between the cavalry squadrons, a new mode which seems to have discomposed the royal horse, accustomed to fight as compact regiments.[1] Rupert himself, though commander-in-chief, kept a directing eye on this wing, and he had his own regiment of horse echeloned on its left rear, which brought up the total strength of cavalry in that quarter to 2500 men. Going east, next came the foot of the centre, of which Eythin seems to have been in general command. On the edge of the ditch were two of the best foot regiments, Lord Byron's and Rupert's own Bluecoats: behind them were three lines of infantry, the third of which was New-castle's Whitecoats, who arrived last on the field. In the rear of this centre was a body of horse, about 1000 strong, which included Rupert's life-guards. Here was probably what he intended to be his *poste de commandement*, from which he could control the tactics of the battle. The left wing was much the same as the right — two lines of cavalry interspersed with musketeers. Lord Goring was in command, and the first line was under Sir Charles Lucas and the second under Sir Richard Dacres. This wing was inferior in strength to the right by perhaps 500 men.[2]

The parliament left, opposite Byron, was under Oliver, and comprised all Manchester's mounted men. It was in three lines, the first two being the cavalry of the eastern association, nearly 2500 strong, and the third the regiments of Scots under David Leslie, which numbered probably less than 1000 men. On this flank were 1000 dragoons, part Manchester's and part Scots. In the left centre were Manchester's three foot brigades under Lawrence Crawford, two in the first line and one in reserve, a total of 4500 men. Before them lay an open ground of attack, for the ditch was flattened out and the hedge was down. The centre, under Lord Fairfax, consisted in the first line of two brigades of his own Yorkshire foot, and in the second line three Scottish brigades. The right centre was the main body of Scottish infantry under Lieutenant-General William Baillie, who was one day to be hunted mercilessly by Montrose, but who on this field won great honour. In the first line he had the regiments of Lindsay, Maitland, Cassilis, and Douglas of Kelhead; in the second, those of Buccleuch, Loudon and Dun-

---

[1] Fuller, *Worthies*, II, 536.

[2] I have followed Sir Charles Firth in these details, *Trans. of R. H. S.*, 1898, 30-35. Rupert's own plan of battle is in the British Museum.

fermline; while the regiments of Edinburgh and Clydesdale were echeloned on his left rear. Baillie himself led the first line, and Lumsden the reserve. The right wing, opposed to Goring, was under Sir Thomas Fairfax, and was composed of Fairfax's own cavalry, 2000 strong, many of the troops being newly raised. He had his men in two lines, and among his Colonels was John Lambert. His reserve in the third line was three regiments of Scottish horse, Leven's own, Lord Dalhousie's and Lord Eglinton's. Leven, as the senior of the three commanders and the leader of the largest army, was in general control, but as he arrived late on the field it is not likely that he had the making of the plan of battle, which may well have been Fairfax's, since he best knew the ground. David Leslie as the senior officer should have commanded the left, but for political reasons, since the Scots were technically not fighting their own but the parliament's battle, he preferred to serve under Oliver.[1]

Neither army was a homogeneous unit. The Fairfaxes had raw stuff in both their horse and foot, and some of Manchester's men were only half trained. Leven's infantry were underfed and a little tired by the winter campaigning and much aimless fighting around York. Leslie's horsemen were mounted on scraggy ponies too light for ordinary cavalry work. On the royalist side many of Rupert's Lancashire levies were uncertain, and Newcastle's rank-and-file had suffered more than the Scots in the desultory manœuvring of the spring. But there were certain troops of superb quality — the veterans of the royalist cavalry, Cromwell's horse of the eastern association, and, among the foot, Newcastle's Whitecoats and the stubborn Covenant levies of Lindsay, Cassilis and Maitland.

All day there had been thunder showers, and the parliament soldiers among the wet rye, who had marched all morning and had eaten little, grew weary of waiting. Rupert had a sermon preached to him, his chaplain taking his text from Joshua, 'The Lord God of Gods, He knoweth, and Israel he shall know; if it be in rebellion, or if in transgression against the Lord, save us not this day.'[2] A multitude of banners shone in the fitful

---

[1] In these dispositions I follow again Sir Charles Firth, as against Mr. Gardiner. There is a conflict of contemporary evidence, but I prefer Ashe and Stockdale to Stewart's *Full Relation* (Th.), and the dispositions given above seem the only ones consistent with the actual incidents of the battle.

[2] Vicars, *God's Ark*, 281.

gleams of sun, including Rupert's great red-cross standard, five yards long from pole to tip. Now and then the low murmur of a psalm rose from the Ironsides on the hill. Five o'clock passed, six o'clock came, but still there was no sign of movement. Rupert grew hungry. Newcastle, who had come out in his stately fashion in a coach and six, agreed that there was no likelihood of an attack that evening. He retired to his equipage to smoke a pipe, while Rupert prepared to sup, and passed the order to his troops to do likewise.

It was the moment for which the parliament army had been waiting. Someone — Oliver perhaps — had prevailed on Leven to order an attack on the first sign that the enemy no longer expected it. It was now seven o'clock, but he may have quoted Fuller's proverb that a summer's evening was as long as a winter's day. In any case the rain had gone, the sky had cleared, and there would presently be a moon. There was time enough, and light enough, for ordeal of battle. 'Is Cromwell there?' Rupert had asked of a prisoner that afternoon. He hastened to his right wing, against which came the flower of the parliament horse, and the man whose name for a year had been on the lips of every soldier.

As Oliver's cavalry thundered down the slopes by Tockwith, Byron, perhaps prompted by Urry, made an ill-judged move. His extreme right was posted behind a slough, to the south of which lay a warren — both ill places for horsemen. It was safe from attack, and was in position to take in flank any charge pressed beyond the ditch. It would seem, however, that in spite of positive orders not to quit his ground, he ordered the right regiment, his own, to advance across the slough, with the result that it was broken up in the mire by Colonel Frizel's dragoons.[1] Meantime against the rest of Byron's first line came the shock of the Ironsides. The royalist musketeers had been cleared from the ditch by the dragoons, but Oliver's men must have crossed it in irregular open order, as they had climbed the warren at Gainsborough, and closed up on the far

[1] The view taken by most historians (Gardiner, Clements Markham, etc.) is that Byron's abortive attempt took place several hours before the main battle was joined. But if it had, in the then mood of the parliament forces it would inevitably have precipitated a general action. It seems to me to come more naturally where I have put it, and I think my view is supported by the authorities. It is true that no parliament account, such as Stewart's *Full Relation*, mentions it; but they had many greater successes to write about. Rupert's Diary (Warburton, *Mem. of Prince Rupert*, II, 468) makes Byron begin the battle, and his action is said to have lost the day for the king in the *Life of James II*, I, 22. See also Fuller, *Worthies*, II, 536.

side. They charged the enemy first line, wrestled grimly for a little with pistol and sword-point, and then, in the words of their scoutmaster, scattered it 'like a little dust.' It was a fine achievement, due to sheer weight and an iron discipline.

But Rupert was now with Byron, and upon Oliver came the shock of the royalist second line, Molineux's regiment and Rupert's own. They were not on the defensive as before, and had room to charge. Oliver's first line was halted and broken, and his second line, now across the ditch, was also stayed. A pistol ball grazed his neck, and the flash of the shot at close quarters blinded his eyes. For some time the issue of the battle hung in the balance, and the parliament horse were on the brink of utter rout. But suddenly the fury of the royalist pressure slackened, for David Leslie with his 800 ill-mounted Scots was attacking their flank. This gave Oliver his chance. Blinded and dazed as he was, he managed to get his retreating first line to face about and renew the attack. For a few critical minutes there was stern hand-to-hand fighting, and then the weight of numbers told and the royalist cavalry broke. Oliver sent Leslie with his Scots — their small light horses served them well in this work — to press the retreat. Into Wilstrop wood they went — even today bullets are dug out of the tree roots — and for three miles down the York road. Rupert himself only escaped capture by a hair's breadth, and his little white dog, Boy, the 'divil dogge pudle' of the puritan pamphleteers, came by its end. Oliver halted and reformed his own regiments, and, having finished with the royalist right wing, fronted them east toward the centre.

It was now after eight o'clock, and on the rest of the front there was no such fortune for parliament. Manchester's foot, under Lawrence Crawford, in the left centre, soon cleared the ditch, and, having open ground before them, and being helped by the rout of Byron's cavalry, defeated Byron's foot regiment and Rupert's Bluecoats, who formed the van of the royalist centre, and turned the flank of the first line. But in the parliament centre Lord Fairfax's infantry were in dire straits. He had met the reserve of the royalist centre, Newcastle's White-coats, had been checked, counter-attacked, and routed, and the two Scottish brigades which formed his own reserve shared the same fate. On the parliament right centre the situation was curious. There fought Baillie with his Scots, and they were in a desperate case, for Lord Fairfax's defeat had exposed their left flank, and their right, as we shall see, was in a still more perilous position. On the Scottish left the regiments of Buccleuch and Loudoun broke, but most of the centre held, and on the right, in the worst place of all, the regiments of Lindsay and Maitland stood like rocks against the royalist attack. Three times their pikeman repelled the charge of Goring's horse, and took prisoner Sir Charles Lucas who commanded the second line. Maitland, as Duke of Lauderdale, was to leave a dark record behind him, but on this day he proved that the Restoration voluptuary had once been a man and a soldier.

The situation of Baillie's right was almost hopeless, for the cavalry of the parliament right wing had been totally defeated. Sir Thomas Fairfax had the most difficult ground of all for mounted work, a maze of furze and ditches and narrow lanes strongly held by the enemy's musketeers. He succeeded in getting part of his horse into open ground and had won a slight success, when down upon him came the full shock of Goring's horse. His raw Yorkshire and Lancashire levies were scattered, but the three Scottish regiments in reserve, Leven's own, Dalhousie's and Eglinton's (some of them had the Borderers' lances [1]) made a gallant fight of it, and partially maintained their ground. Goring's van pursued the runaways far beyond Tadcaster, and rifled the baggage-waggons, while part of his command swung round against the exposed parliament centre. Lord Fairfax fled towards Hull, and Leven towards Leeds (asking, says one wicked tale, the quickest way to the Tweed). Sir Thomas Fairfax, his cheek laid bare by a sword-cut, tore the white parliament favour from his hat and managed to slip through Lucas's horse and join Manchester.

The day seemed lost to parliament. Oliver had beaten Byron, Crawford had won on the left centre, but Lord Fairfax in the centre and Sir Thomas Fairfax on the right wing had been utterly broken, and all that was left there was five Scots regiments fighting a hopeless battle. All three of the army commanders were in flight. When Oliver, still giddy from his wound, heard Fairfax's account and surveyed the field, he realized that the only hope of salvation lay with Manchester's forces. He and his horse were now on the site of Rupert's first *poste de commandement*, and Crawford and the foot was almost level with them. He ordered a general wheel in line eastward across

[1] 'Being lancers, they charged a regiment of the enemies foot, and put them wholly to the rout.' Stewart, *A Full Relation* (1644), 7.

the moor. In front of him were the Whitecoats of the royalist
centre, and beyond them Goring's horse, attacking the remnants of Baillie's Scottish foot. The position was the reverse of
that at the start of the battle, for the parliament men were now
facing more or less to the south and the royalists to the north.

In half an hour the fortune of war was dramatically changed.
Oliver's first task was to deal with Goring. He had some sixty
troops of horse at his command. With Leslie, who had now re-
joined him, in reserve, he flung himself on the victorious royalist
cavalry, and, since they were demoralized and disordered by
their wild pursuit, routed them after a sharp struggle. Then,
with Manchester's infantry and Baillie's unbeaten Scots, he
and Leslie turned on the last of Newcastle's foot. The Whitecoats retreated yard by yard to White Syke Close, and there,
till ten o'clock, an hour after the battle was lost to their cause,
the stubborn pikemen refused quarter and fell fighting. Their
white coats were dyed at last, but not in the blood of their foe-
men. No Borderers in history or ballad ever made a more triumphant end. As the last of them perished there rose from the
battlefield the thanksgiving psalm of the victors.[1]

The triumph of parliament was complete. There were more
than 1500 prisoners, including several officers of high rank;
all the royalist guns were taken, and enough of their gay colours,
said one report, to 'make surplices for all the cathedrals in
England, were they white'; the country people buried on the
field over 4000 bodies, of whom the great majority wore the
badge of the king. Newcastle's army had ceased to be, and
northern England was lost for good to Charles. York surrendered in a fortnight, and Newcastle himself fled overseas.
It was, as we know now, a decisive battle of the war, and even
to the men of the time, to whom the future was still hid, it was
plain that it had decided many things. One was that unless a
makeweight to Leven and his Scots could be found, the royal
cause must go down, and consequently a month later Montrose
crossed the Border on his forlorn enterprise.

[1] The authorities for Marston Moor are many, and will be found set out by Sir
Charles Firth in *Trans. of R. H. S.*, 1898, and by Sir Clements Markham, *The Great
Lord Fairfax*, 176–78. The only matter in real doubt seems to be Byron's conduct
at the beginning of the battle. I have followed Sir Charles Firth's view as to the relative
positions of Baillie and Lord Fairfax in the parliament line, and I have accepted in the
main Colonel Hoenig's interpretation of Oliver's tactics in his *Oliver Cromwell, Der
Reitergeneral Feldherr und Staatsmann* (new ed., 3 vols., Leipzig, 1911), though he is
frequently wrong in his facts, and is inclined to find undue subtleties in Cromwell's
achievement.

It made it clear, too, that a great soldier had arisen in England. On Oliver's share in the victory there was much dispute at the time, and soon it became a partisan question, since all who were hostile to him and his independents decried his prowess in the battle and gave the chief honour to David Leslie. The other side, even Oliver himself, tended to forget the part played by the Scots. In his letter to his brother-in-law, Valentine Wauton, he wrote: 'Truly England and the Church of God hath had a great favour from the Lord in this great victory given unto us, such as the like never was since the war began. It had all the evidences of an absolute victory obtained by the Lord's blessing upon the godly party principally. We never charged but we routed the enemy. The left wing which I commanded, being our own horse, saving a few Scots in the rear, beat all the Prince's horse. God made them as stubble to our swords, we charged their regiments of foot with our horse, routed all we charged.'[1] Leslie himself bore generous witness to the prowess of the Ironsides — 'Europe,' he said, 'hath no better soldiers'; but Oliver seems to have been oblivious of the part played by Leslie's three regiments, by Baillie's foot, and by the horse of Leven, Dalhousie and Eglinton.

A letter of consolation, written in the high emotion of victory, is not a reasoned appreciation of a battle; but was Oliver's view not in substance right? Human nature loves to simplify and to find the culminating drama in a single thing — the heroism of one man, the sudden inspiration of a commander, the intervention of a solitary unit. It is an instinct which is less historical than literary, for victories are not won by a *beau geste*. Parliament fought at Marston Moor with the odds heavily in its favour, and it came within an ace of defeat. The royalist chivalry were fully the equal of any Ironsides, and no infantry ever fought more stoutly than the Whitecoats. Neither Rupert nor Goring made any serious blunder, and no part of the royalist front broke so shamelessly as a large section of the parliament's. Oliver would without question have been beaten but for Leslie's flank attack on Byron, and he could never have turned the tide later without Leslie's help and the stand made by Baillie's Scottish foot. Yet the *causa causans* of victory must be found in his inspiration; the sureness with which in the confusion of battle he divined the right tactics, as

[1] *L. and S.*, I, 176.

in his ultimate wheel upon Goring, and in his complete mastery of his own command, as shown by his rallying of his horse after a check and a rout. Two things are certain. But for the victory at Marston Moor parliament would have gone down, its armies would have melted away, Leven and his Scots would have re-crossed Tweed, and Charles in six months would have been back in Whitehall. And but for Oliver there would have been no victory.

Chapter V

THE NEW MODEL

(1644–1645)

> Know, good mother,
> I had rather be their servant in my way
> Than sway with them in theirs.
> *Coriolanus.*

I

SOME weeks before Marston Moor the younger Vane had been sent by the Committee of Both Kingdoms to the generals lying before York. It was a fateful mission, less military than political, for he came to discover their hearts and to plan out the future. To Vane, as to Oliver, it seemed that no terms could be made with Charles, and that consequently the hope for the land lay not in a peace of exhaustion or a stalemate, but in a crushing parliament victory. He got little encouragement from Fairfax, less from Manchester, and none at all from Leven. These men did not desire revolution; they stood on the old ways, and sought to restore the English polity they had known — reformed, indeed, and safeguarded by many checks and balances, but substantially the same. Leven and his Scots especially were to a man confused monarchists. Oliver, who did not share Vane's republicanism, nevertheless shared his belief in a new birth for England, and he found himself becoming estranged from his army commanders, and acquiring a very vigorous dislike for the Scots. He had also the soldier's conviction that campaigns cannot be won by those who fight not for victory but to acquire assets for some ultimate bargain.

There was another cause which put him out of tune with his leaders. Leven represented the stiff presbyterianism which parliament had accepted for England as the price of the Scottish alliance. Manchester, too, was a presbyterian, as were most of the parliamentary notables. The Westminster Assembly of divines was now busy reconstructing the English Church upon the rigid Scots model. There was to be no toleration, no relief for tender consciences; the grace of God was to be canalized into set channels; it was a new clericalism, Laud with a Scots accent. To Oliver, to whom religion meant a personal communion with his Maker, and who had a stubborn racial pride in his bones, the thing seemed intolerable to Christians and Englishmen. Were all the dreams and sufferings of the people of God to end in an intolerant church built on an alien model, and Charles back at Whitehall with clipped wings but an unchanged heart, and a power for mischief the greater since it would work in secret ways and be inspired by a passion of revenge? The events after Marston Moor confirmed his dissatisfaction. No effort was made to follow up the victory. Leven moved slowly northward to besiege Newcastle, Sir Thomas Fairfax busied himself with reducing certain Yorkshire fortresses, and Manchester went back to his old terrain in the eastern shires. Rupert was in Lancashire with 5000 men, and an open door for supports from Ireland, while Clavering had another 3000 in Cumberland and Westmorland, and the former was to be allowed to recruit his strength unpursued, and to get fresh levies from Wales. Nor was there any attempt to use the victorious army of the north to operate with Waller and Essex against the king. It was not the blame of the London Committee, who had a better notion of strategy than the generals and tried in vain to put speed into their laggard souls; but these generals had always some cogent objection, and the Committee was forced to leave them to their own devices.

Manchester was the chief difficulty, and he and his lieutenant-general of horse were rapidly moving to a parting of the ways. Between the two men there was nothing in common. They belonged to the same Cambridge college, for Edward Montague had entered Sidney Sussex just as Oliver Cromwell left it. In the early days of the Long Parliament they had had a quarrel, in which Oliver had spoken his mind, having no love for a house which had supplanted his own in his native shire.[1] At first in their joint military service they had been friendly enough, for Manchester was a gentle soul and had been docile in Oliver's hands. But now he was leaning more on Crawford, his truculent major-general of foot, for he had become gravely alarmed by both Oliver's military and religious views. He wanted peace by negotiation and not by victory; he wanted a presbyterian church settlement, which satisfied his orderly mind; and he was in terror of the fanatics and sectaries who were his best cavalry and who swore by Oliver.

Above all he was no soldier. Like the other two peers he had

[1] See p. 63, *supra*.

been a fugitive at Marston Moor. He was unhappy in the field, and far more at home sitting as a lay member of the Westminster Assembly or reforming the university of Cambridge. Now he was only playing at war. Instead of reducing Newark, the main cause of trouble in the old debatable land of Lincoln, he was occupying unimportant country-houses, and at Welbeck paying stately compliments to the family of the Marquis of Newcastle. He refused to leave the associated counties, which he maintained that his army had been raised to protect. By early September Oliver was out of all patience with this dilatory grandee. 'We have some amongst us,' he wrote to his brother-in-law, 'much slow in action; if we could all intend our own ends less, and our ease too, our business in this army would go on wheels for expedition. But, because some of us are enemies to rapine and other wickednesses, we are said to be factious, to seek to maintain our opinions in religion by force — which we detest and abhor.'[1]

Small wonder that he was impatient, for since Marston Moor things had gone ill with parliament in the south. Waller and Browne, with their armies of mutinous trained bands, were at a hopeless disadvantage as against the royalist foot, which had now reached a higher professional standard than the horse. In despair the idea of a new model began to stir in the former's brain. 'My lords,' he wrote to the Committee, 'I write these particulars to let you know that an army compounded of these men will never go through with your service, and till you have an army merely your own, that you may command, it is in a manner impossible to do anything of importance.' His considered opinion of his present levies was that they were 'only fit for a gallows here and a hell hereafter.' The House of Commons, alarmed by such a report from so sober a quarter, ordered the enlistment of a new auxiliary army for permanent service. But meantime Essex had marched to disaster. On his appearance Prince Maurice had raised the siege of Lyme Regis and fallen back before him into Devonshire. Essex drove the besiegers from Plymouth, and then was unwise enough to march into Cornwall, where he was presently enclosed by the local royalists and the forces of Maurice and the king. His horse escaped, owing to the fact that Goring, who commanded the royal cavalry, was drunk, and he himself slipped off by sea, but at Lostwithiel,

[1] *L. and S.*, I, 181.

on September 2, Skippon and all the foot laid down their
arms. In spite of Marston Moor the whole organization of
the parliament's forces was breaking down. It had to face
the problem which Washington had to face in 1776, and to
get itself new generals and a different kind of army.

The events of the next two months drove the lesson home.
Charles, no longer needed in the west, moved back towards
the Thames valley, his object being to mark time till Rupert
could join him from the north. In spite of Lostwithiel he was
in a weak position. The Cornish levies would not cross the
Tamar; his own army was mutinous and ill equipped; Wilmot
had just been detected in treachery and had been replaced in
command of the horse by the dangerous Goring: Rupert's
spur seemed to be cold and a lethargy had descended upon
his spirit. Charles's purpose was to relieve certain beleaguered
royalist garrisons, Basing house, Donnington, Banbury, and
then, when Rupert joined him, to attack Manchester in the
eastern shires. Parliament, with far greater numbers at its
command, had a superb chance of cutting him off if only it
could unite its forces. But Waller in Wiltshire pled in vain
for support, and had to fall back before the advancing royalists.
Manchester had only begun to move in the second week of
September towards the rendezvous at Abingdon. With Oliver
well in advance, he reached Reading on September 29, and
there abode for a solid fortnight. On October 19 he was at
Basingstoke, and Charles was forced to turn aside from the
relief of Basing house. The parliament armies, Manchester's,
Waller's, and what remained of Essex's, were now united, and
had got in command of them a council of war, appointed by
the London Committee, which included two civilian members,
and of which Manchester was president since Essex had fallen
sick. The king was on his way to relieve Donnington castle
near Newbury; now was the chance to fall upon him while he
had only ten thousand men to their nineteen thousand. The
council of war decided upon battle.

The Second Battle of Newbury is important on two grounds.
It was the first action in which the parliament made any attempt at tactical manœuvres, and a plan which was bold and
ingenious was brought to nothing by the chaos in the central
command. A mile below the town of Newbury the Lambourne
enters the Kennet from the north. On October 25 the parliament army reached the north bank of the Kennet east of the

town, and next day reconnoitred the king's position. It was a very strong one, which he believed to be impregnable. Roughly he lay across the angle made by the two streams, his right resting on the town, and his left on the Lambourne. Near this latter point the Oxford road crossed the stream, and a fortified manor called Shaw house was a strong point to protect the crossing. North of this line the land rose towards the Berkshire downs, and behind the centre, in open ground, lay the royal cavalry. At its back, on high ground a mile away, and covering it with its guns, stood Donnington castle. To the south-west on the slopes of Speen hill lay Prince Maurice, a covering force echeloned on the main army's right rear.

Clearly the royalists' line could not be assaulted in front, and a flank attack offered no better hopes owing to the difficulties of the ground. Accordingly it was decided by the parliament generals to detail a force to make a wide encircling movement and attack Prince Maurice's rear at Speen, while Manchester at the same moment drove in the royalist left centre at Shaw. On the night of the 26th the force of manœuvre, Skippon's foot from Essex's old army, part of Waller's command, and part of Manchester's horse under Oliver and of Essex's under Balfour, bivouacked in the hills four miles north of Newbury, and by dawn was moving to its battle position at Speen, while Manchester made a feint attack to divert the royalists' attention. But the king was perfectly aware of what was happening, and sent word to Maurice to face westwards at Speen and throw up entrenchments. Skippon and Waller delivered their assault about three o'clock in the afternoon, the foot in the centre, Balfour on the right wing, and Oliver on the left. It was bad ground for cavalry, being much broken up by hedges, and the few lanes were commanded by the enemy's artillery. But by four o'clock the foot had carried Maurice's field entrenchments and taken his guns, and had driven him out of Speen village.

Now was the time for Manchester's supporting attack. But Manchester sat still, while the royalists stripped their front to send help to Maurice. Skippon and Waller nearly succeeded. Their foot were at the last hedge of the stubbornly defended enclosures, Oliver was almost out on the open ground which would have allowed him to hurl his Ironsides at the royal cavalry. But Manchester's supineness saved the king.

He did indeed attack, but too late; the sun had set, and, though there was a moon in its first quarter, clouds came up and the light was too dim to continue the struggle. The battle died away, and in the night the king moved off unmolested towards Oxford.

There followed an aimless and half-hearted pursuit, a meeting of the king and Rupert (who was now made commander-in-chief in Brentford's place), the investment of Donnington by Manchester, and the return of Charles on November 9 to relieve it. Manchester had failed to fight with vigour on October 28, he had refused to pursue with vigour, and on November 9 he declined to fight at all. As for Oliver he had not repeated his exploits of Gainsborough and Winceby and Marston Moor. Anxiety and depression seem to have taken the edge off his spirit. He had done no more than creditably among the hedges at Newbury; he had been partly to blame for the king's easy retreat: he had pressed the need of immediate pursuit with all arms, but had refused to let his horse be distressed by aimless guerilla fighting.[1] He had been for giving battle to Charles on his return to Donnington, but had been rebuked in memorable words. 'If we beat the king ninety and nine times,' Manchester had said, 'yet he is king still, and so will his posterity be after him; but if the king beats us then we shall all be hanged, and our posterity made slaves.' 'If this be so, my lord,' he had replied, 'why did we take up arms at first? This is against fighting ever hereafter. If so, let us make peace, be it never so base.' [2] He knew now the inmost soul of the moderates and the glimpse terrified him. What mattered successes in the north, like the surrender of Newcastle and Liverpool, when their cause was rotten at the core? He saw his task clear; he must expel the half-hearted from the high command as he had expelled them from the ranks, and an army must be constructed after the pattern of his own regiment. What in another would have been a crazy presumption of arrogance was in this man a sober and rather mournful following of duty.

II

In September Manchester had gone to London, and Oliver had followed to discover the mind of parliament. He found

[1] Rushworth, VI, 734.
[2] *Manchester's Quarrel with Cromwell*, 63; Gardiner, *Civil War*, II, 59.

little to comfort him. The majority were presbyterians, not after the Scottish fashion from a passionate belief in presbytery as a thing ordained by God, but simply from a desire to have church as well as king under control of the House. He had failed in his endeavour to have Crawford removed, and the most that he could do was, with the help of St. John and Vane, to get a resolution passed in the interest of his independents, urging an agreement which would provide for a moderate toleration of dissent — 'to endeavour the finding out some way how far tender consciences, who cannot in all things submit to the common rule which shall be established, may be borne with according to the Word, and as may stand with the public peace.' His primary object was military, to prevent that inquisition, desired by Crawford and the Scots, which would deplete his army of its best soldiers. Mr. Robert Baillie could only implore the prayers of his friends, for he saw whither the wind was blowing. 'This is a very fickle people; so wonderfully divided in all their armies, both their Houses of Parliament, Assembly, City and country, that it's a miracle if they fall not into the mouth of the King.' [1]

Then Manchester had proceeded on his leisurely western progress, tarrying for broken bridges and prayer — 'this also being a Fast day I thought it my duty to seek God.' [2] After Second Newbury the crisis could not be shirked. Two matters agitated men's minds. There was the question of the toleration of opinion, a question on which depended the use or disuse of the most vigorous elements in the parliament forces. To Cromwell its military aspect was the chief consideration; Milton, who on November 24th published his *Areopagitica*, argued it on broader grounds. 'Under these fantastic terrors of sect and schism, we wrong the earnest and zealous thirst after knowledge, and understanding which God hath stirred up in this city. What some lament of we should rather rejoice at, should rather praise this pious forwardness among men to reassume the ill-deputed care of their religion into their own hands again. A little generous prudence, a little forbearance of one another, and some grain of charity might win all these diligences to join and unite in one general and brotherly search after truth, could we but forego this prelatical tradition of crowding free consciences and Christian liberties into canons and precepts of men.' And there was the narrower but most

[1] Baillie. II, 230.   [2] *Manchester's Quarrel*, lxiii.

urgent question of the competence of the parliament generals and the quality of their armies.

In November the House of Commons debated the latter point, and on the 25th Cromwell stated his case. He did not mince matters, but set forth mercilessly all Manchester's blunders, delays and hesitations, from the fall of York to the relief of Donnington. These mistakes were due not to accident or to mere improvidence but to 'his backwardness to all action,' and this backwardness sprang less from dulness and lethargy than from an unwillingness to prosecute the war 'to a full victory.' In arraigning Manchester he arraigned the growing peace party, now strong in parliament, the city of London, and the nation, and especially he arraigned the Scots. Manchester replied on the 28th in the House of Lords, not with a defence only but with countercharges against Oliver of factiousness and inertia. More, he attacked him as a political firebrand. Oliver had sneered at the Westminster Assembly; he had declared that he would draw his sword as willingly against the Scots as against the king; he had spoken ill words about the nobility, said he wished there was never a lord in the land, and that it would not be well till Manchester was plain Mr. Montague. The dispute was referred to a committee under the presidency of Zouch Tate, a strong presbyterian, evidence was taken, and a strife began of memorials and counterpleas. The issue was fairly joined — the party that favoured a vigorous prosecution of the war and some freedom in religion against the nobles like Manchester and Essex, the extreme presbyterians in the House like Holles, and the Scottish commissioners. The last named had the happy idea of prosecuting Oliver as an incendiary, but at a secret meeting at Essex house in the first days of December the English lawyers, Maynard and Whitelocke, convinced them that high-flying Scottish views of treason were not agreeable to the spirit of English law.

It was clear that so far as Manchester was concerned Oliver had won his case, in spite of the strength of the presbyterians in the House. But against Manchester himself he had forgotten his grievances. It was not the man that mattered but the system, and the disappearance of one ineffectual leader would be nothing if the system remained. For Manchester's view there was much to be said, but the man who held it should never have taken up arms. He did not believe that the quarrel could be finally settled by the sword, and therein he was right:

no more did Oliver hold that view, but he argued that, since the arbitrament of war had been chosen, it was necessary to fight out the first stage on that basis. The alternative would be no settlement at all, but the acceptance by a vanquished parliament of terms dictated by the king. He realized, if others did not, the desperate plight of the country, and that the only cure for it was a speedy end to the war; that end must come by victory, parliament's or the king's, and he was determined that it should be the former's. Therefore he loathed all the sleepy things that stood in the way of such a victory — grandees (he had already dealt trenchantly with the Greys and Willoughbys who had cumbered him), trimming lawyers, garrulous members of parliament, pedantic Scots lords and divines. Let the army be pruned of this dead wood, and there was hope for England.

On December 9 Tate presented the report of his committee. Then Oliver rose and made one of the most effective speeches of his life. He abandoned his charge against Manchester and left the personal question for greater things.

It is now the time to speak, or forever hold the tongue. The important occasion now is no less than to save a nation out of a bleeding, nay almost dying, condition, which the long continuance of the War hath already brought it into, so that without a more speedy, vigorous, and effectual prosecution of the war — casting off all lingering proceedings, like those of soldiers of fortune beyond sea, to spin out a war — we shall make the kingdom weary of us, and hate the name of Parliament.

For what do the enemy say? Nay, what do many say that were friends at the beginning of the Parliament? Even this — that the Members of both Houses have got great places and commands, and the sword into their hands; and, what by interest in the Parliament, what by power in the Army, will perpetually continue themselves in grandeur, and not permit the War speedily to end, lest their own power should determine with it. This that I speak here to our own faces is but what others do utter abroad behind our backs. I am far from reflecting on any. I know the worth of those commanders, members of both Houses, who are yet in power. But, if I may speak my conscience without reflection upon any, I do conceive if the Army be not put into another method, and the War more vigorously prosecuted, the people can bear the War no longer and will enforce you to a dishonourable peace.

But this I would recommend to your prudence — not to insist upon any complaint or oversight of any Commander-in-Chief upon any occasion whatsoever; for as I must acknowledge myself guilty of oversight, so I know they can rarely be avoided in military matters. Therefore, waiving a strict inquiry into the causes of these things, let us apply ourselves to the remedy, which is most necessary. And I hope we have such true English hearts and zealous affection towards the general weal of our Mother Country as no member of either House will scruple to deny themselves, and their own private interests, for the public good, nor account it to be a dishonour done to them, whatever the Parliament shall resolve upon in this weighty matter.[1]

No speech of Oliver is more full of the man — his realism, his directness, his sense of proportion, the tactical instinct which made him formidable in battle. It had its effect. Tate moved and carried a motion that during the war no member of either House should hold military or civil command. Oliver's enemies voted for it, since, if it disqualified Manchester and Essex, it rid them also of the 'darling of the sectaries.' Two days later the Self-denying Ordinance was passed and sent up to the Lords, and the Commons turned to the duty which on November 23 they had intrusted to the Committee of Both Kingdoms, 'to consider of a frame or model of the whole militia.'

What during this critical time lay at the back of Oliver's mind? He must have faced the possibility that his war service was finished, and that the torch he had lit might be passed to other hands — to Fairfax and Skippon and Balfour, and to the new colonels of horse whom he had trained. It was the only way to get rid of useless litter, and with his uncompromising honesty in the face of facts he took that way. But it is difficult not to believe that he felt that somehow his chance would come again. He was aware that in two years he had made the greatest military reputation in the kingdom and he was conscious of his own genius for war. If a new model army was to be created he may well have hoped that sooner or later the practical good sense of his people would insist on revising the Self-denying Ordinance, once it had served its purpose, and set him again in high command.[2]

III

The early months of 1645 saw little activity in the field, but much at Westminster. The king had begun operations in the

[1] Rushworth, VI, 4. *L. and S.*, I, 186–87.

[2] The documents relating to this crisis are published in *The Quarrel of Manchester and Cromwell* (Camden Soc.), 1875. See also *Camden Miscellany*, No. 8, and, for the Scots view, Baillie, II.

west, where Goring was again besieging Lyme and Plymouth and Taunton. Waller was sent in relief, and Oliver was ordered to join him with his regiment, for the simple reason that the regiment would not go without him. In those weeks, which promised to be the last of his military service, Oliver proved himself a loyal subordinate, for his superior was eager and assiduous if uninspired, and Oliver had no love for indiscipline except in the last extremity. Waller was amazed at the docility of this reputed firebrand. 'At this time,' he wrote afterwards, 'he had never shown extraordinary parts, nor do I think he did himself believe that he had them; for although he was blunt he did not bear himself with pride or disdain. As an officer he was obedient, and did never dispute my orders nor argue upon them.'

The new year brought another vain attempt at peacemaking, preceded by the execution of Laud. The trial of the archbishop had been long dragging on, and, since there was as little hope of a verdict on the impeachment as in the case of Strafford, the same procedure was followed, and a bill of attainder was passed. On January 10, the old man laid down his head on the scaffold, with the prayer, 'I beseech Thee give grace of repentance to all bloodthirsty people, but if they will not repent, O Lord, confound their devices.' Essex had gallantly protested in the Lords against this deed — 'Is this the liberty which we promised to maintain with our blood?' — and Laud's execution, which had no warrant on any view of the public interest but was a mere blind act of revenge, served to make a broader and deeper chasm of the breach in the English polity. It certainly steeled Charles's resolution. 'Nothing can be more evident,' he told the queen, 'than that Strafford's innocent blood hath been one of the great causes of God's just judgements upon this nation by a furious civil war, both sides hitherto being almost equally guilty; but now, this last crying blood being almost totally theirs, I believe it is no presumption hereafter to hope that the hand of justice must be heavier upon them and lighter upon us.' The answer which he had given to the parliament envoys in November was now his fixed creed. 'There are three things I will not part with — the Church, my crown and my friends.'

The negotiations which began at Uxbridge in January were therefore doomed from the start. They were an attempt of the Scottish commissioners to try their hand at making peace. Three propositions were put forward: the king must take the Covenant and accept parliamentary presbytery in England;

he must hand over the militia and the navy; he must give parliament a free hand in Ireland. Charles, having been much pressed at Oxford by the peace party among the royalists, made counter-propositions, which on the ecclesiastical side went far in the direction of toleration. They did not satisfy the presbyterians, and Oliver and his independents very wisely kept clear of the dispute. They believed that the war must be fought to a finish, and that presbyterian intransigence was a certain bar to any premature peace. On February 22 the futile business came to its expected end.

Meantime the making of the New Model army went on. It must be an army for general service, free from local obligations, and therefore it must be paid not from local but from national funds. These were the cardinal points in its structure. The pay must be regular, the supplies ample, and the dress uniform — wherefore the scarlet coat became the rule in England. Conscription was necessary to fill up the ranks, for the new army which mustered on the Windsor meads was fixed at eleven regiments of horse, each 600 strong, twelve regiments of foot, each 1200 strong, a thousand dragoons, and an artillery train. Essex's forces formed the staple, but 600 infantry came from Waller, and the main part of Manchester's army was incorporated. Oliver's own regiment became two, one commanded by his cousin Edward Whalley, and one, under Sir Thomas Fairfax, which ranked first in the cavalry. Officers were required to take the Covenant — an elastic test which only John Lilburne boggled at. They were for the most part of good birth, though there was no social scrutiny. Pride the drayman, Hewson the cobbler, and Okey the ship-chandler have been given undue prominence,[1] since out of thirty-seven senior officers twenty-one were sprung of gentle, and nine of noble, houses. There was little puritanism in the infantry rank-and-file, but the cavalry troopers were largely independents and enthusiasts, and so were the great majority of the officers of all arms.

On February 13 the New Model ordinance was passed into law. A month before Sir Thomas Fairfax had been given the supreme command as captain-general, and Phillip Skippon was major-general in charge of the foot; the post of lieutenant-general in command of the horse was significantly left vacant. Fairfax was now a man of thirty-three, a 'Black Tom,' but not in Strafford's fashion, tall, silent because he stammered badly,

---

[1] 'Most of the colonels were tradesmen, brewers, tailors, goldsmiths, shoemakers and the like.' Holles, *Memoirs*, 149.

with a dark face seamed by old wounds. He was devout, but whether he was presbyterian or independent was a secret between him and his Maker. His men loved him for his gallantry and simplicity, and his enemies never accused him of broken faith. He was a good cavalry soldier, and he was like a flame in battle, but his talent was rather for personal leadership than for any high strategic or tactical flights. The age produced few more sterling and attractive characters, and beyond doubt he was the best man for the post, since he harmonized opposites and roused no antagonisms. Skippon, who had been Essex's infantry commander, was an experienced soldier, and provided the technical knowledge which Fairfax lacked.

The first Self-denying Ordinance, which barred military office to any member of parliament, had been rejected by the Lords, but the second, which enforced resignation within forty days but did not disqualify for future employment, became law on April 3. Under it the chief figures in the parliament's campaign of the past two years laid down their commands — Essex and Manchester, Denbigh and Waller. None were great men, but in this history we shall meet no more honest and dutiful souls. To look on their lineaments on the canvases of Van Dyck and Lely is to see at a glance their virtues and their imperfections. Essex with his bold, stupid Devereux face, Manchester large-featured and vacant, Waller with his heavy cheeks and double chin — they are all of a familiar English type, loyal, kindly, serious, not greatly used to the travail of thought. They have a puzzled air, as if destiny had cast them for parts which they did not comprehend. Set against them the portrait at Hinchingbrooke of Oliver painted early in the Civil War, and mark the difference. The eyes are troubled, but it is with deep reflection. The jaw, the great nose, the full brow are moulded on iron lines. It is the face of a man who knows with utter conviction his immediate purpose. Oliver had learned in these years more than the art of war. He had taught himself to curb his impetuous temper and school his spirit to an infinite patience. Just as in battle he knew where to stop, so he knew in other matters when to speak and when to be silent, when to press forward and when to withdraw. He will accept a little here and renounce a little there provided that it is all contributory to that general aim which is never out of his mind. He does not attempt to penetrate the misty horizon, but he has always his foreground acidly clear. The soldier is acquiring his first instruction in statecraft.

Chapter VI

NASEBY AND AFTER
(1645–1646)

They said this mystery never shall cease:
The priest promotes war, and the soldier peace.
WILLIAM BLAKE.

Γνοῖεν δ'ὡς δὴ δηρὸν ἐγὼ πολέμοιο πέπαυμαι.
Iliad, xviii, 125.

I

THE position of affairs in April 1645, while his opponents' new army was in the making, offered Charles his last chance. He had terribly lost caste with the country. Most of the high-minded gentlemen like Falkland and Northampton and Carnarvon, who had been with him at the start, had now fallen in the field. Rupert had no longer his master's full confidence. The royal cause in the eyes of most men was represented by debauched ruffians like Goring and Sir Richard Grenville, and wandering troops of horse who plundered indiscriminately friend and foe. As the parliament forces improved the others degenerated. 'Those under the king's command,' Clarendon wrote bitterly, 'grew insensibly into all the license, disorder and impiety with which they had reproached the rebels; and they, again, into great discipline, diligence and sobriety; which begot courage and resolution in them, and notable dexterity in achievement and enterprise. Insomuch as one side seemed to fight for morality with the weapons of confusion, and the other to destroy the king and government with all the principles and regularity of monarchy.' The famous royalist cavalry were now definitely inferior to the best parliament horse. On the other hand the royalist foot had attained a high degree of professional skill and were on the whole the finest infantry in the land. Unfortunately too many of them were absorbed in an aimless garrisoning of fortresses.

Yet in spite of all disadvantages the king had still a chance of victory, the last that the fates could offer him. The north, except for a few scattered castles, had gone; but he still had the west, though parliament had the harbours of Plymouth and Pembroke and the inland key-points of Taunton and Gloucester.

He had two armies: that under Rupert, based upon Oxford, about 11,000 strong, and that of the west, under Goring and Hopton, numbering some 10,000; he had also Sir Charles Gerard's considerable Welsh levies. In total numbers he was much inferior to parliament, but the parliament strength was divided, with Leven and his Scots far away on the northern border. Moreover its main army was in process of re-forming, and therefore in a perilous posture. Fortune had given him again the initiative. He might strike at Fairfax before he was ready, or he might push northwards and deal with Leven's depleted command.

For a new factor had entered into the contest which, properly used, might have given Charles the victory. Montrose, as we have seen, had after Marston Moor crossed the Esk almost alone, with the desperate purpose of winning back Scotland for the king. He had prospered miraculously and seemed to be on the brink of complete success. The previous autumn he had routed the Covenant levies of second-line troops at Tippermuir and Aberdeen, and on the second day of February at Inverlochy he had dealt the clan power of Argyll a blow from which it never recovered. Leven had been forced to send north Baillie and some of his best foot regiments, and was now resolutely planted in the neighbourhood of Carlisle, keeping an anxious eye on events across the Border. The king had for a time the notion of joining Montrose, a romantic but impossible enterprise; Rupert, with better judgment, aimed at destroying Leven. Had Charles had the wit to read the situation and the resolution to act upon his conclusion — had he hanged Goring and left the army of the west to Hopton, and marched northward with horse and foot and artillery against the dispirited and half-hearted Scots — history might have taken a very different course. For Montrose was still to win great victories, and, with Scotland under his heel, he could have brought the superb fighting stuff of his Highlanders to the royal side. Such an army, sweeping down from the north, would have fought somewhere in the midlands a very different Naseby.

The New Model was naturally slow to form and at first it was unhandy. Intended for a mobile field army, it did not include anything like all the man-power at parliament's disposal. Besides many garrisons, there were Poyntz's detachment in the north, Browne's in the midlands, Brereton's in Cheshire, and Massey's in the Severn valley. But, apart from this dissipation of strength, there was a serious flaw in the high command. The Committee of Both Kingdoms still directed the strategy, and Fairfax docilely obeyed. Parliament had got itself a noble weapon, but at the start it seemed unable to use it.

Charles did not seize the chance thus offered him. Rupert, who had gone north early in the year to clear the road, had been compelled to deal with a rising of peasants, the Clubmen, in Herefordshire and Worcestershire, which threatened to block his communications with Oxford. Before he could start on his main movement he had to get infantry and an artillery train from Oxford, especially the latter. Parliament, in dread of what Rupert might do before Fairfax was ready, sent against him the only man it possessed who was swift in a crisis. The forty days allowed by the Self-denying Ordinance had not elapsed, and Oliver was still a serving soldier.

His Oxford raid was a brilliant little episode. On April 23 he was at Watlington with 1500 troopers. Next day he routed the royal horse at Islip on the Cherwell, and took Bletchingdon house. Then he swept south-west to Witney and Bampton, till he was halted by the stubborn defence of Faringdon house, whereupon he joined Fairfax at Newbury. He had done his work, for he had carried off all the draught horses in the neighbourhood, so that none were left for the king's artillery train. Charles had to postpone his junction with Rupert till Goring could bring up his troops from the west. The raid was a perfect instance of the strategic use of cavalry, and it had profound consequences for the general campaign.

But the Committee, blind to greater interests, directed Fairfax to march to the relief of Taunton, while Oliver was left to keep in touch with the king. This meant that Oxford could not be watched on every side, and the king slipped out by the northern road. So the Committee recalled Fairfax, after he had sent on a brigade to relieve Taunton, and, on some rumour of treachery within the city, set him to the idle task of besieging Oxford without heavy guns or intrenching tools, while Charles and Rupert were moving towards Cheshire. There was as much indecision in the king's councils. Some would have him turn against Fairfax, others, like Rupert and Sir Marmaduke Langdale, urged the northern march. A foolish compromise was the result. Goring was sent off to Taunton, and the now depleted army tarried to make up its mind. Oxford, with Fairfax at its gates, seemed to be in danger, and Charles did not dare to leave it unguarded. So as a diversion he resolved to attack Leicester, and on May 31 carried and sacked that city.

This event brought the Committee of Both Kingdoms to their senses. The assault on Leicester menaced the eastern association, the holy land of their cause and their best recruiting ground. Oliver, who on May 10th had had his command prolonged for another forty days, was on May 28 despatched to see to the defence of Ely. Moreover word had come of a battle in Scotland, Auldearn, where Montrose had most terribly smitten the Covenant. Fairfax was directed to relinquish the siege of Oxford and use his own discretion, and on June 5 he broke up his quarters and moved towards the king. Meantime Charles hung aimlessly in the Leicester neighbourhood, and was at Daventry on June 7th, anxious about what might be happening at Oxford. He seemed to be oblivious of his danger, and could spare time for a hunt in Fawsley park, the place where Pym had once hatched his plots. He had still a vague idea of marching to Scotland by the vale of York, but he was half-inclined to Digby's plan of concentrating on Fairfax. Also he must arrange for the revictualling of Oxford, and he had summoned Goring from the south-west and Gerard from Wales to join him. He believed that owing to the distractions of parliament he had plenty of time. 'If we peripateticks,' he wrote to Nicholas, 'get no more mischances than you Oxonians are like to have this summer, we may all expect a merry winter.'

He was in a confident mood, as always before disaster. For the New Model he had nothing but scorn. His staff called it the 'New Noddle,' Fairfax was the 'rebels' new brutish general' and this contemptuous view was shared by others than royalists. Robert Baillie reported to Scotland that the parliament army 'consists for the most part of raw, inexperienced, pressed soldiers. Few of the officers are thought capable of their places; many of them are sectaries, or their confident friends; if they do great service many will be deceived.' [1] Richard Baxter, who had better means of judging, was not more favourable. 'The greatest part of the common soldiers, especially of the foot, were ignorant men of little religion, abundance of them such as had been taken prisoner, or turned out of garrisons under the king, and had been soldiers in his army; and these would do anything to please their officers.' [2]

The stage was set for a great battle, and the two armies were

[1] Baillie, II, 264-65.   [2] Rel. Baxt., 53.

moving blindly to a meeting. Since the country people were
hostile in that region, the lack of intelligence was worse on the
king's side. On June 8 Fairfax learned that Charles was at
Daventry and ordered Skippon to prepare a plan of battle. On
that day his council of war petitioned parliament that Oliver
might be appointed to the vacant lieutenant-generalship, since
without him there was no officer to command the horse. 'The
general esteem and affection which he hath both with the officers and soldiers of the whole army, his own personal worth
and ability for the employment, his great care, diligence and
courage, and faithfulness in the service you have already employed him in, with the constant presence and blessing of God
that has accompanied him, make us look upon it as a duty we
owe to you and the public to make our suit.' The Commons,
but not the Lords, assented, and a message was sent to Oliver
at Ely. It was by no means certain that he would arrive in time
for the coming battle, though, as soon as he got the word, he galloped westward with 600 men.

On June 12th Fairfax was at Kislingbury, within eight miles
of the royal army at Daventry. That night the king was at last
aware of the enemy's presence, and on the morning of the 13th
he fired his huts and marched northwards to Market Harborough. Fairfax followed, and, as he struck his camp, a
mighty shout among his soldiers welcomed the arrival of a
body of horsemen from the east. 'Ironsides is come' was the
word that ran down the ranks. Charles's intention was to
march to Belvoir and thence to Newark, but he found that the
parliament van was too close upon his heels. Battle could not
be avoided, but, since his force was heavily outnumbered, he
must find a strong defensive position and await attack. Early
on the morning of the 14th the royal army took up ground on
a long hill two miles south of Market Harborough, in the
midst of open country suitable for cavalry. About eight
o'clock Rupert sent out a scouting party, which reported that
no enemy was to be seen. But Fairfax, who had marched from
Guilsborough at three o'clock that morning, and was now on
the high ground east of Naseby, observed the enemy on a
distant ridge, and deployed his troops from column of route
into order of battle.

The royal army was slightly to his left, so on Oliver's advice
the front was moved further west, since the wind was from that
direction, and it was important not to give the enemy the ad-

vantage of the wind, which would blow the dust raised by them in the faces of the parliament men. The new position was on the edge of a low plateau about a mile and a half north of the village of Naseby, with below it a flat hollow called Broadmoor. Again on Oliver's advice, the line was drawn back slightly from the crest, so as to prevent the enemy from seeing their dispositions and numbers.

It was now about nine o'clock. There had been much rain during the preceding days, but the morning was fine, with a light wind from the north-west which died away as the day advanced. The place was the central boss of the midlands, a country of rolling downs and shallow dales, the water-parting from which streams flowed to both the Atlantic and the North Sea. From springs a few feet distant in Naseby village the Avon ran to the Severn and the Nen to the Wash. The Welland had its rise in the hollow behind the king's position. It was fitting that the battle which was to decide the fate of England should be fought in the very heart of the English land. That it would be a fateful action was understood by both antagonists. Three weeks before Digby had written: 'Ere one month be over, we shall have a battle of all for all,' and he had been hopeful of the issue. Oliver on the other side had no doubts. 'When I saw the enemy draw up and march in gallant order towards us, and we a company of poor ignorant men... I could not, riding alone about my business, but smile out to God in praise, in assurance of victory, because God would, by things that are not, bring to naught things that are. Of which I had great assurance, and God did it.' [1]

II

Rupert, dissatisfied with his scoutmaster's report, rode out himself with a body of horse, and from the high ground above the village of Clipstone he saw the parliament army moving into order of battle. He seems to have misconstrued this as a retreat, for he sent back word at once for the rest of the royalist force to advance with all speed. About ten o'clock it had arrived on the ridge called Dust Hill, looking over the marshy field of Broadmoor to the enemy front drawn up along and behind the crest of Red Pit Hill, which constituted the northern part of the Mill Hill uplands north of Naseby. The king had a

[1] *L. and S.*, III, 247.

total force of some 7500 men, of which 4000 were horse. The foot in the centre was under Sir Jacob (now Lord) Astley, Clarendon's 'honest, brave, and plain man,' full sixty-six years old. He had his regiments formed in solid *tertias*, the old Spanish formation which Tilly had used at Leipsic, pikemen in the centre and musketeers on the wings. On the left flank were the cavalry under Sir Marmaduke Langdale, 'a grave and very thin Yorkshireman, with a long solemn face, brave as a lion and both judicious and enterprising, but with an unfortunate temper.' [1] He had with him his own indifferent Yorkshire horse, and the cavalry from Newark. On the right flank was Rupert, with his own and Prince Maurice's horse, a total of something under 2000. The front was in two lines, but behind the centre was a considerable reserve with the king, both foot and horse, including the royal life guards and Rupert's famous foot regiment of Bluecoats. Apart from the Yorkshire horse the royal army was a veteran one, and especially rich in experienced officers.[2]

The parliament forces on their mile of front numbered the better part of 14,000 men, of whom 7000 were infantry and 6500 horse and dragoons. The infantry in the centre under Skippon had five regiments in first line, and in the second line the three veteran regiments of Rainsborough, Hammond and Pride. The cavalry on the right flank under Oliver were in three lines owing to the constricted ground, but the rest of the battle-front was in two. Henry Ireton as the new commissary-general commanded the horse on the left, and on his left Okey had a thousand dragoons. The parliament position was very strong, for Ireton's flank was protected by a marshy rivulet fringed by what was called the Sulby Hedges, a parish boundary, and a fine station for dragoons. All the rest of the field was open moor or cornland, but on the right there were clumps of gorse and a rabbit-warren, which would cramp a cavalry charge. Here, as at Gainsborough and Marston Moor, the coney played an important part in the war. Many of the horse and no small part of the foot were raw levies, and there was a deficiency of trained officers. Fairfax had shown himself vigorous in movement and a swift marcher, but he was still untried in high command in a field battle. In action he was apt to become transported with excitement and to lose his head.

Rupert, still apparently believing that the enemy was meditating retreat, gave the order to the right wing to charge. The

[1] Markham, *Great Lord Fairfax*, 215.   [2] Sprigge, 325.

hour was about half-past ten. The royal army moved forward, every man with a beanstalk in his hat, crying the watchword of 'Queen Mary,' to be received by a salvo of Fairfax's guns, and the parliament shout of 'God our strength.' As Rupert advanced the whole enemy army appeared over the brow of the hill, and he seems for a moment to have halted his charge. So did Ireton, but Rupert was the first to recover, and, galloping up the hill, he crashed through both the front and the reserve lines of the enemy. Ireton was wounded and made prisoner. Rupert swept on to the baggage lines in Naseby village, had a short tussle with their defenders, and then, remembering Edgehill and Marston Moor, checked the pursuit and returned to the battlefield.

He found things in evil case. Oliver with his 3600 horse had let the royalist left advance well up the slope, and then at the proper moment had launched Whalley's regiment against them, while the rest of his first line made their way down through the rabbit-warren. Whalley, attacking with pistol and the sword, checked Langdale, and the others completed his rout. Then, with that profound tactical good sense of his, realizing that Langdale was no more a danger, Oliver turned against the exposed flank of the royal infantry. For one moment his decision looked like a blunder. Charles, seeing what had happened, led forward the royal horse guards to restore the battle on his left. A fierce charge might have rallied Langdale and routed Oliver's first line, which had been left to watch events. But at the critical instant Lord Carnwath, of the strange and uncertain house of Dalziel, seized the king's bridle, and cried 'Will you go upon your death?' Someone gave the order for a right wheel, and, before Charles could prevent it, the whole reserve had galloped off, and did not halt for a quarter of a mile.

Meanwhile Oliver with his second line had turned against the flank of the infantry battle, while Okey on the other wing had mounted his dragoons for the same purpose. The royal foot of the first line, mostly Welsh levies, though heavily outnumbered had broken the first line of the parliament. Skippon was badly wounded and out of action. Now they were hotly engaged with the reserve regiments of Pride, Hammond and Rainsborough, and Fairfax, who had lost his helmet, was directing the battle. Against them came the deadly flank attack of Oliver, and the heroic infantry could no longer sustain the hopeless odds. Ru-

pert's Bluecoats, the reserves which had been drawn into the
fight, were the last to break. Like Newcastle's Whitecoats at
Marston Moor they died where they stood, and with them
perished the royal infantry of England.

Rupert returned from his chase to find a lost battle. He
joined the king, and with his horse formed a new line of battle
north of Dust Hill. But Fairfax had reformed his foot, and was
advancing with his terrible cavalry wings. Rupert urged a
charge, but he got no response. Oliver's troopers were setting
spurs to their horses, and the royalist remnant broke and fled.
The king himself reached Ashby-de-la-Zouch, twenty-eight
miles off, and others found sanctuary within the walls of Leicester. Five thousand prisoners fell to parliament, of whom 500
were officers, besides the whole royal artillery train, and, what
was more serious, Charles's private correspondence. The parliament army, after its thanksgiving prayer and its psalm of
victory, employed the summer afternoon in murdering the
wretched Irish women who had followed the king, and slashing
the faces of the English female camp-followers, wanton and
reputable alike. It had won a notable triumph but no special
glory, for two to one is heavy odds. The honours of the fight
were with the dead Bluecoats.[1]

III

Naseby was tactically a decisive victory, since it put an end
to Charles's main field force. But it did not end the war, for
there was no nerve-centre in England, pressure upon which
would dominate the whole body politic. The nation was apathetic, perplexed and disintegrated. Charles had still his
cavalry intact, he believed that large Welsh levies would still
appear at his call, he had Goring's army in the south-west, and
he was busy negotiating for troops from Ireland and the Continent. There was a proposal, too, to evacuate the inland fortresses, the garrisons of which would have provided a new

[1] I have taken the numbers at Naseby from Colonel W. G. Ross (*E. H. R.*, 1888, 668,
etc.) whose views are accepted by Gardiner (*Civil War*, II, 379–92). There are contemporary accounts of the battle by Fairfax, Cromwell, Sir Henry Slingsby, Vicars,
Okey, Wogan (in Carte's *Ormonde Papers*, I, 126), and by various pamphleteers, but
the best narrative is Sprigge's in *Anglia Rediviva*. Sprigge gives the battle-plan of both
armies, and there is one of the Royalists reproduced in Warburton's *Rupert*. There is
some uncertainty about the preliminary manœuvring, but none about the main features
of the action.

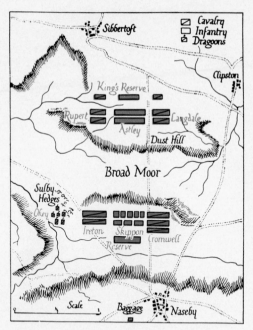

Position at 10.30 A.M.

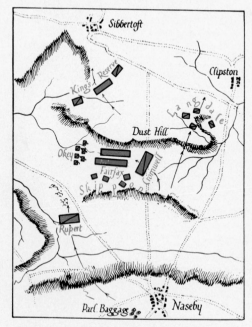

Position about Noon

BATTLE OF NASEBY

field army.[1] But the heart had gone out of his campaigning. He did not evacuate the garrisons or join Goring, but clung feebly to the Welsh border. As for parliament, the revelations in Charles's letters captured at Naseby had driven from the minds of the most moderate any hope of a negotiated peace. A king who was shown as ready to buy foreign aid at any price and as the impenitent foe of the Houses at Westminster could not be treated with, but only routed. Oliver's policy had now triumphed, and Naseby had given him a new authority. On June 16th his lieutenant-generalship was extended for three months, and it was clear that it would be permanent. He was strong enough now to press his political views. In his report to parliament after Naseby he pointed the moral. 'Honest men served you faithfully in this action. Sir, they are trusty; I beseech you in the name of God not to discourage them. I wish this action may beget thankfulness and humility in all that are concerned in it. He that ventures his life for the liberty of his country, I wish he trust God for the liberty of his conscience, and you for the liberty he fights for.' [2]

The campaign of the autumn and winter was for Fairfax a business of 'mopping up.' David Leslie had been left to take Carlisle, and Leven, with part of his unpaid and malcontent Scottish army, was now in the midlands. Fairfax could either move west and face the king in the Severn valley, or join Massey in Dorset to deal with Goring. He wisely chose the latter course, for the Clubmen were becoming dangerous in the southern shires. When Goring heard of his coming, he raised the siege of Taunton and occupied the line of the rivers Yeo and Parret. Fairfax outmanœuvred him, crossed the Yeo, and on the morning of July 10 came up with his main force, drawn up to cover the road to Bridgewater on a hill a mile from Langport, protected in front by enclosures and a marshy valley. He had perhaps 15,000 men to the enemy's 10,000. Goring, having sent off most of his guns to Bridgewater could not reply to Fairfax's bombardment, under cover of which the parliament men crossed the valley and cleared the enclosures. Then Oliver's horse, under Bethell and Disbrowe, charged the royalist cavalry, and broke their front. The infantry following completed the rout, and in an hour Goring was in flight through the burning streets of Langport. It was a far greater feat for the parliament than Naseby, since the enemy had been at-

tacked in a strong position of his own choosing and decisively
beaten by only a small part of Fairfax's troops. The discipline
of the New Model horse was extending to all arms.

Both the royal armies had now been shattered in the field.
Bridgewater was taken before the end of the month, and Fairfax had now a line of garrisons to isolate Devon and Cornwall.
Presently Bath fell, and the strong castle of Sherborne, and
only Bristol remained. Oliver, to whom the rapid training
of the new army must be largely attributed, dealt wisely and
firmly with the Dorset Clubmen,[1] and by the end of August he
was with Fairfax in front of the vast sprawling fortifications
of Bristol, which Rupert was holding with less than 2000 men.
The task of defence was impossible, and after the general assault on September 20th Rupert had no choice but to capitulate.
Oliver, with three regiments of horse and four of foot, was now
given a roving commission to clear Hampshire and Wiltshire,
and Devizes, Winchester and the virgin stronghold of Basing fell
to him before the end of October. Six months earlier in his Oxford raid he had declared that the storming of strong places
was not his business:[2] but he had now learned this branch
also of the art of war.

That autumn hope finally died in the hearts of the wiser
royalists. Charles had been wandering aimlessly in the midlands, now inspired with the notion of joining Montrose, now
cheered by promises of foreign aid. But all his schemes had
come to nothing. Montrose in September had ended at Philiphaugh his year of miracles, and was a fugitive among the
Highland hills, the victim of the feeble strategy of his master.
Rupert had been urging peace, and after the fall of Bristol was
excluded from the royal council, his place being taken by the
civilian Digby, whose dash to the north had a disastrous ending. On November 6 Charles made his way back to Oxford to
begin a fresh tangle of weary intrigues with Leven and the
Scots. The one danger that remained for parliament was the
arrival of foreign support, so Fairfax took the field in the first
days of January 1646, while Devon was still deep in snow.
Goring had gone, and Hopton had his place, but Hopton's wisdom and valour could not achieve the impossible. On January
9th Oliver surprised Lord Wentworth at Bovey Tracey; Dart-
mouth was stormed on the 18th; on Friday 16th Hopton was

[1] See his letter to Fairfax, *L. and S.*, I, 209.
[2] *L. and S.*, I, 194.

defeated at Torrington, and the remnant of his army capitulated
on March 14, while Prince Charles fled to the Channel Islands.
Seven days later the last field action was fought by Lord Astley
at Stow-in-the-Wold. On April 9th Exeter surrendered, and
on May 6th Newark followed. Nothing remained but Oxford.
The king, after making overtures to every possible ally, decided that his best hope lay with the Scots, and on April 27 he
left Oxford for Leven's camp. Fairfax and Oliver were presently before the city, and on June 24 it capitulated on generous
terms, and Rupert and his cavaliers rode over Magdalen bridge
with all the honours of war. Parliament had won that decisive
victory which Oliver from the start had set before him.

IV

He had sheathed his sword before Oxford fell and returned
to his parliamentary duties, now by far the most formidable
figure in England. In January parliament had settled on him
certain forfeited estates of the Marquis of Worcester, designed
to produce an income of £2500, and in April the Commons had
thanked him 'for his great and faithful services.' During the
war his family had been living quietly at Ely, but a country life
was now for him a thing of the past, and he moved his household to a dwelling in Drury Lane. His mother, an old woman of
eighty, lived with him and followed eagerly his career; his wife,
like Napoleon's mother distrustful of sudden greatness, contented herself with domestic concerns and laboured after
small economies in this new expensive mode of life. Of his sons
Robert, the eldest, had died long ago at school, and the second,
Oliver, had perished of small-pox while with the troops at Newport Pagnell in the spring of 1644; Richard was a youth of
twenty, and Henry had already been two years in the army.
Of the daughters Mary and Frances were still little girls, but
Elizabeth was seventeen and was being courted by Mr. John
Claypole, a Northamptonshire squire. Bridget, the eldest,
that very year, while the guns were still busy around Oxford,
had married at the manor-house of Holton, five miles off on the
London road, a man of thirty-six with a great square head,
thick curling hair and deep-set eyes, that Colonel Henry Ireton
who had not been too fortunate at Naseby. From the village
of Forest Hill a mile distant John Milton three years before had
got his wife.

During these four years of war Oliver had known both happiness and peace. He had what the language of his faith called a full 'assurance.' Except when the high command was manifestly incompetent he had not to concern himself with questions of general strategy, and was content to perform the tasks assigned to him. He had a soldier's sense of discipline, and loved, as he once said, to be 'a man under authority.' The gadfly of personal ambition, which tormented the young Napoleon, did not trouble him. The Commons had proposed to the king in December 1645 to create him a baron,[1] but what were such gauds to one whose hope was to sit with Christ on His throne? This happy dedication gave his nature a balance which it did not possess before and which it was soon to lose. He was doing his Lord's work, with no shadow of a doubt, and, though death was ever at his elbow, death was only a messenger to summon him to his reward. Having no fears he was merciful; he was tender with the puzzled Clubmen, and gentle to vanquished enemies. His humanity, too, was notable, for he mixed on familiar terms with all, and could be a merry companion, a lover of horse-play and rough jests and free speech which scandalized the prudish. 'He was naturally of such a vivacity, hilarity and alacrity,' Richard Baxter wrote, 'as another man is when he hath drunken a cup of wine too much.' Had not the Son of Man come eating and drinking?

But his religion dominated every detail of his life. The teaching of his first schoolmaster had borne fruit in a constant waiting upon some sign of the heavenly will. 'He seldom fights,' said Hugh Peters, his chaplain, 'without some text of Scripture to support him,' and a rousing verse of the Psalms was like a cordial to his spirit. No Roman general ever more devoutly took the omens. There was here some psychological necessity, the craving of a slow-moving mind for an external stimulus, and he laboured to make his own need a canon for other people. Mercies must be looked for, for they were a token of the divine approval. 'I have had greater mercies,' he wrote after he took Bletchingdon, 'but none clearer.'[2] He saw in Naseby 'none other but the hand of God.'[3] After the fall of Bristol he told the Commons: 'He that runs may read that all this is none other than the work of God. He must be a very atheist that does not acknowledge it';[4] and after the capture of Winchester,

[1] O. P. H., XIV, 139.   [2] L. and S., I, 193.
[3] Ibid., I, 204.   [4] Ibid., I, 217.

'You see God is not weary in doing you good; I confess His favour to you is as visible, when this comes by His power upon the hearts of your enemies, making them quit places of strength to you, as when He gives courage to your soldiers to attempt hard things.'[1] But in addition to this zealous watching for the hand of the Almighty there was also the duty of constantly entering into mystical communion with the unseen. On the eve of Marston Moor he disappeared, and was found by a girl in a disused room on the top of a tower wrestling in prayer with his Bible before him,[2] and before the sack of Basing he spent hours on his knees. The health of his soul depended upon the frequent renewal of that spiritual experience which had first given him peace.

The style of the letters written during these years is for the most part brisk, emphatic and soldierly. To the men of his faith, who had small literary knowledge behind them, the words of Scripture were the only means of expressing either strong emotion or some high conception of policy. The 'language of Zion' was soon to become a bleak conventional jargon, but it is fair to recognize that it was originally used by simple men for the reason that they could not otherwise express thoughts beyond their daily compass. When Oliver writes about supplies or pay or marching orders his style is the plain and forthright one of the fenland squire. But when he is concerned with deeper things, it becomes interpenetrated with Scriptural rhythms. Now and then he had to deal with profundities, for, as the campaign drew to a close, even his unspeculative mind was forced to read from it certain lessons. He saw the fruits of victory in danger of being wasted, and the liberty he had fought for narrowed into a ritualism not less harsh than that which he had shattered. With a true instinct he had kept himself in the background aloof from controversies, but once and again he was forced to make his testimony. Popery and the anglicanism of Laud he ruled out as hateful to the Almighty, but within the limits of evangelical protestantism he would admit no intolerance. In Richard Baxter's words he was joined to no party but for the liberty of all. In the England of that time such tolerance was not a sedative but an explosive. He stated this belief in his despatch after the capture of Bristol, and the Commons no more dared to print the passage than the similar plea in his letter after Naseby.

[1] *L. and S.*, I, 221.
[2] See Rosebery, *Miscellanies*, I, 94, for the *provenance* of this story.

Presbyterians, Independents, all had here the same spirit of faith and prayer; the same pretence and answer; they agree here, know no manner of difference; pity it is it should be otherwise anywhere. All that believe have the real unity, which is most glorious because inward and spiritual, in the Body and to the Head. As for being united in forms, commonly called uniformity, every Christian will, for peace sake, study and do as far as conscience will permit; and from brethren in things of the mind we look for no compulsion but that of light and reason.[1]

'Light and reason.' Mr. Robert Baillie and his Scottish friends would have called it the outer darkness.

[1] *L. and S.*, I, 218.

Book Three
THE KING-BREAKER

Chapter I

PARLIAMENT AND ARMY
(1646–1647)

Our business is not unknown to the Senate; they have had inkling this fortnight what we intend to do, which now we'll show 'em in deeds. They say poor suitors have strong breaths: they shall know we have strong arms too.

Coriolanus.

I

WHEN after the fight of Stow-in-the-Wold, old Jacob Astley sat on a drum, his white hair blowing in the March wind, he spoke true words to his conquerors. 'You have now done your work,' he told them, 'and you may go play, unless you will fall out amongst yourselves.'[1] Parliament had won the war, but never in history was a victory so indecisive. The settlement of England was still far off. The former sovereignty had crashed, but no substitute of accepted authority had been devised, so the remnants of the ancient régime had, in spite of all up-heavals, a supreme importance. The beaten king was still the most important factor in the problem. But in the empty space created by the disappearance of traditional sanctions new forces had appeared which made it all but impossible to build a fresh structure out of the débris of the old. England was faced with the secular problem which appears after all revolutions — how to graft the revolutionary slips upon the former stock, and preserve that continuity without which a human society descends into chaos.

The two surviving traditional things were the king and parliament. Charles's misfortunes had regained for him the affection of a great mass of the people whom he had once exasperated, but who now, sick of the war and weary of theorizing, longed for peace and order. Only the dreaming few envisaged an England other than monarchical. As for parliament, the nominal victor, it had small hold on public esteem. Its cause had been the war-cry of the triumphant army, but in practice it had grievously impeded that army, and it had in the end been firmly put aside. In 1642 it had been far from representative of the English commons, and now it was less so than ever. It

[1] Rushworth, VI, 140.

contained no royalists, though the majority of Englishmen were still royalist.[1] Elections had been held during 1645 and 1646 and about one hundred and fifty new members had been added, but this recruitment had not changed its character. It represented in the main the monied classes and the more rigid types of dogma in politics and religion. It was wholly insensitive to public opinion outside Westminster. Victory had made it arrogant, though it had had but a small part in the winning of victory. In the confiscation of royalist and ecclesiastical lands it had shown great harshness and little honesty; many members had feathered their nests, and bribery was the order of the day.[2] Also, it had no leaders like Pym and Hampden, and no parliamentarians of special talent. The younger Vane had succeeded to only a shred of Pym's mantle, for he led a group rather than a party.

But when Oliver in the summer of 1646 cast his eye over the Commons he saw certain faces which gave him hope. The presbyterians were in the majority; Denzil Holles, Stapleton and Maynard, Glyn the lawyer, and soldiers like Massey and Sir William Waller. But on the benches he observed old friends like Vane and St. John, and the weather-beaten countenances of new members who had been his comrades in the field. Skippon had come in for Barnstaple and young Algernon Sidney, Lord Leicester's son, for Cardiff. His own son-in-law Henry Ireton sat for Appleby, and Robert Blake, the defender of Taunton, for Bridgewater. There were famous colonels of the New Model, Edmund Ludlow for Wiltshire and Charles Fleetwood for Marlborough, there was John Hutchinson, the governor of Nottingham — all men of his own school of thought. There were wilder figures, visionaries and enthusiasts like Thomas Harrison for Wendover and Thomas Rainsborough for Droitwich, for whose dreams and truculences he had a half-ashamed tenderness. Such men would see that the toil of the past years did not issue in barrenness. Fairfax, too, his old commander, was the popular hero, and, when he came up to London in November, to be his neighbour in Queen Street, he was given an almost Roman triumph. Fairfax was a just man, who might be trusted to do honestly by the commonweal.

---

[1] Just as at almost any time in the later sixteenth century manhood suffrage would have brought back the Pope, so between 1642 and 1660 it would have brought back the king.

[2] Cf. Lady Verney's experience. *Verney Memoirs*, I, ch. xxvi.

Yet when in the intervals of his military business — for he was still lieutenant-general of the army — he surveyed the public scene he saw much to disquiet him. His slow mind had been coming to certain conclusions. Order must be established, order on a basis of toleration, and there must be peace; but there were strong forces making for tyranny, disorder and the renewal of war. The land was in a grievous state, burdened with taxation, groaning under all manner of exactions and for-feitures, with trade at a standstill and the prospect that year of a miserable harvest. Let us set out the elements in the situa-tion, most of which were now clear to Oliver's mind.

The presbyterians, a majority in parliament, very strong in the city of London, and with a great following among the coun-try gentry and the middle classes in the provinces, were consti-tutional monarchists and advocates of a popularly controlled church. Unlike their Scottish brethren they were determined that the laity and not the clergy should have the final word in church government — which Robert Baillie called 'but a lame Erastian Presbytery.'[1] The best exponent of what was of value in their creed was, surprisingly enough, the Scotsman Argyll in his famous speech in the Lords on June 25th, in which he pleaded for a certain elasticity in the new ecclesiastical system which had been made the law of the land.[2] The blunder-ing of their leaders should not blind us to the fact that it was their view which in substance ultimately triumphed. They killed the old monarchy and the old Church of Laud; the king who was restored in 1660 had none of his former absolutism, and the Church then re-established was subject in the last re-sort to parliament and therefore to the laity. Their weakness was that they had no deep roots among the English people, and were forced to support themselves by foreign intrigues; and that the pattern of their church was to the last degree strait and intolerant. They could with impunity prohibit a prayer-book which had still no great hold on English affections, and even establish their own directory and confessions, but they were on dangerous ground when they sought to compel all men to bow to the letter of their worship. To their leaders toleration was 'the Devil's masterpiece' and to 'let men serve God according to the persuasion of their own conscience' was 'to cast out one devil that seven worse might enter.' Their ec-clesiastical rigidity set the independents in eternal opposition,

[1] Baillie, II, 362.   [2] L. J., VIII, 392.

and their political blunders arrayed against them the ancient pride and loyalties of England.

The next factor was Scotland — that northern land where English creeds were held with an ominous difference, and its mercenary army, which had made parliament's victory possible but which was now much out of love with the men who had hired it. The Scottish leaders desired the establishment of presbytery in England, but they were lukewarm over the other items in the parliament's creed. Having no belief in tolerance they hated the independents, and, being monarchists of an antique school, they were apathetic about constitutional niceties; had the king been willing to accept the Covenant they would have gladly restored to him most of his prerogatives. Here was a chance for a man like Charles who was an adept at playing one irreconcilable against the other. Small wonder that the tale of the next three years is a bewildering network of intrigue.

There remained the two most vital factors of all, the first still obscure and hard to assess, the second daily becoming more assertive. Parliament had created a royalism which in 1642 had scarcely existed. Confiscations and persecutions had made Laud a saint to thousands who had once detested him, and had endeared anglicanism to many who had once been its bitter critics. Driven for the most part underground, a sentiment had come into being which was the strongest thing in the land — a desire for an old order which had been replaced by chaos, an abhorrence of all that was windy and fantastic. A nationalism, too, which refused to serve either Edinburgh or Geneva or Paris. When in June Hyde and Capel and Hopton refused to accompany the Prince of Wales to France, they exhibited the spirit which was one day to triumph — the royalism which declined to intrigue with any sect or faction or foreign Power, and was content to wait till England recovered what Hyde called 'its old good manners, its old good humour, and its old good nature.' He believed that the incompatibles would sooner or later destroy each other. 'Therefore I expect no great good from either till they have bettered their understandings and reformed their consciences by drinking deep in each other's blood; and then I shall be of your opinion that whosoever shall by God's blessing be able to preserve his conscience and his courage in a very few years will find himself wished for again in his country, and may see good days again.' [1]

[1] Hyde to Nicholas. *Clarendon S. P.*, II, 285.

The second was the army, that crop of dragons' teeth. Certain local troops were disbanded, but so long as the Scots lay on English soil with the king in their keeping, the bulk of the New Model must be kept intact. Most of the men no doubt thought only of their arrears of pay, and, had they got them, would gladly have returned to the farm and the shop. But there were many who conceived themselves to be prophets of a new dispensation. The presbyterian clergy, who had been the first chaplains, had soon returned to their parishes, and spiritual sustenance had been supplied by independent preachers or by the fighting men themselves. In the long periods of idleness which are found in all campaigns the army's thoughts had been directed into strange channels, and it had become a factory of high explosives in Church and State. Having a hundred queer faiths, it demanded toleration as against the presbyterians. Having beaten the gentry of England, it had lost its respect for rank and birth. 'What were the lords of England but William the Conqueror's colonels, or the barons but his majors, or the knights but his captains?' [1] It had no great reverence for parliament, having witnessed its muddling, and it declared not for parliamentary sovereignty but for the sovereignty of the people. The consciousness that it had saved English liberties made it little inclined to submit to ill treatment, and the comradeship established in the field compacted all the various strains into one formidable unit, when it was a question of soldiers' rights. More and more it was beginning to listen to fire-brands like John Lilburne, whom Oliver with his odd fondness for cranks and his hatred of injustice had always befriended, and who, whether in prison or out of it, poured forth his subversive pamphlets. Presently the army was quoting his writings 'as statute law.' If this formidable and incalculable power was not wisely handled parliament might find a more deadly enemy than the king.

II

The first business before the new *de facto* government was to come to terms with Charles, since without him no lasting settlement could be made. In July negotiations began with the presentation of the Nineteen Propositions to him at Newcastle.[2] It was a bad start, for the proposals had no hope of acceptance.

[1] *Rel. Baxt.*, 51.   [2] Gardiner, *Const. Docs.*, 290-306.

Charles was required to take the Covenant and enforce it upon the nation; to accept the abolition of episcopacy; to hand over the army and navy to parliament for twenty years, and then to let the Houses decide upon their future disposal; to suffer parliament to appoint all high officers of state, and to consent to the proscription of many royalists.

It is needless to recount the foolish diplomacy of the next few months. The king did not categorically reject the proposals, but endeavoured to gain time. He was in treaty with France, and Mazarin, busy with the Spanish Netherlands, and anxious to keep England weak and divided, had no wish for a speedy settlement. Had Charles been wholly honest or wholly dishonest he would have been more fortunate. Two things he would never surrender — his kingly duty, as he conceived it, and the anglican Church. Had he been a complete dissembler he might have accepted the parliament's proposals, in the certainty that in practice they would rouse such violent antagonisms as to prove unworkable. Had he been straightforward about his creed, he would have won the respect of the honest extremists, and a way of accommodation might have been discovered, which would have saved his personal scruples while safeguarding the nation. But, being neither, he merely exasperated his opponents, and created for himself a colossal repute for duplicity. After eight futile months the patience of the Scots was exhausted. In the first week of 1647, having received a payment on account of half the amount due to them, they handed over the king to the parliamentary commissioners, and Leven's carts began to rumble across the Border. On February 3 Charles set out for Holmby house in Northamptonshire, being received with acclamations on the road, and being courteously greeted by Fairfax at Nottingham. He had offered to grant the establishment of presbytery for three years and the control of the armed forces for ten; and, though this had been unsatisfactory to the Scots and to parliament, he had evidence that the House of Lords might accept it and that a majority in the Commons might soon take the same view. He had some reason to be confirmed in his belief that he was indispensable. 'Men will begin to perceive,' he wrote, 'that without my establishing there can be no peace.' He had never been nearer to success.

The situation was dramatically changed by the quarrel which broke out with the army. Had the army been peaceably disbanded, the independents would have been left at the mercy of the parliamentary majority, which was now moving towards a kind of presbyterian royalism. In January 1647 Ormonde offered to hand over his lord-lieutenantship to the English parliament, which would now have the duty of conducting the Irish campaign. This gave parliament the chance of proceeding to that disbandment which had been due in the previous October, but which had been postponed because of the strained relations with the Scots. An armed force, largely independent in creed, was a constant menace to the presbyterian section, and moreover the nation could not afford it, since, along with the navy, it absorbed three fifths of the national revenue. The obvious course was a drastic reduction, and the transference of most of the troops to the Irish service.

In February parliament propounded its scheme and in March it was accepted by both Houses. The infantry in England was to be confined to troops required for garrison work, about 10,000 in all, while the horse was fixed at 6600. An Irish force of 12,600 was to be raised from those who should volunteer for that service. Fairfax was to be retained in his command, but the independent officers of the New Model were to be got rid of, since no officer was to be employed who was not a presbyterian, and no member of parliament was permitted to hold a commission — a provision clearly directed against Oliver. No mention was made of the monies due to the troops, though the pay of the infantry was eighteen weeks in arrear and that of the horse forty-three weeks — a total of some £330,000. When the parliament commissioners visited Fairfax's headquarters at Saffron Walden to explain the proposals and call for volunteers for Ireland, they discovered that the manifest inequity of the terms had stirred the army to its depths. Some were furious at the treatment of their officers, some saw in the whole affair a presbyterian plot, but all were united on the question of arrears of pay and on the need of an indemnity for what had been done in the late war.

Oliver found himself in a position of grave embarrassment. Since the fall of Oxford he had taken little part in public affairs. In the autumn and winter months he had sat in his place in the House and had supported the independents in their policy of getting rid of the Scots. He had striven in vain to prevent parliament from passing an ordinance forbidding laymen to preach and expound the Scriptures in public. The few letters

that remain from this period show him busied in looking after
the interests of brother officers, and interceding with a royalist
gentleman on behalf of certain poor neighbours, and writing to
Bridget Ireton about her own spiritual state and that of her
sister Elizabeth. To Fairfax he writes in December of the
dangerous temper of the city and its hostility to the army.
'But this is our comfort, God is in heaven, and He doth what
pleases Him; His and only His council shall stand, whatever
the designs of men and the fury of the people be.'[1] In March
the situation is graver. 'Never,' he tells Fairfax, 'were the spirits of men more embittered than now. Surely the Devil hath
but a short time. Sir, it's good the heart be fixed against all
this. The naked simplicity of Christ, with the wisdom He
please to give, and patience, will overcome all this.... Upon
the Fast day divers soldiers were raised (as I hear) both horse
and foot... to prevent ——[2] from cutting the Presbyterians'
throats. These are fine tricks to mock God with....[3] Parliament's disbandment proposals, aimed directly at himself, saddened him by their contrast with the old loyal army spirit. 'It
is a miserable thing,' he told Ludlow, 'to serve a parliament, to
which, let a man be never so faithful, if one pragmatical fellow
amongst them rise and asperse him, he shall never wipe it off;
whereas, when one serves a general, he may do as much service,
and yet be free from all blame and envy.'[4]

All winter he had been unhappy and out of health, and in
February he had a serious illness, the ague of the fens acting on
a body wearied by four years' campaigning. He was a disillusioned man, though he preached hope and patience. The world
was full of 'pragmatical fellows,' and there was no concord
among Christian folk. Parliament, for which he had drawn
the sword, was not the devout and sagacious sanhedrin of
which he had dreamed, but an assembly of pedants who would
deny the great principle of Christian liberty and by their per-
verseness forfeit all that the war had won. There was rumour
of presbyterian intrigues with France, with the Scots, with the
king; there might soon be a restoration which would bring
back the old evil days. Worse still, their blunders were an-
tagonizing the army that had saved them, and this quarrel
might soon lead the country into anarchy or a second war. For

[1] L. and S., I, 248.
[2] The word is obscure in the original: perhaps 'sectaries.'
[3] L. and S., I, 252-53.   [4] Ludlow, I, 145.

a moment he despaired of England. Any ambition which might have been growing up at the back of his soul had withered, and he asked only for a simple task where he could have scope for his talents in God's service. That must be soldiering, for he was but a novice in politics. He had a plan to transfer himself with some of his colonels to the service of the Elector Palatine, and in the defence of the German Calvinists to strike a blow for the toleration which seemed to be a lost cause in England.

He abandoned the notion from his own sense of duty, and partly, no doubt, from the persuasion of his friends. In the new unfamiliar world of politics he found two men on whom he could lean. One was the younger Vane, who like him stood for toleration in religion and would accept no settlement which stultified the toil of the past four years. The other was his son-in-law Henry Ireton, who shared his own intense religious faith, and who had the same passion for spiritual liberty. Ireton had many things that Oliver lacked. His nature was narrower, more dogmatic, less visionary, infinitely less humane; but he was a trained lawyer, he had a quick logical mind, and he could move securely among these constitutional tangles which to Oliver were puzzling and repellent. Above all he was supremely explicit; he had a reason for everything he did, and he had the pen of a ready writer. To a perplexed soul feeling its way among the débris of old institutions and principles Ireton's luminous intelligence was like a lamp in the night. Here was one of whose purity of purpose he was confident, and whose intellect was a staff on which he could happily lean. Than Oliver no man ever made his first venture into the civil arena with greater modesty. Before he had only been a subaltern in politics, but now he was conscious that he might be forced to show the way.

His chief dread was anarchy. Parliament with all its imperfections must be the centre of government, and he abhorred the notion of military dictation. Deep in his bones he had the English respect for law. 'In the presence of Almighty God before whom I stand,' he told the House, 'I know the army will lay down their arms at your door, whenever you will command them.'[1] These words were a bitter disappointment to the extremists within the army and outside it, who had pinned their faith to him as a maker of revolutions. John Lilburne implored the Lord to open his eyes, and was 'jealous over him with the height of godly jealousy,' beseeching him not to be 'led by the

[1] Walker, *Hist. of Independency*, 31.

nose by two unworthy covetous earth-worms, Vane and St. John.'[1] But Oliver, when his mind was clear, was not to be diverted by friend or foe. The soldiers at Saffron Walden rejected the terms of the parliamentary commissioners, and drew up a petition to Fairfax in which with great moderation they set out their demands. Oliver disapproved of the petition, as inconsistent with army discipline, and the House lost its temper and passed a furious declaration against it. This was deeply resented at Saffron Walden, and a second parliamentary commission succeeded no better, either in enlisting volunteers for Ireland or in conciliating the troops. Mutiny was imminent, and since Fairfax had to go to London for medical treatment, there was no controlling influence to prevent it. To the legitimate grievances of the soldiers there were now added many extreme political doctrines, and early in May they were talking of going to Holmby to fetch the king. The next stage was the appointment by the cavalry regiments of agitators, or agents, to state their grievances, and, since parliament would have none of them, they made their appeal to their generals. This was too grave a matter for even the blind parliamentary majority to disregard; the House capitulated, and sent down four of its members, Skippon, Oliver, Ireton and Fleetwood, to reason with the malcontents.

Oliver did his best as a peacemaker. The commissioners had authority to promise an indemnity and an immediate payment of part of the arrears, and for a week he laboured with the agitators, honourably fulfilling his instructions from parliament. They presented a declaration of the army, which vindicated its conduct and made certain reasonable proposals as to the details of a settlement. Oliver was convinced of the substantial justice of the soldiers' claims, but he gave no countenance to indiscipline. He emphasized the control of parliament. 'Truly, gentlemen,' he told the officers, 'it will be very fit for you to have a very great care in the making the best use and improvement you can... of the interest which all of you or any of you may have in your several respective regiments — namely, to work in them a good opinion of that authority that is over both us and them. If that authority falls to nothing, nothing can follow but confusion.'[2]

Unhappily that authority fell to nothing by its own folly. Parliament had made up its mind that the power of the

[1] *Jonah's Cry out of the Whale's Belly* (Th.).   [2] *C. P.*, I, 72.

army must be crushed once and for all. 'They must sink us, or we sink them.' [1] This meant an appeal to force, and ultimately that renewal of war which Oliver feared. The city militia was remodelled on a purely presbyterian basis, and secret negotiations took place with the French ambassador and the Scots with the view of bringing David Leslie's army to England. There was to be a settlement with the king on the understanding that he need not take the Covenant, but would accept presbyterianism for three years and hand over the militia for ten, and Lauderdale was permitted to visit him at Holmby. Rumours of these doings reached the army, and the agitators circularized the regiments, pointing out that, after disbandment, they might be 'pressed away for Ireland or hanged in England.' [2] A petition to parliament by the fanatics who followed John Lilburne proposed a scheme of social and political reform which scared the presbyterian formalists to the marrow. On May 21 Oliver presented his report to the House, and for a moment he seemed likely to guide the majority in the path of wisdom. But members presently relapsed, they did not believe in his assurance that the army, if fairly treated, would disperse peaceably, and they resolved upon an immediate disbanding and the bringing of the artillery train from Oxford to London that it might be under their control. Secretly they were planning to get the king, the trump card, into their hands. 'I doubt the disobliging of so faithful an army will be repented of,' Ireton wrote to Oliver. 'It shall be my endeavour to keep things as right as I can, but how long I shall be able I know not.' [3]

The army was already in revolt. It refused to disband, and the parliamentary commissioners were greeted as enemies and bidden take their 'twopenny pamphlets' home again. Fairfax, torn between his belief in parliamentary authority and his loyalty to his men, had virtually surrendered his command. The agitators were now in charge. Oliver, who had hoped against hope that parliament would be reasonable, was compelled to a decision, and he decided, as he always did, on what he understood to be the facts of the case. Military disorganization must be prevented, for that spelt anarchy: the presbyterian intrigues with the Scots must be crushed, for they meant a second civil war.

A certain Cornet Joyce, once a tailor but now high in the

[1] Rushworth, VI, 515.   [2] C. P., I, 87.   [3] Ibid., I, 100.

army's confidence, had been ordered by the agitators to act in the two urgent matters, the prevention of the removal of the artillery train and the securing of the king's person. Oliver, hearing of the project, summoned a meeting at his house in Drury Lane on May 31, and, as Fairfax's second-in-command, gave Joyce his marching orders. He was to proceed to Oxford to see that the artillery was in safe hands, and then with five hundred horse to ride to Holmby and prevent Charles's removal by Scots or presbyterians, carrying him if necessary to a place of greater security. This last instruction was either explicit or implied, but it did not involve the bringing of the king to the army. Joyce did his errand at Oxford, and on June 2 arrived at Holmby.[1] There he found a situation which alarmed him, and he decided to remove the king to a place where he would be directly under the army's eye. Fairfax had no cognizance of this purpose, and it clearly exceeded Oliver's general instructions. Early on the morning of June 4 on the Holmby lawn took place the famous dialogue between the king and the cornet. Charles asked to see his commission, and Joyce could only point to the troopers at his back. 'It is as fair a commission,' said the smiling king, 'and as well written as I have seen a commission in my life — a company of handsome, proper gentlemen.'[2] Charles chose Newmarket as his new abode, and to Newmarket they went.[3]

The king was in a good humour, for he saw his enemies falling out, and when Colonel Whalley, despatched posthaste by Fairfax, tried to induce him to return to Holmby, he answered that he preferred Newmarket. Meanwhile, Oliver, deciding that Westminster was no place for him, had joined the army. At a rendezvous near Newmarket the soldiers' grievances were presented in a 'Humble Representation' and a 'Solemn Engagement,' and a council was formed to negotiate on behalf of the army, the only way to curb the agitators and prevent anarchy. This was certainly the work of Oliver, and it brought him little favour from John Lilburne and his band. 'You have robbed by your unjust subtilty and shifting tricks the honest and gallant agitators of all their power and authority, and

[1] Holmby or Holdenby was then regarded as the largest country-house in England. It was built by John of Padua for Sir Christopher Hatton, Elizabeth's chancellor, and was purchased in 1607 by James I as a summer residence.

[2] Rushworth, VII, 573.

[3] I have followed Gardiner's evidence for the part played by Oliver in Joyce's raid. *Civil War*, III, 266–74.

solely placed it in a thing called a council of war, or rather a cabinet junta of seven or eight self-ended fellows, that so you may make your own ends.' Oliver's object now was to use the army to defeat the presbyterian intrigues, but at the same time to keep it under strict control.

Parliament at the news of Joyce's doings and of the truculence of the troops at Newmarket, had a brief moment of discretion, especially as it was beset by old soldiers of Essex and Waller, the so-called 'reformadoes' who had also grievances. But the loss of confidence between the disputants was now complete. The army asked for more than a redress of its wrongs; it desired security for the future by some limitation of the power of a tyrannical parliament. It began the task of constitution-making, and it moved towards London. The letter written by the generals on June 10 to the city authorities, who had been seeking powers to raise a force of cavalry, was probably Oliver's work, and is a significant proof of his desire to give revolution a legal and conservative colouring.[1] The army, it said, was not acting as soldiers, but as Englishmen. They desired a settle-ment under the ægis of parliament, but parliament must not do violence to the moral sense of the nation. Some have seen in this letter evidence of Oliver's deep duplicity of character, and others of his fundamental intellectual confusion. But it should be noted that the letter bore also Fairfax's signature, and that its main argument was that of Edmund Burke. 'I see no other way but the interposition of the body of the people itself, whenever it shall appear, by some flagrant and notorious act, by some capital innovation, that these representatives are going to overleap the fences of the law and establish an arbitrary power.'[2]

On June 15 Fairfax had moved to St. Albans, and that day was issued the 'Declaration of the Army,' the views of the soldiers on current politics.[3] It was the work of Henry Ireton and showed all the vigour and lucidity of that most masculine mind. Its main point was that absolutism must at all costs be guarded against, and that an oligarchical parliament was as dangerous as a tyrannical king. It accepted the view of Lil-burne that the people were the source of power, and that the popular will should prevail in all government. To ensure this, parliaments must be made more representative, and their du-

---

[1] L. and S., I, 266–69.   [2] Thoughts on the Present Discontents.
[3] Rushworth, VI, 564.

ration should be shorter. As for the immediate question, the present parliament must be purged of those who had abused their office, and especially of those who had wantonly libelled the army. There was no plenary power in king or parliament but only in the English people. For the first time the creed of a later democracy, long maturing in secret places, had found a mouthpiece.

Events now followed fast. The army specifically charged eleven members, including Holles, Sir William Waller, Stapleton, Massey and Glyn. The Commons refused to consider the charges, and the army moved nearer, to Uxbridge. On June 26 the eleven members withdrew with the consent of the House. For a fortnight negotiations dragged on, and Oliver had much ado to restrain his hot-heads, who would have marched forthwith to London and taken order with the presbyterians, especially as every day brought rumours of a coming Scots invasion. He was engaged with Ireton and Lambert in drawing up heads of an agreement, and he would permit no use of force. 'Whatever we get by a treaty,' he declared, 'it will be firm and durable, it will be conveyed over to posterity as that that will be the greatest honour to us that ever poor creatures had.... We shall avoid the great objection that will lie against us that we have got things of the Parliament by force.' [1]

Parliament yielded, appointed Fairfax to the command of all the forces in England, declared against the employment of foreign troops, and put the London militia in the hands of those whom the army trusted. But the city, stirred up perhaps by the eleven members, was in a truculent mood. It became obsessed with a strange blend of presbyterian and royalist fervour, threatened the Houses, and forced the two Speakers and those peers and members who were reckoned independents to flee to the army for refuge. For a moment it seemed as if the Londoners under Massey would defy the veterans of Naseby. But Fairfax's advance to Hounslow brought them to reason. On August 4 the city capitulated, and on August 6 the army escorted the fugitive members back to Westminster, each soldier with a leaf of laurel in his hat, and at Hyde Park and Charing Cross Fairfax was welcomed with wry faces by the city fathers. Next day Oliver rode through the streets at the head of his cavalry, and Fairfax took over the constableship of the Tower. But parliament had forgotten nothing and learned nothing.

[1] *C. P.*, I, 202.

In a week the majority, still presbyterian, were again stupidly at odds with the soldiers. Only the objection of Fairfax prevented Oliver from drastic purging. 'These men,' he said, 'will never leave till the army pull them out by the ears.' [1]

III

In five months Oliver's repute had begun to take a new shape in the popular mind, as is evident from the contemporary pamphlets and broadsheets. The most formidable soldier of the day had hitherto held in the main aloof from politics, but now he was coming to be recognized as a political leader. Aforetime he had been plentifully bespattered with royalist abuse, which harped on his supposed brewing ancestry, his copper nose, his deeds of sacrilege ('the Devil's groom that turns churches into stables'), his alleged cowardice in battle.[2] But now the bottle-nose was forgotten and the charges flew higher; it was hinted that the brewer was aiming at a throne.

> Thou art the King of our New State
> And worthy to undoe us.[3]

'I hope Cromwell will not imagine himself a King, though in this Trago-Comedy he personates a King.' [4] In various parodies of the creed England was enjoined to worship 'no God save Oliver,' and to confess its belief in 'Cromwell, the Father of all Schisms, Heresy and Rebellion, and in his only son Ireton.' [5] From another angle the presbyterians were accusing him of trampling upon parliament, and of being an *agent-provocateur* with the army, though posing as a peacemaker; while John Lilburne, crazy with dreams and self-conceit, was raving against him as a turncoat and a traitor. He had acquired the first warrant of statesmanship, a motley of contradictory oppositions.

One fact was clear to him. His strength lay in the army which he had led, and in no other quarter. One principle, too, was taking shape in his mind. He still firmly believed in government by parliament as Pym had expounded it, but he no longer

[1] Ludlow, I, 148: see Gardiner, *Civil War*, III, 350 *n*.
[2] See *e.g. Ad Populum, or a Lecture to the People*, 1644; *The Character of a London Diurnall*, 1645; *A Case for the City-Spectacles*, 1647 (Th.); *Cromwell's Panegyrick*, 1647.
[3] *The Cities' Welcome to Colonel Rich*, etc., 1647 (Th.).
[4] *Mercurius Pragmaticus*, Sept. 1647 (Th.).
[5] *The Parliament's Ten Commandments; The Cities' Ten Commandments*, 1647 (Th.)

believed in this parliament. Ireton had given him words for a vague faith which had always been at the back of his head; sovereignty lay in the people of England, and in a parliament only in so far as it truly represented them. But the English people must also be the people of God, and for the moment that happy combination was best exemplified in the army. The problem was how to give a civil form to this fundamental authority, for it was the duty of a patriot and a Christian once for all to sheathe the sword. One centre of stability had failed him, since parliament had become a mere fossilized relic, a travesty of its great beginnings. His mind was beginning to turn more happily to the other traditional centre, the king.

Chapter II

ARMY AND KING

(1647–1648)

Others apart sat on a hill retired,
In thoughts more elevate, and reason'd high
Of providence, foreknowledge, will, and fate;
Fix'd fate, free will, foreknowledge absolute;
And found no end, in wandering mazes lost.

MILTON, *Paradise Lost.*

Les natures profondément bonnes sont toujours indécises.

Renan. *St. Paul.*

I

THE next six months were among the most difficult of Oliver's
life. They saw him compelled to take the lead in intricate and
fruitless negotiations where he won a repute for crooked purposes which never left him. To his enemies his doings seemed
the ingenious shifts of an ambitious man manœuvring for position. But a closer study reveals a very different case. In these
months, passionately desirous of peace, he tried tool after tool,
all of which broke in his hands. His sluggish conservative mind
was forced to the unfamiliar tortures of thought, and slowly,
by a process of trial and error, he was driven to conclusions
against which all his instincts revolted, but which were hammered into his soul by the inexorable pressure of facts.

Hitherto he had been vaguely a monarchist. To the claims
which had first brought the country to war he was as resolutely
opposed as ever; there could be no overriding royal and ecclesiastical prerogatives; the representatives of the people in
parliament must have the final say. But to him, as to most
Englishmen, a king seemed an indispensable part of the mechanism of government, and he was in hopes that this king
might now have bowed to the logic of events. He thought that
'no men could enjoy their lives and estates quietly without the
king had his rights.' Since he himself stood for freedom of
conscience he was prepared to be tender about Charles's religion, and it seemed to him that army and king had much common ground, since both desired toleration, and neither would
assent to the dictation of a presbyterian parliament. This was
Ireton's view, and it was also Fairfax's. The latter was no

political theorist, but from a rough draft of a treaty which he has left we know that, after taking security for the rights of parliament and for liberty of conscience, he would have restored both king and bishops.[1] Accordingly the army granted Charles privileges which had hitherto been denied him. He was allowed to have his own chaplains about him. Royalists like Sir John Berkeley and Ashburnham passed freely between him and the army chiefs. Above all he was permitted to see his children, James, Elizabeth and Henry, who were in the custody of parliament.

In July army headquarters were at Reading and Charles nearby at Caversham, and to Caversham the children were brought on a visit. There Oliver met the king — the first time since his far-off boyhood. He saw his meeting with his family and was deeply touched. He felt the strange glamour which Charles could cast over the most diverse minds, the sad graciousness of one who had suffered grievously but whose soul was at peace with itself. As to Montrose on a similar occasion a new man seemed to be revealed. He, who knew something of such matters, recognized the sincerity of Charles's faith. The king, he told Berkeley, 'was the uprightest and most conscientious man of his three kingdoms.'[2] They talked of policy, and found themselves in agreement on the presbyterian demands. Oliver had still his doubts; he could have wished for greater frankness, and he did not like the king's bondage to narrow maxims; but he believed that there was room for a true understanding, and he urged Ireton, to whom the task had been entrusted, to lose no time in presenting his terms.

Ireton had them ready in the 'Heads of the Proposals,'[3] which he had been preparing all summer, and which, having been passed by the army council, were on July 23rd submitted to the king. Changes had been made in the original draft after preliminary conversations with Charles. The main feature of this remarkable document was that it imposed limitations both on Charles and on the existing parliament, but provided ampler powers for a future king and a future parliament; it sought to be a remedy for the present difficulties, and also a scheme for the ultimate governance of England. The king was to be responsible to parliament, and parliament to the people. On the religious side episcopacy was to be maintained, but the hierarchy

[1] Markham, *Great Lord Fairfax*, 299.   [2] Berkeley, *Memoirs*, 26.
[3] The text is in Gardiner, *Const. Docs.*, 316-26.

was deprived of all coercive power. The Covenant was to be dropped, and toleration was to be universal, except for papists. On the political side, the present parliament was to dissolve itself, and thereafter there were to be biennial parliaments elected on a reformed franchise with equal electoral districts. There was to be a council of state nominated by agreement, to sit for seven years, to share with the king the management of foreign affairs, and to have control of the militia, subject to parliamentary approval. For ten years executive officers were to be appointed by parliament, and after that chosen by the king out of parliament's nominees.

It was in substance the Revolution settlement, but on broader and wiser lines. It anticipated the Toleration Act of 1689, cabinet responsibility, and the whole future constitutional monarchy. It would have secured the good will of the great bulk of the English people, for, though royalists were temporarily excluded from office, their fines were to be reduced and only a few were to be exempted from the general amnesty. The army leaders were wholly sincere in their policy. They laboured in the cause of conciliation, and even altered their proposals to meet the king's criticisms. They declared that if he accepted them he should be asked for no further concessions. They assured him that they had both the will and the power to clinch the bargain, whatever difficulties the parliamentary rump might raise. Ireton, as the author of the scheme, was especially emphatic. The army, he said, 'would purge, and purge, and purge, and never leave purging the Houses, till they had made them of such a temper as to do his Majesty's business; and, rather than that they would fall short of what was promised, he would join with French, Spaniard, Cavalier, or any that would join with him to force them to do it.' [1]

But Charles would not agree, beyond expressing a tepid preference for the 'Heads of the Proposals' over the Newcastle Propositions. Ireton's scheme was by far the most favourable ever put to him. It could not be wholly palatable, since it involved some diminution of the royal power, but that diminution was no greater than what he had already expressed his willingness to accept, and it safeguarded his church and his religion. But the truth was that Charles was in no mood to negotiate. He was in high spirits, for the clouds at last seemed to

[1] This is the evidence of Major Huntingdon, who was in the confidence of both Charles and Oliver.

be breaking. The London mob, hitherto his enemies, seemed to be swinging round to his side. He believed that the army would support him; if the army chiefs had offered so much they could be constrained to offer more. Wise counsellors like Berkeley warned him not to trespass too much on the army's patience, but he did not listen. 'I shall see them glad ere long,' he said, 'to accept more equal terms.' 'They cannot do without me,' was the burden of his talk. Ireton on one occasion spoke plain words. 'Sir,' he said, 'you have the intention to be the arbitrator between the parliament and us, and we mean to be it between your Majesty and the parliament.' At another time Charles declared that he would play the game as well as he could, and Ireton replied, 'If your Majesty has a game to play, you must give us also the leave to play ours.' The king had indeed a game of which he made no mention in these discussions. He was deep in intrigues with Lauderdale and others, and his hope was for a Scottish army to set him once again without conditions upon his throne.

It was soon clear that the 'Heads of the Proposals' had failed, but Oliver and Ireton did not lose hope. If one line of argument was rejected by the king they would try another, and with exemplary patience they set themselves to knit up the broken threads. They laboured to induce parliament to put itself into direct touch with the king; and they secured the defeat of Henry Marten's motion that no further addresses should be made to him. They permitted Charles to call his friends like Richmond and Ormonde to a council at Hampton Court. Oliver himself attempted a compromise with the presbyterians in parliament, but it shipwrecked on the matter of toleration. Meantime his own position was rapidly becoming impossible. He could still carry the army council, but it was doubtful if he would long be able to hold the army. On every side he had to face mistrust and hostility. Charles's prevarications had roused against him many of the soldiers who had once been eager for an agreement, and the wilder ones were advancing in prestige, the men who talked of him as an Ahab whose heart God had hardened, a man of blood who must be brought to justice. The moderates had lost hope; 'they are cold,' said a royalist letter, 'and there is another faction of desperate fellows as hot as fire.' The controversy was now to move from the solid practical levels to the volcanic heights of abstract dogma and apocalyptic vision.

II

In early October five cavalry regiments cashiered their agitators, appointed new ones, drew up a manifesto under John Lilburne's influence called 'The Case of the Army truly stated,' and on the 18th laid it before Fairfax. A new party had formed itself, popularly known as the Levellers, and a new creed had been officially promulgated in England. The 'Case' dealt not only with practical steps such as the dissolution and purging of parliament; it laid down a revolutionary philosophy of politics the echoes of which are still loud in the world. England, nearly a century and a half before the French Revolution, was offered the Revolution's dogma. All power, it was maintained, was 'originally and essentially in the whole body of the people of this nation.' The monarchy and the House of Lords were therefore excrescences and must be removed, and government must be by a single chamber biennially elected under manhood suffrage. These provisions were to be a 'law paramount,' which could not be tampered with by any parliament — a written constitution with no proviso for any future change. The conservative lawyers who had argued as against Pym the sanctity of the 'law fundamental' now found strange supporters. Coke joined hands across the ages with Rousseau.

To Oliver, with his contempt for abstractions, his distrust of all talk of natural and inalienable rights, and his instinct for building upon old foundations, the proposals seemed the last word in folly. On the 20th he expounded for three hours in the House of Commons his belief in a limited monarchy. But he realized that the Levellers had become a power in the army, and that it was necessary to meet them squarely. The new agitators had summarized their demands succinctly and more modestly in a document called 'The Agreement of the People,' [1] and a meeting of the army council was called in Putney church on October 28th to consider it. The council consisted of the generals, and four representatives, two officers and two soldiers, from each regiment. One or two civilians were admitted, including Wildman, who had been a major in a disbanded regiment. Fairfax was sick, so Oliver took the chair.

The session lasted for three weeks, with fervent prayer-meetings interspersed, and during these weeks Oliver's mind went through many painful transitions. He found himself compelled

[1] Gardiner, *Const. Docs.*, 333-35.

to formulate what had hitherto been vague beliefs, and in formulating them to revise them. The Levellers' case had a terrible cogency. Oliver and Ireton, they said, had striven to reach an agreement with king and parliament, and had notably failed. As practical men therefore they must look elsewhere, and appeal to the people at large.

Oliver met them on two grounds. First, a clean slate was impossible, since they were bound by certain engagements to parliament and people. Wildman argued that such engagements were not binding since they were not just and honest, and Ireton ironically reminded him that the pith of their case against parliament was that it had violated engagements. Oliver asked for the appointment of a committee to look into these obligations, and meantime stated his second objection. The question was not whether the proposals were good or bad, but whether they were practicable. The way to perfection, as Sir John Evelyn had declared in parliament two years before, did not lie through confusion, and confusion must follow any reducing of things to first principles. Under this method there was no end to the plans that might be put forward. There could be no unanimity and no finality. 'Would it not make England like the Switzerland country, one canton against another, and one county against another?' There was also the consideration of ways and means. A scheme academically perfect on paper was nothing; the real point was, could it be put into effect; would the spirit and temper of the nation receive it? On this score he saw endless difficulties. 'I know a man may overcome all difficulties with faith, and faith will overcome all difficulties really where it is. But we are very apt to call that faith that perhaps may be but carnal imagination and carnal reasoning.'

This brought up the Levellers, for it touched the heart of their creed. Such timidity and dilatoriness, said Wildman, was a dishonouring of God. You talk of difficulties, said Rainsborough, but if difficulties were the point, why was the war ever begun? You condemn our scheme as an innovation, 'but if writings be true, there have been many scufflings between the honest men of England and those that have tyrannized over them, and if people find the old laws do not suit freemen as they are, what reason can exist why old laws should not be changed to new?'

Presently the debate was in a morass of abstractions. Wildman declared that any arrangement with the king would be a breach of the natural rights of the people. Ireton answered scornfully that there were no such things. 'There is venom and poison in all this. I know of no other foundation of right and justice than that we should keep covenant with one another. Covenants freely entered into must be freely kept. Take that away, and what right has a man to anything — to his estate of lands or to his goods? You talk of law of nature! By the law of nature you have no more right to this land or anything else than I have.' So the dispute raged, Ireton making his debating points hotly and cleanly, and Oliver striving to conciliate and to find common ground. He was not 'wedded and glued to forms of government,' and was prepared to admit that 'the foundation and supremacy is in the people'; the problem was how to marry this doctrine with the existing form of the English commonweal, not how to devise a visionary Utopia. Here another practical man put in his word. 'If we tarry long,' said a certain Captain Audley, 'the king will come and say who will be hanged first.'

But Oliver failed, his scheme for a committee on engagements was shelved, and the council proceeded to examine the 'Agreement of the People.' That document contained only four provisions — more equal constituencies, the dissolution of the present House, biennial parliaments in future, and the acceptance of an unchangeable law paramount, which would provide for religious liberty, freedom from compulsory military service, and legal equality. On this the controversy waxed fiercer than ever. 'In the government of nations,' Oliver had already said, 'that which is to be looked after is the affection of the people.' He was well aware that the manhood suffrage which Rainsborough demanded would mean an overwhelming royalist victory, but he left Ireton to reply. 'I think,' said Rainsborough, 'that the poorest He that is in England hath a life to live as well as the greatest He, and therefore, truly, sir, I think it clear that every man that is to live under a government ought first, by his own consent, to put himself under that government.' But, said Ireton, if every man has a right to political power, every man must have a right to property. Clearly Ireton's view impressed an assembly mainly composed of country gentlemen and solid burgesses. Oliver clinched the impression by admitting that, while he thought that universal suffrage 'did tend very much to anarchy,' he was prepared for a liberal extension of the franchise, and begging the assembly to get away from abstract theories. For the moment he had regained his influence. On the 30th a committee was appointed to turn the 'Heads of the Proposals,' supplemented by the 'Agreement of the People' into a set of propositions to be offered to parliament, and in the re-drafting the more extravagant items were omitted. Though Rainsborough was on the committee, the moderates won their way, and the new constitution was to be based on an understanding with the king and not on a direct ukase of the people.

But the trouble was not over, and Oliver's own mind had been slowly changing. His hopes of an agreement with the king were daily becoming more tenuous. Charles at Hampton Court had refused to renew his parole, and London was humming with rumours of Scottish intrigues; the king, it was reported, had already fled with a thousand Scots horse. The anti-monarchist sentiment in the army blazed high, and the army council resumed its meetings on November 1 in an atmosphere of suspicion and religious exaltation. The first question raised was the relation of the people to king and Lords, both of which the Levellers sought to abolish. Oliver argued as he had argued in the House of Commons three weeks before, but with less conviction. He admitted that both parties to the contract had been in fault. 'Let him that was without sin amongst them cast the first stone.' Then he turned to the broader question, the need for some authority. If they did not accept parliament with all its faults, there was no discipline left in the nation, and it would follow that there would be none in the army. Parliament should be reformed, but it must have the last word in deciding the governance of England, and must not be dictated to. 'If they be no parliament, they are nothing, and we are nothing likewise.' In the present storm they must make the best of what anchors they had. Therefore, he concluded, 'I shall move what we shall centre upon. If it have but the force of authority, if it be but a hare swimming over the Thames, I will take hold of it rather than let it go.'

He was arguing in a circle, for he knew that he was avoiding the vital point — whether the authority for which he strove could be made to work. He wished to maintain, after certain reforms, the historic polity of England, which he believed to be desired by the people at large. That happened to be monarchy, but he set no particular store by any form of government for its own sake. Had not the Jews been governed successfully at different times by patriarchs, judges and kings? The important thing was the popular assent, and the securing of a wholesome and orderly national life. A change in formal authority was, he declared, 'but dross and dung in comparison with Christ.' But, since he could give no assurance that his proposed compromise would work, he opened the door to the extravagances of the Levellers, which on this point raised ugly doubts in his own soul.

Goffe arose and declared that a voice from heaven had revealed to him that they had sinned against the Lord 'in tampering with His enemies.' Oliver replied with a personal confession and a halting deduction, for this point touched him very close. 'I am one of those,' he said, 'whose heart God hath drawn out to wait for some extraordinary dispensations, according to those promises that He hath held forth of things to be accomplished in the later times, and I cannot but think that God is beginning of them.' But it was one thing to judge of God's will by the things He had brought to pass, and another to trust to personal revelations. The latter way lay confusion, and 'certainly God is not the author of contradictions.' It might well be that God meant to overthrow the king and the Lords, but He would reveal the manner of it in His own good time, and it must not come about through a breach of faith on the part of the army dictated by the imagined visions of hasty men. It was dispensations, actual events, that he believed in, not visions. Yet he argued with a divided mind, for he knew how earnestly he had himself sought for such divine intimations. Much of his sympathy was with Goffe and Wildman and Rainsborough, and his opposition was half-hearted. He remembered Gamaliel's words: 'Refrain from these men, and let them alone: for if this counsel or this work be of men, it will come to nought; but if it be of God ye cannot overthrow it; lest haply ye be found even to fight against God.'

He had his way. The 'Agreement of the People,' which was to be presented to parliament for its consideration, was so modified that universal suffrage became only an extended franchise, the Commons were given the main authority, and the king and the Lords were retained. But meantime it had become clear that the feeling against Charles was growing in volume and bitterness, and on November 11 Oliver warned his cousin Whalley at Hampton Court to see that there was no attempt on the royal life. He did not like Harrison's savage scriptural parallels. That very night, accompanied by Berkeley, Ashburnham and Legge, the king escaped from his gaolers.

III

For weeks Charles had been in treaty through Legge with Berkeley, Ashburnham and the Scottish envoys. He was in a confident mood, for he believed that he held the master card, but to play it he must be in a position of greater freedom. His purpose was, in Mr. Gardiner's words, to 'put himself up for auction to the Scots and the officers at the same time'; if neither bid high enough, he must have a way of escape open for him by sea to the queen in France. He was aware that the extremists were clamouring that he should be brought to trial, and that some were actually plotting his assassination — it did not need Oliver's letter to Whalley to tell him that; but anxiety for his life played a small part in the thoughts of one who knew little personal fear.

The view that Oliver deliberately frightened him into escape to further his own ambition was widely held at the time, and has been given currency by Andrew Marvell, who was more puritan than royalist.

> Twining subtle fears with hope
> He wove a net of such a scope
>   That Charles himself might chase
>   To Carisbrooke's narrow case,
> That thence the royal actor borne
> The tragic scaffold might adorn.

It is a view for which there is no atom of proof. We have Charles's own admission that his flight was not caused by Oliver's letter.[1] His advisers had differed about the sanctuary he should aim at. Ashburnham would have had him go to London and throw himself boldly on the royalism of the city; some counselled Scotland; Berkeley advised France, and he himself had at first a preference for Jersey. Divided counsels led to bungling, and the choice in the end was narrowed to Carisbrooke castle in the Isle of Wight, the governor of which, Robert Hammond, was believed to be not unfriendly. Oliver had nothing to gain by the escape wherever the king's steps turned. If he went to London he would swell the rising royalist

[1] *L. J.*, IX, 520.

tide. In Jersey he would be next door to France, and from France it would not be hard to reach Scotland. As for Carisbrooke there was no security there. It was true that Hammond was a kind of cousin of his own, since he had married John Hampden's daughter, but he was also the nephew of a famous royalist divine, and had lately been moving towards the king's side. Oliver had heavy thoughts about the fortitude of his dear Robin.

Meantime there was a task waiting for him which he understood. On November 8 the sittings of the army council were suspended, and the agitators sent back to their regiments. He knew that he had incurred the deep hostility of the Levellers, since he had foiled their plans, and the odium attaching to him for his long negotiations with Charles was increased by the news of Charles's flight. There were plots to murder him in his bed, and Marten and Rainsborough talked of impeachment. No more than Charles did he trouble himself over his personal risk, but he was gravely concerned with the condition of the army, which was in danger of becoming an armed mob. On the 15th at Corkbush field, near Ware, there was a review by Fairfax, the whole force having been divided into three brigades for the purpose, of which this was the first. Fairfax in general orders had already insisted on the importance of maintaining discipline, and had promised to support the soldiers in their just demands, and to work for the reform of the House of Commons on the lines which Oliver had accepted at Putney. In return he asked for a written pledge of adhesion to the army council and himself. On the 15th there was no trouble with most of the regiments, but Harrison's and Robert Lilburne's appeared on the field with copies of the 'Agreement of the People' stuck in their hats, shouting for England's freedom and soldiers' rights. Both had driven away most of their officers. The former was easily induced by Fairfax to submit, but the latter proved contumacious till Oliver laid hands upon it. He heard that they meant to seize him, so he took the offensive. Riding down the ranks with a drawn sword, he bade the men tear the papers from their hats. The sight of the bright steel and the grim face and the memory of what Ironside had done cowed the mutineers. They did as they were bid and pled for mercy. Three of the ringleaders were condemned by a court-martial to death and, after dicing for their lives, one was shot. Four days later Oliver announced in parliament that the army was at peace.

There followed six months of public diplomacy which was manifestly futile, and of underground intrigues which at odd moments came, like moles, to the surface. Charles from Carisbrooke at once began his policy of putting himself up to auction. He wrote to parliament offering the establishment of presbytery for three years, after which the divines would be consulted as to a final settlement, which must be a modified episcopacy. During these three years there should be complete toleration for all forms of worship. He was prepared to surrender the militia for his own life, provided that the control of it should return to his successors. By way of a sop to the army he advised the Houses to consider favourably the soldiers' demands anent parliamentary reform. Finally he asked that he should be admitted to a personal treaty with the Houses in London. To the army chiefs he sent the same proposal.

But the question was no longer one of paper terms. Both parliament and army in view of recent events had come to distrust profoundly the king's honour. Ugly rumours were current of secret dealings with the Scottish commissioners, and of plans to escape from Carisbrooke. Ireton was driven to extend his distrust of the House of Commons to the king. About the middle of the month he was heard to declare that he hoped that any peace that might be made would be such as would permit him with a clear conscience to fight against both. His suspicion was soon to receive dramatic confirmation. There was word of a secret letter from Charles to the queen, and one night he and Oliver, disguised as troopers, sat drinking in the tap-room of the Blue Boar inn in Holborn. The messenger arrived and, while he was refreshing himself, the two generals ripped up his saddle and found the letter. Of its contents all we know is that it revealed Charles's leaning to the Scots and his intention to keep no promises made under duress 'whenever he had power enough to break them.' [1]

In such an atmosphere the army could only return a curt answer to the king, while parliament prepared an ultimatum which he was required to accept before negotiations could go further. This ultimatum contained four terms, borrowed from the Newcastle Propositions; the militia was to be under parlia-

---

[1] The story, which there is every reason to believe, comes from Lord Broghill, afterwards Earl of Orrery, who was on intimate terms with Oliver. See Morrice's life prefixed to his edition of *A Collection of State Letters by Roger Boyle, first Earl of Orrery* (1742); Gardiner, *Civil War*, IV, 27–30.

ment for twenty years, and thereafter the Crown should only control it with the assent of the Houses; the present parliament was to be allowed to adjourn itself to any place it pleased.[1] The terms were put forward primarily as a test of the royal sincerity, for, once accepted, they would preclude any coercion of parliament. The propositions were turned into bills, passed in their Houses through all their stages, and presented to the king on December 24th.

But now Charles had other fish to fry. The Scots commissioners were at Carisbrooke, and three days later he signed with them the secret treaty known as the Engagement. Under it he agreed to confirm the Covenant by act of parliament, though it was not to be made compulsory, to establish presbytery for three years, and in the meantime to suppress the independents and other sects. In return he was to have control of the militia, the army was to be disbanded, the present parliament was to be dissolved, and if necessary a Scots force was to be sent into England to replace him on the throne.[2] No clearer proof could be desired of Charles's duplicity, for a month before he had proposed religious toleration to parliament and now he was covenanting with the Scots for its opposite. Next day he rejected the four bills and set about preparing his escape to France. But he was too late. On the news of his refusal his guards were doubled and Carisbrooke became a prison.

Oliver had come to a decision. He was still a monarchist, but Charles was impossible as king. In his revulsion he blamed himself for going too far on the path of conciliation. If we are to believe Berkeley [3] he told his brother-officers that 'the glories of this world had so dazzled his eyes that he could not discern clearly the great works the Lord was doing; that he was resolved to humble himself, and desired the prayers of the saints, that God would be pleased to forgive his self-seeking.' This was the manner of speech he used whenever he acknowledged a mistake. If the Throne was to be preserved, it must find another occupant, and his mind turned to the Prince of Wales and the Duke of York. Charles must be set aside, and when the king's answer to the four bills was debated in parliament on January 3 he supported, along with Ireton, the proposal for his impeachment in order that he might be deposed.[4] When the Commons passed the 'no addresses' resolution, cut-

---

[1] Gardiner, *Const. Docs.*, 335–47.   [2] *Ibid.*, 347–53.
[3] *Memoirs*, 75.   [4] Walker, *History of Independency*, 74.

ting off all further negotiations with the king, the motion which
he had opposed when Martin brought it forward four months
earlier, he spoke strongly in its favour, and described Charles in
the Harrison vein as 'an obstinate man whose heart God had
hardened.' Probably the rumour of the king's perfidy about
toleration and his surrender to the Scots (for it is clear that the
terms of the Engagement soon leaked out) were the things that
determined his change of view. Like all Oliver's changes, it
was slow in coming but decisive when it came. He bent himself
to unite the army and parliament, and he rejoiced when the
latter unanimously abolished the Committee of Both Kingdoms
and put the management of affairs into the hand of the purely
English Committee of Derby house. He wrote to Hammond,
urging him to search out any 'juggling' at Carisbrooke, and
especially Scots intrigues.[1] But, as always with Oliver's mental
conflicts, this one left its marks on his body. Early in 1648 he
fell dangerously ill, and for a little believed that he had received
his death sentence. 'It's a blessed thing to die daily,' he wrote
to Fairfax, 'for what is there in this world to be accounted
of.'[2]

Not much at the moment certainly, for to his eyes the skies
must have seemed very dark. The faith of even the staunchest
was failing. There was some light indeed on the far horizon,
had he had eyes to see it. His cherished creed of spiritual liberty was not supported by the sectaries only, for in the previous
year a great royalist divine, Jeremy Taylor, had published his
Liberty of Prophesying, which went very far on the same road.
But the first fine ardour was flagging among the reformers,
and there was no longer a single purpose. One half of the army
was preaching anarchy, and perhaps a quarter was huzzaing
for Charles. Honest men, who had an eye to the instant needs
of the nation, were being shouted down and written down
by noisy sciolists — John Lilburne with his republicanism on
one side, and William Prynne with his pedantic conservatism
on the other.[3] The nation was as sick of constitutional argument as it had ever been of war, and in its craving for order it
was turning back to the old ways.

In the war the solitary royalist news-sheet, the *Mercurius
Aulicus*, had been issued in Oxford; but now the king's press

[1] *L. and S.*, I, 290.   [2] *Ibid.*, 295.
[3] Cp., *e.g.* Prynne's *The Levellers Levelled* (Th.), with its defence of the House of
Lords.

came boldly to London, and royalist pamphlets and news-sheets circulated everywhere — a bevy of *Mercuries*, *Melancholici* and *Pragmatici* and *Elenctici*.[1] The mobs in London and the provinces were for the king, and on Christmas day 1647, there were serious riots. In January Fairfax had to send an armed force to occupy Whitehall for the protection of parliament. Stage-plays were starting again, with crowded audiences. Cavalier and presbyterian were coming together owing to their common fear of the independents. The anniversary of the king's accession was celebrated in London with more bonfires than had been seen for thirty years. Worse still, a sentimental royalism was growing which might soon sway the popular mind. Charles among the seagulls of the Isle of Wight was a far more attractive figure than Charles ranging England with Rupert and Goring. The thought of his losses and disappointments and his fall from his high estate, the stories of his gentleness and piety, easily misled those who had no knowledge of his maddening duplicity. Already three-fourths of the men and most of the women of England were seeing in the Carisbrooke prisoner a type of suffering innocence, whom it was not blasphemous to liken to Christ.

> Causeless they like a bird have chased me;
> Behold, O Lord, look down from Heaven and see,
> Thou that hearest prisoners' prayers, hear me!
> Never was grief like mine.[2]

A second war was inevitable, and Oliver realized that, in face of the apathy and hostility of the nation at large, it was necessary that army and parliament should be united. The army was a simple task. There was an amnesty for insubordinate officers, and the quarrel between himself and Rainsborough was patched up. In the House he did his best to conciliate the presbyterians, and he also strove to come to better terms with the city of London. The news of the outbreak in South Wales, and the more alarming tidings which came at the end of April of a Scottish army preparing to cross the Border, were cogent arguments for unity. The spirit of nationalism awoke in the House at this threat of alien dictation. Oliver still held by monarchy, though he was daily becoming

---

[1] For the journalistic activities of that time see W. M. Clyde, 'Parliament and the Press': *Transactions of the Bibliographical Society*, March and June, 1933.

[2] An imitation of George Herbert's 'Sacrifice.'

more bitter against Charles, for, as always, he wished a settlement to be accompanied by the minimum of change. On the
question of a republic he differed not only from Ludlow and
Marten, but from his bosom friend, the younger Vane. He
gave a dinner to the theorists, and afterwards the old barren
question was argued in the old barren way. Ludlow complained that Oliver and Ireton 'kept themselves in the clouds,
and would not declare their judgments either for a monarchical,
aristocratical or democratical government, maintaining that
any of them might be good in themselves, or for us, according as
Providence should direct us.' It was the secular dispute between the practical opportunist and the impractical doctrinaire, and there was no hope of agreement. The debate ended
with Oliver flinging a cushion at his antagonist, and being
pelted in return by Ludlow as he ran downstairs.[1]

But before war began again, he got his will. The House of
Commons by a large majority agreed not to alter the fundamental governance of England by king, Lords, and Commons,
though significantly there was no word as to who the king
should be. In religion there was to be a presbyterian settlement.
Oliver's mind was now for the moment at ease about parliament, and he was satisfied with the condition of the army. In
recent months all local and superfluous troops had been disbanded. Most of the veteran officers had been retained by the
system of reducing the strengths of the troops in the cavalry
and of the regiments in the infantry, but increasing the number
of regiments both of horse and of foot — the first hint of the
modern system of weak cadres which in a crisis can be readily
enlarged. Having seen that the powder was dry, he turned to
the other side which, to borrow from the saying attributed to
him by tradition, we may call trust in God. On April 29 he attended a great prayer-meeting at army headquarters.

That Windsor meeting was for Oliver politic as well as de-
votional, for there he made his peace with the hotheads. He
and his brother officers humbled themselves before the Lord,
and strove to discover what were their sins and imperfections
which had led to the heavy judgment of a new war. For three
days, with preaching and prayer and copious tears, they
examined themselves. In this solemn inquisition Oliver was
the leader. Major Goffe began with the text from Proverbs,
'Turn you at my reproof; behold, I will pour out my spirit upon

[1] Ludlow, I, 184-85.

you, I will make known my words unto you,' and their searching of heart revealed that their sin had been too much reliance
upon carnal wisdom in an effort to make terms with the king,
and an ignoring of the plain providences of God. In the end
they came to two firm conclusions. 'We are led,' says the narrative of one of them, 'to a clear agreement amongst ourselves,
not any dissenting, that it was the duty of our day, with the
forces we had, to go out and fight against those potent enemies,
which that year in all places appeared against us, with an
humble confidence, in the name of the Lord only, that we
should destroy them. And we were also enabled then, after
serious seeking His face, to come to a very clear and joint resolution... that it was our duty, if ever the Lord brought us back
again in peace, to call Charles Stuart, that man of blood, to
an account for that blood he had shed, and mischief he had
done to his utmost, against the Lord's cause and people in
these poor nations.' [1]

The gage had been thrown for battle. With the first resolution Oliver heartily agreed; from the second he did not dissent,
since all his political views, which he had laboriously hammered out with Ireton, were again in the melting pot. His illness of the spring, following upon the mental perturbation of
the autumn, had left him with tense nerves and a mind now
moved to a stern exaltation and now sunk in the slough of
despond. For the past year he had steered a difficult course,
which to most men seemed a miracle of inconstancy. He had
been first for parliament against the army, and then for the
army against parliament. He had gone to the utmost lengths to
obtain an agreement with Charles, so that extremists like Wildman could declare that he had prostituted 'the estates, liberties
and persons of all the people at the foot of the King's lordly
interests.' [2] He had won for himself the unhesitating distrust
of royalists, presbyterians, and republicans. To reasonable
people like Hyde he seemed to be a man with a single purpose
of overmastering personal ambition, to further which he was
prepared to snatch at any means however crooked and shameless. He was looked askance at by old friends like Vane, and
suspected by colleagues like Haselrig. 'If you prove not an
honest man,' said the latter, 'I will never trust a fellow with a

---

[1] Adjutant-General Allen's pamphlet (published in 1659) is in *Somers Tracts*, VI,
499–501, and in *L. and S.*, I, 307–10.
[2] *Putney Projects or The Old Serpent in a New Form*, 1647, (Th.).

great nose for your sake.' With a large part of the nation the name of Cromwell replaced that of Machiavelli as a synonym for a dissembler.

He was well aware of the discredit into which he had fallen, but he did not answer the attacks; that was never his way. 'I know,' he told a friend, 'God has been above all ill repute, and will in His own time vindicate me.' The truth was almost the opposite of the common belief; his trouble was that he no longer had a fixed purpose. All the marks by which he had steered had been destroyed. He certainly had not the pole-star of personal ambition. One of Charles's reasons for distrusting him was that he appeared to want nothing for himself. His much quoted reply to the French envoy Bellièvre, 'No one rises so high as he who knows not whither he is going,' [1] which made De Retz think him a fool, was merely an epigrammatic form of that cautious, provident realism which was his working philosophy. For an ambitious man he played his cards wondrous ill. He was content to negotiate a marriage for his eldest son with the daughter of a small country squire.[2] He showed no haste to be rich, and when in March parliament settled on him an estate with a rental of £1700, he offered £1000 a year for the expenses of the Irish war.

It was a time of profound unhappiness. From this date began for him a period of bodily and spiritual maladjustment, which in certain natures falls in the middle season of life. Once again he was *valde melancholicus*, as he had been in his young days at Huntingdon. A line in one of the many pasquinades of the year was not without its truth —

Madnesse mixt with melancholy.[3]

The happy unquestioning activity of the campaigns had gone, and he found himself stumbling in a dark land where he had neither chart nor star. He was perplexed with the kind of doubts which he had lamented at the Windsor prayer-meeting — whether his worldly common sense had not been a forsaking of the 'simplicity of Christ,' whether he had not come near the sin of Meroz. He was aware that he had used arguments and consented to expedients which his conscience had questioned, and that daily he had been crushing down fears which might

[1] De Retz, *Mémoires*, III, 242.   [2] *L. and S.*, I, 292, 300.
[3] *Mercurius Bellicus*, May 30–June 6, 1648 (Th.).

have been sent as warnings from Heaven. He could tell Fairfax, 'I find this only good, to love the Lord and His poor despised people,' but he knew in his soul that he had no longer this forthright faith and the old unbroken communion. The bloom had gone from his spiritual life.

Chapter III

THE RENEWAL OF WAR
(1648)

A purpose wedded to plans may easily suffer shipwreck; but an unfettered purpose, that moulds circumstances as they arise, masters us, and is terrible. Character melts to it like metal in its steady purpose. The projector of plots is but a miserable gambler and votary of chances. Of a far higher quality is the will that can subdue itself to wait and lay no petty traps for opportunity.

GEORGE MEREDITH, *Evan Harrington*.

I

IF Oliver's spirit was disordered, his mind had acquired a wider scope and stronger powers. The mental toil of the past year had given an edge to what had hitherto been a massive but blunt intelligence. When he resumed the business of war, it was not as one under authority but as an independent commander, who had to direct not one element of a battle but a whole campaign. He is no longer only the incomparable trainer and leader of cavalry, the man with an eye for a turning-point of a fight, the executor of other men's schemes, but the general who must take all England into his survey and plan his operations with a view to the moral as well as the physical victory which the crisis demanded. He is a soldier now on the grand scale, strategist as well as tactician, statesman as well as fighting man, and it is by this new phase of his military career that his place is to be adjudged in the hierarchy of the great captains.

What is called the second Civil War was, in England, strictly a royalist revolt. Most of the king's officers in the earlier struggle had given their parole not to take up arms again against parliament, and some of the best of them, like old Lord Astley, refused to break their pledged word, and stood aside. The rising depended upon local bodies of irreconcilable cavaliers, and upon ex-commanders of the parliament forces who had some personal grievance as to dismissal and disbandment: its leaders based their hopes on the widely spread crypto-royalism of the nation, the very general discontent with parliament, and the prevalent fear of a military tyranny. The danger would have been greater if Fairfax had not at the close of the first struggle most wisely dismantled or weakened most of the fortresses, with a view to saving the expense of garrisoning them. Had there been more Pembrokes and Colchesters and Pontefracts, he and Oliver might have been fatally entangled in sieges while the Scottish army came south to their destruction.

The outbreak began in South Wales, where the gentry were royalist and the townsmen presbyterian, and all alike were hostile to the army. In February, Poyer, the governor of Pembroke, an alcoholic presbyter, was superseded in his command. He refused to leave, and declared for the king; and next month Laugharne, the general commanding the district, also revolted. His men had grievances about pay and disbandment, and had been affected by the temper of the countryside. The flame spread fast, and presently other castles, Tenby, Chepstow, Carmarthen, were in royalist hands. On May 3 Oliver was dispatched by Fairfax with two regiments of horse and three of foot. But before he arrived Poyer and Laugharne had been soundly beaten on May 8th by Colonel Horton at St. Fagans. The rebel leaders fled to Pembroke, and the campaign relapsed into a slow business of sieges. Ewer stormed Chepstow on May 25th. Tenby surrendered to Horton on the 31st, but Oliver at Pembroke had a more difficult task. The place was too strong to be taken by assault, and its garrison fought as desperate men with the gallows before them. He had no siege train — it was wrecked in the Bristol Channel — so he was compelled to rely on a new type of big mortar; moreover the neighbourhood was hostile, and supplies were hard to come by. It was not till the 11th of July, after six weary weeks, that Pembroke surrendered and Oliver was free to face the storm in the north.

The fire in Wales had burned fiercely, but there was insufficency of dry fuel to keep it going. The same was true of the other sporadic outbreaks in England, but their wide local distribution proved how uncertain was the temper of the nation. In the north the strong places of Berwick and Carlisle were seized by the royalists. Pontefract was surprised by a party of Newark cavaliers disguised as drovers, and Scarborough castle declared for the king. There were outbreaks in Cornwall, in Northamptonshire, and even in those eastern shires which were the puritan stronghold. More serious, the appointment of Rainsborough to the fleet caused a mutiny in the navy in the Downs, and the revolting ships put themselves under the command of Prince Charles, and dominated the Cinque Ports. Most serious of all, Kent, at the very gates of the capital, rose for Charles.

This was towards the end of May, and the situation was desperately critical. Oliver was far away in South Wales, at the slow business of reducing fortresses. Lambert at York had slender forces with which to check the royalist risings and the imminent Scots. Fairfax, much troubled by gout, was in London with the greater part of the army, about to march for the north. He acted with vigour and decision, assembled his troops at Blackheath, and swept eastward. He had some 8000 men against the 12,000 of the insurgents, but the latter were mostly untrained country labourers. They held the line of the Medway, but Fairfax had no difficulty in crossing the river, and on June 1 he took Maidstone and had Kent at his mercy. Meantime the elder Goring, now Earl of Norwich, with a part of the insurgent army, made a bold attempt on London. He found that the citizens would have none of him, but he had better hopes of Essex, so with 500 cavaliers he crossed the Thames, and, being joined by Lord Capel, Sir Charles Lucas and Sir George Lisle, threw himself into the strong place of Colchester. He had performed a notable strategic feat in pinning down Fairfax to the south-east of England, the more as there was presently a rising in Surrey under Lord Holland and the young Duke of Buckingham, and the mutinous ships were hanging about the mouth of the Thames. Colchester did not fall till August 27th, and on July 8 the Scots army crossed the Border with only Lambert's scattered levies between them and the capital.

The defence of the north therefore fell to Oliver, who three days later finished his task at Pembroke. He had done it competently, and his letters show how clear was his view of the situation and how firm his handling of the most minor operations.[1] They also show him consumed again with a crusading fervour, and looking for guidance to dispensations and not to fine-spun arguments. 'I pray God,' he wrote to Fairfax, 'teach this nation, and those that are over us, and your Excellency and all that are under you, what the mind of God may be in all this, and what our duty is. Surely it is not that the poor godly people of this kingdom should still be made the object of wrath and anger, nor that our God would have our necks under the

[1] See especially *L. and S.*, I, 315, etc.

yoke of bondage; for these things that have lately come to pass have been the wonderful works of God; breaking the rod of the oppressor as in the day of Midian, not with garments much rolled in blood but by the terror of the Lord; who will yet save this people and confound His enemies, as in that day.' [1]

II

Strange ferments had been at work in the witch's cauldron beyond Tweed. The Engagement made with Charles at Carisbrooke the previous year was now bearing fruit. Hamilton had formed a party of those in Scotland who accepted those two incompatibles, the king and the Solemn League, who feared the army and hated the sectaries. The Engagers dominated the Estates when they assembled in March, and were authorized to raise an army to deliver Charles from that captivity into which a year before they had sold him. They at once entered into negotiations with the Prince of Wales in Paris, but would have nothing to do with the exiled Montrose. On May 3 a summary demand was made to the English parliament for the restoration of the king, the disbandment of the army, the enforcement of the Covenant, and the suppression of all forms of worship save presbytery.

Matters had already come to the breach. A united Scotland could probably at the moment have dictated to a distracted England, but Scotland was sharply divided. Argyll went into opposition, and with him many of the Covenant lords, Eglinton, Elcho, Cassilis, Balmerino, and presently Loudoun the chancellor. Most of the ministers followed Argyll, for, though they hated the sectaries, they were in terror of the king, and there was an armed rising in Ayrshire in May which Middleton suppressed with difficulty. The one bond among the Engagers was the old Scottish crypto-royalism and an intense dislike of the English government. This bitter nationalism, which gave them a shadow of coherence, did something also to unite England, or at any rate to immobilize forces which might have otherwise been sympathetic. 'If we must have a government,' said Henry Marten, 'we had better have this King and oblige him, than to have him obtruded on us by the Scots.' [2] John Lilburne was ready to come to terms with Oliver, 'lending a hand to help him up again, as not loving a Scotch inter-

[1] See especially *L. and S.*, I, 321.　　　[2] *Hamilton Papers*, 170.

est.[1] The English royalists, however strong their ill-will to parliament, could have small love for those truculent northern allies who accepted only one article of their creed; 'so many monstrous concessions that, except the whole Kingdom of England had been likewise imprisoned in Carisbrooke castle with the King, it could not be imagined that it was possible to be performed.'[2]

Hamilton, the generalissimo, was a man without military talent, and his character was shallow and tortuous. He had no moral authority, and was dictated to by Callander, his second-in-command, who was a martinet and little more. Middleton was a better soldier, and with the foot was Baillie, Montrose's old antagonist, who at any rate knew something of the art of war. David Leslie, the ablest soldier then in Scotland, was on the side of Argyll. Leven's old army had been long ago disbanded, and most of the best fighting stuff in officers and men refused to brave the ban of the Kirk. Hamilton could only recruit the rawest troops, and that by the methods of the press-gang.[3] The finest infantry in Britain at the time, the Highlanders with whom Montrose had 'conquered, were beyond his reach. It was a slow business filling up the regiments, and a slower getting ready an artillery train. He had no money, and his supply organization was embryonic. He was leaving behind him a country so hostile that his brother Lanark, not without reason, urged him first to deal with Argyll and the ministers before crossing the Border.[4]

Yet had Hamilton been a different man, had he had one tithe of the speed and genius of Montrose, he might have altered the course of history. For at midsummer he had a supreme chance, which with each hour of delay grew weaker till it altogether departed. Fairfax was pinned down at Colchester, and Oliver at Pembroke. Holland was about to rise in Surrey; the fleet was mainly for the king; London was largely royalist. Carlisle and Berwick, the two keys of the Border, as well as Scarborough and Pontefract, were in royalist hands. Parliament seemed to be divided in opinion as to whether the invading Scots were friends or enemies, and from it no vigorous action could be expected. Had Hamilton struck before the end of June, he might well have swept Lambert from his path, united the

---

[1] *The Legal Fundamental Liberties*, 32 (Th.).   [2] Clarendon, *Hist.*, X, 167.
[3] See Sir James Turner, *Memoirs*, 53, 55.
[4] Burnet, *Mem. of the Hamiltons*, 351.

royalists of the north, and, with Pontefract as a base, advanced upon a distracted south, compelling Fairfax to leave Colchester untaken and Oliver Pembroke, and confronting with a strong field army the weary and widely separated forces of parliament. Such would without doubt have been Montrose's strategy, had he been in command, and the odds are that it would have succeeded. Even the dissensions in Scotland would not have nullified a resounding victory in the English midlands.

But Hamilton tarried, and meanwhile Lambert, the young general of twenty-nine, made gallant efforts to close the northern door. He had under him three or four regiments of regular cavalry, and he set himself to recruit troops in Yorkshire and Lancashire, which were for the most part poor stuff. His problem was intricate. The barrier of the Cheviots must force a Scottish invasion to take the road at either end, by Berwick and Newcastle, or by Carlisle and the western shires. The first route was made difficult by Newcastle, held by Haselrig for parliament, and by York, but it was the direct road to Pontefract and the shortest path to London. If Hamilton came that way, it was for Lambert to hinder him in Northumberland till he got reinforcements. If he took the western road — which was probable in view of the strong royalist feeling in Westmorland and the presence there of Sir Marmaduke Langdale with some 4000 local levies — then the problem arose of his route after he had passed Carlisle. The Pennine range, the watershed of northern England, ran at right angles from the western end of the Cheviots, and in its length of one hundred and twenty miles was pierced by few roads. One followed the line of Hadrian's wall, one ran by Settle and Skipton from Lancaster to York, and a third in the south led from Rochdale to Leeds. But there were various practicable hill passes which could be traversed by troops, by Brough moor from Appleby to Barnard castle, by the springs of Lune, and by the upper Ribble. It was Lambert's business to hold this lateral barrier and keep the invaders out of Yorkshire by pinning them to the alley between the Pennines and the sea.

Lambert did his work brilliantly, but in Sir Marmaduke Langdale, who acted as the advance guard of the Scots, he found a capable opponent. That lean, solemn and irascible catholic was no inconsiderable soldier, and he and his troops had an intimate knowledge of the countryside. His object was to recruit men and collect supplies and to keep the road open for

Hamilton, so he avoided a field action. Early in June Lambert crossed the Pennines, took Appleby and Penrith, and drove Langdale back to the shelter of Carlisle. On the last day of the month one of his detachments, under Robert Lilburne, won a useful victory on the Coquet and cleared Northumberland of royalist troops. But on 8th July Hamilton crossed the Border, and Lambert was obliged to retire before his superior numbers. Hamilton had written to him declaring that his quarrel was only with the parliament, and that he meant no harm to Lambert or to the kingdom, and Lambert had replied that the parliament was no concern of his, but that since the duke had come 'in a hostile way into England, he would oppose him to the utmost, and fight him and his army as traitors and enemies to the kingdom upon all opportunities.' [1] The war had become a contest not of sects and parties but of nations.

Hamilton had over 10,000 men, Langdale had the better part of 4000, and any hour Sir George Monro was expected from Ulster with 3000 Scottish veterans. Lambert with less than 5000 horse was compelled to retire through the Brough pass to Bowes and Barnard castle. Hamilton moved slowly — naturally, since he was waiting for Monro and further Scottish levies — and there was constant quarrelling in his command. Langdale, who was for instant action, was allowed to act independently as an advanced guard. When Hamilton reached Kendal on August 2, he threw out scouting parties which pushed past Dent on the road to Wensleydale. This turned Lambert's position on the Tees, so he fell back on Richmond, and then to Knaresborough, to cover Pontefract and await help from the south. He was convinced that Hamilton meant to cross the watershed from Ribble to Aire and take the road through Yorkshire.

Meantime there was marching to his aid one who was as swift as Hamilton was slow. On July 11 Pembroke surrendered and on the 14th Oliver set out for the north, having sent on most of his horse ahead. His infantry were shoeless and ragged, and the second half of July was one long deluge of rain. But by the 31st he was at Warwick, and on August 5 he was at Nottingham, where his troops received shoes from Northampton and stockings from Coventry. He reached Doncaster on August 8th, where his men were paid, and rested for three days to await the artillery train from Hull. He had marched two hundred and fifty miles in twenty-six days through a difficult country in foul weather, and he was six days ahead of the time he had allotted. Near Knaresborough, on Saturday, August 12, he found touch with Lambert.[1]

At Kendal Hamilton was joined by Munro, but the Ulster commander was in a difficult mood. He refused to serve under Callander and Baillie, and Callander would not consent to his having an independent command. There was trouble too with some of the English royalists under Sir Philip Musgrave, so the best that Hamilton could do was to make a strong rear-guard of Musgrave's horse and Monro's veterans, a foolish squandering of the best fighting stuff in his army. He advanced with the main body to Hornby, where Langdale, who had been acting as flank guard among the hills, appeared with news of the parliament concentration in Yorkshire. He seems to have heard a rumour that Oliver had arrived:[2] but he did not make the significance of the news clear to his colleagues.[3] Hamilton behaved as if his great antagonist were still two hundred miles away. The council of war at Hornby debated whether to cross the watershed into Yorkshire or to continue down the Lancashire couloir. Middleton and Turner were for the former, Callander had no decided view, and Hamilton and Baillie were for Lancashire, apparently in the hope of getting support from the town of Manchester and from Lord Byron. The duke's view prevailed, and on the 13th the long line of the invasion began to straggle southwards. It numbered well over 20,000 men; some 15,000 under Hamilton and Callander, 3000 under Langdale, and the better part of 5000 foot and horse with Monro and Musgrave.

On the evening of the 16th Hamilton had reached Preston and the north bank of the Ribble. Callander and Middleton with the bulk of the Scottish horse were south of the river, strung along the fifteen miles of the road to Wigan. Monro and Musgrave were a day's march behind. Langdale, who had

[1] Oliver's march against the Scots is sometimes taken as an example of the strategy of 'indirect approach.' He was to use this effectively later, but this was not an instance of it. It is clear that he took the road he did, partly because he had to get supplies in the midlands and artillery from Hull, and partly because he believed that he would meet the Scots in Yorkshire. He must have got his intelligence from Lambert, and in early August Lambert expected Hamilton to cross the Pennines. (Gardiner, *Civil War*, IV, 180 n.) It was not till August 13 that Hamilton's council of war decided to continue through Lancashire. Cf. the evidence of Langdale (*Civil War Tracts of Lancashire*, 267) and of Sir James Turner (*Memoirs*, 62).

[2] *Fairfax Correspondence*, II, 60.   [3] Turner, *Memoirs*, 63.

ceased to be an advance guard, was acting as a flanking force to the east in the Ribble valley. The Scots army was still under the delusion of security. Langdale, who was best placed to get information, had rumours in plenty of the enemy advancing from the east, but they seem to have been so indefinite that they carried no conviction to his superiors, who set down the movements as demonstrations by the Lancashire militia. Clearly no one, not even Langdale, can have believed that Oliver was upon them.

Yet that night he was only a few miles off. On the 13th he set out to cross the hills, leaving his artillery train behind him. He had a total of 8600 men, including 2500 of his veteran horse and about 4000 of his veteran foot.[1] He had no precise strategic plan; his business was to defeat Hamilton without delay, for he dreaded what might happen should the latter join hands with Byron and the rebels, actual and potential, in North Wales and the midlands. His lack of accurate intelligence compelled him to draw the bow at a venture. He did not yet know the road that the enemy meant to take; but if it was towards Yorkshire he would meet him and fight him somewhere in Craven, and if by the Lancashire alley, he would cut in on his flank. On the night of Monday the 14th, he was at Skipton, and next night at Gisburn in the Ribble valley, where his scouts probably brought him news of the decision taken at Hornby, and of Hamilton's van at Preston. On the 16th he was at the bridge which spanned the Hodder just above its junction with the Ribble. Here he had an important strategic decision to make. Should he cross and take the north bank of the river to Preston, or should he make a detour to the south by Whalley, so as to place himself between the invaders and the midlands. He chose the first course, for it was his principal aim to make Hamilton fight, and he believed that the duke would stand his ground at Preston in order to wait for Monro. But he had another and a weightier reason. If he met Hamilton squarely, attacking from the south, and defeated him, he would only drive him back upon his supports, and leave him still to make mischief in Scotland and north-east England. But if he could force the main Scots army southward, away from its reserves, he might annihilate it, and remove for ever that root of bitterness.[2] So he marched

---

[1] *L. and S.*, I, 343.

[2] 'Upon deliberate advice we chose rather to put ourselves between their army and Scotland.' *L. and S.*, II, 215.

down the north bank of Ribble, and that night lay in Stonyhurst park, nine miles from Preston, and perhaps three from Langdale's outposts.

Next morning, Thursday, August 17th, was 'St. Covenant's day,' the anniversary of the signing of the Solemn League, which had created most of the trouble. Hamilton had just given directions to Baillie with the foot to cross the Ribble on the march to Wigan, when news arrived that Langdale was being furiously attacked. The duke, believing that the enemy was only Assheton or some minor parliament leader or being overborne by Callander, did not stop Baillie, but contented himself with retaining two infantry brigades and some 1500 horse to protect the town.

By this time Oliver was more precisely informed about the situation. He knew that Monro was not with Hamilton; he knew that the Scottish van was far south of the Ribble; he realized that his first business was to bring Hamilton's centre to action. Langdale with 3000 foot and 600 horse was drawn up to cover Preston on the east, among a nest of small fenced fields and enclosures. He was out numbered by two to one, he was in the dangerous position of having his front parallel to his communications, and he had no reserves except the small force left behind by Hamilton in Preston. Early on the Thursday morning, Oliver attacked from Ribble Moor, drove in his outposts, and came up against his foot lining the hedges. There was a lane running from the moor to the town, and at the entrance to it he posted his own and Harrison's regiments of horse. Then, strengthening his right so as to outflank Langdale and prevent his withdrawal northwards, he proceeded to clear the enclosures.

It was a repetition of Second Newbury, but now he had the most veteran soldiers in Europe for the task. For four hours Langdale stood his ground heroically — one of the finest feats of arms in the war — but in the end he was driven back into the town, with Oliver's horse at his heels. Hamilton's two infantry brigades which he had left there shared in the rout. The duke himself, who never lacked personal courage, made an attempt to check the pursuit with his handful of horse, but Oliver had possessed himself of the Ribble bridge, and there was nothing to do but fly. Hamilton and a few of his officers swam the river, and Oliver's cavalry pressed the pursuit till they had taken also the bridge over the Darwen. Langdale's foot were annihilated, and the remnant of his horse fled north to Monro.

The rearguard in Preston was gone. A thousand men were dead and Oliver had 4000 prisoners. He had driven an iron wedge into splintering timber, and the invading army was cut in two.

All day it had rained in torrents, and Friday the 18th opened in a downpour. Hamilton, south of the Darwen, had lost all grip of the situation. He had still forces superior to Oliver's in number, six or seven thousand foot with him, besides Middleton's horse and Baillie's vanguard at Wigan. But the council which met in the dripping night was without heart or purpose. Baillie was for making a stand, but Callander was for a further retreat, and Hamilton as usual followed Callander. The foot straggled southward in the dark, and Middleton, who had been sent for, was given unintelligible instructions and missed them on the road. He found only the ashes of their camp-fires, and, pressing the pursuit, Oliver with 3000 foot and 2500 horse.

Oliver realized that his task was only half done, and that he must sweep up with all speed the disjointed members of the invading army. Hamilton had relinquished his train, including most of his ammunition, his men having only what they could carry in their flasks. Assheton was left to hold Preston with the Lancashire militia, his orders being to put his prisoners to the sword if he was attacked by Monro. A possible line of retreat by way of Whalley was strongly guarded, and Oliver pushed on after the main enemy body. Middleton's horse did well as a rearguard, and Wigan was safely reached by the fugitives on the evening of the 18th. There it was at first proposed to make a stand, but the Scots were to a man drenched and famished, and they had little powder, so, when the sky cleared in the night and the moon rose, Hamilton ordered a further retreat to Warrington, hoping to put the Mersey between him and his enemy. The edge, too, was a little taken from the pursuit, for the parliament troops were also wet and weary. They had lost Colonel Thornhaugh, and Middleton and Turner were adroit rearguard skirmishers.

On Saturday morning, the 19th, the Scottish foot made its last stand at Winwick, three miles from Warrington. They resisted for several hours till, with a loss of 1000 killed and 2000 prisoners, they were beaten from the field. After that nothing remained but the mopping up of jaded fugitives by pursuers who were scarcely less jaded. 'If I had a thousand horse,' Oliver wrote, 'that could but trot thirty miles, I should not doubt but to give a very good account of them, but truly we are so harassed and haggled out in this business that we are not able to do more than walk at an easy pace after them.'[1] Hamilton gave Baillie and his foot leave to surrender, and Oliver, knowing the difficulty of the Mersey crossing at Warrington, offered fair terms. Hamilton with 3000 horse moved into Cheshire, hoping to join Byron, but Lambert with four regiments was in pursuit, and the countryside, even the gentry, was rising against him. He drifted into Staffordshire, apparently aiming at Pontefract, but on the 25th at Uttoxeter he was forced to surrender to Lambert. Middleton and Langdale were taken with him, and Callander alone escaped. Meanwhile Oliver had turned north to deal with Monro, but Monro did not await him. In spite of the protests of Sir Philip Musgrave, he made his best speed across the Border.

Preston was thus far Oliver's most overwhelming victory, and it marks a new stage in his mastery of the art of war. He was for the first time in sole command of a major campaign and he made no single false step. It is unnecessary to read undue subtleties into his strategy. The subtlety was rather with Lambert, who in the weeks before Oliver's arrival used the physical configuration of the western defile to brilliant purpose, not attempting a frontal defence, but perpetually threatening the invaders' communications from behind the flanking mountains Oliver marched into Yorkshire because he believed that he would meet Hamilton there; his dash through Craven and down Ribble was not intended as a flank attack to pierce the line of advance, for he knew little of Hamilton's dispositions till he was within a few miles of him. The poverty of his intelligence department compelled him to improvise his strategy. It is also true that he was opposed to a general who lacked the rudiments of military capacity, and who squandered idly his many assets, and that his veteran troops were better fighting material than even Langdale's north of England men, and infinitely better than the half-hearted Scottish levies. But these facts scarcely detract from the splendour of Oliver's positive achievement. He succeeded, by attacking a superior force in detail, in fighting always at a numerical advantage. His tactical dispositions were masterly, as in his assault on Langdale, where it was essential to get the business quickly over. And he made one bold and far-sighed strategical decision — when he resolved to cut Hamilton off not from the English midlands but from Scot-·

[1] *L. and S.*, I, 342.

land: for his success meant not only the annihilation of the invader, but the immobilizing, at any rate for a season, of certain perilous forces beyond Tweed.[1]

III

The temper had hardened of that fraction of the people, which, because it was armed and disciplined, controlled the fate of England. In the first Civil War both sides had looked upon their opponents as theoretically traitors, but in practice as mistaken fellow-countrymen who should be leniently dealt with. There was no such tolerance at the close of the second struggle. The army regarded its opponents less as belligerents than as outlaws.[2] The royalist leaders had violated their parole; the ex-parliamentarians who had fought for the king had apostatized;[3] all had broken the peace, and had been the cause of the shedding of blood. This feeling was strong in the ranks, and it was shared by every commander, even by the gentle Fairfax. Two facts increased its strength in the minds of the more thoughtful. They knew the precarious ground on which they walked. Parliament, both Lords and Commons, was hostile to them and for the present was attached only by a slender bond of self-interest; the nation as a whole was apathetic, or unfriendly and suspicious; their natural exasperation was sharpened by an ever-present fear. Again, the Thirty Years War was drawing to a close, and the Continent was on the eve of the Peace of Westphalia. Unless they acted swiftly and decisively, France and Holland would be in a position to give Charles those allies for whom he had so long intrigued. So, when Colchester fell on August 28, there was little mercy shown to its defenders. Sir Charles Lucas and Sir George Lisle

---

[1] The battles from Preston southward offer no point of serious difficulty. Oliver's own account will be found in his letters (*L. and S.*, I, 329–47) and on the parliament side we have also the *Autobiography of Captain John Hodgson* (1882). There is a vivid description of the Scots advance in Sir James Turner's *Memoirs* (1829) and Langdale's narrative is in *Civil War Tracts of Lancashire* (Chetham Soc., 1844). See also Burnet, *Mem. of the Hamiltons* (1677).

[2] As Grant ordered Sheridan to regard those concerned in the fighting in Texas in May 1865, after Lee's surrender.

[3] Cf. Cromwell to the Speaker after the surrender of Pembroke: 'The persons excepted are such as have formerly served you in a very good cause, but, being now apostatized, I did rather make election of them than of those who had always been for the king, judging their iniquity double, for they have sinned against so much light. *L. and S.*, I, 324.

were shot by order of a council of war. These executions were perhaps as legal as anything else in that season of suspended law. Fairfax defended them on two grounds — the satisfaction of military justice, and the need to avenge innocent blood,[1] but the heroic deaths of Lisle and Lucas made a deep mark on the English mind. The peers were left to the sentence of parliament, and Hamilton, Holland and Capel went to the block, while Norwich [2] was only saved by the casting vote of the Speaker. The subordinate officers and the private soldiers were sold as 'redemptioners' to the West Indies, that is to a terminable period of slavery, or as conscripts to the service of the republic of Venice.[3]

Meantime the strained mood in which Oliver had begun the new campaign had not relaxed, and the shadow of the Windsor prayer-meeting was still heavy on his spirit. During the actual operations the need for swift action and for the exercise of his strong intelligence had given him a certain peace. A proof was his mercifulness, for he was always merciful when he was not tormented. At Pembroke he had been gentler to his prisoners than Fairfax at Colchester. Though he had the heartiest dislike of the Scots, and those in England who favoured their invasion — 'This is a more prodigious treason than any that hath been perfected before; because the former quarrel was that Englishmen might rule over one another, this to vassalize us to a foreign nation' [4] — yet after Preston he had not shown himself vindictive. Hamilton, at his trial, bore witness to the generosity of his treatment: 'Indeed he was so very courteous and so very civil as he performed more than he promised, and I must

[1] Rushworth, VII, 1243. The matter is fully discussed in Gardiner, *Civil War*, IV, 205 n., and Markham, *Great Lord Fairfax*, 328, etc.

[2] It is reasonably clear that Hamilton had been captured, and had not surrendered to quarter, and that his execution was therefore not a breach of military justice. Norwich, though a better man than his ruffianly son, was no very elevated character, but, like most people in that age, he could write noble English. Take his letter to Lady Campion after her son's death at Colchester. 'Madam, to offer set comfort upon so inexpressible a loss would be no less indiscretion in me than importunity to you. I shall therefore only beg this one favour of you, for his sake that your Ladyship loved most and I next, that if you can any way find wherein I may sacrifice ought to his memory, at the hazard of all I am or ever may be, your Ladyship shall then see, by the passion with which I shall undertake it, how really I was his, and how sincerely, Madam, your Ladyship's all vowed faithful humble servant,' Lipscomb, *Hist. and Antiquities of County of Buckingham*, I, 87.

[3] Carter, *A Most True Relation... of Colchester* (1650), 203: *The Moderate Intelligencer*. (Th.)

[4] *L. and S.*, I, 387.

acknowledge his favour to those poor wounded gentlemen that I left behind, that were by him taken care of, and truly he did perform more than he did capitulate for.' He was merciful towards the Preston prisoners, letting the pressed men go, and selling only the volunteers to the plantations or foreign service, though he lent himself to the abominable practice of handing over batches of them to private individuals to dispose of for their profit.[1] In some of his letters at this time there is the familiar note of tenderness; he writes to Lord Wharton to congratulate him on the birth of an heir — 'My love to the dear little lady, better to me than the child'; [2] and amid all his distractions he finds time to press upon Fairfax the duty of looking after the family of a dead comrade-in-arms.[3]

But, whenever the guns were silent, his thoughts turned back upon themselves, and he was unhappy, for his mind had no clear prospect. He saw an instant duty, the crushing of the rebellion, but nothing beyond. There was always in him an element of rustic cunning. When an urgent need confronted him, especially a military need, he would fall back upon the arts of the horsedealer, and forget everything but the immediate purpose. In the spring he had used many devices, some of them disingenuous enough, to keep parliament quiet. He had spoken smooth things to both Leveller and presbyterian. 'The chief of these levellers, following him out of the town to take their leave of him, received such professions from him, of a spirit bent to pursue the same just and honest things that they desired, that they went away with great satisfaction, till they heard that a coachful of presbyterian priests coming after them went away no less pleased.' [4] In August the Lords examined a certain Major Huntingdon, formerly one of his friends, who deponed that, in addition to other extreme statements, Oliver had declared to him that it was 'lawful to play the knave with a knave.' [5] He may well have used the words. He had a country licence in his speech, and there were times when he was prepared to flatter fools in their folly, if he thought that such craft would further his purpose.

He was now to give a signal example of this audacious opportunism. The clearing of northern England after Preston was done with his accustomed precision and economy of force. Then he marched to the Border, for he must make sure that for

[1] Cf. L. and S., I, 378.   [2] Ibid., I, 353.   [3] Ibid., I, 356–57.
[4] Hutchinson, II, 126.   [5] L. J., X, 408.

a season at any rate the fires in Scotland were dead. Every step he took in this, his first Scottish visit, was nicely calculated. He sternly repressed any looting by his army, though it was ragged and penniless, and addressed the Covenanting lords in a high strain of devout courtesy. Events north of the Tweed fell out fortunately. Eglinton and Loudoun organized the Whigamore Raid of Ayrshire peasants, and, with the help of Argyll, seized Edinburgh. The Estates capitulated to the Kirk. Argyll and Loudoun welcomed Oliver when he crossed the Border on September 21, and on October 4 he arrived in Edinburgh to find a party in power which execrated Hamilton and repudiated the Engagement. It was agreed that no Engager should hold office, and Lambert was left with three regiments of horse to strengthen Argyll's hands. Carlisle and Berwick were surrendered, and Monro was sent back to Ireland.

His aim was to patch up a peace between his English independents and Scottish presbytery, and he found his task easier than he had hoped. In Argyll and his friends he discovered 'nothing but what becomes Christians and men of honour,'[1] and he wrote to Fairfax that there was hope of a 'very good understanding between the honest party of Scotland and us here, and better than some would have.'[2] He was lavishly entertained, lodged at Moray house in the Canongate, and feasted by old Leven in Edinburgh castle. But he was too shrewd a man not to see the fires grumbling below the surface — the fires of a sentimental royalism and of an intolerant presbytery. David Leslie paid him a perfunctory visit the first morning, and never again came near him.[3] As for the ministers who greeted him, he cannot have been blind to the great gulf between his purpose and theirs. He seems to have talked strangely; told them that he was in favour of monarchical government in the person of the king and his posterity, and that he was not wedded to religious toleration; but he refused to give his own views on church government. He did not greatly impress them: they liked Lambert's 'discreet, humble, ingenuous, sweet and civil deportment,' but not Oliver's. Mr. Robert Blair, who had been a nuisance to Strafford in Ireland and was later to desire to die with Charles on the scaffold, thought him 'an egregious dissembler, a great liar... and a greeting deevil.'[4]

An exact report of those conversations in Moray house

[1] *L. and S.*, I, 371.   [2] *Ibid.*, I, 373.

[3] *Hist., MSS. Comm.* (Lord Braye), 72.   [4] Row, *Life of Blair*, 210, etc.

would be an illuminating document. The truth was that Oliver won nothing in Scotland but the alliance of Argyll, and that was due to the victory of Preston and to Lambert's regiments. He did not scratch the hard shell of Covenanting intolerance. But it is a proof of the confusion in his own soul that he made many disingenuous concessions in his pleading, and that he believed that he had succeeded. If he failed to hoodwink the ministers he succeeded in deceiving himself. This was his justification to his independent critics in England:

> I desire from my heart — I have prayed for — I have waited for this day to see — union and understanding between the godly people — Scots, English, Jews, Gentiles, Presbyterians, Anabaptists, and all. Our brethren of Scotland — sincerely Presbyterians — were our greatest enemies.... Was it not fit to be civil, to profess love, to deal with clearness with them for the removing of prejudices; to ask them what they had against us, and to give them an honest answer? This we have done and no more... and we can say, through God, we have left such a witness amongst them, as, if it were not yet, by reason the poor souls are so wedded to their Church government, yet there is that conviction upon them that will undoubtedly have its fruit in due time.[1]

Little he then understood the rigidity and subtlety of the Scottish presbyterian creed or the intractable spirit of its defenders. Three years later he was to realize that it could not be bent, but only broken.

IV

In the middle of October Oliver re-crossed the Border, and set himself down to the siege of Pontefract, with one eye upon London where parliament was again in treaty with the king. He was in a curious temper, at once exalted, anxious and confused. He had settled the military question, and by his arms and diplomacy had put Scotland temporarily out of action. But he realized how far victories in the field were from solving the problem of his country. His view was that of Milton's sonnet to Fairfax:

> O yet a nobler task awaits thy hand,
> (For what can war but endless war still breed?)
> Till truth and right from violence be freed,
> And public faith cleared from the shameful brand
> Of public fraud. In vain doth valour bleed,
> While avarice and rapine share the land.

[1] Cromwell to Hammond, Nov. 6, 1648. *C. P.*, II, 49.

He could put a name to rapine and avarice — the untamable royalists, the hair-splitting parliamentarians. And one figure, the king, was beginning to fill his unwilling thoughts as the prime begetter of all mischief.

A proof of his perplexity is that in his letters, except when he is reporting a military operation, he has begun to use more copiously the language of Zion.[1] He is always pointing excited morals — after Preston, from Scotland, from Yorkshire. He abases himself before God — 'The best of us are poor weak saints, yet saints; if not sheep, yet lambs, and must be fed' — but he issues his practical commands like pistol-shots. The gist of his moralizing is that in the fog of things the only beacons are the dispensations which God has vouchsafed. 'Surely, sir, this is nothing but the hand of God'; — 'God, who is not to be mocked,... hath taken vengeance on such profanity even to astonishment and admiration'; — 'Give me leave to tell you, I find a sense among the officers concerning such things as the treatment of these men to amazement, which truly is not to see their blood made so cheap as to see such manifest witnessings of God, so terrible and so just, no more reverenced.' Pembroke had been such a witnessing, and Preston and Colchester, and the crumbling of the Hamilton faction in Scotland, and not less the wind which on the last day of August blew the Prince of Wales and his fleet out of the Thames. His concrete mind clung to such providences as rocks in the yeasty tides. A man, he held, might interpret the whisper of his own corrupt heart as a message from Heaven, but actual events, battles won, difficulties surmounted, could not be misconstrued; he forgot that the same fallible human mind which misread a dream might also draw a fantastic moral from a fact. Vane seemed to him too cold on this vital matter, 'I pray he make not too little, nor I too much, of outward dispensations.'[2]

He was in indifferent health, and he was very weary. 'Our rest we expect elsewhere,' he wrote to St. John; 'that will be durable. Care we not for tomorrow, nor for anything.' But a devout apathy was not for him, and he tortured himself with thought. Finally, on November 25 from Pontefract he poured out his soul to his kinsman, Robert Hammond, the king's warder

[1] It should be noted that his constant attribution of his successes to the Lord and his many pious ejaculations were largely conventional, designed to avert the nemesis which follows arrogance, just as people write 'D.V.' or touch wood.

[2] *L. and S.*, I, 350. In his quarrel with Oliver in 1656 Vane referred to this message. See *The Proceeds of the Protector... against Sir Henry Vane*, 1656 (Th.).

in the Isle of Wight.[1] In this extraordinary letter may be found the whole history of his inner life while he was sweeping over northern England like a flame — fragments of Ireton's old philosophy, some of the Levellers' speculations which had been creeping into his mind, his own perplexed musings over Scripture texts.

He begins with his doctrine of providences. Hammond had complained of the difficulties of his task. 'Seek to know the mind of God in all the chain of Providences, whereby God brought thee thither, and that person (the king) to thee,... and then tell me whether there is not some glorious and high meaning in all this, above what thou hast yet attained.... I dare be positive to say it is not that the wicked should be exalted.' Then he sets himself to answer his cousin's conservative scruples — that the powers that be were ordained of God and that these powers in England were king and parliament. It is lawful, he says, to resist such powers if they do wrong, since they are of human institution. The true question therefore is 'whether ours be such a case.' On that point he asks his correspondent to look into his heart, and then he propounds three further questions. Is *salus populi suprema lex* a sound doctrine? Will the proposed treaty between king and parliament secure the safety of the nation, or will it not frustrate the whole purpose of the war? May not the army be itself a lawful authority ordained of God, and therefore entitled in a good cause to oppose both king and parliament? He does not answer these conundrums, but returns to his providences. 'Surely they mean somewhat. They hang so together, have been so constant, clear and unclouded.' It is these providences, and not the logic of fleshly reasoning that must be the guide. God may be tempted as much by diffidence as by over-confidence. He and his army of the north are waiting upon God, striving to construe His dispensations.

The letter has no conclusion. It was not such as Oliver would have written to Vane or Ireton, but the outpouring of a distracted mind to an irresolute kinsman, who might be trusted to keep it private. Yet it is fortunate for us that it has survived, for it shows Oliver in undress, with all his emotional tenderness, his confusion, his sophistical subtlety, and above all his residuum of caution. It is the letter of a man who is groping among shadows in an unfamiliar cosmos, awfully lit up at moments by apocalyptic lightnings. But it is plain in what direction he is moving — towards a breach with the canons and traditions of the old orderly world which he loved.

[1] *L. and S.*, I, 393–400.

Chapter IV

THE THIRTIETH OF JANUARY
(1648–1649)

Not all the water in the rough rude sea
Can wash the balm off from an anointed king.
Richard II.

I

THE last act of the drama had come, and events marched with a tragic speed. The different protagonists acted according to their types, puppets in the hands of destiny. The presbyterian majority in parliament, delivered by Fairfax and Oliver from all fear of a royalist triumph, set itself to spike the guns of the other object of its dread, the army, and hastened to negotiate with the king. On September 18 began the futile venture known as the treaty of Newport. Charles was first asked to withdraw all his declarations against parliament; he hesitated for some time, but finally agreed. Then followed a slow duel about terms, in which Holles put the extreme presbyterian case, and Vane pled for toleration, and Charles revelled in dialectical subtleties. There were pleas and counter-pleas, rebutters and surrebutters. Charles offered to accept the establishment of presbytery for three years, and after that a limited episcopacy, and to give parliament the control of the militia for ten. He eventually extended this latter term to twenty years, and surrendered Ireland wholly to parliament. On the question of exempting royalists from pardon he stood firm. He had granted all that he could be expected to grant, and, although on October 27 the Commons rejected his proposals, the negotiations dragged on, for the ordinary parliamentarian saw in the royal answers some hope of an ultimate agreement.

But in truth there was none, for Charles was not sincere. At the start of the discussions he had made the ominous stipulation that nothing which he conceded should be valid unless a complete agreement were reached on all points, and, since he did not believe that a final understanding was possible, his concessions on details were meaningless. He had shaken off the lethargy of the summer, and was in a brisker mood, more careful in his dress, and with his 'hermit beard' now neatly trimmed. He negotiated merely to gain time, for he was dreaming of escape. There was good hope of succour from abroad, and his queen was planning a great stroke in Ireland. To his host in Newport he wrote with the utmost candour:

> I pray you rightly to understand my condition, which, I confess, yesternight I did not fully enough explain through want of time. It is this: notwithstanding my too great concessions already made, I know that, unless I shall make yet others which will directly make me no King, I shall be at best but a perpetual prisoner. Besides, if this were not, of which I am too sure, the adhering to the Church — from which I cannot depart, no, not in show — will do the same. And, to deal freely with you, the great concession I made this day — the Church, militia and Ireland — was made merely in order to my escape, of which if I had not hope I would not have done; for then I could have returned to my strait prison without reluctancy; but now, I confess, it would break my heart, having done that which only an escape can justify. To be short, if I stay for a demonstration of their further wickedness, it will be too late to seek a remedy; for my only hope is that now they believe I dare deny them nothing and so be less careful of the guards.[1]

If escape failed, he had resolved upon the ground to which he must stand, and he would stand the more firmly now, because he had already strained his conscience by too much diplomatic shuffling. On the Church especially he was in deadly earnest. On November 29th, when his hopes of escape had grown dim, he spoke a solemn farewell to the peers among the parliamentary commissioners. 'My lords, you are come to take leave of me, and I believe we shall scarce see each other again. But God's will be done. I thank God I have made my peace with Him, and shall without fear undergo what He shall be pleased to suffer man to do unto me.'[2] The time for finesse was gone; he must now stand overtly by that creed to which he had always been faithful at heart.

There was a like stiffening among the true rulers of England. The army had changed its character in the past three years. The New Model which had conquered at Naseby had gone. Few of the old colonels remained, and the men who had taken their place, Ewer and Pride and Hewson and Harrison, were of a darker and wilder strain. Fairfax had not his old authority,

---

[1] Wagstaffe, *Vindication* (1711), 160. For the plans to escape see Hillier, *Narrative of Attempted Escapes of Charles I* (1852).
[2] *Perfect Weekly Account*, Nov. 29–Dec. 6, 1648 (Th.).

and the real commanders were Oliver, strangely absent in the north, and Ireton, ceaselessly busy at St. Albans and Windsor. Ireton had become a different man from the patient *politique* of the summer of 1647. Then he had been a bold innovator and a daring speculator on the foundations of government, but he had been essentially conservative, seeking not a breach with the past but an organic evolution. He had been a staunch monarchist as against the republican theorists. But the second Civil War had opened his eyes. There could be no agreement with such a man as Charles, since no conceivable form of words would bind him. 'We know... what Court maxims there are amongst the King's party concerning some fundamental rights of the Crown which the King cannot give away, and their common scruple whether the King granting away such or any other hereditary crown rights can oblige his heirs and successors, or exclude their claim; but if all other pretexts fail, their non-obligation to what is wrested from them by force in a powerful rebellion, as they count it, will serve such a king's conscience for a shift to make a breach where he finds its advantage.' [1] These weighty words were the conclusion forced by a study of Charles's character on the mind of one who had been not unfriendly to him. To Ireton, as to Oliver, the Newport conferences were only 'ruining hypocritical agreements.' The king must be brought to trial for the blood he had shed and for his treason to the liberties of England; both for the sake of abstract justice, and as a warning to all kings who should dare to set themselves above human law.[2] His temper had hardened not only against the man but against his office, and he began to give ear to the radical doctrines of the Levellers. Ireton is an example of the thinker with a strong sense of law and logic, who, when the premises on which he has founded himself are proved untenable, rejects them ruthlessly and accepts their precise opposite. There is no extremist so convinced as the disillusioned moderate.

He found it hard to convince Fairfax, and he met with strong opposition in the council of officers, but the bulk of the army was with him, for the ordinary soldier saw ruin for himself in any agreement between king and parliament. In October he drew up his first draft of a 'Remonstrance of the Army,' in

---

[1] *A Remonstrance of his Excellency, Thomas Lord Fairfax... and of the General Council of Officers*, St. Albans, Nov. 16, 1648 (Th.), 32.

[2] *Ibid.*, 27.

which he laid down a constitutional scheme built upon the
sovereignty of the people — that is, of the middle classes who
had a stake in the country. Any future monarchy must be
based upon contract, a trust granted by the nation on terms,
and no king should have a right to veto the decision of the
people's representatives. It was Ireton's version of John Lilburne, and it struck at both Charles and the present parliament. At first Fairfax would have none of it, so, at Oliver's
suggestion, Ireton took to lobbying — conferences of the independents in the army and the chief men of the Levellers. A new
version of the 'Remonstrance' was produced, a blend of the old
'Heads of the Proposals' and the old 'Agreement of the People.'
Meantime the council of officers submitted its terms to Charles
on November 16, terms which involved concessions not for a
period of years, but for perpetuity. The present parliament
must be dissolved, and its place taken by biennial parliaments
with a reformed electorate, and the militia must be in the
charge of a council of state, while parliament should appoint
the great officers of the Crown. Charles, buoyed up by hope of
escape, rejected the proposals, and the council of officers thereupon accepted Ireton's 'Remonstrance.' The army was now
virtually at one. Oliver approved of the last version of the
'Remonstrance,' which seemed to him, as he told Fairfax, to
have 'nothing in it but what is honest, and becoming honest
men to say and offer.' On the 20th it was presented to the
House of Commons; the House paid no attention to it, but continued its sterile logomachy with Charles.

The patience of the army had been strained to breaking-point.
Fairfax was passive, Ireton was resolute and he had with him
most of the new fighting colonels, and Oliver at long last was on
Ireton's side in demanding the king's trial and the dissolution of
a farcical parliament. Action must be swift or Charles would
outwit them and escape to his foreign friends. Ireton was not
slow to strike. On December 6, Hammond having been removed from his post, the king was carried from Newport to the
blockhouse called Hurst castle, on the Hampshire coast. There
for more than a fortnight he was left in rough lodgings, with no
means of exercise except walking on the shingle beside a bleak
winter sea. He was in a placid temper, however, and amused
himself by watching the ships in the Solent. On the 19th he was
conducted by a party of horse to Winchester, where he had a
great popular reception, and he slept the next night at Farn-

ham, where he was received by Harrison, a splendid figure in a new buff coat and a crimson silk sash. Charles's hopes had risen again. When he learned that his destination was Windsor, he could not believe that the army intended him any harm, since, as he said, they were moving him from the worst of his castles to the best. Harrison's appearance reassured him, though that darling of the sectaries took occasion to remind him that justice had no respect of persons. 'He looked like a soldier,' was the king's comment, 'and that, having some judgment in faces, if he had observed him so well before, he should not have harboured that ill opinion of him.' [1] He was also in hourly expectation of a rescue. But the horse, the swiftest in England, which was awaiting him at Bagshot, fell lame, and on the 23rd he arrived at Windsor. As he entered the castle he was met by the doomed Hamilton, who fell on his knees and stammered 'My dear master.' Charles raised him and embraced him. 'I have been so indeed to you,' he said.

The army had parliament to deal with as well as the king. On December 2 it marched from Windsor to London, and had reached Kensington when Fairfax received a letter from the Speaker forbidding him to enter the city. The cavalry took up their quarters in the royal Mews (now Trafalgar Square). Whitehall was the headquarters, with Hewson's regiment lodged there, while Pride's regiment occupied the other royal palace of St. James's. In face of this menace parliament showed an unexpected independence. When the House of Commons met on Monday the 4th, it protested against the removal of the king without its consent or knowledge. On the 5th by 129 votes to 83 it decided that the king's answers were a good ground for further negotiations, a decision in which what was left of the House of Lords unanimously concurred. This determined the army's action. That evening the council of officers consulted with the independents in parliament, and in deference to the view of the latter it was decided to purge rather than to dissolve the House. [2] Next morning, December 6, Pride with a body of musketeers appeared in the doorway of St. Stephen's. He dismissed the usual guard of trained bands, and, Lord Grey of Groby with his lists helping him, prevented some hundred odd members from entering the House, and sent forty-one of the more recalcitrant to be confined in a tavern called Hell, in Old Palace Yard under Exchequer Chambers. A rump of from

[1] Sir T. Herbert, *Memoirs* (1702), 98.   [2] Ludlow, I, 209.

forty-five to fifty was left. 'Since Tophet,' said Henry Marten, 'is prepared for kings, it is fitting that their friends should go to Hell.' Pride's Purge was the only course before the army if its purpose was to be achieved, and at the same time some semblance of a parliament retained, for it is certain that, if dissolution had been preferred, the election which followed would have returned to vast royalist majority. But it meant the final shattering of all constitutional authority and a naked appeal to force. Hugh Peters was right when, being asked his warrant, he pointed to the great sword with which he had girt himself.

On this point Oliver had no doubts. That night he arrived in London from the north, having left Lambert to finish with Pontefract. He had been consulted on, and had approved of, the march of the army to London, but, since the decision for a purge had only been taken at the last moment, there had been no time to inform him of it. 'He declared that he had not been acquainted with their design, yet since it was done, he was glad of it, and would endeavour to maintain it.' [1] Next day he sat among the three-score or so of the remnant and was thanked for his services in the field. Fairfax, shocked and flustered, confined himself to the task of preserving discipline in an army which was loathed by nine out of ten of the London citizens, and to Oliver and Ireton was left the shaping of policy. Let us try from the slender evidence that remains to us to trace the process of the former's thoughts.

It is unfortunate that the events of that mid-fortnight of December are so deep in shadow, with only a few pinpricks of light in the gloom. Plainly Oliver when he arrived in London had made up his mind on two things — that further negotiations with Charles were impossible, and that the safety of the realm required that his power for mischief should be curbed once and for all. He was convinced, too, that it would be just to bring the king to trial. Beyond that he had no clearness. The issue of any trial must be condemnation. What then? They might condemn the king and hope that the prospect of death would compel his surrender. But was that likely? He had learned enough of Charles to realize the stubbornness of his convictions and his ultimate core of stark courage. They might depose him — but after that? If they banished him they would make a future invasion inevitable; if they imprisoned him, they

[1] Ludlow, I, 211.

would set up in England a perpetual focus of strife, a magnet to draw to itself all the elements of discontent which were only too strong in the hearts of the people. There remained the desperate, the irrevocable step of execution, to follow Essex's maxim that stone dead had no fellow, the course desired by the strongest forces in the army. 'Nothing in all the known world of politics is so intractable as a band of zealots, conscious that they are in a minority, yet armed by accident with the powers of a majority.' [1]

Now that the crucial moment had come he was undecided. So also was Ireton, for even the latter's hard logic shrank from the extreme conclusion. Ireton was clear on the need for a trial and a verdict in the hope of extorting adequate concessions. Oliver, with his strong practical sense, was doubtful even of a trial, however much he might admit its justice, for he was afraid of its upshot. Anyhow he wished it deferred in order that other methods should be first attempted. There was a sharp division in the council of officers, with Oliver as leader of the moderates. He won a momentary victory, for on the 21st the council by a majority of four rejected a proposal for the king's death. He induced Pride to put in a curious plea that it was foolish to kiss Charles I when a Charles II would be at large, 'to exchange a king in their power for a king out of their power, potent in foreign alliances, and strong in the affection of the people.' He had interviews with Lenthall and Widdrington and Whitelocke, all lawyers and cautious parliament men, in order apparently to make some use of the House of Commons rump as against the extreme party in the army.[2] The House on the 23rd appointed a committee to consider the procedure of the king's trial, but this was intended as only a tactical step in negotiations. Charles was to be given a last chance.

The king was spending a dismal Christmas-tide at Windsor. He had been permitted to order new clothes, but he was allowed no Christmas fare, most of his attendants had been dismissed, and he had himself to read the church service, since he had no chaplain. On Christmas day or on the day following he was waited upon by the last deputation that he was to receive from his people. The envoy was Denbigh, who, as Hamilton's brother-in-law, could pay a visit to Windsor without rousing suspicion. What the conditions he offered were we do not know, but we may assume that they included the abolition of the royal

[1] Morley, *Cromwell*, 277.   [2] Whitelocke, 357.

veto and such a policy towards Church lands as would make a farce of episcopacy in its old sense. Oliver seems to have looked for much from this mission, and on the 25th he urged the council of officers to spare the king's life if the conditions were accepted. He was doomed to disappointment. Charles refused to see Denbigh, having come to the end of his concessions. Weariness and despair had produced a final obstinacy. He would not yield up the ancient rights of the throne or consent to the spoliation of a Church of which he believed himself the divinely appointed head. On the 27th, when the news of this refusal reached London, the council of officers was at last unanimous. There was no way out of the tangle but the king's death.

To his innumerable critics, royalist and presbyterian, Oliver's conduct seemed to be due to dark motives of personal ambition. 'I have been assured,' wrote one of them, 'that Cromwell is retreating from them (*i.e.* the extremists), his design and theirs being incompatible as fire and water, they driving at a pure democracy and himself at an oligarchy; and it will appear that the wild remonstrances and the present design of taking away the King's life is forwarded by him only to make the Levellers vent all their wicked principles and intentions; that, having declared themselves, they may become the more odious and abominable, and so be the more easily suppressed when he sees the occasion to take them off and fall openly from them.' [1] 'Give me leave to jest a little,' wrote another. 'Doth not Oliver and the rest of the grandees, think you, that set them on work, laugh in their sleeves at these nasty Levellers and their remonstrances? Yea, and when time serves, will kick them off both together; and his own reason must needs prompt him to shield that sacred head, without which there can be no ease, health, nor safety to the members.' [2]

But Oliver had no dreams of an oligarchy dominated by himself, with a king as a sort of Doge of Venice. For him the matter was narrowed down to the immediate problem of Charles. What was to be done with this troubler of the peace, who, as long as he lived, made impossible the building of Jerusalem? He had in his bones a love of tradition and a respect for legalities, and he had also the slow prudence of his race. He had delayed returning to London, when he could have handed over the army of the north to Lambert, that he might remain de-

<hr>

[1] Quoted by Gardiner, *Civil War*, IV, 282.

[2] Marchamont Needham in *Mercurius Pragmaticus*, Dec. 19–26, 1648 (Th.).

tached from minor controversies and have peace to think. He
was a merciful man, who would never seek vengeance on a fallen
enemy. He realized the strength of English royalism, and the
breach which the king's death would make between army and
country. He saw the folly of making a martyr out of a bungler.
He had been a reluctant convert to Ireton's 'Remonstrance,'
for he saw where it would lead, and at Pontefract he had been
labouring in a bog of constitutional dogmas which he could not
reconcile. These he presently relinquished, and thought rather
of the personality of Charles. Here was one against whom the
Lord had witnessed; here at any rate was a plain rock of offence
which must be removed. This man, who for nine months had
slept bare, and now tossed 'in one of the king's rich beds at
Whitehall,' began to move towards the conclusion that so long
as the king lived there could be no peace in Israel.

It was a tardy and painful transformation, for it meant that
one who had been a monarchist and had despised republican
whimsies had to found his case openly on what he disliked.
Even Ireton's logic did not wholly persuade him, though Ireton's energy in the cause to which he had been converted had
its effect upon his slower and profounder mind. One thing he
shared with him, his belief that a summary act of justice might
be a lesson for all time to encroaching kings, a perpetual *vindi-
ciae contra tyrannos*. Oliver disliked all fatted things, loving
the plain, homely appurtenances of life, and seeing human
grandeur as trivial against the vast background of eternity.
The two campaigns had made him more than ever impatient of
folly, and intolerant of claims of rank and prerogative. He had
come to feel for the royal line of England the contempt he had
felt for the Manchesters and Willoughbys and Essexes who
clogged his path in the first years of war. There was no sanctity
in kingship unless it were truly kingly. He was no Leveller or
egalitarian, for the world could not do without its masters, but
why reverence a brocaded puppet larded by a priest with oil,
when there were men who needed no robes or sacring to make
them kingly? Teach the Lord's Anointed his mortality, and
there would be hope in the years to come of a true anointing.

But still he was not clear. Fairfax whom he reverenced,
Vane whom he loved, were against Ireton; the arguments
seemed to balance with a dreadful nicety. He could only wait
for a sign, and the sign was given him. The king's rejection of
Denbigh turned the scale. The psychology was that of a sudden

conversion, familiar to men of his religious faith, whereby by an act of God the soul swung round and marched on a different road. Having cast behind him all fleshly reasonings and politic considerations, and having throttled his common sense, he was in the extravagant exalted mood of one with a direct commission from his Maker. A few days later he told the House of Commons: 'If any man whatsoever hath carried on the design of deposing the King and disinheriting his posterity; or if any man hath yet such a design he should be the greatest traitor and rebel in the world; but, since the Providence of God hath cast this upon us, I cannot but submit to Providence.' He talked of deposition and disinheritance, but he knew well that the true word was death.

II

On January 1, 1649, the remnant of the Commons, now the obedient satellites of the army, passed an ordinance to set up a high court of justice for the trial of the king. The court was to consist of Rolle, chief justice of England, St. John, chief justice of the Common Pleas, and Wilde, chief baron of the Exchequer, with a jury of 150 commissioners, including six peers. Next day it was sent up to the Lords, accompanied by a resolution which declared that 'by the fundamental laws of this kingdom it is treason for the King of England for the time being to levy war against the Parliament and the kingdom of England.' The Lords, now only twelve in number, summarily rejected both ordinance and resolution. Manchester argued that without the king there could be no parliament, and that therefore the king could not be a traitor to himself. Northumberland declared that the vast majority of the people of England were 'not yet satisfied whether the king did levy war against the Houses, or the Houses against him.' Denbigh swore that he 'would rather be torn in pieces than have a share in so infamous a business.' [1] Also the judges nominated refused to take part in the trial. So on January 6 the Commons passed a new act by a majority of six, which arrogated to a single House the legislative power. [2] The court established by it consisted of one hundred and thirty-

[1] *L. J.*, X, 641; Blencowe, *Sydney Papers*, 42; Firth, *H. of L.*, 207–08.

[2] On the 4th a resolution was passed that, since the people were the origin of all just power, the Commons, as representing the people, could pass binding laws without consent of king or Lords. *C. J.*, VI, 110, etc.

five commissioners, with no judges among its members, and no peers. The act set forth that Charles Stuart had wickedly designed to subvert the ancient laws and liberties of the people, and had shown himself impenitent in these causes; wherefore he must stand his trial 'for prevention of the like and greater inconveniences, and to the end no chief officer or magistrate whatever may hereafter presume traitorously and maliciously to imagine or contrive the enslaving and destroying of the English nation, and to expect impunity for so doing.' [1] These words in which we may detect the influence of Oliver, put the thing in its true light as a political act, to meet a present emergency and to provide for the future — a step founded not on legal or constitutional niceties but on a desperate need.

Under any possible definition of law there was no shadow of legality in the business. It was an act of state based upon that necessity which is assumed to be above the laws, an act of war like a drumhead court-martial. The commissioners were army officers, members of parliament, and aldermen of London. Since there was no judge to preside, an obscure lawyer of Gray's Inn, one John Bradshawe, was chosen as president. There were independent colonels like Pride and Whalley and Harrison, and other parliamentary commanders like Ludlow and Hutchinson and Grey of Groby. Fairfax and Ireton and Oliver were members. But when the first meeting was held in the Painted Chamber on January 8 only fifty-two attended. Half of the nominees refused the task. Some were aghast at the constitutional absurdity of a tribunal founded upon a resolution of a disconsidered fragment of a single branch of parliament. Others felt the scandal of an action taken professedly in the name of the English people, when the people by a great majority were notoriously hostile to its originators. Others dreaded the tyranny of the army, remembering perhaps that clause in the Petition of Right which forbade martial law. Fairfax attended the first meeting, but no others, and some of his old officers, like Skippon, Lambert and Disbrowe, followed his example. The court, after several sparsely attended meetings, decided that the trial should begin on the 20th.

On the 19th Charles was brought from Windsor to the palace of St. James's, guarded by troops of horse, and with Hugh Peters prancing in mountebank triumph before his coach. London was in the grip of a black frost and its Christmas had

[1] Gardiner, *Const. Docs.*, 357.

been dismal. Troopers were everywhere, riding in grim posses, or off duty and sombrely puffing tobacco, vast silent men, lean from the wars. The citizens did not linger in the streets, for none knew his neighbour's mind. Whitehall was full of soldiers, and now and then there was an outbreak and broken heads. St. Paul's, if we are to believe the royalist journalists, was a curious spectacle; 'they have turned it into an ale-house, a barber's shop, a smith's forge, a scullery, and, I blush to think of it, into a bawdy house.'[1] Everywhere there was an epidemic of preaching, Hugh Peters and his friends in St. Margaret's and the Whitehall courtyard, while the London ministers, like Marshall and Calamy, from their own pulpits fulminated against the army.

Meantime the great hall of Westminster had been set in order for the trial. That hall remains today though all its environs have suffered change, and it is easy to reconstruct the scene. The booths of the tradespeople were cleared from the floor, and the south end, where the courts of Chancery and King's Bench usually sat, was filled with a wooden platform, divided from the rest of the hall by a partition three feet high. Beneath it was a broad gangway, and another ran at right angles down to the main door, and both gangways were to be lined with pikemen and musketeers. The spectators were to be crowded in the space between the gangways and the walls, but there were also two little galleries above the dais itself. The judges were to sit on benches covered with scarlet cloth at the back of the dais under the great south window. In the middle of the front row was a raised desk for the president; the clerks sat at a table beneath him, where lay the mace and the sword of state; at the edge of the dais there were pews for the prosecuting counsel and a crimson-velvet armchair for the king, who would sit with his back to the body of spectators. On the left of the dais, looking towards the judges, a door led to St. Stephen's Chapel where the Commons met; at the back there was a way through by the Court of Requests to the Painted Chamber, splendid in gilding and frescoes and black-letter Scripture texts, where the court held its private sessions. The windows of the Painted Chamber looked out on the gardens of Sir Robert Cotton's house, where the king was to lodge.

About two o'clock on the 20th Charles was carried to Whitehall in a sedan-chair and thence by water to Cotton house. The

[1] *Mercurius Melancholicus*, Jan. 1 (Th.).

KING CHARLES THE FIRST
As he sat before the High Court of Justice

commissioners in the Painted Chamber saw him arrive before they had decided upon the authority on which they should found their case, for they were well aware of its legal flimsiness. A certain Sir Purbeck Temple, a royalist who was planning the king's escape, was hidden behind the arras, and at the trial of the regicides deposed as follows:

> When their prayer was over there came news that the King was landing at Sir Robert Cotton's Stairs, at which Cromwell ran to a window, looking on the King as he came up the garden. He turned as white as the wall. Returning to the board... he said thus: 'My masters, he is come, he is come, and now we are doing that great work that the whole nation will be full of. Therefore I desire you to let us resolve here what answer we shall give the King when he comes before us, for the first question that he will ask will be by what authority as commissioners we do try him.' To which none answered presently. Then after a little space Henry Marten rose up and said: 'In the name of the Commons in Parliament assembled, and all the good people of England.' [1]

We may discredit certain details, such as Oliver's white face, but there is no reason to disbelieve the substance of the tale. Headed by Bradshawe in his shot-proof hat, the court, having got its formula, marched with its men-at-arms and ushers into Westminster hall.

Charles, in a dark suit and wearing the insignia of the Garter, remained covered and paid no respect to the court. When the roll of judges was called sixty-eight responded; when Fairfax's name was spoken Lady Fairfax in one of the galleries called out that he had too much wit to be there. While the charge was read the king's stern face relaxed, and he laughed when he heard himself proclaimed a traitor. He tried to interrupt the clerk by touching him with his cane; its silver head fell off and he had to pick it up himself. Bradshawe called on him to answer, using Henry Marten's new-made formula. Again there was an interruption, a woman's voice crying out, that it was a lie, that not a half nor a quarter of the people of England was with them, and that the charge was made by rebels and traitors.[2] There was a delay while the gallery was cleared, and then Charles asked the expected question — by what authority he

---

[1] *Exact and Impartial Accompt of the Indictment... of the Regicides* (1660), 248.

[2] It is not quite clear whether the woman was Lady Fairfax or Lady De Lille. See *State Trials*, V, i, 146, and Archbishop Sancroft's correspondence quoted by Muddiman, *Trial of King Charles*, I, 80–81.

was being tried. England, he said, had never been an elective kingdom; he was monarch not by election but by inheritance, and to acknowledge a usurped authority would be a betrayal of his trust. As he was removed the soldiers by order shouted 'Justice,' but the mass of the spectators cried 'God save the King.'

He was next brought before the court on the 22nd, and again refused to plead. His objection was unanswerable by those who tried to give a colour of legality to what was an act of revolutionary statecraft. 'It is not my case alone, it is the freedom and liberty of the people of England, and, do you pretend what you will, I stand more for their liberties. For if power without law may make law, may alter the fundamental laws of the kingdom, I do not know what subject he is in England can be assured of his life or anything he can call his own.' So completely did the court fail to overawe the prisoner that Hewson, one of the commanders of the guards, is said to have lost his temper and spat in Charles's face. 'God hath justice in store,' said the king gently, 'both for you and me.' Again on the 23rd he was before the court with the same result. The commissioners accordingly sat in private in the Painted Chamber, and heard condemnatory evidence in the absence of the prisoner — how he had been seen in arms against the parliament and had invited foreign armies to enter England. All this was farcical, but time was needed to convince doubting members of the court. On the 25th it was resolved in a small house that they should proceed to sentence against the king as tyrant, traitor, murderer and public enemy to the commonwealth of England, and that the sentence should be death; and a fuller court next day confirmed the decision. The king was to be brought into Westminster hall on the morrow to hear his doom.

That day, Saturday the 27th, saw the end of the judicial travesty. That morning Bradshawe's wife implored her husband to spare the king, and was told that he would do him no harm save what the Lord commanded. Bradshawe believed sincerely that he had a good legal case, and, when four years later the rump of the Commons was turned out on the ground that it was no parliament but an oligarchy, he is said to have lamented, 'If this be no parliament, then am I the king's murderer?' When he took his seat in a scarlet gown that afternoon in Westminster hall there was further interruption by women. Charles demanded that he should be heard in his defence by the Lords and Commons, since he had something to say 'most material for the peace of the kingdom.' What that something was we cannot tell, but it may be that he meant to offer to abdicate in favour of his son on certain terms. One of the commissioners, John Downes, was inclined to agree to the proposal, but the rest of the court refused. Bradshawe delivered a vast rambling speech, in which he quoted the Scriptures and the classics, mediæval lawyers like Bracton, Mariana, Father Parsons and George Buchanan, and made but a poor job of it. Charles asked permission to answer him, but was told that it was too late. The clerk read the sentence, and the prisoner, still struggling to speak, was removed by the guards. The soldiers in the hall and outside it, pursuant to orders, shouted 'Justice' and 'Execution' and blew tobacco-smoke in his face. 'Poor souls,' said the king, 'for sixpence they would do the same for their commanders.' But in the streets the common people were weeping.[1]

As the news of the verdict flew abroad, and the first trestles were set up outside the Banqueting House in Whitehall, a silence of horror fell upon the city. The death-sentence was not the work of the people of England; it was carried through by a small, resolute and armed minority in the face of a stupefied nation. Visionaries besieged the council of officers with commands from Heaven for Charles's safety. All that was most stable in the land, all who were reverent of old sanctities and 'fearful for the laws' were shocked to the core not only by the barbarity of the deed but by its futility. Many pointed out — not quite truly — that England's true grievance was not against the king's person but against 'the power that is made up in the kingly office by the corrupt constitution';[2] the sword could end Charles's life, but not the monarchy. Staunch reformers and tried servants of parliament went into opposition. Fairfax was one; he did his best in his slow way to save the king's life, and, like Montrose, he wrote verses of passionate regret to his memory.[3] Vane was another, and he had gone to

---

[1] The records of the trial are voluminous and there is a bibliography of them in Muddiman's *Trial of Charles I*, who prints for the first time Bradshawe's *Journal* (*S. P. Dom*, Car., I., vol. 517, Record Office). Other official accounts are the *Perfect Narrative, etc.*, by C. W. (Jan. 22, 1649), reprinted in *State Trials*, IV, and V, and Nalson's transcript of John Phelps's *Journal of the High Court of Justice* (1684). The evidence at the trial of the regicides, which must be accepted with caution, will be found in the *Exact and Most Impartial Accompt* (1660).

[2] See Major White's letter to Fairfax. Gardiner, *Civil War*, IV, 303.

[3] See Fairfax's *Short Memorials* (reprinted in *Somers Tracts* and *Stuart Tracts*) and Markham, *Great Lord Fairfax*, 352.

extreme lengths in his anti-monarchist fervour. Lawyers like St. John and Pierrepoint were naturally hostile, and young Algernon Sidney put the thing squarely to the judges — 'First, the king can be tried by no court; second, no man can be tried by this court.' The presbyterians were scandalized and enraged; the Scottish commissioners in London made vigorous protests; the Assembly of Divines pled for a respite, as did the London clergy. The gentility, the reason, the moderation, the wealth of England were flung into one scale.

Fruitlessly, for in the other was the sword. A knot of determined men, who see their course with the terrible simplicity of the fanatic, and have armed forces to do their bidding, are more than a match for a million puzzled civilians. They were so deeply in earnest that they made a sacrament out of their vengeance. 'The gentlemen that were appointed his judges,' Lucy Hutchinson wrote, 'and divers others, saw in the King a disposition so bent on the ruin of all that opposed him, and of all the righteous and just things they had contended for, that it was upon the conscience of many of them that, if they did not execute justice upon him, God would require at their hands all the blood and desolation which should ensue by their suffering him to escape, when God had brought him into their hands.'[1] Against such assurance there could be no argument, for it had the compelling power of a mandate from Heaven. The logic of events had convinced both Ireton and Oliver, but they saw it not as a conclusion of cold reason but as a flash of divine revelation.

But Oliver, unlike his colleagues, had the plain good sense of the countryman and a mind ruled more by instinct than by syllogisms. He had reached his decision by crushing down his practical wisdom and closing his eyes to ultimate consequences. He had no doubts, but the consciousness that his certainty had been won by doing violence to other sides of his nature left him in a strained, neurotic temper. He argued his case fiercely to Fairfax, to the Scots, to every doubter; his inflexible will coerced the waverers, and it is said that in the signing of the death-warrant he guided some of their pens.[2] The strain of rustic buffoonery in him came out, for on that same grim occasion he inked Henry Marten's face and got his own inked in return. It was the natural rebound from his long months of torturing indecision. The man, too, was physically and mentally over-

<hr>

[1] Hutchinson, II, 152.   [2] State Trials, V, i, 219.

strung; an indecent nervous hilarity was the proof of his new-won confidence, and he dismissed with horse-play or with a horse-laugh the scruples of the timid. 'I tell you,' he boasted to Algernon Sidney, 'we will cut off his head with the crown upon it.' [1]

III

On the evening of the 27th, after sentence, Charles was taken to Sir Robert Cotton's house, and thence to Whitehall, where he spent the night. His spirits were equable, almost gay. He gave orders that his dogs should be removed and sent to his wife, that nothing might distract his mind from grave contemplation. On Sunday Juxon, who had been bishop of London, was permitted to attend him, and the day was spent in prayer. Charles refused to see any of his friends on the ground that the time left to him on earth was short and precious. He sent for a little casket of jewels, which was in the care of his laundress, and which was all that he had to bequeath to his children. On the Sunday evening, through a sudden mercifulness in his gaolers, he was taken to St. James's palace that he might not hear the scaffold being hammered together in Whitehall. Colonel Hacker, who commanded his guards, was induced also to keep the soldiers out of his room, so that the last nights of his life were spent in peace. All that Sunday the London pulpits rang with presbyterian denunciations of his judges, while Hugh Peters of St. James's poured forth Hebraic frenzies in their honour. He found an apt text — 'All the kings of the nations, even all of them, lie in glory, every one in his own house. But thou art cast out of thy grave like an abominable branch, and as the raiment of those that are slain, thrust through with a sword, that go down to the stones of the pit; as a carcass trodden under foot. Thou shalt not be joined with them in burial, because thou hast destroyed thy land, and slain thy people.' [2]

On the Monday the king set about disposing of his few belongings, while the scaffold was rising in Whitehall, and the commissioners were playing strange pranks to secure an adequately signed death-warrant.[3] To his family and his friends he gave his books and jewels. His two younger children were admitted to see him, Princess Elizabeth and the Duke of

[1] Blencowe, *Sydney Papers*, 237. [2] Isaiah xiv. 18-20.
[3] For this see Gardiner, *Civil War*, IV, 316, etc.

Gloucester. He took them on his knees, dried their tears, and gravely comforted and counselled them. The delicate little girl of thirteen has left her own record of his words: 'He wished me not to grieve or torment myself for him, for that would be a glorious death he should die, it being for the laws and liberties of this land, and for maintaining the true Protestant religion. He bid me read Bishop Andrewes's sermons, Hooker's Ecclesiastical Polity, and Bishop Laud's book against Fisher, which would ground me against Popery. He told me he had forgiven all his enemies, and hoped God would forgive them also, and commanded us and all the rest of my brothers and sisters to forgive them. He bid us tell my mother that his thoughts had never strayed from her, and that his love should be the same to the last.' To the boy he spoke more simply, for he was only ten. 'Sweetheart, now they will cut off thy father's head; mark, child, what I say: they will cut off my head and perhaps make thee a king. But mark what I say. You must not be a king so long as your brothers Charles and James do live; for they will cut off your brothers' heads when they can catch them, and cut off thy head too at the last, and therefore I charge you do not be made a king by them.' 'I will be torn to pieces first,' was the child's answer. He shared among them his trinkets, which were mainly broken Georges and Garter stars.

Tuesday the 30th dawned grey and very cold; so keen was the frost that ice-floes jostled in the Thames. Charles rose shortly after five. He bade Herbert dress him carefully, giving him an extra shirt; 'by reason the season is so sharp as probably may make me shake, which some will imagine proceeds from fear. I would have no such imputation. I fear not death, death is not terrible to me. I bless my God I am prepared.' Herbert told of a dream he had had in the night of Laud entering the room, but Charles only said that it was remarkable; he was more concerned about his clothes, which were black (but not mourning), and he put on the George and the Garter riband. 'This is my second marriage day,' he said. 'I would be as trim today as may be, for before night I hope to be espoused to my blessed Jesus.' Presently Juxon arrived to pray with him and read the lesson of the day, and a little later Hacker knocked at the door and bade him get ready to go to Whitehall.

In the bitter morning, attended by Juxon and Herbert and a guard of halberdiers, the king walked across the park, briskly, as was his custom. He arrived at Whitehall about ten o'clock.

There was no chance of talk on the way, for drums beat continually. At Whitehall he received the sacrament from Juxon and was allowed to rest in a bedchamber for some hours, while parliament was passing an act to forbid the proclamation of any successor. He was offered a meal but refused; the bishop, however, warned him that he might faint in the cold, so he ate a crust of bread and drank a glass of claret.

About half-past one Hacker summoned him to die. He walked to the Banqueting House through the Whitehall galleries which were lined with spectators; most of them were praying, and the guards did not forbid them, 'seeming by their silence and dejected faces afflicted rather than insulting.' From one of the windows he stepped out on to the scaffold.[1] This was railed in, and it and the railings were covered with black cloth. In the centre was the low block. Charles's refusal to plead had led to the fear that he might resist at the last moment, so staples had been fixed in the floor so that if necessary he might be held down by ropes. By the block lay the axe, brought from the Tower, perhaps the very one which had been used at Strafford's death, and beside it stood two masked men, dressed in close-fitting tunics, rough-looking fellows like sailors or butchers, one of them short, and one of them tall with a grey wig. Around the scaffold were lines of horse and foot, and beyond them a packed multitude, while every window and housetop was crowded.

On the scaffold were six figures, the king and Juxon and the two headsmen, Colonel Hacker and Colonel Tomlinson. Since Charles could not speak to the people, he addressed himself to Tomlinson and Juxon. Remembering Strafford, he said that an unjust sentence to which he had been a party was now punished by an unjust sentence upon himself. He submitted himself humbly to God's judgment. He prayed that his enemies might be pardoned, and that the land should be freed from the tyranny of the sword. There could be no peace till men paid their duties to God, people and king. And then in a few sentences he expounded his political philosophy, sentences which afterwards must have come ominously to Oliver's mind.

> For the people I desire their liberty and freedom as much as anybody whomsoever; but I must tell you that this liberty and freedom consists in having government, those laws by which their lives and goods may be most their own. It is not their having a

[1] Generally taken as the middle window, but see Muddiman, *op. cit.*, 139–42.

share in the government, that is nothing pertaining to them. A subject and a sovereign are clean different things; and, therefore, until you do this — I mean that you put the people in that liberty — they will never enjoy themselves.... If I would have given way to have all changed according to the power of the sword, I needed not to have come here; and therefore I tell you (and I pray God it be not laid to your charge) that I am the martyr of the people.

With the assistance of the executioners he put his long hair under a white satin nightcap. For a little he spoke aside with Juxon, handing him the George which he took from his neck, with instructions for its disposal. He removed his cloak and doublet and laid himself down on the scaffold with his head on the block. For a few minutes he lay there praying, his eye, said a watcher, 'as brisk and lively as ever he had seen it.' Then he stretched out his hands, and the grizzled executioner brought down the axe and severed his head. The other held it up in silence to the people. A groan of horror rent the stillness, and the next minute troops of horse were on the move, splitting up the crowd and driving it towards Charing Cross and Westminster.

Then followed a hideous scene. Men and women were permitted — on payment — to dip their handkerchiefs in the king's blood, and his long locks were shorn and sold as keepsakes. The body was put in a plain deal coffin costing six pounds, covered with a black velvet pall, and remained for some days in a Whitehall bedroom. Then it was embalmed, the head being sewn on, and afterwards removed to St. James's palace. An application to bury it in Henry the VIIth's chapel was refused, but permission was given to lay it in St. George's chapel at Windsor. Thither on Friday, February 9th, it was taken by Herbert and Juxon, Richmond and a few other nobles attending, and placed in the vault which held the remains of Jane Seymour and Henry VIII. No service was read, for the governor of Windsor would not permit the use of the prayerbook. The prophecy of Merlin was fulfilled, and Charles, who had chosen to be crowned in white, went in white to his tomb. 'This is memorable,' Herbert wrote, 'that at such time as the King's body was brought out of St. George's hall the sky was serene and clear; but presently it began to snow, and fell so fast as, by the time they came to the west end of the royal chapel, the black velvet pall was all white (the colour of innocency) being thick covered with snow. So went the white King to his grave, in the forty-eighth year of his age and the twenty-second year and tenth month of his reign.'[1]

IV

In Bossuet's great sermon at the funeral of Henrietta Maria he spoke some words of her husband. 'I am scarce able to contemplate the greatness of his courage in those last trials; but assuredly he plainly evidenced that it is not in the power of rebels to make a king who knows himself lose his majesty.' The tribute was just. None of the shortcomings of Charles's life can detract from the splendour of his death. He had the gift of his strange race of leaving the world with a noble gesture, with no act or word to mar the final tragic perfection. On the paradoxes of his character men will argue till the end of time. Of his personal charm there is no doubt; on that Clarendon and Philip Warwick have written with a lover's passion. Nor are his virtues and vices in dispute — his piety and fortitude; his inability to read a plain lesson, his lack of candour, his craze for blundering intrigues, his gentle but unshakable obstinacy. He was a tragic figure, because he was born into times which he could not understand and to a task which was too hard for him. The tragedy is there rather than in his death, for his execution was largely his own blame. It was beyond his power, beyond the power of anyone, to revive the Tudor monarchy, and Charles realized this; he was willing to make concessions, and it is certain that during the first nine months of 1647 he could have got from Oliver and Ireton and the army terms which would have safeguarded the things for which he ultimately died, episcopal government and a reasonable degree of royal authority. But in his folly he tried to bluff those with whom he dealt, the game went against him, and after the second Civil War men's tempers were soured and all hope of accommodation departed. As a legal act his death was a travesty of justice; as an incident in a revolutionary war it was as just or as unjust as the other details of that war. Charles lost and had to pay the penalty; if he had won, Oliver, Ireton and many others would have been shorter by their heads.

Such has been the rough verdict of history. Oliver himself regarded the deed differently. Having been driven to it by a mystical interpretation of providences, he saw it apocalyptically

[1] *Memoirs*, 135-44.

as a bolt from the armoury of Heaven. The stories of his behaviour — how he prised open the coffin lid with his sword to
gloat over the dead face of the king; how Southampton saw him
at midnight in the Banqueting House murmuring 'Cruel necessity!' [1] — may be disbelieved, but they point to his having been
in the view of his contemporaries in a strange, unbalanced
mood, half of exultation and half of melancholy. On the deed
itself he never wavered. In after years he spoke of it as the
'great fruit of the war,' a thing which for all time would make
saints rejoice and tyrants tremble, and he was to argue its justice hotly against the Edinburgh presbyterians. But he had
reached that view only by stifling his practical wisdom, and the
consciousness of this was like a thorn in the flesh, to fever his
body and distemper his mind. His spiritual life coarsens for a
time; in his piety he is more declamatory and flamboyant, but
he loses the old assurance and the old tenderness. For he knew
in his inmost heart that he had compelled a deed which had lost
him for good the 'middle folk,' the plain citizens with whom he
had the closest affinities. A 'bleeding head' in Marvell's phrase,
would remain to trouble the architects of a new England. He
had drawn a sword which he would not be permitted to sheathe.

The zealots of the camp, the republican dogmatists, the hot
gospellers of the sects might approve the king's death,[2] but it is
plain that it shocked the soul of England. It was not only fear
of a military dictatorship and of revolutionary violence; there
was in the feeling something which sprang from profounder
human instincts. The intolerable pathos of Charles's last hours,
expounded straightway by the most potent pamphlet in English
history, the meekness of his demeanour, his behaviour on the
scaffold, certain horrid incidents of parted garments and hands
dipped in his blood, seemed, even to the most reverent, to have
some kinship with the sufferings of Christ. The shadow of his
misdeeds and failings was dispelled by the fierce light of martyrdom. Not to royalists only, but to all who had a care for the
human decencies, it seemed that a cruel wrong had been done
and that innocency had been outraged. The disturber of England's peace was admitted into the hierarchy of England's

[1] The first tale comes from the royalist Richard Symonds (*Harleian MSS.*, 991).
The second is from Spence's *Anecdotes*, 286. Spence got it from Pope, and Pope's in-
formant might have got it direct from Southampton. It seems to me worthy of less
contempt than it has received.

[2] Oddly enough Samuel Pepys, then a schoolboy at St. Paul's, was in favour of the
execution.

saints. More, out of the primeval depths of the folk-heart there welled another feeling, the more perilous because it was intermingled with those ancient things which are beyond reason. It is clear, from contemporary letters and parish records and the diaries of obscure folk, that there fell on the land the horror of a great sacrilege. The priest had been sacrificed, the god slain at the altar. The Middle Ages came to a second birth. That January day in Whitehall did not wash the balm from kingship but gave it a new anointing.

Book Four
THE LORD GENERAL

Chapter I

THE IMPROVISED REPUBLIC
(1649)

> To sequester out of the world into Atlantic and Utopian politics, which never can be drawn into use, will not mend our conditions, but to ordain wisely in this world of evil, in the midst whereof God has placed us unavoidably.
>
> MILTON, *Areopagitica.*

ENGLAND had ceased to be a monarchy; for a little it looked as if she might cease to be a nation, and, the foundation-stone having been removed, might soon clatter down in fragments. Oliver's practical instinct revived in this dire emergency, and, having for a month been in a fever of mind, he became again the wary politician. Like another soldier-statesman of later date he was determined that somehow or other government should be carried on. He had broken irrevocably with the royalists, and he was consistently opposed to leniency in the case of the royalist prisoners taken in arms:[1] but he held firmly by such poor shreds as remained of the constitution in the hope of patching them into a serviceable fabric. He had that trait which is said to mark the true conservative: change, the most drastic change, he would face if it were proved to be inevitable, but he had no liking for change for change's sake; he did not seek, in Marvell's phrase, to 'ruin the great work of Time'; if it were necessary to 'cast the kingdoms old into another mould,' the new one should be as like as possible to the former. A proof of his recovered sanity is his behaviour about the marriage settlement of his eldest son. With Mr. Richard Mayor of Hursley he argued about dispositions as if he had been a country squire whose sole object was to see his family well established in life. 'I have two young daughters to bestow, if God give them life and opportunity. According to your offer, I have nothing for them: nothing at all in hand. If my son dies, what consideration is there to me, and yet a jointure parted with?'[2] All this while the ground was quaking under the commonwealth, and half the nations of the earth were gathered against it.

The new republic could only live by rejecting every principle

[1] *C. J.*, VI, 159.   [2] *L. and S.*, I, 424-25.

on which it had been professedly founded. 'There is something superior to law,' Bradshawe had said at the king's trial, 'the parent or author of the law, and that is the people of England.' But the people of England had no say in this government, which was an oligarchy composed of the remnant of a nine-year-old House of Commons, which was in turn the protégé of a bitterly unpopular army. Arbitrarily this fragment recast the constitution of England. In February, though Oliver would have had it otherwise, it abolished the House of Lords and the office of king as 'unnecessary, burdensome, and dangerous to the liberty, safety and public interests of the people of this nation,' and in May it established a republic. 'England,' so ran the act, 'should henceforth be governed as a Commonwealth, or a Free State, by the supreme authority of this nation, the representatives of the people in Parliament, and by such as they shall appoint and constitute under them for the good of the people.' The word 'representatives' was meaningless. There were about ninety members in the House, and of these London had only one, Wales had only three, while great shires like Hertfordshire and Lancashire had none at all. The new fabric might be oligarchy or aristocracy, but it was certainly not representative government, and still less was it a free state, since its whole authority rested upon the army. Its justification lay in the fact that it was a new experiment, which must be nursed, as Henry Marten said, by 'the mother who brought it forth,' and could not yet be submitted to the rude winds of popular judgment. The paradox was that it would only endure with the army's support, and that this prop meant high taxation and deep popular discontent.

But the makers of the republic, if they could not give England self-government, were determined to give it that government which Charles in his dying words on the scaffold had declared was the chief desideratum. A Council of State of forty members was formed as the main executive authority, with Oliver as its first president. It was in substance an annually elected committee of parliament, and its recommendations had to be approved by the House, but since it was a microcosm of the House this approval was a foregone conclusion. Its early sittings were in Derby house, but presently it moved to Whitehall. Its members were squires, merchants, a few lawyers, and one or two professional soldiers; Bradshawe, Fairfax, Whitelocke, Marten, Ludlow and Vane had seats on it. For its working it resolved itself into committees, each undertaking a special department. A new High Court of Justice was established to try Hamilton and the other prisoners, but it was soon found possible to induce sufficient judges to continue in office to carry on the ordinary work of the King's Bench and the Common Pleas. In matters of finance the republic had more than three times the revenue of Charles, but it had to face a far heavier naval and military expenditure, so it had to keep the level of taxation high, and, since much of its income came from fines upon delinquents and the sale of confiscated lands, the collection of revenue was laborious, costly and unpopular. Special attention was given to the fleet. Under the admiralty committee of the Council there was a board of experienced navy commissioners, the sailors were better paid, and within three years no less than forty-one new men-of-war were added to the navy. The army was now a standing professional force, numbering forty-four thousand men. The machinery of local government went on as usual, sheriffs and justices being appointed in the old manner. There was a rigid press censorship, a comprehensive system of espionage, and harsh punishment of delinquents, but it may fairly be said that the work of the new constitution-makers was efficient. Within a month or two they had put the machine in working order again, and many parts of it were a vast improvement on anything known before. Let Mazarin's agent bear witness: 'They are economical in their private affairs, and prodigal in their devotion to public affairs, for which each man toils as if for his private interest.'

But this capable bourgeois parliament got little credit for its toil. It depended for its very existence upon the army, and from the army came its severest critics. Parliament could not face a dissolution, since that would mean the end of the republic; it must carry on its task at all costs till by good government and some easing of taxation it might hope to acquire a modest popularity. But to the plain soldier this tactical necessity seemed a defection from honest principles. If England was a free state, the people must be free to govern themselves. The half-truths of democracy were held by him with the same conviction as his religious faith, and he demanded an answer to his awkward question. In January the army had drawn up a new form of the 'Agreement of the People,' which embodied its simple creed. The present parliament was to dissolve itself in April; a new parliament was to be elected every two years,

and to sit for only six months in the year; there was to be manhood suffrage, apart from paupers and menials, and equal
electoral districts; freedom of conscience and worship, no compulsory recruitment, and equality before the law were to be
regarded as articles of an unalterable 'law fundamental'; finally
the whole arrangement was to be embodied in a written constitution. Parliament received the 'Agreement' with thanks and
did nothing. It might admit the merits of the scheme, but it
knew well that the first step taken to give it effect would fling
the country into anarchy or royalism.

If the army was critical, the bulk of the community was hostile or contemptuous. The royalist gentry, broken by fines and
forfeitures, were uncompromising foes, though impotent for the
moment, as were all ranks of the disinherited episcopal clergy.
The average man and woman, with no strong party affiliations,
was deeply moved by the king's death as portrayed in *Eikon
Basiliké*, to which the sonorous prose of Milton's *Eikonoklastes*
was but a feeble answer. The presbyterians, lay and clerical,
refused to acknowledge the 'heretical commonwealth.' They
had seen the solid lump of presbytery in parliament forcibly
dissolved, and they had no love for what remained.

But the most virulent opposition came from a different quarter — the dreamers and theorists hatched out by the heats of
revolution. Three parties are to be discerned in what Carlyle
has called 'the submarine world of Calvinistic Sanscullotism.'
There were first the religious enthusiasts, known as the Fifth
Monarchy men, who held that the reign of the saints, the fifth
of the world's monarchies, had come, and that government
should be in the hands of the godly. Instead of a written constitution they were content with the Word of God. With their
general views Oliver had some sympathy, but not with so crude
a statement. More dangerous at the moment than such enthusiasts were the Levellers, who had a communist and a political wing. The communists, who called themselves the True
Levellers, were a species of Anglo-Israelites, who held it their
business to 'restore the ancient community of enjoying the
fruits of the earth, and to distribute the benefits thereof to the
poor and needy, and to feed the hungry and clothe the naked.'
They proposed to confine their operations to waste and common ground, and in April fifty of them, led by Everard and
Winstanley, started digging on some desert land at St. George's
Hill in Surrey. They were arrested and brought before the

Council, where they proved to be gentle visionaries, who neither sought to appeal to force, nor had any force to appeal to, for English sentiment was strongly for individual rights of property.

The political Levellers were a more formidable affair. They repudiated communism, and took their stand on the army's creed, complete religious freedom, annual parliaments, and manhood suffrage. Their case in logic was irrefutable, for their principles were those in whose name the revolution had been effected. Milton might appeal to 'the old English fortitude and love of freedom,' but they asked with reason what chance these qualities had under the present régime. They stood for a restriction of the powers of government and ampler rights for the individual, and in John Lilburne they found a potent leader. For Lilburne himself there is not a great deal to be said. He was without dignity of character, for when he was not abusing parliament he was petitioning it for compensation. He had a narrow cast-iron logic, and a blustering declamatory courage, but his whole being was one clot of diseased vanity. He was the type of man who earns the sobriquet of 'honest' or 'blunt' or 'free-born,' but in whom there is no true honesty, the egotist whose valour is chiefly stupidity and self-love. Wise men fought shy of him, for, even when they agreed with his creed, they deplored his antics. A contemporary pamphleteer summed up the better opinion about him when he urged that his proper fate was to be confined in a high tower where his ambition could harmlessly burn itself out, to be girt with a wooden sword, and to be fed on the carcasses of ravens, 'because he had made such fatal music and was still croaking.'[1]

But the croaker was a bellman who rang up a great following. He was the god of the common soldier, interpreting his simple-minded democracy. In his manifestoes he put into words what a vast number of humble citizens were feeling — their disappointment that the monarchy had been followed by a tyranny, their surfeit of state supervision, their impatience with taxes on which they had never been consulted. All spring and summer there was trouble with the army. When in April a mutineer was put to death in front of St. Paul's he was given a popular funeral, at which even respectable burgesses wore the sea-green ribbons of the Levellers. The soldiers' grievance is set forth in the publication *The Hunting of the Foxes from Newmarket to Whitehall by five small beagles late of the Army* — 'The

[1] *Looke about you*, 1647 (Th.).

old King's person and the old Lords are but removed, and the new King and the new Lords with the Commons are in one House, and so we are under a more absolute arbitrary monarchy than before.'

It was no more than the truth. The justification of the new régime lay in the razor edge on which England stood — anarchy on the one side and a Stuart restoration by foreign help on the other. The infant republic had countless enemies at home, and not a friend in the outer world. John Milton, hitherto a good deal at variance with parliament over the matter of press censorship, was brought in as secretary to the Council, and in his stately Latin made the best of a hopeless diplomatic task. All Europe had gasped with horror at Charles's death. The English envoy was murdered at the Hague, and no attempt was made by Holland to avenge him. France refused to recognize the republic, put an embargo on English imports, and sent out privateers to prey on English commerce. Russia imprisoned English merchants and impounded their merchandise. In protestant Germany, Scandinavia, and the United Provinces the pulpits rang with denunciations of the regicides. Only catholic Spain, out of hostility to France, preserved an uneasy neutrality. All northern Europe was filled with royalist fugitives, waiting the chance of revenge. Montrose was collecting troops for a descent on Scotland. Scotland itself was making extravagant demands upon the republic, the refusal of which meant war. In Ireland Ormonde had made terms with the Confederate Catholics, and was threatening Dublin with a formidable army. At any moment to Scotland or Ireland might go the young Charles to launch a counter-revolution.

Oliver, on whom the chief burden of the new civil régime fell, had for the moment forgotten his malaise of mind and body in facing instant needs. He was aware that he was the chief target of popular dislike — it was from his coach that the linch-pin was taken during the official visit to the city on June 7 — and the knowledge braced him to a prodigious energy.[1] In that energy

---

[1] During these months the pamphlet literature of the opposition reached its high-water mark of scurrility. Most of it is merely obscene or abusive, but there are certain illuminating traits. One is the hopes which the royalists entertained of Oliver's absence in Ireland; see especially *Mercurius Elencticus*, July 9–16 (Th.); *Mercurius Pragmaticus*, July 10–17 (Th.); *Man in the Moone*, No. 15, July 25–Aug. 2 (Th.); and *Balaam's Asse, or The City-Fast for Blessing the King and Cursing Oliver* (Th.). Another is the general expectation that he would presently seize the throne, for which see *Earl of Pembroke's Speech to Nol-Cromwell* (Th.) (an excellent skit upon that feeble nobleman); *A Remonstrance to the People*; *The Right Picture of King Oliver from Top to Toe*; and

there was much that was fevered and morbid, but his practical
acumen and his swift instinct were unimpaired. 'You shall
scarce speak to Cromwell about anything,' Lilburne complained, 'but he will lay his hand on his breast, elevate his eyes
and call God to record. He will weep, howl and repent, even
while he doth smite you under the fifth rib.' To the main arguments of the Levellers he knew there was no logical reply, but
their irrelevance, at that hour of national crisis, broke his temper. In February there was a scene in the House of Commons
between him and Henry Marten, when he drew his dagger and
'clapping it on the seat by him, expressed great anger against
Harry and his Levelling crew.'[1] He detested, too, the implications of their creed, which 'tended to reduce all orders and
ranks of men to an equality' — a pleasing prospect, no doubt,
for poor men and 'truly not unwelcome to all bad men.' When
Lilburne was brought before the Council in March he listened
to Oliver speaking through the door. 'I tell you, no,' he heard
him say, thumping the table. 'You have no other way to deal
with these men but to break them, or they will break you; yea,
and bring all the guilt of the blood and treasure shed and spent
in this kingdom upon your heads and shoulders, and frustrate
and make void all that work that, with so many years' industry,
toil and pains you have done, and so render you to all rational
men in the world as the most contemptible generation of silly,
low-spirited men in the earth to be broken and routed by such
a despicable, contemptible generation of men as they are.'

Oliver did not succeed in smiting Lilburne under the fifth
rib, for no court would convict him, and he had to be left yet
awhile to continue his career as a public and not unpopular
nuisance. But when the same spirit revealed itself in the army
he dealt with it faithfully. The trouble in London in April was
followed in May by an outbreak at Banbury and then at
Salisbury among the troops destined for Ireland. Fairfax and
Oliver reviewed their own regiments in Hyde Park, and the
latter made a candid appeal to them to trust parliament to
settle arrears of pay and to dissolve as soon as its immediate
task was completed, and not to give England's enemies the

many others. Most of the pamphlets are trash, but there are one or two amusing
parodies of Oliver's prayers and sermons. If anyone desires to see into what depth of
filth his opponents could descend, he may refer to the two parts of *A Tragi-comedy
called New-market-Fayre* (Th.), and *A New Bull-Bayting, or A Match Play'd at the
Town-Bull of Ely by Twelve Mungrills* (Th.).

[1] *Mercurius Pragmaticus*, Feb. 27–Mar. 5, 1649 (Th.).

chance of victory by demanding a change of horses when they were crossing the stream. The men were convinced, and the green ribbons were torn from their hats. Then the two generals set out in pursuit of the mutineers, fell upon them at Burford in Oxfordshire, took four hundred prisoners and shot three as an example. Few military insurrections have been quelled with so little bloodshed.[1]

But to restore army discipline was only one of Oliver's tasks. He tried — and failed — to conciliate the presbyterians by offering to consent to the establishment of presbytery if it were combined with toleration, and to re-admit to the House the members excluded by Pride's Purge. He laboured to convert some of his querulous friends like Robert Hammond and Lord Wharton. No doubt there had been irregularities in the way the republic had come to birth, but who were they to cavil at the methods of the Almighty? 'It is easy to object to the glorious actings of God if we look too much upon instruments. Be not offended at the manner; perhaps there was no other way left. What if God accepted their zeal as He did that of Phineas, whom reason might have called before a jury?... What if the Lord have witnessed His approbation and acceptance to this also — not only by signal outward acts but to the heart too?' It is his old doctrine of 'dispensations,' with the addendum that they must carry the conviction of their divine origin to the Christian spirit.

These spring and summer months of diplomacy and police work must have put a cruel strain upon his temper, for he was eager to deal with the republic's most instant peril, the threat from Ireland and Scotland. Of the two he was convinced that Ireland was the more urgent problem. Prince Rupert with eight ships was on the Munster coast. The king's death seemed to have united protestant and catholic in a common abhorrence of his executioners. The strong places held for parliament were being one by one surrendered by parliament's own officers. The native Irish clans, the gentry of the Pale, and the protestants of Ulster and Munster seemed to have composed their quarrels. Every since the rebellion of 1641 had been quelled in blood and fire the catholic Irish in self-defence had had their Confederacy, which disputed the government of Ireland with the lord-lieutenant. Charles had intrigued to his own dis-

---

[1] At Oxford on their return journey Fairfax and Oliver were made Doctors of Civil Law, and Harrison, Hewson and Okey, Masters of Arts.

advantage with these Confederates, and the royalist hopes of Ireland had been weakened by the arrival of the papal legate Rinuccini, who laboured to make the quarrel one wholly of religion and Irish nationality. Ormonde, the lord-lieutenant had in despair surrendered his office to parliament, Michael Jones was put in command at Dublin, Inchiquin routed the Confederates in Munster, and George Monk took charge of Ulster. But by the beginning of 1649 the situation had changed, and a new alliance under Ormonde was formed, which involved all the elements, catholic and protestant, which were prepared to stand by the monarchy. Monk was forced to leave the country, and only Dublin, Drogheda and Londonderry remained to the new republic. Presently Drogheda fell to Inchiquin, and Ormonde with 7000 foot and 4000 horse was besieging the capital. At midsummer that year it looked as if Ireland had become a compact royalist state, and would demand in every part a laborious reconquest.

To Oliver the matter was not only one of the republic's defence. It raised the question which was never far from his mind — whether the three parts of Britain should remain a united nation, and whether England should be the predominant partner in the trinity. On March 15 the Council of State nominated him to the Irish command. At first he hesitated, for he was determined to make sure that, if he undertook the task, he should have a free hand and should be properly equipped and supported; and it was not till March 30 that he formally notified his acceptance. On March 23 in a speech to the council of officers at Whitehall he explained the reason for his hesitation. He would not have soldiers follow him to Ireland out of personal loyalty and affection, unless he was certain that they would be well provided for. Then he turned to the larger question. 'It matters not who is our commander-in-chief if God be so.' Formidable as their enemies were the chief menace lay in dissension among themselves. Ireland was the first task, for with it was bound up the future of their republic, their religion, and the ancient pride of Englishmen.

> If we do not endeavour to make good our interest there, and that timely, we shall not only have... our interest rooted out there but they will in a very short time be able to land forces in England, and to put us to trouble here. I confess I have had these thoughts with myself that perhaps may be carnal and foolish. I had rather be overrun with a Cavalierish interest than a Scotch interest: I had

rather be overrun with a Scotch interest than an Irish interest; and I think of all this is most dangerous. If they shall be able to carry on their work, they will make this the most miserable people in the earth, for all the world knows their barbarism.... Truly it is come thus far, that the quarrel is brought to this state, that we can hardly return unto that tyranny that formerly we were under the yoke of, which through the mercy of God hath been lately broken, but we must at the same time be subject to the kingdom of Scotland, or the kingdom of Ireland, for the bringing in of the King. Now that should awaken all Englishmen, who perhaps are willing enough that he should have come in upon an accommodation, but not that he must come from Ireland or Scotland.[1]

Such an appeal did not fall upon deaf ears, and there was no trouble about the twelve thousand men of the expeditionary force. But there was a good deal of trouble with the financing, transport and supply. On these points Oliver was adamant, and four months were wasted on the business. In June an act was passed to provide £400,000 from the excise, and to authorize the floating of a loan for £150,000, but the city merchants would not take up the loan, and indeed offered odds of twenty to one that the expedition would never start. Meantime he left no stone unturned to insure success. He was privy to Monk's armistice with Owen Roe O'Neill, and he got into touch with the royalist Lord Broghill, the son of Lord Cork and a power in Munster, and won over to his side one who detested the native Irish more than he loved the king. In April his mother, now well on in the eighties, was seriously ill, and he could not leave her,[2] but as soon as she recovered he set about moving troops towards the western seaboard. Three regiments of foot and one of horse were sent to Chester as reinforcements for Dublin, while the main army was concentrated at Bristol on its way to Milford Haven. His first intention had been to send the whole force to Munster and to accompany it in person, but news from Dublin made him change his mind; two-thirds of the army should go to Munster under Ireton, while he himself with the remainder sailed for the Irish capital. In the west of England there were signs of indiscipline among the troops which he must correct before his departure.

On Tuesday, July 10, he left London for the west, charged with the duties of lord-lieutenant and commander-in-chief in

[1] The speech is in *C. P.*, II, 200, and *L. and S.*, III, 400.
[2] *L. and S.*, III, 406.

Ireland for three years, with a salary of £13,000; nominally under the authority of Fairfax, but in reality with powers limited only by the embarrassments of the exchequer. He left the capital in state — 'himself in a coach with six gallant Flanders mares, whitish-grey; divers coaches accompanying him, and very many great officers of the army; his lifeguard consisting of eighty gallant men, the meanest whereof a commander or esquire, in stately habit; with trumpets sounding, almost to the shaking of Charing Cross, had it now been standing.'[1] This was policy, not ostentation. Oliver cared nothing for pomp for its own sake, but he was determined that the republic should be honoured in its principal servant; therefore he, whom Ormonde and others called a John of Leyden, would set out on his high mission with all the state of a king.

In Bristol he was detained a week or two waiting a supply of money from London. There his wife was summoned to join him, for Oliver became the more dependent upon family affection when his public purpose was grim. Thence he wrote to Richard Mayor at Hursley about his new daughter-in-law: 'I am very glad that our children have also good leisure to make a journey to eat cherries; it's very excusable in my daughter. I hope she may have a very good pretence for it.' As for his son Richard, 'I wish he may be serious, the times require it'; and in a later letter, 'I would have him mind and understand business, read a little history, study the mathematics and cosmography: these are good, with subordination to the things of God. Better than idleness, or mere outward worldly contents. These fit for public services, for which a man is born.'[2] At the end of the month the army moved westward, and a free market was ordered in the villages around Milford Haven, ready money being promised for all purchases.[3]

On August 12, as he waited for a favourable wind, he was cheered by good news. Michael Jones had sallied from Dublin and at Rathmines had decisively beaten Ormonde. Next day Oliver embarked, and from on board ship wrote to his daughter-in-law, in reply to a letter from her. 'I like to see anything from your hand, because indeed I stick not to say I do entirely love you.' She had recently had a miscarriage, and he begs her not to trust herself to a jolting coach, but, if she must travel, to borrow a sober family nag. Then with grave kindliness he speaks of intimate things.

[1] *Cromwelliana*, 62; in the *Sidney Papers* the mares are 'reddish-grey.'
[2] *L. and S.*, I, 448–51.   [3] *E. H. R.* (1887), 140.

I desire you both to make it above all things your business to seek the Lord: to be frequently calling upon Him that He would manifest Himself to you in His son, and be listening what returns He makes to you, for He will be speaking in your ear and in your heart, if you attend thereunto. I desire you to provoke your husband likewise thereunto. As for the pleasures of this life and outward business, let that be upon the bye. Be above all these things, by faith in Christ, and then you shall have the true use and comfort of them, and not otherwise.... The Lord is very near, which we see by His wonderful works, and therefore He looks that we of this generation draw near Him. This late great mercy of Ireland is a great manifestation thereof. Your husband will acquaint you with it. We should be much stirred up in our spirits to thankfulness. We much need the spirit of Christ to enable us to praise God for so admirable a mercy.[1]

These are words which cannot jar upon us and which can never be out of date, the true language of personal religion. There was to be little of such tenderness about Oliver's public deeds for many a month.

The flotilla took a day and two nights for the journey, reaching Dublin on August 15th. 'The lord-lieutenant,' wrote Hugh Peters, 'was as sea-sick as ever I saw a man in my life.'

[1] *L. and S.*, I, 452-53.

Chapter II

IRELAND

(1649–1650)

But the prince would make no payment of amends; he bade them look for no
payment, but for the strong storms, for the grey spears, and for the rage of Odin.
Lay of Helgi.

I

OLIVER'S first act after landing in Ireland was to issue proclamations by which all men might know the spirit in which he
meant to conduct the campaign. Jones's Dublin army had got
a little out of hand, and discipline must be restored. His proclamation of August 24 warned those under his orders that
he would tolerate no looting or 'cruelties upon the country
people,' that peaceable folk must be protected in their avocations, and that all supplies must be duly paid for. The previous
day he had enjoined the citizens of Dublin to abjure their
faults of 'profane swearing, cursing and drunkenness,' offences
which would be punished with the extreme rigour of the law.[1]
He intended to carry out his task with sober justice, and with
such mercy as was compatible with justice. Even with Drogheda behind him he believed that he had been faithful to this
standard. To the enemy commander in Ross he wrote on
October 17: 'Since my coming into Ireland I have this witness for myself that I have endeavoured to avoid effusion of
blood... this being my principle, that the people and places
where I come may not suffer except through their own wilfulness.'[2]

Before we consider what is by general consent the darkest
episode in Oliver's career, it is important to recall his intellectual
and emotional background. But first we may note a physical
fact. He was in bad health. Before Christmas he had an actual
breakdown, some form of malaria which was the country
epidemic, but from the start his bodily condition was abnormal.
It had been so ever since the difficult days before the second
Civil War, and it was to continue so, with interludes of serious
illness, till after Worcester. He took a doctor with him, a step

[1] The proclamations are in *L. and S.*, I, 456–57, and III, 410.
[2] *Ibid.*, I, 490.

which in the old days he would have scorned.[1] The balance of
his nature was maladjusted; mind preyed upon body, and body
distempered mind.

The chief thing to remember is that he regarded the immediate conquest of Ireland as of desperate importance for the
future of Britain. Apart from his repugnance to the idea that
England should be dictated to by an alien nation, there was the
fact that for the past eight years Ireland had been a perpetual
menace to what he regarded as the work of God. From it
Charles had time and again threatened the success of that
work, and now the peril was greater than ever. The republic
was on a needle point; the forces of darkness were massing
against it; at any moment the young king might land in Scotland and set that country aflame: if Ireland were still uncon-
quered England would then be between two fires. Speedily and
once and for all he must stamp out the embers of revolt, and in
such a cause extreme severity was a right and a duty. Here was
no longer the chivalrous war of Marston Moor and Naseby,
when leniency was a military as well as a political necessity.
Now it was surgery, the more merciful if the sharper. Carlyle's
rhodomontade, preposterous enough as an historical judgment,
does not in fact misrepresent Oliver's temper: 'Armed Soldier,
terrible as Death, relentless as Doom; doing God's Judgments
on the Enemies of God. It is a phenomenon not of joyful
nature; no, but of awful, to be looked at with pious terror and
awe.' With awe, doubtless, but also with pity, for it is Oliver
perverted, forced by his overmastering sense of practical needs
out of his normal humanity.

In the second place the Irish seemed to him, as to all Englishmen of that time, to be a lower race, something beneath the
level of mankind. To Milton, judging by hearsay, they were
'indocible and averse from all civility and amendment.'[2] To
Raleigh long before they had been like the savages of the
Guianas. The gentle Spenser could paint a picture of misery
which has few equals in literature: 'In one year and a half
they were brought to such wretchedness as any stony heart
would have rued the sight. Out of every corner of the woods
and glynns they came forth on their hands, for their legs could
not bear them — they looked like anatomies of death, and

[1] This was Jonathan Goddard, who became Warden of Merton. See Aubrey, *Brief
Lives* (ed. Clark), I, 268.
[2] *Observations on the Articles of Peace,* 1649.

spoke like ghosts crying out of the grave; they flocked to a plot
of watercresses as to a feast, though it afforded them small
nourishment, and ate dead carrion, happy when they could find
it, and soon after scraped the very carcases out of the graves.' [1]
But Spenser goes on to urge that Essex should harden his
heart, and reduce other parts of the land to the same condition.
A hideous blindness seems to have afflicted even the best
Englishmen in the Tudor and Stuart periods where the native
Irish were concerned. They were outside the human pale, below even the standards of the beast, sunk in a brutish barbarism and in blasphemous idolatries. When in 1655 the massacre
of Protestants took place in the Piedmont valleys, Fleetwood
found a more heinous offender than the Savoyard troops. 'It
was less strange to us when we heard that the insatiable Irish
had a hand in that bloodshed.'

Again, to this racial contempt there was added a complete
misreading of recent Irish history. To Oliver it was a design in
snow and ink — innocent and honest English against murderous and treacherous Irish. His views seem to have been gathered from Thomas May, whose parliamentary history had been
published in 1647.[2] He had a memory of the Irish rebellion of
1641, which had been swollen into a monstrous legend. It is
clear that the atrocities of that rebellion were grossly exaggerated, and that Irish barbarities were at least balanced by the
cruelties of the English retaliation.[3] For the rest he was unconscious of the long black history of spoliation and oppression,
legal chicanery and military violence — the horror of the past,
the misery of the present and the darkness of the future. Let us
take the judgment of an unemotional historian. 'Behind the
people,' Lecky has written, 'lay the maddening recollection of
the wars of Elizabeth, when their parents had been starved by
thousands to death, when unresisting peasants, when women,
when children had been deliberately massacred, and when no
quarter had been given to the prisoners. Before them lay the
almost certain prospect of banishment from the land that re-

[1] *View of the State of Ireland*, 1596.
[2] See Gardiner, *Comm. and Prot.*, I, 148.
[3] An instructive document is the report of the commission of seven Protestant ministers in 1641–42 which, with the best will in the world to put the case high, makes it clear
that there was no general massacre. It was published in London in 1642. For the
measures of retaliation see *A True Relation of the Proceedings of the Scots and English
Forces in the North of Ireland in* 1642, which Parliament ordered to be burned. See also
Prendergast, *Cromwell's Settlement of Ireland*, ch. II.

mained to them, of the extirpation of the religion which was
fast becoming the passion as well as the consolation of their
lives, of the sentence of death against any priest that dared to
pray beside their bed of death.'

Of all this Oliver seems to have been unaware. He had forgotten, too, what he must have known — that the scutcheon
of parliament had not been unstained with horrors — the murder of Irish women after Naseby, and the butchery of women
and non-combatants after Philiphaugh by the parliament's
Covenanting allies. When in December the twenty Irish prel-
ates at Clonmacnoise made their appeal to the Irish people he
replied in a high strain of angry rhetoric and aggrieved innocence. The bishops had warned their flocks that unless the
Irish people were united against the common enemy their
religion would be extirpated, their property confiscated, and
they themselves slain or banished — all incontrovertible de-
ductions from England's past policy. Oliver replied with another picture which, though ludicrous as history, undoubtedly
represented his sincere belief.

> Who is it that created this common enemy? I suppose you mean
> Englishmen. The English? Remember, ye hypocrites, Ireland was
> once united to England; Englishmen had good inheritances which
> many of them purchased with their money, they or their ancestors
> from many of you and your ancestors. They had good leases from
> Irishmen for a long time to come; great stocks therefrom; houses
> and plantations created at their cost and charge. They lived peace-
> ably and honestly among you; you had generally equal benefit of
> the protection of England with them, and equal justice from the
> laws — saving what was necessary for the State, for reasons of
> State, to put upon some few people apt to rebel upon the instigation
> of such as you. You broke the union. You, unprovoked, put the
> English to the most unheard-of and most barbarous massacre,
> without respect of sex or age, that ever the sun beheld, and at a
> time when Ireland was in perfect peace, and when, through the
> example of English industry, through commerce and traffic, that
> which was in the natives' hands was better to them than if all Ire-
> land had been in their possession and not an Englishman in it; and
> yet then, I say, was this unheard-of villainy perpetrated by your
> instigation who boast of peace-making and unity against the com-
> mon enemy. What think you by this time? Is not my assertion
> true? Is God — will God be with you? I am confident He will not.[1]

It is a strange farrago — the loss of civil and religious liberty

[1] *L. and S.*, II, 7–8.

can be compensated for by material prosperity — but it has the accent of complete conviction. It was in accord with what Clement Walker tells us was the policy of the independents — 'the papists of Ireland rooted out and their lands sold to adventurers.' There was no warrant for it in statesmanship, for statesmanship does not apply to brute beasts, but there was a strong warrant in military necessity. The Irish were to be permitted to live only in so far as they consented to become English. If not — death or the overseas plantations. He would tolerate opinion but not that worship in which opinion must be embodied — which was only a cruel quibble. 'I meddle not with any man's conscience,' he was to write to the governor of Ross. 'But if by liberty of conscience you mean the liberty to exercise the mass, I judge it best to use plain dealing, and to let you know where the Parliament of England have power, that will not be allowed of.'[1] He had come, he told the bishops, to avenge innocent blood, to break the power of lawless rebels who were enemies to human society, and to introduce the blessings of English liberty, whether they wanted them or not. The first and third pleas were more rhetoric, but the second was vital. He had to get rid as speedily as possible of an armed menace to the new, precarious commonwealth.

II

When Oliver landed in Ireland the military problem had become suddenly simplified. Blake, no longer a soldier but now entering upon his great career as an admiral, had driven Rupert from Kinsale, and the Commonwealth held the seas. Jones's victory at Rathmines on August 2nd had left Ormonde with but the shadow of an army. He could not hope to face Oliver in the field. But outside Dublin only Londonderry was for the republic. All the fortified places were held by the royalists, English cavaliers, Scots veterans, and native Irish levies. Inchiquin was in Munster with an army largely of protestants, Clanricarde led the catholics of Connaught, and in Ulster Owen Roe O'Neill had terminated the arrangement he had made with Monk, and was ready to fight for the king. He was a catholic first, a royalist second, and an Irishman third, and now all his loyalties were combined. Too little praise has been given to those Irish leaders who in the face of betrayal and

[1] *L. and S.*, I, 493.

neglect maintained their royalism. 'I wonder,' Henrietta Maria
had written to her husband in 1647, 'that the Irish do not give
themselves to some foreign king; you will force them to it in the
end when they see themselves offered as a sacrifice.' But when
the news came of the Rathmines disaster O'Neill's chivalrous
soul turned to the losing side. 'To demonstrate to the world,' he
told his officers, 'that I value the service of my King and the
welfare of my nation, as I always did, I now forget and forgive
the Supreme Council and my enemies their ill practices, and all
the wrongs they did me from time to time, and will now embrace that peace which I formerly denied of a good intent.' [1]

To make this help from Ulster available the fortresses must
be held which stood between that province and Dublin. The
garrisons of Trim and Dundalk were strengthened, and into
Drogheda, at the mouth of the Boyne, Ormonde put the flower
of his army — his own regiment under Sir Edmund Verney,
three regiments under Colonels Byrne, Wall and Warren, of
which one was mainly English in composition, and seven
troops of horse. If he could hold these fortresses he might
afford to wait till he was joined by O'Neill and could venture
upon a field action. For the rest there was no difficulty about
recruiting fresh troops, for the land was full of armed banditti,
but there would be the utmost difficulty about pay and supplies, for his war-chest was empty. He did not know that Owen
Roe had less than three months of life before him, for he was
dying of a disease in the knee, poisoned, as his friends believed,
by the gift from some traitor of russet-leather boots.

Oliver had at his command a compact, disciplined and well-
equipped army. He had ready money, though he had constantly to wring fresh supplies out of parliament, and he could
maintain an open market wherever he went to which the country people flocked, so that his troops were far better supplied
than the enemy. The main lines of the problem, as he saw it,
were simple. Now that Ireton had arrived, he disposed of some
10,000 foot and 5000 horse. He was opposed by an enemy,
numerous, amorphous and inorganic, offering no single nerve-
centre at which to strike, always ready to disappear into bog
or forest. Therefore he must have a number of light, swift
columns with which to hunt down each enemy nucleus. But if
there was no single nerve-centre there were a number of lesser
bases which must be destroyed. He knew that Ormonde was

[1] Gilbert, *Cont. History of Irish Affairs*, III, 211.

too weak to relieve these garrisons by an assault upon the besiegers — the most he could do was to re-victual and reinforce
them. Again, Ireland was an island, and he controlled the sea.
Every port he took could be made a new base, and so he would
not be troubled with long lines of communication. Once the
ports had been mastered it would be his business to clear the
valleys of those rivers which were almost the only means of
transport, the Barrow, the Nore and the Suir, the Blackwater,
and ultimately the Shannon. All must be done at racing speed,
for he knew how narrow was his limit of time.

But first he must capture the half-way houses which lay between him and Coote in Ulster, who might presently have to
face O'Neill. Chief of these was Drogheda, which Ormonde had
garrisoned with 2500 men under the command of Sir Arthur
Aston, while he himself lay up the Boyne at Trim waiting for
supports from Munster and Connaught. Aston, a grim old
catholic veteran with a wooden leg,[1] had fought at Edgehill,
defended Reading against Essex, and had been governor of
Oxford. The place was very strong, and it was believed could
hold out against any force for at least a month. It lay on both
sides of the Boyne, and so was impossible to invest. When
Oliver reached it on September 3, he decided to assault it only
on the south side, and he had to spend some days in erecting
batteries and waiting on the arrival of his siege train by sea.
On the 10th he summoned the town, and on Aston's scornful
rejection of his demands he opened his cannonade.

The high mediæval wall of the south front was protected
on the east by a deep ravine, and within the south-east angle
stood St. Mary's church. At the western end there was a re-
entrant angle, strengthened at its apex by an artificial hillock
called the Mill Mount. By the evening of the 10th Oliver had
made two small breaches in the south wall, and destroyed the
the church steeple. Neither breach was yet practicable for
troops, but Aston realized what the next day's bombardment
would bring forth, and he also knew that he could not hope
for help from Ormonde. He saw that his case was desperate,
and during the night he threw up a triple line of interior
earthworks running west from behind the church. Next
day, the 11th, the cannonade was resumed, and about five

---

[1] 'It's said that upon a salley he lost his wooden instrument, which made many of the
soldiers to cry out, *A Chyrurgion, A Chyrurgion*; but stout-hearted Ashton replyed, *A
Joyner, A Joyner.*' *Moderate Messenger*, Sept. 10–17, 1649 (Th.).

in the afternoon Oliver gave the word to storm. The three regiments of assault were twice repulsed, and one of their commanders slain. Oliver in person led the column to a third assault and the defence broke. The supplementary entrenchment was soon carried, and the garrison fled, pursued by Oliver's horse, partly across the bridge to the north part of the town, and partly to Mill Mount. At first quarter was granted, but, when the assault on Mill Mount began, by Oliver's own order it was thereafter refused. All the royalists on the Mount were massacred, including Sir Arthur Aston, whose head was battered in with his own wooden leg. Then pike and sword swept north through the narrow streets, leaving death behind them. The heaviest slaying was around St. Peter's church, where a thousand died. Some eighty took refuge in the steeple; Oliver ordered it to be burned, and those who escaped the flames perished by the sword. With the coming of darkness the siege of Drogheda was over, but not the killing. On the 12th some refugees were driven out of two towers on the wall, the officers slain and the rest shipped to the Barbadoes. Every friar found in the place, save two, was knocked on the head. The surviving royalist leaders were hunted down and with Oliver's consent slain in cold blood, among them, possibly, Sir Edmund Verney,[1] son of him who had fallen at Edgehill bearing the king's standard. Inevitably in the confusion a certain number of civilians perished.

Such are the bald and indisputable facts of this hideous business.[2] Let us see how Oliver viewed them. He arrived before Drogheda on September 3, which was to be the day of Dunbar, and of Worcester, and of his death. That year it was a fateful day for him in another sense, for Drogheda revealed him, for the only time in his career, rapt into a mood

---

[1] Mr. Gardiner accepts this version of Verney's death, but I think it more likely that he perished on Mill Mount, where he was with Aston. The only authority for his subsequent murder is a letter written two months later by a Mr. Buck (*Verney Memoirs*, I, 413), which I find frankly incredible, and a letter written to Ormonde by Inchiquin (Gilbert, *op. cit.*, II, Pref.), who had no means of learning the truth. I have had the privilege of reading an excellent MS. study of Cromwell at Drogheda by Mr. W. M. Clyde of St. Andrews, which confirms my suspicions from a careful study of the evidence.

[2] The authorities are Oliver's own dispatches in *L. and S.*, I, 464–72, the royalist letters in Gilbert, *Cont. Hist. of Affairs in Ireland*, Vol. II, and in the *Carte MSS.*, and the accounts by Hewson and others in *Perfect Occurrences* (Th.), *The Perfect Diurnal* (Th.), and *The Kingdom's Faithful and Impartial Scout* (Th.). See also Gardiner, *Comm. ana Prot.*, I, 114–25, Murphy, *Cromwell in Ireland*, ch. VII and VIII, and Bagwell. *Ireland under the Stuarts*, II, 122–26.

of blind animal ferocity. Hear him to Lenthall on the actual events:

> The enemy retreated, divers of them, into the Mill Mount: a place very strong and of difficult access, being exceedingly high, having a good graft, and strongly palisaded. The Governor, Sir Arthur Ashton, and divers considerable officers being there, our men, getting up to them, were ordered by me to put them all to the sword. And indeed, being in the heat of action, I forbade them to spare any that were in arms in the town, and I think that night they put to the sword about 2000 men, divers of the officers and soldiers being fled over the Bridge into the other part of the Town, where about one hundred of them possessed St. Peter's church-steeple, some the west gate, and others a strong round tower next the gate called St. Sunday's. These, being summoned to yield to mercy, refused, whereupon I ordered the steeple of St. Peter's church to be fired, where one of them was heard to say in the midst of the flames: 'God damn me, God confound me; I burn, I burn.' [1]

There is no shirking of responsibility — 'I ordered' — 'I forbade' — but there is a hint of apology, 'being in the heat of action.'

Let us hear his reasons. It was, he is persuaded, a 'righteous judgment of God upon these barbarous wretches, who have imbrued their hands in so much innocent blood.' Strange history, for it is highly improbable that any man in Drogheda had a hand in the old rebellion.... It was the direct work of the spirit of God. 'That which caused your men to storm so courageously, it was the Spirit of God, who gave your men courage and took it away again, and gave the enemy courage and took it away again, and gave your men courage again and therewith their happy success.' Strange theology, for the Holy Spirit was in that case responsible for his heat of temper at the Mill Mount, for which he implicitly apologizes.... But he has a better reason. 'It will tend to prevent the effusion of blood for the future, which are the satisfactory grounds to such actions, which otherwise cannot but work remorse and regret.' And to Bradshawe: 'The enemy were filled upon this with much terror. And truly I believe this bitterness will save much blood through the goodness of God.' [2] Through the heavy coating of pious commonplaces there juts this one piece of intelligible and practical reasoning. The work had to be done fast and extreme severity would expedite it.

[1] *L. and S.*, I, 468–69. [2] *L. and S.*, I, 468–69, 420, 465.

Drogheda had in fact that immediate effect. Trim and Dundalk were at once evacuated, Venables was dispatched to Ulster to support Coote, and Carlingford and Newry soon surrendered. Oliver's next objective was in the south, Wexford on the Slaney in the first place, the home of the pirates who had preyed upon English trade. On October 1 he was before the town, with an army which, in spite of troops detached for garrisons, numbered some 7000 foot and 2000 horse. The place was duly summoned, and at first there seemed to be a hope of surrender, but Castlehaven succeeded in getting some 1500 foot into the town and the governor changed his mind. But parleys continued, with the result that the defence was in confusion; the castle was yielded by accident or by treachery, but there was a blind resistance in barricaded streets and in the market-place, where some 2000 soldiers and civilians were slaughtered. There was also a great butchery of friars. It was an affair of the rank-and-file of Oliver's army, maddened by what they regarded as senseless resistance and exasperated by long exposure to autumn rains. He himself had no direct responsibility for the massacre as he had had at Drogheda, but he was not prepared to question the ways of the Almighty. 'Indeed!' he told Lenthall, 'it hath not without cause been set upon our hearts that I was intending better to this place than so great a ruin, hoping the town might be of more use to you and your army, yet God would not have it so; but, by an unexpected providence in His righteous justice, brought a just judgment upon them; causing them to become a prey to the soldier, who in their piracies had made preys of so many families, and made with their bloods to answer the cruelties which they had exercised upon the lives of divers poor Protestants.' [1]

From Wexford Oliver moved to Ross, at the head of the estuary of the Nore and the Barrow, which capitulated on liberal terms. From now on we may note a certain slackening of the fierce temper of Drogheda. The country malaria had descended upon his army, and was decimating its ranks. 'I scarce have one officer of forty amongst us that hath not been sick, and how many considerable ones we have lost is no little thought of heart to us.' [2] Among the dead was that Colonel Horton, who had done much to save the situation in South Wales in the summer of 1648. Oliver himself fell ill. All these were disquieting providences, the meaning of which was not

---

[1] *L. and S.*, I, 486–87.   [2] *Ibid.*, I, 506.

plain, and it behoved a man to walk before the Lord in fear. His mood has become patently gentler. He finds time to send a kindly letter to Fairfax,[1] and to beg Mr. Mayor at Hursley to get Dick and his young wife to write to him. 'As for Dick I do not much expect it from him, knowing his idleness, but I am angry with my daughter as a promise-breaker. Pray tell her so; but I hope she will redeem herself.... I desire you to call upon my son to mind the things of God more and more: alas, what profit is there in the things of this world; except they be enjoyed in Christ, they are snares. I wish he may enjoy his wife so, and she him; I wish I may enjoy them both so.'[2]

The weather was vile. The sickness among his troops was no longer malaria and dysentery but spotted fever, that plague which turned men's bones to water. But he dared not rest, for he knew that at any moment a crisis east of St. George's Channel might cut short his work. The fear inspired by the Drogheda cruelties was ebbing and being replaced by a sullen fury. He failed to take Duncannon, at the mouth of the estuary which led to Waterford. When in November, in a short spell of better weather, he attacked Waterford itself he found himself too weak to storm it, and was compelled to go into winter quarters. Michael Jones, his lieutenant-general, died in December of plague — a staunch fighting man who had had sore scruples over the king's execution. 'What England lost thereby,' Oliver wrote, 'is above me to speak. I am sure I have lost a noble friend and companion in labours.... indeed we are a crazy company, yet we live in His sight, and shall work the time appointed to us, and shall rest after that in peace.'[3]

But there were elements of hope in the prospect. O'Neill in Ulster was also dead, and his army was leaderless; in October Cork had declared for the republic, to be followed in November by Youghal, Kinsale, Bandon and other strong places. By the end of the year the coast of Ireland from Londonderry to Cape Clear was, with the exception of Waterford, free of the enemy. The Munster protestants were breaking with their allies, and daily desertions were thinning Inchiquin's forces. The bishops at Clonmacnoise in December had identified the revolt with their church, and made it hard for protestant royalists to continue in arms. Ormonde was in an impossible position, though on paper he still disposed of larger numbers than his opponents. There was no cohesion in his following, he was suspect

[1] *L. and S.*, III, 411.   [2] *Ibid.*, I, 498.   [3] *Ibid.*, I, 515.

alike by the protestant and catholic elements, and he was
steadily being forced into commitments which were contrary
to his political views. In December Oliver wrote to Lenthall
that, though the cup was mingled, mercies had been abundantly
vouchsafed, and he urged his doubting brethren on all sides to
agree at least in praising God. His mind was always on the
major problem at home awaiting settlement.

> If it will not yet be received that these are seals of God's approba-
> tion of your great change of government — which indeed were no
> more yours than these victories and successes are ours — yet let
> them with us say, even the most unsatisfied heart amongst them,
> that both are the righteous judgements and mighty works of God....
> And let them not be sullen, but praise the Lord, and think of us as
> they please.[1]

The first task of the new year — apart from Waterford —
was to clear the southern river valleys by capturing the interior
Munster fortresses. Rumour had reached Oliver that his recall
had been decided upon, and he must make the most of the time
left. The small places soon fell, but Kilkenny on the Nore, the
old seat of the Catholic Confederacy, proved a tough business.
Defended by Sir Walter Butler, it beat off every attack and
ultimately capitulated with all the honours of war. The same
thing happened at Clonmel on the Suir. It was held by Ulster
troops under Hugh O'Neill, the nephew of the dead Owen Roe,
'an old surly Spanish soldier,' and Oliver's assault was repulsed
with a loss to him of something like 2000 men. Ireton considered
the check 'the heaviest we ever endured either in England or
here.' 'They found,' wrote Whitelocke, 'in Clonmel the
stoutest enemy their army had ever met in Ireland, and that
there was never seen so hot a storm of so long continuance and
so gallantly defended, either in England or Ireland.' The
garrison, having exhausted their ammunition, managed to slip
out in the night and take the road for Waterford. Next day
the mayor handed over the place, and Oliver, though he was
angry when he found the soldiers gone, observed the conditions
of surrender.

That was on May 10. On May 26 Oliver at last obeyed the
summons to return home, which parliament had issued on the
8th of January, leaving Ireton to complete the subjugation of
Ireland. He was received in England as a conquering hero,

[1] *L. and S.*, I, 512.

who had delivered his country from an ancient fear. 'So much,' said Marvell's ode —

> 'So much one man can do,
> That does both act and know.'

The praise was deserved. Oliver had fulfilled his task, and, though the war lingered on for another two years, the back of the resistance was broken. He had captured nearly all the ports and cleared the main river valleys. More important, he had driven a wedge into the enemy, separating out the protestant and English elements, and leaving the opposition no longer a royalist one, but exclusively native Irish and catholic — a thing which could not be easily linked up with the English and Scottish foes of the republic. The young Charles, watching events from Jersey, saw that his restoration could not come from Ireland and turned elsewhere. On the technical side Oliver had shown a firm grasp of the obvious strategic elements of the situation. Tactically he had exhibited no special brilliance, but he had revealed his old power of handling transport and commissariat, and that gift of leadership which could keep an army together in the face of sickness, the extremes of discomfort, and a watchful and ubiquitous enemy. 'Forty years later, when the conquest of Ireland was undertaken by a former marshal of France and a king long schooled in a war against the first generals of the time, they were glad to search out Cromwell's plans for his Irish campaign and follow them at such distance as they might.'[1]

But his success was won at the expense of his repute with later generations. Oliver's Irish campaign is admittedly the chief blot on his fame. We have seen the mood in which he landed at Dublin and its psychological background. The main count is his severity at Drogheda, which even so grim a fighter as Ludlow thought 'extraordinary.'[2] In what did that severity consist?... He ordered the slaughter of all men found in arms. The excuse is that by the law of war, as it stood then and stood for many a day, the defenders of a fortress, which was duly summoned and then stormed, had no claim to mercy, the more so if the fortress was patently indefensible. Wellington considered that he would have done rightly if he had put the garrisons of Ciudad Rodrigo and Badajoz to the sword: 'If I had done so to the first it is probable that I would have saved 5000

[1] Fortescue, I, 238.   [2] Ludlow, I, 234.

men in the assault of the second.' [1]... He appears to have ordered, at Mill Mount and afterwards, the killing of men who had been admitted to quarter; it is necessary to put it tentatively, for it is not certain how far he knew the fact. In defence it may be said that this admission to quarter had not been authorized, and that Oliver never showed the sanguinary madness of some of his contemporaries who held the breaking of a promise of quarter was a religious duty.[2]... He allowed prisoners to be butchered later in cold blood. It may be argued that that followed from his original no-quarter order.... He was the cause of the death of many civilians. The reply is that that was one of the inevitable consequences of a sack, and that it was never his policy. 'Give me an instance,' he asked the bishops, 'of one man, since my coming into Ireland, not in arms, massacred, destroyed or banished, concerning the massacre or destruction of whom justice hath not been done, or attempted to be done.'... Finally he permitted a wholesale slaughter of friars. The defence would be that he regarded catholic priests as in the nature of combatants, the men who were the backbone of the whole resistance.

But it is idle to defend him by reference to the current practice of war, to his mildness as compared with Tilly, or to the opinion of Wellington. He was built on other lines than Tilly or even Wellington, and must be judged by other standards. In Ireland he was false to his own creed. Never in the English wars, except at Basing, had he been anything but merciful. He knew that he had erred and therefore he tried to justify his conduct to Lenthall, a thing, it may fairly be said, that no other soldier of the day would have dreamed of. His confusion of spirit is shown by his excuse of a heat of temper, which in his sober moments he would have held to be a sin. It is shown by his childish tale of the blasphemy of some poor creature in the agony of burning, as if that justified the enormity. He is trying to batter his soul into complacence.

He had erred grievously and he knew it. Moreover his instinct told him that he had sinned not only against humanity but against military wisdom. Duncannon, Waterford, Kilkenny and Clonmel convinced him that his doings at Drogheda were proving an incentive and not a deterrent to the enemy. From Wexford onward he reveals a different temper. At Fethard the

[1] *Wellington Despatches*, I, 93.
[2] *e.g.* the Covenanters of 1646, for whom see *A. P. S.*, VI, i, 249.

terms were easy and the clergy were protected. At Kilkenny no priest died, and he complimented the garrison on the gallantry of their defence. So too at Carrick and Clonmel. Almost his last act in Ireland was to write to Hewson, the governor of Dublin, to secure civil treatment for the young royalist Lord Moore who had recently surrendered. After one furious lapse he returned to his natural reasoned mercifulness.

III

Oliver lives in history as the hammer of Ireland, and justly, since he set the example, but the bulk of the fighting was left to Ireton and Ludlow. Soon there was no Irish army, and the campaign became a series of sieges, raids and ambuscades. In the summer of 1650 Waterford fell to Ireton, as well as Carlow and Duncannon, and Coote and Venables in Ulster destroyed the remnant of Owen Roe's levies. Only Limerick, Galway and Athlone remained, controlling the river valleys of the west. In October Ireton laid siege to Limerick, but the coming of winter forced him to desist. In December Ormonde left Ireland, handing over to Clanricarde his hopeless task. He had shown infinite patience and fortitude,

> Doing the king's work all the dim day long.

His was not the iron hand to mould the fate of nations, but it may be truly said that he had a task beyond human powers, and that in honesty, faithfulness and purity of purpose he was, after Montrose, the noblest of the cavaliers.

In June 1651 Coote took Galway and Ireton again sat down before Limerick. It did not yield till after a five months' siege, and then rather to sickness and treachery than to arms, and as the garrison marched out two of its members fell dead of the plague. Ireton himself caught the infection and died in November — an extraordinary man who had fretted his body to fragility by incredible labours, one who never undressed in the wars except to change his linen, who would toil even when in a high fever, 'pen, tongue, head, or both or all, incessantly at work.' He would have been a great man in history, had he not been fated to be first-lieutenant to a greater. In May 1652 Galway, the last enemy stronghold, surrendered to Coote, and Ludlow, the new commander-in-chief, received weekly the surrenders of the Irish leaders, who were for the most part permitted to transfer themselves and their followers to foreign service. When Fleetwood, who had married Ireton's widow, arrived in September to succeed Ludlow, the war was virtually over.

Such was the Cromwellian conquest of Ireland. It was followed by the Cromwellian settlement, which even more than the war has made the name of Oliver an object of unrelenting hate. This is not the place to elaborate the details of that melancholy blunder. Oliver did not originate the principles behind it, which were mainly an extension of the Tudor policy of conquest and English settlement, and which had been laid down in 1642 by the Long Parliament after the rebellion. The actual working out was in the hands of Fleetwood. The claims of the adventurers who had lent money for the campaign and of the soldiers who had taken part in it were met by a wholesale confiscation of Irish land. The dispossessed were provided for by grants in the desolate wastes of Connaught. It took six years to complete the formal settlement, which found only a feeble resistance, since Ireland had lost one-third of her population, and the best of her native leaders were in exile. Two-thirds of the soil passed to new owners. Catholic rites were proscribed, and priests were hunted down and imprisoned or exiled. An attempt was made at extensive protestant propaganda and ministers were invited from New England and elsewhere. Ireland, regarded now as a piece of England overseas, was accorded equal trading rights and was not discriminated against in taxation, and presently she was given parliamentary union with England. There were one or two enlightened elements in the scheme. The administration of justice was purged of corruption, some attempt was made to promote the education of the people, and Trinity College was endowed with the lands of the old Dublin archbishopric, while the Irish army subscribed for and bought Archbishop Ussher's books as the nucleus of a public library.

It was a dogma of the older liberalism that violence can never achieve anything, and that persecution, so far from killing a thing, must inevitably nourish it. For such optimism there is no warrant in history; time and again violence has wholly achieved its purpose, when it has been carried to its logical conclusion. But Oliver and his colleagues, having many other grave matters on hand, left the Irish business unfinished, and the half-achieved extirpation resulted in the confounding of all their aims. The attempted conversion of the

Irish proved a farce, and the catholic church drew fresh strength from its sufferings. The grandees among the new landed gentry remained loyal to the English connection, but the lesser settlers became in time more Irish and more catholic than the natives. Among all classes a nationalism grew up which soon made the parliamentary union unworkable. The stricter administration of justice did nothing to conciliate, since the law administered was fundamentally unjust. 'Justice,' Sir Charles Firth has written, 'combined with forfeiture and proscription, and without equal laws, was a legal fiction which had no healing virtues.'

Any scheme of government based solely on the interests of the resident alien is doomed in the long run to failure, unless by massacre and banishment such aliens are made the bulk of the population. Oliver's conception was simple. Ireland was to be an appanage of England, governed by Englishmen, and the native Irish were awkward chattels to be moved about at their superiors' pleasure. In 1655, when Jamaica was taken and his son Henry was Lord Deputy, he tried to arrange for a thousand 'young Irish wenches' to be collected and sent out for the use of the new settlers there. The truth is that he never gave his mind to the subject; he accepted blindly the ancient legends and prejudices, and, detesting the people, used his full powers only in their conquest. In his later years he is generally in an Irish problem to be found on the side of mildness, but such isolated sparks of benevolence could do nothing to illumine the darkness. On Ireland only two men of the seventeenth century had the larger vision. Ormonde, himself an Irishman, would have made the country a comfortable neighbour to England by tolerating her religion and accepting a reasonable nationalism. Strafford had a different creed, for he would have made Ireland prosperous in the English way by giving her law and order and fostering her industries; he believed in settlement by Englishmen but on wise lines, and he would in no way discriminate between native and newcomer; he hoped for the growth of protestantism, but it must grow on its merits, and in the meantime he refused to attack the church or the land; he understood Irish conditions and realized that change must come gradually, through patient statesmanship and the slow process of time. In both of these creeds there was hope, but in Oliver's there was none. The best that can be said for him is that he was no blinder than the rest of the English people.

Chapter III

DUNBAR

(1650)

And Ehud... blew a trumpet in the mountain of Ephraim, and the children of Israel went down from the mount, and he before them.

And he said unto them, Follow after me: for the Lord hath delivered your enemies the Moabites into your hand.

Book of Judges.

I

ON THE first day of June Oliver was welcomed on Hounslow Heath, soldiers and parliament men uniting to do him honour; two days later he was officially received in the city; on the 4th he was offered the thanks of the House of Commons, and on the 11th he made his report on Ireland. He had no civilian authority; now that his appointed task was over he was only a soldier awaiting further employment; but, since such employment was assured, he was in effect the chief figure in the state, and of this all men were cognizant.

He was aware of it himself, and in the few weeks allowed him in London did his best to study the complexion of affairs. The improvised government had been a model of energy, swearing in the citizens to support the new régime, raising funds by the sale of royalist estates, reforming laws and morals, grappling with the difficulties abroad which were blowing up like sand-storms in the desert. It was not loved, but nine out of ten people tolerated it since they were very weary of strife.[1] The tenth, if he were a royalist, was deep in intrigues with Charles abroad or with potential west-country rebels. If he were a Leveller he was in furious opposition to the government, and if he were somthing short of that, one of the old guard of puritanism, his distrust was chiefly of Oliver himself. Lucy Hutchinson reflects such suspicions. 'Now had the poison of ambition so ulcerated Cromwell's heart that the effects of it became more apparent than before, and, while yet Fairfax stood an empty name, he was moulding the army to his mind,

---

[1] Much on the principle of the ex-royalist Marchamont Needham's *The Case of the Commonwealth of England Stated*, May 1650 (Th.), which urged the provident man to accept the existing state of things rather than risk further trouble.

weeding out the godly and upright-hearted men, both officers and soldiers, and filling up their rooms with rascally turncoat cavaliers, and pitiful sottish beasts of his own alliance, and others such as would swallow all things and make no questions for conscience sake.'[1] She gives instances of his subtlety, and we have another to hand in his treatment of Ludlow. Oliver wanted Ludlow in Ireland, partly because he was a good man for that kind of work, and largely because he was certain to make trouble if he were left in England. In a long interview he achieved his purpose, playing adroitly cards like the safety of the republic and the reform of the laws which he knew would influence Ludlow, and finishing with an ecstatic discourse on the 110th Psalm.[2]

He had to keep his mind firmly fixed on practical necessities, for he found all his slowly distilled theories again evaporating, and he had not Ireton beside him to fortify his mind. The Levellers were preaching doctrine which was having its effect even on moderate minds. There was a passage in one of John Lilburne's pamphlets, which had greatly influenced the court at his trial.

> The ancient and famous magistracy of this nation, the Petition of Right, the Great Charter of England, about thirty times confirmed in open and free Parliament, with all other the fundamental laws, safeties, and securities of the people, which our ancestors with an extraordinary dear rate purchased for the inheritance of us and the generations after us, and for which you pretendedly took up arms against the late King and his party, are now all subverted, broken down, and laid waste, the military power being thrust into the very office and seat of civil authority: — the King not only most illegally put to death by a strange, monstrous, illegal arbitrary court such as England never knew, monarchy extirpated not rectified, without and beside the consent of the people, though the actors of that bloody scene have owned and declared them to be the original of all just human authority; but even our Parliaments — the very marrow and soul of all the native rights of the people — put down, and the name and power thereby transmitted to a picked party of your forcible selecting, and such as your officers, our lords and riders, have often and frequently styled no better than a mock Parliament, a shadow of a Parliament, a seeming authority or the like, pretending the continuance thereof but till a new and equal Representative, by mutual agreement of the free people of England, could be elected; although now, for subserviency to their exaltation

[1] Hutchinson, II, 163.   [2] Ludlow, I, 245-47.

and kingship, they prorogue and perpetuate the same, in the name and under colour thereof introducing a Privy Council, or as they call it a Council of State, of superintendency and suppression to all future successive Parliaments for ever, erecting a martial government by blood and violence impulsed upon us.[1]

Apart from the words about the king's death — ominous words coming from that quarter — Oliver could not deny the truth of the indictment. All the principles of Pym and Hampden had been shattered into fine dust. He might rail with Ludlow against the lawyers, but he believed in the reign of law; he might defend the sword as the sword of justice and of the Lord, but he knew well in his heart that no polity of which it was the main instrument could endure.

The new régime was not only arbitrary and unpopular, it was not really efficient. The Council of State, intertwined as it was with parliament, was not a strong executive. In the spring one member, Sir John Danvers, had suggested that there need not be a constant reference of its decisions to the House, and had been snubbed for his pains. But the idea was in the air. Young Isaac Pennington, whose father was himself a member of the Council, had urged that what the country complained of in the administration was the 'multitude of affairs, prolixity in your motions, and want of an orderly government in your own body,' and had suggested as the remedy the separation of the legislative and executive powers.[2] Oliver agreed. He had been feeling his way to some such conclusion, and in that direction a way might be found to provide a strong civilian polity. But in the meantime the truth in Lilburne's charges must be disregarded and the army must continue to be the essential power, for the long-expected storm was breaking in the north.

The king's death had set all Scotland in revolt against his executioners. Charles II had been at once proclaimed king of the whole of the British islands, and the truculence of the Scottish envoys had secured their expulsion from England. But it was easier to quarrel with the new republic than to make terms with Charles. When he saw that Ireland offered him no help, he returned to Holland, and had long and embarrassed conclaves with the Scottish emissaries. He was asked to do that which he loathed, and, being helpless and penniless, he was compelled

[1] *An Outcry of the Young Men* (Th.).
[2] *A Word for the Commonweal*, 1650 (Th.)

in the end to agree; those who bargained with him were perfectly aware that he accepted in his heart none of the tenets to which he did lip-service, and that he would assuredly break the pact if fortune gave him the chance. On May 1st he signed an agreement at Breda, which pledged him to take both Covenants, to force presbytery upon England and Ireland, to use its forms in his own household, and to extirpate the popish religion from his dominions. There was further bickering on the voyage to Scotland, and matters were not finally settled till his ship had anchored at Speymouth on June 23. It is not easy to blame him for his dissimulation, granting his antecedents and the difficulties of his position; he thought the throne of Britain worth a Covenant or two, as his grandfather Henri IV had thought Paris worth a mass; an honest man among the Scottish commissioners confessed that they were more to blame for the hypocrisy of the transaction than the king.[1]

A graver charge is that by his conduct he sacrificed his best friends. His undertaking about the catholic religion made Ormonde's position in Ireland impossible, and the mere signing of the treaty sent Montrose to his death.[2] When the young king entered Aberdeen he saw mouldering on a high place a limb of the greatest of his followers. His treachery brought its punishment, for he handed himself over to the keeping of men who for the most part regarded him with aversion, and who laboured to make his life a burden. Argyll was on his side, as two years before he had been on the side of Oliver, since all his schemes had come to naught and he clutched blindly at the last straw. Scotland was royalist because she was nationalist — the dead king had been a poor thing but her own; because she sought in self-protection to force her own form of church government upon England; and because she bitterly hated the English army and the sectaries who gave that army its strength. Her royalism was certainly not due to any love of the long, dark boy whose crooked smile seemed always to be making mock of her solemnities.

Very early in the summer it was clear to parliament that a war with Scotland could not be averted, since a Scottish invasion of England was imminent. It resolved on June 12th

---

[1] Jaffray, *Diary*, 55. The documents recording the agreement are in *Clarendon S. P.*, II.

[2] See Buchan, *Montrose*, 362–63; Lang, *Hist. of Scotland*, III, 221–26; Gardiner *Comm. and Prot.*, I. 190, etc.

that in that event Fairfax should command in chief, with Oliver as his lieutenant-general Fairfax at first accepted, believing that it only meant a campaign in the north of England, but when he found that an offensive was intended across the Scottish Border he developed doubts. A committee was appointed to reason with him, including Oliver, Whitelocke, St. John, Lambert and Harrison, and no one of them was more urgent than Oliver. Fairfax argued that an invasion of Scotland would be a breach of the Solemn League, since it was not absolutely certain that the Scots meant to enter England. Oliver gave the sound practical answer that in war some probabilities were to be taken as certainties. 'Your Excellency will soon determine whether it is better to have this war in the bowels of another country or of your own, and that it will be one of these I think it without scruple.' There can be no doubt of the sincerity of his pleading. Lucy Hutchinson admits that 'he laboured for it almost all the night with most earnest endeavours,'[1] Mazarin's agent believed the same, and even the suspicious Ludlow confessed that Oliver 'acted the part so to the life that I really thought him in earnest.'[2] Indeed there was every reason why he should be. Oliver's chief aim was to find a common ground of agreement between the presbyterians and his independents, to see royalism crushed in the north, and the Scottish people ranged alongside England in the making of a Christian polity. Fairfax was not a controversial figure and he had few enemies; he liked the presbyterian form of worship and his wife and his secretary were presbyterians. To set Fairfax in command would be a gesture of conciliation, while with himself, the arch-independent, as general, it would look like war to the uttermost.

But Fairfax had come to the end of his tether. The reason he stood by was that a high probability was not sufficient ground to make war upon covenanted brethren, but to prevent trouble he gave his official grounds as 'debilities both in body and mind occasioned by former actions and businesses.' The truth was that he was altogether out of sympathy with the new current of events. He had opposed the king's execution, and he now shrank from its inevitable consequences: he loved too many of the things that had been broken, and in any case his was not the mind and temper that could rebuild out of frag-

---

[1] Hutchinson, II, 166. Colonel Hutchinson was present.

[2] Ludlow, I, 243.

ments.[1] Oliver was forced to accept that which he had never sought. On June 26 parliament decreed the advance on Scotland and appointed him 'Captain-General and Commander-in-Chief of all the forces raised or to be raised within the Commonwealth of England.'

The expeditionary troops consisted of 10,500 foot and 5500 horse, a force superbly disciplined, and largely veteran both in officers and men. Oliver took with him Fleetwood as his lieutenant-general of horse and Lambert as major-general in command of the infantry. George Monk, the ex-royalist, who had been unfortunate in Ireland, had impressed him with his military talents; he offered him as colonel to a vacant regiment, but the men would not have him, so he formed a new regiment for him out of companies from the garrisons of Berwick and Newcastle.[2] Harrison was left behind to command the troops in England, and for a greater security a new act reorganized the militia in every county.

Oliver had no illusions about the difficulty of his task. He had seen the fighting quality of the Scots, both horse and foot, at Marston Moor, and had witnessed how gallantly many of them had stood, though outnumbered and outflanked, in the rout of Preston. He had experience, too, of the abilities of David Leslie, the Scottish commander in the field, for Leven, the nominal general-in-chief, was now too old for war. Word came that the Scottish parliament had authorized levies to the number of 40,000, and later news made it clear that Leslie would dispose of something like 27,000 foot and 5000 horse. Some of this would doubtless be raw stuff, but the numbers were formidable, for they were double his own, and they would be fighting in a familiar country. There was good material among the officers at Leslie's command — presbyterians of the old rock like Strachan who had taken Montrose at Carbisdale, and Wemyss the general of artillery, and, abler still, men like John Middleton, and Massey who had once defended Gloucester for the parliament. But he was convinced that Leslie could not

[1] The best tribute to Fairfax's loyalty and simplicity of character is in the lines of his son-in-law, the Duke of Buckingham, written after the Restoration.

> 'He never knew what envy was, nor hate;
> His soul was filled with worth and honesty,
> And with another thing quite out of date,
> Called modesty.'
>
> *Somers Tracts*, V, 397.

[2] This was the beginning of the oldest existing English regiment, 'the one complete relic of the famous New Model,' the Coldstream Guards. See Fortescue, I, 240.

make use of all his assets. An intolerant Kirk was in power, which would be suspicious of all Engagers and might exclude them from serving, and which could not call upon the best fighting material in Scotland, the Highland clans. The Kirk would be certain to do what he had never done, though often accused of it by his enemies, and appoint men as officers because of their religion rather than their military value, 'placing in command ministers' sons, clerks, and such other sanctified creatures, who hardly ever saw or heard of any sword but that of the Spirit.'[1] There was no such homogeneity in the Scottish army as in his own.[2] Leslie could not trust his forces, and therefore he would stand on the defensive, no doubt in front of Edinburgh. Between the capital and the Border the land would be cleared of supplies; therefore the invaders must be provisioned by sea. That demanded a harbour somewhere between Berwick and Leith, and there was only one, Dunbar. Oliver's first step was to do as he had done in Ireland, and make an advanced base of a seaport.

II

Oliver went north in another mood from that in which a year before he had sailed for Dublin. The Scots were not the Irish: 'God hath a people here fearing His name, though deceived.'[3] He was fighting not against a nation or a race, but against a sudden perversity which had seduced honest men into folly. It was his task to split up an unhallowed combination, separating the misled from the irreconcilables before taking stern order with the latter. For this purpose he must show himself patient and tactful, must set his case fairly before the people of Scotland, and must treat that people, as distinct from their army, not as enemies but as misguided friends. He was therefore in a gentle temper. From Alnwick on July 17 he wrote to Richard Mayor for news of his son Dick's first child. 'I should be glad to hear how the little brat doth. I could chide both father and mother for their neglects of me: I know my son is idle, but I had better thoughts of Doll. I doubt not her husband hath spoiled her; I pray, tell her so from me. If I had as good leisure

---

[1] Walker, 162.

[2] The Scots had, or were about to have, the embarrassing choice of three several rallying cries, 'Presbytery and King,' 'Presbytery and No King,' 'King and No Presbytery.' Douglas, *Cromwell's Scotch Campaigns*, 26.

[3] *L. and S.*, II, 109.

as they, I should write sometimes.' [1] He issued declarations 'to all the saints and practitioners of the faith of God's Elect in Scotland,' and proclamations to the Scottish people, couched in a tone of grave and kindly reproach. He put upon his troops the most stringent discipline in their behaviour towards civilians. He could laugh again. When a soldier got his head jammed in a Scots churn he guffawed as loudly as the youngest private.[2]

On July 22 he crossed the Border from Berwick and saw the beacons flaring on the Lammermuirs to warn Edinburgh of his coming. The land had been stripped to the last boll of meal; the men had been mostly drawn north to fight; only the women remained, 'pitiful sorry creatures clothed in white flannel,' in terror of their lives from the English soldiery, whom they credited, as they had credited Montrose's kerns, with nameless atrocities. They had better reason in this case for their fears, for they had heard the tale of Drogheda and Wexford. Oliver picked up supplies from his ships at Dunbar on the 26th, as Wellington was to do in the Peninsula, and on Sunday the 28th, at Haddington, he had news of Leslie's vedettes. That night his whole army lay at Musselburgh, four miles from the capital.

He had hoped that Leslie might have given him battle on the open ground of Gladsmuir, but next day it was plain that the Scottish commander had no such intention. Oliver, advancing over the old battlefield of Pinkie, found the Scots firmly entrenched on a line running from Leith past the foot of the Canongate, the Calton hill lying inside their works, and the trenches being supplemented in rear by a great rampart of earth. Clearly to one who had only field guns and no siege train the main position was impregnable, especially as it was defended by double his numbers. The weak point was its southern end, the little eminence of St. Leonard's (now built over, but then a cornfield), which was only occupied by a body of sharpshooters. Oliver's trained eye told him that here lay his only chance, so, while his ships bombarded Leith, he detached a force to occupy the St. Leonard's height. At first he was successful, but Leslie sent the Lawers regiment [3] to regain the

[1] *L. and S.*, II, 70.   [2] Hodgson, 130.

[3] This regiment was reputed 'the stoutest regiment in the Scots army' (*Memorie of the Somervilles*, II, 315). Montrose annihilated it at Auldearn, but it was soon reconstituted, and was present at Alford.

position, the English were driven out, and were only saved from destruction by the arrival of their cavalry.

The night was stormy, and the English troops, whose tents had to be left behind, spent a comfortless time on the wet ground. It was clear that nothing could be done against Leslie's left and centre, and the south side of the city offered no better opportunity for assault, while Oliver had failed to seize a position on the high ground which was essential for observation. On the 30th he gave orders to retire to Musselburgh. The retirement was made good, though his rear was harassed by the Scottish horse, and fantastically enough by some English cavaliers of the old Newark garrison, who charged to the cry of 'Remember Pontefract.'[1] That night a Scottish force, led by Strachan, made a vigorous attempt to beat up the English quarters.

For the better part of a week Oliver sat still in Musselburgh. The Lammas floods were at their height, and the western gales made it hard for his ships to make the little port. On August 5 he was compelled to fall back to Dunbar. Meantime on the 3rd he had issued one of the most famous of his manifestoes — that to the ministers of the Kirk. He knew his most potent enemies, and he attacked them with their own artillery. He bade them read the twenty-eighth chapter of Isaiah, which tells how 'the priest and the prophet have erred through strong drink.' Theirs had been the strong drink of spiritual vanity, the 'spiritual fulness which the world may call drunkenness.' Every sentence in his indictment could have been comprehensively annotated from the history of the past decade.

> By your hard and subtle words you have begotten prejudice in those who do too much (in matters of conscience, wherein every soul is to answer for itself to God) depend upon you.... Your own guilt is too much for you to bear; bring not therefore upon yourselves the blood of innocent men, deceived with pretences of King and Covenant, from whose eyes you hide a better knowledge.... Is it therefore infallibly agreeable to the Word of God all that you say? I beseech you in the bowels of Christ think it possible that you may be mistaken.... There may be a Covenant made with death and hell.[2]

---

[1] The presence of southern cavaliers with the Covenanting army is one of the dramatic ironies of history. The dying words of one of those who fell the next day were 'Damme, I'll go to my King.'

[2] *L. and S.*, II, 78-80.

No words of Oliver's could shake the iron front of the Kirk against the doctrine of toleration and religious freedom which he specially represented, but it was not wholly comfortable about the alliance in which it found itself. In particular it was uncomfortable about the king. On the 29th Charles had visited Leith hoping to win that popularity with the army which he could never win with the ministers, but at the urgent request of the Committee of Estates he had soon withdrawn himself. The ministers were uneasy at the number of Engagers and malignants in the Scottish ranks, and could not believe that a blessing would attend such unsanctified allies. Oliver's retreat to Dunbar gave them their chance, so, while the Edinburgh pulpits rang with sermons on the text 'The wicked flee when no man pursueth,' they induced the Committee of Estates to undertake a drastic purge. There had been a nominal purging six weeks before when the army was first raised, but this was a very different business. They had been glad enough to have the help of avowed cavaliers while Edinburgh was threatened, but they could dispense with them now that the enemy had failed. In three days eighty officers and more than three thousand men were dismissed.

Oliver at Dunbar had serious thoughts. The first honours had fallen to Leslie, who held an unshakable position, and had three-fourths of Scotland behind him for supplies. No argumentative wedge could be driven yet awhile into his command, for, though word had come of a purge of malignants, the Kirk was still firm on the side of the now-covenanted king. Oliver himself was having grave trouble with a commissariat dependent upon small ships in precarious weather, and his difficulties were increased by his having to feed, true to his policy of conciliating the nation, the starving people of Dunbar out of his own stores.[1] In such circumstances the ordinary general of that age would have secured his communications with England and fortified a 'leaguer' at Dunbar. But Oliver was no leisurely professional man of war. He had to finish his task and finish it soon, for none could tell how soon a storm might blow up in the south. He must have a speedy peace, and for that Leslie must be brought to battle and defeated. Having replenished his stores, he was back at Musselburgh on August 12.

It may be that his first intention was simply to assault

[1] He sent the Scottish wounded back to Edinburgh in his own coach after the raid on Musselburgh.

Leslie's entrenchments from the rear, and come in upon the west
side of Edinburgh.[1] But if such a notion was in his mind two
days of reconnoitring to the south of the capital convinced him
that it was impracticable, for Leslie moved rapidly to conform.
A bolder plan suggested itself. If he marched round Edinburgh
and got in touch with his ships at Queensferry, he would be in
a position to cut off the Scots' supplies. The fertile lands of the
south-east were now closed to them, and they could only feed
their army, and the Edinburgh citizens, from the midlands,
from the west, and especially from the rich fields of Fife. In
that way Leslie might be driven to fight a battle. On the 13th
Oliver was in camp on the Braid hills.

Thereafter he moved slowly. One of his reasons no doubt
was policy, for he had word from Leslie himself that Charles
was to be required to sign a declaration admitting his humiliation for his father's sins and his mother's idolatry. There was
a faction in the Scottish army, men like Strachan, Holbourn,
Gilbert Ker and Sir John Brown, who were as intransigent in
religion as any minister. There was so much matter for dissension in the enemy camp that he may have wished to give it
time to gather to a head. But there was also the difficulty of
the country, since the wet August had made a bog of every
hollow, and elaborate reconnaissance was needed. He was
nervous, too, lest Leslie might take the chance of breaking
south for England, as Loudoun desired. Whatever may have
been the cause, it was not till August 18 that the westward
move seriously began. Leslie, perfectly conscious of his enemy's
purpose, had occupied Corstorphine hill, with an outpost at
Redhall to watch Oliver's outpost at Colinton.

Once again there came a stalemate, while the English army,
though it now had tents for its accommodation, was ravaged by
dysentery. It was not till the 27th that movement was resumed,
after Redhall had delayed it for forty-eight hours. The Water
of Leith was crossed, but Leslie only side-stepped his army
further west. He was in an unassailable position, occupying the
high ground between Oliver and the sea, and barring the way
to Queensferry, while between the two forces lay impassable
stretches of lake and bog. Clearly he could not be forced to
fight, and on August 28th Oliver fell back on Musselburgh. He
had been handsomely outmanœuvred, and his one chance —
of reaching Queensferry by a swift dash about the 13th — had

[1] The point is discussed in Douglas, *Cromwell's Scotch Campaigns*, 54–56.

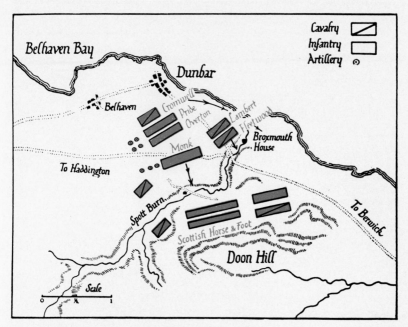

Position about 4 A.M.

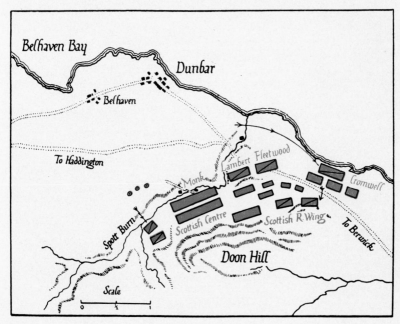

Position about 5.30 A.M.

BATTLE OF DUNBAR

been flung away. Leslie had made no mistakes. He had taken
full advantage of his superiority in position and numbers and
knowledge of the ground, and he had made skilful use of his
horse and flying squadrons of light infantry like the Lawers
regiment. Moreover the religious and political dissensions in
his camp had quieted down. Charles had signed the required
declaration with a wry face, and peace had fallen upon
Israel.

Musselburgh was no place to abide in. Leslie had pressed the
retreat hard and might at one moment have blocked it; but he
did not hurry his men, for he had another and a better plan.
At Musselburgh on the 30th Oliver's council of war decided to
fall back on Dunbar and fortify a base there. The sick were
shipped under his personal superintendence, but a considerable
quantity of stores had to be left behind. On the afternoon of the
31st he struck camp and made Haddington during the night,
his rearguard harried by Leslie's horse. He dared not turn and
strike, for the Scots had 22,000 men to his 12,000 and the latter
were weary and ill-fed, 'a poor, shattered, hungry, discouraged
army.'[1] Next day, Sunday, September 1st, he reached Dunbar and a temporary refuge, the Scots having pressed less vigorously owing to their disinclination to fight on the Sabbath. The
English forces lay along the base of the little peninsula on which
the town stood. 'This now is all the ground that Oliver is lord
of in Scotland. His ships lie in the offing, with biscuit and transport for him; but visible elsewhere in the Earth no help....'[2]
That day Leslie sent a detachment south which seized the pass
at Cockburnspath and so controlled the land route to England.
That night he had his army on the hill called the Doon, where
the heather of the Lammermuirs fell in bent and cornlands to
the sea. He had manœuvred the invaders into a trap from
which they could not retreat, and where, if they fought, it must
be against odds which spelled certain disaster.[3]

[1] Hodgson, 143.   [2] Carlyle, *L. and S.*, II, 90.
[3] The authorities for the Scottish campaign before the retreat to Dunbar are Oliver's
dispatches (*L. and S.*, II, 73–76, 87–88, 102–05); Hodgson; Walker; Balfour, III, IV;
Baillie, III; Whitelocke; Nicoll, *Diary* (Bannatyne Club); *Memorie of the Somervilles*,
II; *Charles II and Scotland* (ed. Gardiner, S.H.S.) *Mercurius Politicus* for August 1650;
Maidment, *Historical Fragments*; *Cromwelliana*; *Ancr. and Loth. Corr.*, II. The best
modern account, done with exact topographical knowledge, is in Douglas, *Cromwell's
Scotch Campaigns*.

III

Oliver was not blind to his critical position. On Monday the 2nd he wrote to Haselrig, the governor of Newcastle: 'We are upon an engagement very difficult. The enemy hath blocked up our way at the pass at Copperpath, through which we cannot get without almost a miracle. He lieth so upon the hills that we know not how to come that way without great difficulty; and our lying here daily consumeth our men, who fall sick beyond imagination.' Haselrig, he knew, had not the strength at the moment to march north and clear the road at Cockburnspath, but he begged him to raise what men he could and get further levies from the south; to tell Vane of the predicament, but not to make it matter of public knowledge. 'All shall work for good,' he added. 'Our spirits are comfortable (praised be the Lord), though our present condition is as it is.' [1] He may at one time have entertained the thought of pushing on to Berwick, but now that was patently impossible. He was badly caught, with his line of land communication a prolongation of his front, and double his numbers sitting on the hills above him. The most he could do was to fortify Dunbar, trust to the sea for his supplies, and wait on Haselrig. He had bungled the Cockburnspath business, and must pay the penalty. But there were the unpredictable chances of war, of which he had often taken advantage and which he called the arm of the Lord. [2] He had no intention of retreating one further yard.

What meantime was in Leslie's mind? He had hoped that Oliver would only halt for a night at Dunbar and continue his march south, in which case he meant to fall on his rear from the Doon — a project of which, were the southern passes held, the success seemed assured. But when on the Monday the enemy showed no sign of moving, his views began to change. His men had no tents and the Sunday night on the Doon in the rain had been dolorous. He was anxious about his supplies. East Lothian was devastated, the Lammermuirs were an unfruitful waste of heather, and everything had to be brought from Edinburgh. He could not continue indefinitely perched on these uplands. Moreover he was alarmed by the prospect of Oliver

[1] *L. and S.*, II, 92–93.
[2] Cf. the letter of Colonel George Fenwick to Bradshawe: 'The Lord is still the same to those that rest upon Him: He is the God of the Hills as well as of the valleys.' *Carte MSS.* (Bodleian), xviii, 417.

fortifying Dunbar. The enemy could easily make it too strong to be taken by assault, and with the sea behind him and supports coming in time from England there would be a weary winter before the Scottish army. That army, also, was not in the best of tempers. It was large enough, for it had just got Lumsden's northern levies, but much of it was raw and ill-trained, and there was a perpetual bickering in the high command. The Committee of the Kirk and Estates which accompanied it were anxious to make war according to the simple methods of the Books of Joshua and Judges, and even his council of war was divided. Could he trust such a command to play the waiting game which it looked as if Oliver meant to force upon it? Those veteran Ironsides were capable of enduring a diet of salt junk and biscuit from their ships till his own motley concourse broke up in chaos.

On the Monday morning he was still unresolved, but two things happened then which brought him to a decision. The first was that he got the notion that Oliver was shipping his guns and part of his forces — at any rate his fishing question to a prisoner suggests this.[1] In that case there would be some confusion, and a chance for the offensive. The second was the strong pressure from the politicians and ministers of the Committee, whose imagination had been heated by the memory of Old Testament precedents. We know that Johnston of Wariston was one of them, and that strange youth, part lawyer, part mystic, and part madman, was a power among his brethren.[2] He was probably supported by men like Ker and Strachan and Holbourn in the council of officers, who saw in the situation a chance of repeating Essex's overthrow in Cornwall six years before.[3] But it is likely that Leslie was not an unwilling convert.[4] There was good reason why he could not stay on the hill, and as the day wore on his spirits rose at the prospect of forcing a battle. So far he had had the better of his great adversary, and now the omens were happier than ever. 'Leslie missed the best chance that ever man had of beating Oliver Crom-

---

[1] Cadwall's narrative in Carte, *Ormonde Papers*, I, 382.

[2] Wariston is not an attractive figure, but his sternest critics must be moved by the broken-hearted passages in his *Diary* on the death of his young wife.

[3] They forgot a less happy parallel — that on that very Doon hill in 1296 a Scottish army, which was unwise enough to descend and give battle, was destroyed by Warenne (Hailes, *Annals*, I, 289).

[4] This seems to have been Lord Orrery's view, *Art of War*, 149.

well because he had just before beaten Oliver Cromwell so
thoroughly.' [1]

Sometime on the morning of Monday the Scots began their
descent. The Doon hill on its north-east side fell steeply to the
glen of the Brock or Spot burn, a grassy gully about forty feet
deep. This ravine became shallower at one point about a mile
and a half from the burn's mouth, where a cart-track crossed it
beside a small cottage. There it ran mainly due east, but lower
it bent again to the north and was crossed by the highroad to
Berwick. In all its lower course the ravine was flattened out,
and that part of the Doon which lay south and east of it was a
gentle slope where cavalry could operate. North of the highroad, bounded on the east by the burn, lay the policies and
house of Broxmouth, belonging to Lord Roxburgh. The English forces on the Monday lay across the peninsula, with their
left resting on Broxmouth, and with an outpost in the cottage
in the Brock burn glen. They expected attack, and that portion
of the 7500 foot and 3500 horse which was not on duty at the
harbour stood to their arms.

During the afternoon it became plain that the Scots were
astir. The many cornets bearing the cross of St. Andrew and
the motto 'Covenant, Religion, King, and Kingdom' were
slowly moving down the hill. Presently news came that the
outpost at the mouth of the ravine had been seized by the
enemy. Oliver, having written his letter to Haselrig, went into
Dunbar to dine, and when he returned after four o'clock he
watched with Lambert the Scots' doings. Beyond doubt Leslie
was preparing to offer battle. He was drawing up the bulk of
his troops on the gentle slopes east of the burn and south of the
Berwick road. He evidently thought that the enemy might
attempt to escape by that road, and intended to dispute the
passage. That meant an attack in the early morning. Oliver
observed another thing. Leslie was massing most of his strength
on his right wing where the burn, though swollen by the rains,
was easy to cross. His left wing rested securely on the deep
upper ravine of the Brock, but it was cramped and in no position
to give assistance elsewhere in the field; the centre also was too
crowded together for free movement; therefore if the Scottish
right were beaten, it would get no help from the rest of the

---

[1] Douglas, *op. cit.*, 106. The evidence for the pressure of the Committee is Burnet,
who was Wariston's nephew (*Own Time*, I, 54-55); Baillie, III, 111; Oliver himself,
L. and S., II, 113; and Major White's statement in the House, *C. J.*, VI, 464.

army, and if it were routed its flight in that narrow space would create wild confusion. But to beat that right wing meant that he would, somehow or other, have to pass the bulk of his army across the enemy front. Were his veterans capable of so difficult a manœuvre? He thought so. 'I told him (Lambert) I thought it did give me an opportunity and advantage to attempt upon the enemy, to which he immediately replied he had thought to have said the same thing to me. We called for Colonel Monk, and showed him the thing; and coming to our quarters at night, and describing our apprehensions to some of the colonels, they also cheerfully concurred.' [1]

It was decided to forestall the Scots by an attack before dawn. As soon as night fell Lambert, who was to command on the left, began to move his men. The Scottish outposts in the twilight observed only that troops were being drawn up resting on Broxmouth house, the natural position for a defensive. But in the darkness fateful things were happening. The fretting of the sea on the reefs and the flying scurries of sleet drowned the movement of great masses of men. Lambert and Fleetwood had six regiments of horse lining the burn where it was easiest to ford, and facing the Scottish right. Monk had a brigade of three and a half regiments of foot opposite the Scottish centre. A body of horse on the extreme right, where the ravine was deep, was to make a feint against the weakened Scottish left, supported by the heavy guns. Most vital of all, two brigades of foot under Pride and Overton, supported by the Lord General's own regiment of horse, were to cross the Brock far down and after a wide circuit to fall upon the extreme Scottish right.

It was a wild night, cold and wet and gusty, and the moon did not show itself till four o'clock. Leslie's position was the out-fields and in-fields of the two farms on the Doon, and, since the harvest that year had been early, the oats and bear were already in shock. The Scots had not had the hardening experience of Oliver's men in recent weeks, and spent a night of misery crouching among the sheaves. Many of the officers left their men and sought shelter. Holbourn, making his rounds about two, ordered the foot to extinguish their matches, except the file leaders — a dangerous economy in face of so near an enemy, but probably the rain had already extinguished many. Before dawn most of the Scots had fallen into an uneasy slum-

---

[1] Cromwell to Lenthall, Sept. 4, *L. and S.*, II, 106. Hodgson (*op. cit.*, 144), says that at first there was some doubt about the venture in the council of war.

ber, and the command to stand to would be limpingly obeyed. To this slackness perhaps more than to the descent from the hill is to be attributed the eventual disaster. Such was Leslie's view. In his letter to Argyll of the 5th he sets down the Scottish defeat to 'our own laziness.' 'I take God to witness we might have as easily beaten them as we beat James Graham at Philiphaugh, if the officers had stayed by their troops and regiments.' [1]

Things were very different beyond the burn. At first there was intense activity as the troops got into position, and the allotted two field-pieces were brought up to each infantry regiment. Then for a space there was quiet, but little sleep. The veterans were praying, having done all that man could do to ensure victory. One officer overheard a cornet at his devotions. 'I met with so much of God in it as I was satisfied deliverance was at hand.' Oliver himself rode all night through the regiments in the rain. In 1704 died one Henry Hudson who fought at Dunbar, and he used to tell how he saw the Lord General the night before the battle 'riding by torch-light upon a little Scottish nag, biting his lip till the blood had run down upon his chin.' [2] Oliver was in the same mood of confident ecstasy as he had been before Naseby. Serious and prayerful folk wondered to hear him laughing.

About four o'clock the moon struggled through the clouds and the moment had come. The English guns opened on the far right where the Brock ravine was deep, and under their cover a small body of horse crossed and attacked the Scottish left. Lambert was directing this movement when a trumpet sounded among the Scots, and Oliver, waiting to begin the main attack on his left, grew impatient, for he feared that the chance of surprise would be lost. Presently Lambert arrived, and his cavalry and Monk's foot crossed the stream, while Oliver started his flanking force on its wide circuit.

A little before five the battle was joined. Trumpets rang out on both sides, and from the English rose the cry of 'The Lord of Hosts,' and from the Scots 'The Covenant.' While the east was lightening into dawn, Lambert and Fleetwood and their horse, and Monk on their right with his foot, attacked the serried lines of the Scots on the slope beyond the burn. The first charge of the English cavalry pressed back men who were in a hurried and

[1] *Anc. and Loth. Corr.*, II, 298.
[2] *Archaeologia Aeliana*, 4th Ser., X, 66. Cf. Aubrey, *Miscellanies*, 113.

disorderly formation, but Monk could do nothing against the infantry of the centre.[1] He was forced back to the channel of the burn, for his opponents were among the best pikemen in the world.[2] Lambert's success, too, was short-lived, for the Scottish horse came up to support the foot, and, having the greater numbers and the slope in their favour, checked the Ironside cavalry and compelled them to give ground. They had lances in the old Border fashion, terrible weapons with iron pegs on the side, so that if the point broke they could be used like a Lochaber axe. For a moment or two it looked as if Leslie were the victor.

But as the watery first light crept up the sky, there came a sudden change in the scene. Oliver with his three foot battalions and his own regiment of horse had completed his circuit, and was coming in upon the extreme Scottish right. That right endeavoured to change front to flank, but it was not given the time. Lambert's horse recovered from their check, as Oliver's had done at Marston Moor, and charged again. There was a desperate struggle with one Scottish regiment, the famous Highlanders of Lawers,[3] but in the end a cavalry charge routed it. The Scottish front began to roll up from right to left, and in that congested space no help could be got from its unbeaten left wing. Monk's infantry rallied and poured into the gaps, and the battle became first a rout and then a shambles. 'I never beheld,' wrote Rushworth, 'a more terrible charge of foot than was given by our army, our foot alone making the Scots foot give ground for three-quarters of a mile together.' Just then the sun rose out of the sea beyond St. Abb's, and Oliver, in a voice which rang above the din, cried, 'Let God arise, let His enemies be scattered!' And again, 'They run, they run — I profess they run.'

By six o'clock the battle was over. Leslie's horse was driven back on his foot, and the foot, penned in between the enemy and the upper ravine of the burn, was a helpless mob: much of it had never come into action. Some fled towards Cockburnspath, but more across the hills towards Haddington. Oliver, before the pursuit began, halted his men and sang the 117th Psalm, and the ministers who, says Sir Edward Walker, were the first

---

[1] Lambert had some 2200 horse against between 4000 and 5000. Monk was opposed by at least three times his numbers.

[2] They were also armed with skeans and dirks for close-quarters fighting.

[3] They were armed with flint-locks, and so did not suffer like most of the Scottish infantry from having their matches unlit.

to flee, heard behind them words which they had often used to other purposes:

> O give you praise unto the Lord,
> All nations that be;
> Likewise you people all accord
> His name to magnify.

> For great to us-ward ever are
> His loving-kindnesses;
> His truth endures for evermore:
> The Lord O do ye bless.

Bewildered souls they must have been, for their Lord had strangely forsaken them; Ehud had duly descended from the mountain of Ephraim, but the Moabites had falsified the promise of the test. Three thousand Scots were slain, and not more than a score or so of English; ten thousand prisoners were taken, two hundred colours, and the whole of the Scottish baggage and artillery. The wounded among the prisoners were released, but 5000 were dispatched to Haselrig in the south, where some died of fever and dysentery, some were sent to the salt-pans or made to teach the Northumbrians how to weave linen cloth, and the rest were shipped to America.[1]

Leslie was safe in Edinburgh by nine o'clock. Leven, now an old man of seventy, straggled in about two. But, if we may trust an English news-letter, the capital received tidings of the battle in a more dramatic form. A certain Mr. Haig was conducting the daily service, and in his sermon promised his hearers a glorious victory, and rhapsodized over the destruction of the sectaries now in progress.... Suddenly he faltered. The eyes of all turned to the door, where stood one of Leslie's troopers, ashen white and swaying with fatigue. Minister and congregation knew the truth.[2]

[1] The sending of the Dunbar prisoners beyond the Atlantic led to the establishment of the Scots Charitable Society of Boston, the earliest Scottish society in America. Some of them founded distinguished families; a MacLachlan, for example, was the progenitor of the Claflins, who gave a governor to Massachusetts and became eminent merchants in New York.

[2] The authorities for Dunbar are those cited in note 3 on p. 301. I am indebted to Sir Charles Firth's article in *Trans. of R. H. S.*, XIV, (1900), which contains a full bibliography, and Payne Fisher's plan of the battle from the Bodleian.

Chapter IV

THE CAMPAIGN OF WORCESTER
(1650–1651)

The Pict no shelter now shall find
Within his parti-coloured mind.
ANDREW MARVELL.

I

THE news of Dunbar reached London on September 7th. Whitelocke heard it at Charing Cross as he was going to his coach to Chelsea. 'Oh, my lord,' said Cadwall the messenger, 'God hath appeared gloriously for us in Scotland.' Whitelocke dispatched him to the Council of State, and next day, a Sunday, every pulpit proclaimed the victory. On the 10th, when parliament met, a public thanksgiving was decreed, and a medal was ordered to be struck with Oliver's head on it — against which undesired honour Oliver in vain protested.[1] To the nation at large it was a triumph in which all parties could share, since it had crushed an arrogant threat by a foreign people. But there were dissentient voices. Prynne wailed in a pamphlet about the 'invasive war against our Presbyterian Protestant Brethren in Scotland,' and some of Oliver's own intimates mingled doubts with their felicitations. St. John reminded him that the Scots were not the Irish but slightly perverse children of God, and Ireton counselled him to be forbearing and patient. Victories over brothers, even misguided brothers, were not things to glory in.

These considerations Oliver had fully in mind, but he was too much of an Englishman not to rejoice that he had taken order with those who had attempted to dictate to England, and too human not to be proud of his own handiwork. For the first time in his military career he shows some personal pride. He gives the glory to the Lord, but he cannot conceal his sense that he has performed a considerable feat of arms. So he writes to everybody — not only to Lenthall the Speaker and Bradshawe the Lord-President of the Council, but to Haselrig at Newcastle, to Ireton in Ireland, to the wavering Lord Wharton, to Richard Mayor at Hursley (with messages to Doll and Dick), and to his

[1] *L. and S.*, II, 175.

wife. 'My weak faith,' he told the last, 'hath been upheld. I have been in my inward man marvellously supported; though I assure thee, I grow an old man, and feel infirmities of age marvellously stealing upon me.' [1]

He had received a great refreshment, but his bodily strength was running low. He turned, with increased spiritual vitality but with ebbing physical powers, to a task which he knew well was only half done. In asking for horse and foot from Haselrig at Newcastle — and incidentally begging him to treat the wretched prisoners humanely — he expressed the hope that Dunbar might 'produce a peace to England and much security and comfort to God's people.' [2] In one respect the situation was changed. Dunbar saw the failure of the last attempt at theocracy in Britain. The ministers as national leaders were discredited, and the ordinary man in Scotland was fain to bid them get back to their proper sphere. The cause for which Montrose had fought had been carried to victory by other hands. 'Surely it's probable the Kirk has done their do,' Oliver told Haselrig. 'I believe their King will set up on his own now, where he will find many friends. Taking opportunity offered, it's our great advantage, through God.' [3] It was his business to drive a further wedge into an unnatural amalgam, and to make the enemy the Scottish royalists, and not the Scottish people.

So he set himself to press home the lesson of Dunbar to hearts which he believed must be profoundly disquieted. He was changing his opinion about Scotland. He had never liked the nation, but he had thought the bulk of them unpleasing fellow-Christians, condemned by Providence to inclement weather and a niggardly soil. Now he was coming to think differently. 'I thought I should have found in Scotland a conscientious people and a barren country; about Edinburgh it is as fertile for corn as any part of England, but the people generally given to the most impudent lying and frequent swearing, as is incredible to be believed.' [4] There was a blatant hypocrisy which must be exposed, and the leaders of the Kirk seemed inclined to play into his hand. Nine days after Dunbar the Commission of the General Assembly published a declaration.[5] It began with an

[1] L. and S., II, 102-19.   [2] Ibid., III, 271.
[3] Ibid., II, 112.   [4] Ibid., II, 137.
[5] Balfour, IV, 98, etc. Mr. Lang (Hist. of Scotland, III, 243) appropriately compares this to Swift's Prophecy taken down from the Mouth of a Man killed by the Mohocks. 'Concerning these things neither do I know, nor do ye know, but I only.'

extraordinary sentence: 'Albeit the Lord, Whose judgments are unsearchable and Whose ways are past finding out, has brought the land very low under the hand of our prevailing enemy, yet must we not forbear to declare the mind of God, nor others refuse to hearken thereto.' The result of their researches was that the judgment was due to the sins of the king and his father, the inadequate purging of malignants, the professional arrogance of army officers, the profanity of the king's horse-guards, the neglect of family worship among the great, and the general backsliding of the people. But they had no doubt about their course. There must be an implacable resistance, till such time as the dews gathered again on the mountains of Gilboa. 'Albeit the Lord has suffered that army of perfidious and blasphemous sectaries to prevail, yet God forbid that the land should comply with them, whatever may be the plausible and fair carriage of some of that enemy.' There was a crazy magnificence about their blind, unwavering perversity.

Oliver set himself to reason with them in public, not in the hope of converting men like Mr. James Guthrie and Mr. Patrick Gillespie, but in order to get behind them to ordinary reasonable folk. His correspondence with the governor of Edinburgh castle was in substance an appeal to the Scottish people against the prophets who had misled them. He made his points clean and hard. The ministers professed to stand for a glorious Reformation, and had laid 'the foundation thereof in getting to themselves worldly power, and can make worldly mixtures to accomplish the same, such as their late agreement with their king, and hope by him to carry on their design.' That kind of Zion was built with untempered mortar. Again, they had interpreted their Covenant, and claimed a papal infallibility for their interpretation, 'so to serve whatever worldly ends they happened to desire.'... He broke off to touch on a different matter. He had given all ministers the right to perform their duties undisturbed, but the Kirk had complained, in a kind of trade-union spirit, that his soldiers were also preaching. 'I thought,' he replied with scorn, 'the Covenant and those "professors" of it could have been willing that any should speak good of the name of Christ; if not, it is no Covenant of God's approving.'... They were afraid that, if dissent were tolerated, heresies might creep in. That was like prohibiting all wine in a country to prevent drunkenness. 'It will be found an unjust and unwise jealousy to deny a man the liberty he has by nature upon a

supposition he may abuse it. When he doth abuse it, judge.'
He concluded with an unanswerable question: 'Whether, if your
Reformation be so perfect and so spiritual, be indeed the kingdom of the Lord Jesus, it will need such carnal policies, such
fleshly mixtures, such insincere actings as to pretend to cry
down all malignants, and yet to receive and set up the head
of them, and so act for the kingdom of Christ in his name.'
Was there not here something of dissimulation and hypocrisy? [1]

On matters like these Oliver wrote with far greater clarity
and ease than on political topics, for questions of religion and
conduct were constantly revolving in his mind. His words had
their effect. His attack upon the Kirk's tyranny went home to
the ordinary man, for it was what a great multitude had long
been thinking but few had dared to utter. His charge of hypocrisy occasioned heart-searchings even among the extremists.
The Covenant *bloc* began to split asunder. A section of the
army, led by men like Strachan and Gilbert Ker, drew away
from the Committee of Estates, and, while fighting against
Oliver, would own no allegiance to Charles. Among the ministers Guthrie and Gillespie found their followers shrinking.
Johnston of Wariston and his group would have no dealing
with malignants, and at Dumfries in October a Remonstrance
was issued, whose supporters took their stand upon the old intransigence of Andrew Melville. But it was a dying cause. The
lay mind in Scotland was beginning to wake out of sleep and
assert itself. A national patriotism was arising, and a national
cause was being substituted for a Covenanting cause. The
extremists were also becoming locally segregated — in the
west country, the scene of the old Whigamore Raid. Moderate
folk, lay and clerical alike, were prepared to admit anyone into
their ranks who would help to oust the invaders. Men who were
royalists *sans phrase* had watched the issue of Dunbar without
regret, for it meant the downfall of the Kirk and the end of the
crazy purging. They saw that now the guidance of affairs would
fall to them, for Leslie, their general-in-chief, had become
anathema to the preachers. At Stirling they had the gate of the
north, and, while Cromwell might sweep the Lowlands, so long
as they held the bridge of Forth the Highlands were safe. Further recruits to the Scottish army could only come from the
north, and the north was royalist.

[1] *L. and S.*, II, 122-33.

Argyll at long last had joined the moderates. Charles had laid himself out to cultivate him, though he never trusted him. He had agreed to pay him the £40,000, which was the unpaid balance of the arrears of the Scots army when they surrendered his father at Newcastle. He had promised to make him a duke and a knight of the Garter. It was rumoured that he was to marry Argyll's daughter, Lady Anne Campbell, and so unite Kirk and Throne. 'It pleased the Marquis of Argyle to present him (Charles) with six Flanders mares for his coach; and if our royal news prove truth, the seventh will be his daughter.' The young Lorne was the captain of the royal bodyguard, and Argyll was the greatest figure about the shabby little court. But he was a miserable man, for he knew that his real power had gone. That had been built on the Kirk; he had been its leader against Montrose, the chief opponent of the Engagement, the pillar of a narrow presbytery in which he devoutly believed. He had been Cromwell's ally after Preston. Now he had forsaken his old associates and had become only a common courtier, the rival of men who were far more congenial to Charles. The ablest statesman in Scotland had entered upon the slippery steep which was to lead to the block.

The campaign of the autumn and early winter was a slow business. Leslie at Stirling, defended by water and bog, decided to play the game which had been so successful at Edinburgh before Dunbar. Oliver had Leith and the capital, but not the castle, and, after marching to Stirling, he decided that the place was too strong for a direct attack. His comparative supineness at this time was partly due, perhaps, to his hope of winning over the ultra-presbyterian group under Ker and Strachan in the west.[1] But his diplomacy proved fruitless. The westlanders, having quarrelled with the Committee of Estates, continued what was virtually an independent war, and by their activities at Dumfries and on the western Border threatened one line of Oliver's communications with England. There was nothing for it but the lesson of the sword. On December 1 Ker attempted to surprise Lambert at Hamilton, and was himself soundly beaten and taken prisoner. Strachan laid down his command, surrendered himself to Oliver, and presently died of religious mania. That was the end of the Remonstrants in the field. Meantime the siege of Edinburgh castle went slowly on. The miners who had been brought from

[1] This was Sir Edward Walker's opinion.

Derbyshire failed to do much, so recourse was had to battery by heavy mortars. The governor of the castle, Dundas, was no hero, and after many parleys he surrendered the keys on December 24.

Lambert the while was engaged in reducing the Lowland castles one by one, and in curbing a sudden outbreak of moss-trooping in the Lothians. The old pre-1603 spirit seemed to have revived, and under one Wat from Tweeddale, and one Augustin, a German soldier of fortune, the prickers cut up convoys and destroyed lonely garrisons. Lambert and his colonels had many a weary hunt among the morasses of Moorfoot, Lammermuir and Cheviot. They were in an unfriendly country, and in constant danger, as happened at Jedburgh, of being attacked in rear. For a moment we are back again in the world of the Border ballads, a world of defiant adventure, and when a month or two later Hume castle was summoned the governor replied in the old manner with the child's rhyme of 'Willie Wastle.' But by the end of the year the Lowlands, if not pacified, were strongly held. Oliver ate his Christmas-eve supper in Moray house with the ex-governor of the castle as his guest, and of a Sunday listened to Mr. Stapylton, his chaplain, hold forth in the High Kirk. If there was no local society for himself, his men had plenty of it, for we are told that almost every day in that season the bagpipes skirled at the weddings of Scottish girls and English soldiers.

The chief interest of these months lies in the doings of Charles. The young king had read correctly the signs of the times, and saw a chance of uniting the bulk of Scottish opinion in his support. He desired especially to bring to his side those royalists who had been the backbone of Montrose's party. Middleton was his chief hope, and he planned to escape from Perth, and gather the gentry of Angus and Aberdeen. But Buckingham or some other friend talked indiscreetly, the Committee of Estates heard of the escapade in time, and he was overtaken on the South Esk, 'over-wearied and very fearful, in a nasty room, on an old bolster above a mat of sedges and rushes.' He was brought back to Perth, was much preached at, and given an ill-omened lodging in the house where the Gowrie conspiracy had been hatched.

But the cavaliers of the north were not to be put down, the Ogilvies especially were in arms, and a bond was entered into by men who declared that they would maintain the Covenant, but meantime were determined to fight for the king — Huntly, the Lord Lewis Gordon of Montrose's day, Seaforth, Mackenzie of Pluscardine, Sir George Monro of Preston fame, Atholl, and Airlie, and Middleton, Sir David Ogilvy, and Black Pate of Inchbrakie, who had been Montrose's most loyal henchman. Leslie marched against them, but meantime the Committee of Estates had issued an indemnity which the insurgents accepted. The result was now a coalition of all the anti-English groups except the westland Whigs, which, accepting the resolutions of parliament, was henceforth the Resolutioners as against the Remonstrants. Engagers and every type of royalist were welcomed to the country's service and released from sentence of banishment and incapacity, though to please the Commission of the General Assembly they had to do public penance for past misdeeds. It must have been an edifying spectacle to see Lauderdale on the stool of repentance at Largo, and Middleton and Huntly in the kirk of Dundee.

The new alliance was not slow to act. It ordered a brisk levy in the north, in which there was no purging, for it was designed to include every variety of religious and political creed,[1] and it set about crowning the king. The nation was called on December 24th to a day of fasting, and on the 26th Charles publicly humiliated himself for his own sins and those of his father — 'I think,' he said, for he was very weary of penitence, 'I must repent too that ever I was born.' On the first day of January there was a solemn gathering in the kirk of Scone. Mr. Robert Douglas preached the sermon, and Charles subscribed again the two Covenants, carrying himself, said the ministers, 'very seriously and devoutly.' Argyll then put the crown on his head, and the other nobles swore fealty. In age the new king was still five months short of twenty-one, and much dissimulation may be forgiven to an embarrassed and hunted boy.

II

Leslie was getting himself a more compact army, and his wisdom was clearly to wait yet awhile in his strong position at Stirling. Oliver, eager to bring the war to an end and faced at last with an enemy about whom he need have no punctilios, desired to renew hostilities at once, and, after a week's rest for his troops, took the field, as he had done in Ireland, before the end of January. But the Scottish weather was more inclement than the Irish, and Leslie more formidable than Ormonde. Yet it was not the climate which made the operations of the first six months of 1651 languid and aimless. Oliver saw clearly the strategical problem before him — he must somehow or other cut Leslie off from his supply-grounds of food and men, and these were Fife and the north. Attempts were made to lay the foundations of a plan — fighting at Linlithgow which was on the road to Stirling, an effort of George Monk, which failed, to take Burntisland on the north shore of the Firth, a dash which also failed against the fords of the upper Forth. But nothing was done vigorously beyond the capture of a few castles, while Leslie was steadily pushing his outposts further south and training his new levies. The reason for this inaction lay in Oliver's health.

In February he fell ill after marching back from Kilsyth in a storm of hail and snow. It was his old enemy, the ague of the fens, and he was weakened by nearly three years of heavy physical toil and incessant travail of mind and spirit. The malady came and went, but it was not till the early days of June that he was truly recovered. More than once he was at death's door, so much so that it was rumoured among the refugees in France and Holland that he was dead, and by his own hand. Mr. Robert Baillie in Glasgow noted the news in his diary, which came on a Sunday when he was busy praying against him.[1] When word of the repeated relapses reached London the Council became alarmed; dispatched to him two London doctors, Bate and Wright, whom Fairfax accommodated in his own coach, and begged him to return to England for a change of air. His staff were relieved to see the experts arrive, for Oliver was a bad patient — 'My lord is not sensible that he is grown an old man.' 'I am glad,' ran one letter to London, 'that your doctors can come down, because, though Dr. Goddard is a very able and honest man, yet they will be able with more majesty to overcome my lord for his health, and will be some stay to his overworkings of his affection to go out to the army too soon.' He found that the *haars* and east winds of an Edinburgh spring suited him ill, but now and then came a fine day when he could walk and take the sun in the southward-sloping gardens of Moray house.

[1] Baillie, I, cix.

These were months of bodily and mental discomfort, much chafing at the delay which his sickness interposed, the boredom of an active man who is suddenly tied by the leg. He had no company except his staff and his generals, and military talk must have palled on one who was cut off from the practical business. He had no friends among the Scottish people. He tried hard to get into touch with the ministers, but they naturally fought shy of him. On his first visit to Glasgow, when Mr. Robert Baillie fled incontinent to the Cumbraes, the whimsical Mr. Zachary Boyd preached against him in the cathedral, and it was said that Oliver replied by bidding him to dinner. On the second visit he listened to sermons from three ministers who stoutly testified against him. Oliver invited them to a conference, which was also attended by Mr. Guthrie and Mr. Gillespie, and they seem to have had a friendly discussion.¹ But no argument of his could pierce the armour of their prejudice. Indeed there was nobody in Scotland with whom he could have profitably conversed. The only minister of that age who revealed a tincture of statesmanship, Mr. Alexander Henderson, was dead; the only lay statesman, Argyll, was in Charles's camp; while the head of the one Scotsman who shared something of his own creed, Montrose, was rotting on the Edinburgh Tolbooth. His isolation distressed him, for he always desired to be patient and persuasive and to seek the best in his fellow-men. Five years later he was to write to his son Henry in Ireland: 'Take care of making it a business to be too hard for the men who contest with you. Being over-concerned may train you into a snare. I have to do with these poor men, and am not without my exercise. I know they are weak, because they are so peremptory in judging others.' ² Only rarely could he get under the guard of his enemies. There is a pleasant tale of how, in returning from one of his Glasgow journeys, he called at Allenton house for a guide, and was entertained by Lady Stewart and her delicate boy. Oliver let the child play with the handle of his sword and called him his 'little captain,' had in better wine from his own baggage for the household, and begged the mother to send her son for his health to a softer climate.

¹ Oliver always welcomed plain speech. When he visited Perth in August 1651, a certain Andrew Reid presented a bond of the King for some Coronation expenses and asked for payment. He was told: 'I am neither heir nor executor to Charles Stuart'; to which Mr. Reid replied: 'Then you are a vicious intromitter.' Oliver laughed, and said it was the boldest speech ever made to him. *Mem. of Montrose*, II, 317.

² *L. and S.*, II, 486.

Ever after that the Stewarts, a staunch royalist house, spoke no ill word of Oliver.[1]

He had his regular posts from England and they brought him mixed news. He heard of Blake's blockade of Rupert in Lisbon, which had begun before he crossed the Scottish Border, of the fight with Portugal's Brazil fleet, of Rupert turned pirate and his harrying along the capes of Spain, and of his final refuge in Toulon. That was well, for the British flag had been carried into the Mediterranean. Spain had recognized the commonwealth, and it looked as if France were coming to heel. Soon there was further word of Rupert in the Atlantic bound for the West Indies, a pirate now in the grand tradition. That must be looked to, for Oliver had large ideas about the British possessions beyond the Atlantic. He heard of the troubles of the Prince of Orange with the States-General and then of his death from small-pox — good news, for William II had been no friend to the commonwealth — and of St. John's mission to Holland. From London he had tidings that parliament had taken the hint he gave it in his Dunbar dispatch, and was seeking to relieve tender consciences and to redress legal abuses. There were royalist risings, in Norfolk and in Lancashire, which showed that there was an uncomfortable amount of loose powder about, and that no Scottish invasion must be allowed as yet to supply the spark. The new militia was being pushed on, and Haselrig come up from Newcastle to concoct plans of home defence. Things were going passably well, though the difficulties of the problem did not diminish, and in spite of the high taxation there was always a struggle to make ends meet. The new secretary to the Council, Mr. Milton, had been busy, and had written a tract called *A Defence of the People of England*, with a special eye to the criminality of the royalist-presbyterian. It was in Latin and a little beyond Oliver, but his learned friends spoke well of it.

[1] Coltness Collections (Maitland Club), 9. There is a curious suggestion of another royalist friendship — with the Dowager Countess of Wintoun. Oliver had stayed at Setoun on his first visit to Scotland, and Sir Edward Walker reports that 'in a gallantry' he sent her 1000 prisoners as a present after Dunbar. This was probably only gossip, but the gossip points to some kind of friendship which was a matter of public knowledge. Lady Wintoun, who was then in her early forties, was a catholic, born Elizabeth Maxwell, only daughter of John, 6th Lord Herries of Terregles. Her husband, George, the 3rd Earl, died in 1650, and her stepson, the 4th Earl, had a fine of £2000 reduced to £800 three years later. Her own son John was noted for piety and good works (see Balfour Paul, *Scots Peerage*, VIII, 595, etc.). Oliver seems to have had a kindness for the family of Setoun, which was shared by the Cromwellian writer of the letter printed in *Charles II and Scotland*, 134–40, for Lady Wintoun is the only person in Scotland to whom he gives a good name for hospitality.

He had much work to do besides the business of war, small things as well as great. Every type of old soldier, some of them ex-royalists, applied to him for help in getting justice, and he rarely turned a deaf ear. Oxford university desired to make him its chancellor in succession to Pembroke, and with much hesitation he accepted. There was a scheme for a new college in Durham, to support which he wrote at length to Lenthall. And there were anxious epistles from his wife, who was kept informed by one of his staff of the ups and downs of his sickness. She had Richard and Dorothy visiting her at the Cockpit (Dick, having got into debt, was glad of free quarters), and she was in a sad taking over her husband's health. Just after Christmas she had written to beg for more letters, and to complain, as wives do, that he never answered her questions. She kept a watchful eye on his interests, and counselled him to write more often to certain people, in particular to St. John, Bradshawe and Lenthall. — 'Indeed, my dear, you cannot think the wrong you do yourself in the want of a letter, though it were but seldom.'[1] But after March his health was her only concern, and he replied reassuring her as well as he could — 'Indeed I love to write to my dear, who is very much in my heart' — and sending messages to the children, especially to his favourite Elizabeth. 'Mind poor Bettie of the Lord's great mercy. Oh, I desire her not only to seek the Lord in her necessity, but in deed and in truth to turn to the Lord, and to keep close to Him, and to take heed of a departing heart, and of being cozened with worldly vanities, and worldly company, which I doubt she is too subject to.'[2] Betty was pretty and quick-witted and not yet twenty-three.

At last the weary spell of ill-health came to an end. By the first week in June Oliver was himself again, and by the middle of the month he could mount a horse. There was much leeway to be made up. Leslie was waiting patiently at Stirling for a chance of fighting a battle at an advantage, while the cavaliers around him were clamouring to be led into England. This Fabian game could not be permitted to go on, and Oliver set himself to precipitate a crisis. There was one encouraging omen — the Scots were showing signs of movement. Charles was the nominal general-in-chief, but Leslie, his second-in-command, was the true leader, with Middleton commanding the horse and Massey the English contingent. During June

[1] *L. and S.*, II, 169. [2] *Ibid.*, II, 190.

the Scottish outposts were far south, for Falkirk and Callander house were in their hands, and Augustin the moss-trooper, now a regular officer, took a raiding party as far as Dumfries. Now on the 28th of that month their main army left Stirling and marched to the Torwood over the holy land of Scottish arms, and only the little river Carron divided it from its opponents. The young king, splendid in a new buff coat and the blue riband of the Garter, was riding tirelessly among the ranks heartening his men. Was the long-threatened march into England now to be undertaken, or was this merely a move to forestall an English attempt at seizing the upper fords of Forth?

Whatever the Scots' purpose they must be brought to battle, for Oliver knew well that another dismal Scottish winter would be the ruin both of his army and of the commonwealth. He stormed Callander house, and cunningly tested the strength of the enemy. A direct attack was impossible, for Leslie had an impregnable position and he was not likely to repeat the blunder of Dunbar. 'We cannot come to fight him,' Oliver wrote to the Council, 'except he please, or we go upon too manifest hazards, he having very strongly laid himself, and having a great advantage there.' [1] To turn his right flank by the upper Forth would only drive him back to another strong position, and would not cut him off from his supply-grounds. Oliver conceived a bolder plan; he would turn the Scots' left flank by way of Fife and the Firth, and force them to accept battle or make a dash for England. That would mean cutting loose from his base and transferring his whole force to the enemy's rear. Now that the new English militia was embodied and the various royalist revolts had been suppressed he thought that he could trust his own country. There was a nationalism in England which in the event of a Scottish invasion would, he believed, rise superior to religion or party.

So began a series of manœuvres which were Oliver's greatest achievement as a soldier, for now he rose to the height of his strategical genius. At first he moved cautiously. He ordered Colonel Overton with 2500 men to cross the Firth in boats at Queensferry. They reached the north shore on the early morning of July 17, and established a *tête du pont* there. Leslie heard of the venture at once and sent off Sir John Brown of Fordell with 4000 men to oppose it. Lambert presently arrived with two regiments of foot and two of horse as reinforcements.

[1] *L. and S.*, II, 207.

Brown had made the mistake of letting his opponents land in safety, and on Sunday the 20th he had to face Lambert with a force equal in size to his own, firmly posted on the peninsula of Inverkeithing. The English attacked, and after a short and desperate struggle utterly routed the enemy; some of the officers like Holbourn may have been traitors, but the foot fought gallantly to the end, and five hundred Macleans from Mull died to a man. Two thousand Scots lay on the field, and fourteen hundred were taken prisoner: relatively to the numbers engaged Inverkeithing was a more crushing defeat than Dunbar.[1]

It was also a decisive battle, for its result determined the success of Oliver's plan. Leslie fell back on Stirling, and seemed resolved to march his whole army against Lambert. But Oliver was too quick for him. He menaced the Scots in front, thereby causing Leslie to retreat inside his entrenchments. On the 24th the Scottish post on Inchgarvie surrendered and on the 29th Burntisland was taken; Oliver had now complete control of the Firth. He began to pass his whole army across to Fife, having entrusted to Harrison, whom he had summoned to meet him at Linlithgow, the defence of the Border and the duty of watching the Scots if they took the road left open to them. On August 2nd he received the surrender of Perth. He had cut off Leslie from his chief area of supply, and intervened between him and the Gordons that Middleton was bringing from the north.

Leslie, had he had his will, would no doubt have preferred to play a cautious game. He had 20,000 men to Oliver's 13,000 or 14,000, and might have attempted to cut the communications between the English at Perth and Edinburgh, thereby forcing a battle in which, if Oliver were defeated, he would have had behind him the unfriendly north. But Charles and his cavaliers overbore him. They believed that England was waiting to rise for their cause, royalists and presbyterians alike; that once across the Border they would receive an immense recruitment and would be opposed by nothing but raw militia, since Oliver and his New Model would be left far behind in the Scottish entanglement. They trusted their army, for it was now of one type and one temper. 'All the rogues have left us';[2] it was 'truly noble and generous and purged from phanatical frenzy'; it had in its ranks those Highland clansmen with whom Mont-

---

[1] The Scottish campaign of 1651 up to Inverkeithing has been carefully studied by Douglas, *op. cit.*, who musters all the authorities.

[2] The phrase was Hamilton's. Cary, *Mem. of the Great Civil War*, II, 305.

rose had wrought his miracles. On July 31st Charles broke up
the camp at Stirling and ordered the march for England. By
August 5th he was close on the Border.

It was the beginning of one of the most brilliant pursuits
in the history of British arms. Having accepted the bold
strategical venture, Oliver organized to the minutest detail its
execution. On the 2nd he left George Monk with 6000 men to
deal with Stirling, and by the evening of the 4th had the bulk
of his army back in Leith. Harrison was already at Newcastle
with a force of foot and mounted infantry, on the left flank of
the invader. On the 5th Lambert started with 4000 horse to
co-operate with Harrison. On the 7th the militia was called out
in England, Fleetwood was drawing together at Banbury the
midland contingents, and Fairfax himself was raising Yorkshire. The *retiarius* was swinging his net; Oliver himself moved
south with the trident.

But first he must prepare the mind of the Council for his
audacious strategy. On August 4th he wrote to Lenthall ex-
plaining his purpose. It was the only way to move the enemy;
no doubt there would be some alarm in England, and some inconvenience, but he trusted the fortitude of his own people:
England had been far more unsteady before Preston, and he
had taken the same risk then. 'Upon deliberate advice we
chose rather to put ourselves between their army and Scotland,
and how God succeeded that is not well to be forgotten. This is
not out of choice on our part, but by some kind of necessity,
and it's to be hoped will have the like issue, together with a
hopeful end of your work; in which it's good to wait upon the
Lord, upon the earnest of former experiences, and hope of His
presence, which only is the life of your Cause.' [1]

On the 9th Charles was at Kendal. He had long ago shed all
the half-hearted, Argyll, Loudoun and the rest, and he found
that the 20,000 he started with were swiftly decreasing. He
received no recruits in England — only Lord Derby and Sir
Philip Musgrave with a boat-load or two came over from the
Isle of Man — and he had word of the militia rising steadily in
front of him. Everywhere he met scowling or apathetic faces.
On the 15th he was at Wigan, and next day he crossed the
Mersey at Warrington after a slight skirmish. Lambert and
Harrison had joined hands and were there — the former had
marched 200 miles in ten days — but it was not their business

[1] *L. and S.*, II, 214–15.

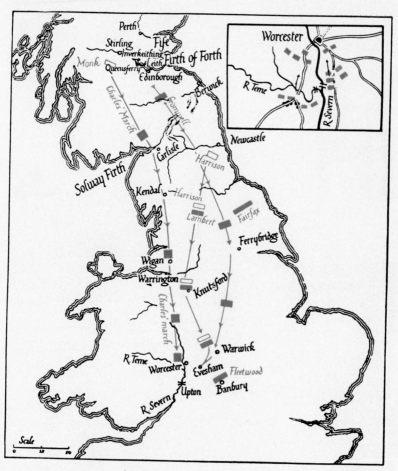

CAMPAIGN OF WORCESTER

to offer battle; they were only hounds to harass and bay the deer. Oliver was following fast by the eastern road; he had reached the Tyne from Edinburgh in seven days and had since then covered twenty miles daily in blazing heat: he was at Ferrybridge in Yorkshire on the 19th, and was being welcomed as a deliverer, the country folk running beside his troops to carry their loads.

After Warrington Charles changed his plans. He could not march straight to London, for he knew that Lambert and Harrison were in front of him at Knutsford, and Fleetwood at Banbury, and Oliver on his left rear. The decisive battle would not be fought between Lichfield and Coventry, as had at first seemed likely. He would turn to the west, which had always been the mainstay of his house. His men needed rest, and in the Severn valley, while Derby tried to rouse the loyalists of Lancashire, he must take up some strategical position, covering the gates into Wales. Massey might do something with the presbyterians of Gloucester — he had once been their idol — and Wales had never failed to rally to his cause.

On the 22nd he reached Worcester with something under 16,000 weary and footsore men. He set about repairing the half-demolished fortifications, and sent out parties to recruit in Gloucester and Hereford. Apart from the garrison in the city most of his troops were encamped on the west bank of the Severn, a mile and a half from the walls, and for greater security Massey had broken down the bridge at Upton, six miles down the river. Meantime on the 24th Oliver joined Lambert and Harrison at Warwick, and presently moved to Evesham, lying between Charles and London with over 30,000 men. He had no doubt about the coming battle, and took measures well in advance to block the enemy's retreat and intercept the fugitives. The issue had been decided a month before when he manœuvred Leslie out of Stirling. He had double the Scottish strength and he was confident in his men. He could afford to disregard all the conventions of war, and divide his army, and put a wide and deep river between the halves. On the 28th Lambert repaired the Severn bridge at Upton, and moved 11,000 men to the west bank. The Teme enters the Severn from the west a mile and a half below the city. This was the Scots southern line of defence and Oliver's plan was for a sweeping advance on both sides of the Severn, for which purpose it was necessary to have a bridging train both for the main river and its tributary. The Thirty Years War began and ended at Prague; the war of 1914–18 on the western front began and ended at Mons; for it seems the destiny of great campaigns to come full-circle. So the Civil War was to end where nine years before, at Powick bridge, there had been the first clash.

The *retiarius* had done his work, and on the 3rd of September came the moment for the trident. It was a day of cloudless skies and a fierce sun. That morning Oliver flung a bridge of boats across the Severn just above the mouth of the Teme. All was now ready for the northward sweep. He himself with four of his picked regiments attacked on the east bank, while Fleetwood forced the line of the Teme, bridging it near its junction, as Oliver had done the greater river. The two separate forces now swept northward, driving the outnumbered Scots from hedge to hedge. The western suburb of St. John's was carried, and its defenders were driven across the bridge into Worcester city.

Charles, watching the fight from the cathedral tower, saw how the main battle was going beyond the river. His one chance was to take advantage of Oliver's division of his forces, and defeat the half which was on the east bank. Out of the Sudbury gate he led his horse, which had scarcely been in action, and what foot he could collect, and flung himself on Oliver's right wing. For three hours there was a determined struggle, and Oliver recrossed the river to direct it. But in the end numbers told, and soon the Scots were being driven back into the city. The fort at the Sudbury gate was stormed and its guns used against them. Oliver was in the forefront of the mellay, 'riding himself in person to the enemy's foot to offer them quarter, whereto they returned no answer but shot.' In the streets there was a dreadful carnage, for the Highlanders knew that they could expect no mercy in this far country, and fought stubbornly to the end. 'As stiff a contest for four or five hours as ever I have seen,' [1] wrote Oliver, who was no stranger to desperate battles.

All was over by the early afternoon. From this Sedan there was no escape. Over 10,000 prisoners were taken, including half the nobility of Scotland, for every leader of note was made captive on the field or afterwards — Hamilton who got his death wound, Leslie and Middleton, Massey and Derby and

[1] *L. and S.*, II, 223.

Lauderdale.[1] Macruimen's prophecy came true and the High-landers returned no more to their own country. The army, which had been born among the bleak stone towns and the dark hills of the north, was scattered like a vapour in the orchard closes and cornlands of Severn side. Only its leader escaped, when Charles took the Kidderminster road and disappeared into the greenwood. The ceremony at Scone eight months before had, as the queen of Robert the Bruce said of her husband, made him 'but a king of the May, such as boys crown with flowers and rushes in their summer sports.'[2]

III

With Worcester ended Oliver's life as a soldier. Thereafter he was to decree the operations of armies, but not to lead them. We may pause to consider his place in the roll of the great captains.

He was a pioneer, as he was bound to be, for he did not belong to the hierarchy of professional men-at-arms. Like Cæsar he took the field as an elderly party politician,[3] but Cæsar began with the rudiments of a soldier's training, and Oliver had none. He had no military bible behind him, as Gustavus had the *Cyropædia*; he had no practical experience in arms; therefore he did not begin with a body of doctrine, which Napoleon seems to have valued higher than experience, since at St. Helena he declared that he had fought sixty battles and had learned nothing that he did not know at the outset. Fortunately he lived in a transition period of the art of war, and the traditional technique was largely in the melting-pot. He brought to the business a clear notion of what arms must effect, and he set himself to learn the best way of doing it. He had certain natural assets. One was the practical man's power of organization, acquired from his ordinary life, a kind of training which is given to few soldiers. Another was a knowledge of the hearts of his countrymen. These two gifts made him an effective recruiting officer, and an incomparable trainer of

[1] Derby was executed; Massey and Middleton escaped later; and Leslie and Lauderdale remained in prison till the Restoration.

[2] The authorities for Worcester are Oliver's dispatches (*L. and S.*, II, 225–26); *Cromwelliana*; Cary, *op. cit.*; Whitelocke; and contemporary news-sheets like the *Weekly Intelligencer* and *Mercurius Politicus* (Th.). See also Willis Bund, *Civil War in Worcestershire*, etc. (1905).

[3] Condé began at 22, Gustavus Adolphus at 27, and Turenne at 33.

troops. He gave England in eight years a new military organization, built up on the direct needs of the case, and he gave his men a compactness and a discipline which had not been matched since the Roman legions. That is his first claim to military greatness. As a maker of English soldiers only Sir John Moore is a possible rival.

In the second place he was a superb cavalry leader. He was always a lover of horses, and his practical instinct taught him at the start the importance of cavalry. That indeed was the creed of his age, which believed, as Polybius wrote of Cannae, that 'in actual war it is better to have half the number of infantry and the superiority in cavalry, than to engage your enemy with an equality in both.' He had studied the *Swedish Intelligencer* and followed Gustavus's reforms, but when he came to handle troops he improved upon the latter. The King of Sweden had made his cuirassiers reserve their fire till they saw the whites of their opponents' eyes, and then set on with the sword. But this could not be true shock action, for the mere act of firing meant a check in the pace. Oliver, like Rupert, increased the speed of a charge, and relied largely on the weight of horses and men and their cumulative impetus. He kept, too, his troops strictly in hand, and never, as Rupert did, let a charge carried too far ebb into impotence. He established so close a grip on his men that he could check them in the wildest dash, and re-form them after a rebuff and attack again. At Grantham he learned what a determined charge could do even against odds, and at Gainsborough he led his men to the attack against an enemy in formation, after they had been disordered by difficult ground, and withdrew them later by detachments in face of all Newcastle's army. That was at the beginning of his career, and every month increased the effectiveness of his force, which became an instrument responsive to his slightest will. No commander in history has ever handled cavalry with more freedom and precision.

In the matter of tactics he had the supreme gift of judging the crucial moment and the critical point in a battlefield. Two principles guided him. He never tied himself to a preconceived idea, but altered his plans to suit changing circumstances; also he never exhausted his resources, but kept always something in hand till it was certain that resistance was over. His aim was to win not a section of a battle, but the whole battle; not to defeat the enemy but to destroy him. He could judge to a nicety a situation, and decide, as at Marston Moor and Dunbar, the right method for meeting it; his pursuits, as at Naseby, Langport and Dunbar, were as deadly as the actual combat. He had in the fullest degree the gift of many highly-strung temperaments of acquiring in the heat and confusion of battle a strange composure, and of seeing every detail in the cold white light of reality.

But it was only when he came into sole command that he revealed his full powers. He appeared now as a strategist on the grand scale, something far more than the skilled tactician, or the trainer and leader of cavalry. Now his business was not to win battles but to win campaigns, and with a supreme economy of means he directed himself to this purpose. He realized that his task was to break the enemy's will to resist, to strike at his nerve centres; and since in the then state of England the only nerve centre was the armies, he must strike at the armies. But his method was not the clumsy one of frontal attack; he would not fight until he was morally certain of victory, and his first duty was to manœuvre the enemy into a position which gave him this certainty. If the numerical odds were against him, he laboured to engage the enemy piecemeal so as to counterbalance these odds, and to direct his maximum against his opponents' minimum. Unlike other soldiers of his age and most of his successors he disregarded the lure of fortresses, and permitted no distraction in his purpose. For example, after Naseby, he paid no attention to Oxford or Bristol or the other royalist strongholds on his flanks, but moved straight against Goring at Langport. When both the enemy armies had been defeated then he turned to the fortresses.

He had always the larger vision, for he saw the ultimate needs, and he had the strength of mind to subordinate the lesser advantage to the greater, whatever the risks. At Preston he deliberately put his army between the Scots and Scotland. In the Worcester campaign, which von Hoenig ranks as equal to any achievement of Moltke or Napoleon, he opened the door to the invader, and by a precise concentration at the right point made victory certain. He could be very bold, and also very cautious; he was a master of the strategy of indirect approach, and also of manœuvre in bulk — both novelties in his day. So obvious indeed his methods seem that we are impressed by their simplicity, and are apt to attribute his successes largely to the stupidity of his opponents. But that is the highest tribute that can be paid to a great captain. No great step, whether in war and statesmanship seems to us otherwise than inevitable in the retrospect. The supreme gift of the soldier is the power to simplify amid confusion, to make a simple syllogism which, once it is made, seems easy and unquestionable, but which, before it is made, is in the power only of genius.

It is idle to attempt to give Oliver rank in the military hierarchy of his age, for he was a new kind of soldier. He did not fight to score points in a game. He was primarily a statesman to whom war was an incident in policy; the phrase 'absolute war' would have seemed to him wicked and foolish, and in all his fighting he had an eye on post-war aims. That is why he was so swift and resolute — he could not afford to have a campaign indecisive. He carried on the tradition of William the Silent and Gustavus, who fought for a principle or religion or statecraft, but he was not weighted as they were by the baggage of the past, and he could work out a new technique which would exactly fit his problem. He was as unlike Condé and Turenne as his New Model was unlike the magazine-tied, fortress-bound armies of the eighteenth century. He is the first great soldier of a new world, and he had to wait half a century for his successor.

IV

Parliament bestowed upon the victor of Worcester an additional £4000 a year and gave him a royal palace, Hampton Court, for his country home. The whole land acclaimed him, for the cause in which he had triumphed was the cause of England. He had soared beyond the leadership of a faction, and become the pillar of the hopes and the centre of the desires of a people. For an hour, but only for an hour, the dark shadow of sacrilege was, even for most royalists, dispelled by the blaze of patriotic glory. He was saluted as *Imperator* and *Dominus* by a bad poet, and there was no complaint. 'This man,' said Hugh Peters, who understood the popular mind, 'will yet be King of England.'[1] Conjectures about what might have been are a futile business, but it seems certain to me that if Oliver, at this supreme moment of his fame, had announced that England demanded a monarchy and had offered himself as the monarch, both army and nation would have submitted with few dissenters.

[1] Ludlow, I, 344.

But such thoughts were far from his mind. He made a leisurely journey towards London, through the vale of Avon which drowsed in the mellow September light, revelling in the sights and scents of his familiar fields — he who for so long had been an exile. The malaise of body and mind was over. Some reconciliation had been wrought in his spirit between the things of time and the things of eternity, and he had recaptured his delight in the visible world. After all his exaltations and agonies he was again the genial countryman. At Aylesbury he was met by a dignified deputation from parliament bearing compliments, but also by someone more to his liking, for Mr. Winwood, the member for Windsor, was there and had brought his falcons. Joyfully as in his old fenland days the Lord General went 'out of the way a-hawking.'

Chapter V

THE END OF A MOCKERY
(1651–1653)

> Let the counsel of thine own heart stand; for there is no man more faithful unto thee than it.
>
> For a man's mind is sometimes wont to tell him more than seven watchmen, that sit above in an high tower.
>
> *Ecclesiasticus.*

I

OLIVER was welcomed in London like a king returning from the wars, with salvos of musketry, and the whole city jubilant in the streets. He was in an equable enjoying mood, at peace with himself and with his fellows. When he spoke of his battles he would not talk of his own work but only of the valour of his army. When his friends marvelled at the vast concourse which greeted him, he observed that there would have been a still bigger gathering to see him hanged. Worcester had been to him a 'crowning mercy,' a proof that his labours were blessed of Heaven, a time of reconciliation between his soul and his God. It had given him back not only spiritual peace, but the heritage of the natural world and delight in the human comedy. All his impulses were towards mercy. He pled that Lord Derby's life should be spared, and his first demand was for an Act of Oblivion. He had had enough of storm and strife, and for himself asked only for rest — not the rest of a sick man, but of one newly alive to the joys of ease. The familiar landscape, the familiar air had laid their spell upon him; his mind hankered after his horses and his hawks and his hounds, and the gracious routine of the countryman's life; there was the business of draining the Fens, too, in which he wished to have again a hand. Later he used often to say that after Worcester he longed to withdraw himself from public affairs, for he had none of the vanity of power. He would fain have followed Thomas Tusser's advice:

> Far from acquaintance kest thee
> Where country may digest thee....
> Thank God that so hath blessed thee,
> And sit down, Robin, and rest thee.

But he knew that these dreams were foolishness. He had climbed too high. Petitions were flowing in from all England not to parliament but to him. Foreign emissaries were coming like Nicodemus by night to his house at the Cockpit. He was a rich man now, with an income equal to some £30,000 today; he was compelled, whether he desired it or not, to live on an ampler scale, and his wife was now too full of domestic cares to be anxious about his relations with the parliament men, as she had been during the Scottish exile. His victories had solved one problem but no other — they had removed the menace of a foreign invasion and the return of Charles — they had not answered the riddle of the governance of Britain. The warning which Milton embodied in a sonnet to him the following year was always in his mind:

> Cromwell, our chief of men, who through a cloud
> Not of war only, but detractions rude,
> Guided by faith and matchless fortitude,
> To peace and truth thy glorious way hast ploughed,
> And on the neck of crownèd fortune proud
> Hast rear'd God's trophies, and his work pursued,
> While Darwen stream with blood of Scots imbrued,
> And Dunbar field resounds thy praises loud,
> And Worcester's laureat wreath. Yet much remains
> To conquer still....

Much indeed remained. He had never penned a dispatch after a victory without pointing a moral to the Council of State. He had written thus after Dunbar: 'Disown yourselves, but own your authority and improve it to curb the proud and the insolent, such as would disturb the tranquillity of England, though under what specious pretence soever; relieve the oppressed, hear the groans of poor prisoners in England; be pleased to reform the abuses of all professions; and if there be any one that makes many poor to make a few rich, that suits not a Commonwealth.' [1] And after Worcester he had prayed that this mercy should 'provoke those that are concerned in it to thankfulness, and the Parliament to do the will of Him who hath done His will for it and for the nation... and that justice and righteousness, mercy and truth may flow from you, as a thankful return to our gracious God.' [2]

He was adrift again from all constitutional theories, and Ireton was dead before Limerick and could not help him. Some minds, lucid, analytic and comprehensive, draw confi-

[1] *L. and S.*, II, 108.   [2] *Ibid.*, II, 226.

dence from the masterful clearness of their vision of things. Others have an overruling personal ambition which clarifies their outlook. Oliver was unlike both. He was not ambitious in the common sense, and his intellect had no easy lucidity. His assurance came from his belief in the Power behind him who had called him to his task, and who, if he had faith, would guide him through the mist. His mind was like a large vague vapour from which came ultimately a precipitate of belief. This slow distillation was once again in process, but so far he had reached only two conclusions. The first was that which he was to express two years later to his parliament — 'the necessity... to divest the sword of the power and authority in the civil administration.' [1] The second was that the land was rank with scandals and miseries.

The condition of England, as he saw it, was very ill. It was a good world for nobody but the lawyers. The overseas commerce, which was the life of the land, was crippled by piracies and by the hostility of the continental Powers. At home the wars had all but reduced society to chaos. Hundreds of thousands had been beggared, and the roads were full of honest folk turned vagrants. Trade was bad and unemployment widespread. The country gentry were in a pitiable condition, and those of them who were royalists had not only been ruined by fines and confiscations, but were in hourly expectation of new burdens. The prisons were full of debtors, for the old relations of landlord and tenant, creditor and debtor, had comprehensively broken down. There were many barbarous legal relics still in force, and a man could be hung for a theft of six-and-sixpence. The Church was in chaos, there was no regular provision for worship, and all the abuses of the old régime luxuriated alongside the abuses of the new. Only the army was flourishing, for it had now grown to a force of thirty regiments of foot, eighteen of horse, and one of dragoons, a total of some 50,000 men, besides the independent companies in garrison and the regiments borne permanently on the Irish establishment: but it was a parasite feeding on the life-blood of England, since the cost of its upkeep (a million and a half a year, and a million for the navy) compelled a weight of taxation never known before. The old merry England had gone, and its place had been taken by a famished, dishevelled land full of undernourished and careworn men.

[1] L. and S., II, 289.

He got no more comfort from his survey of parliament. The problem which had come between him and his sleep — where to find the true ultimate authority — was still unsolved; but, leaving that aside, it was not easy to be satisfied with the provisional arrangement. Parliament was the most unpopular thing in England, for none trusted its integrity. There were honest men in it, but a multitude not so honest. It was known to be full of lawyers and scriveners who acted as brokers of pardons and abatements of fines, milking the unhappy royalists; one member had already been expelled for taking bribes and sent to the Tower, and it was believed that he was only one of many. The army had dark tales of politicians enriched by monopolies, pluralities and extravagant salaries self-voted, and the rumours, though exaggerated, had an ugly core of truth. He was forced to the conclusion that a majority of the House were more bent on using their position to increase their fortunes than on the public welfare. In his conversation with Whitelocke in November 1652, Oliver summarized the conclusions to which a year's patient observation had brought him.

As for members of Parliament the Army begins to have a strange distaste against them, and I wish there were not too much excuse for it. And really their pride and ambition and self-seeking, ingrossing all places of honour to themselves and their friends, and their daily breaking forth into new parties and factions; their delay of business and design to perpetuate themselves, and to continue the power in their own hands; their meddling in private affairs between party and party, contrary to the institution of Parliament, and their injustice and partiality in these matters, and the scandalous lives of some of the chief of them; these things, my lord, give much ground for people to open their mouths against them and to dislike them. Nor can they be brought within the bounds of justice and law or reason, they themselves being the supreme power of the nation, liable to no account to any, nor to be controlled or regulated by any other power.[1]

The man who controlled the army was the *de facto* ruler of Britain, and Oliver could not be blind to his responsibilities. But in his home at the Cockpit and in his place in the House of Commons he was still the patient inquirer, unwilling to act or speak till his mind was clear. His mood for eighteen months after Worcester was curiously gentle and deliberate: it was as if the mercies vouchsafed to him had been so great that he must

[1] Whitelocke, 524.

walk humbly. In a letter written in 1652 to Fleetwood, who had married Oliver's daughter and Ireton's widow, he bade the lady beware of a 'bondage spirit' and preached her a simple and beautiful little homily. 'Fear is the natural issue of such a spirit; the antidote is love. The voice of Fear is "If I had done this, if I had avoided that, how well it had been with us!" I know this hath been her vain reasoning — poor Biddy!' [1] He was prepared to be very patient and considerate, but he was bound some day to act, for his countrymen looked to him.

The first thing he did was to force parliament to fix a date for its dissolution. Parliament was nervous in his presence, for it was understood that he also meant to press for a return of the expenditure of public monies by all officials,[2] and it agreed to his proposal by only small majorities; but on November 18 the day of dissolution was finally put at three years later, on November 3, 1654. Oliver accepted this as the best he could get, though he chafed at the delay, since he thought that the moment offered the best chance likely to arise of getting a new constitutional settlement with the consent of the nation. He set himself to see what could be done with the existing parliament, and on December 10 called a conference of officers and parliamentary lawyers at the Speaker's house.[3]

The slow precipitation was beginning, for the conference revealed the germ of a policy in Oliver's mind. It was not yet rounded and formed, but it was taking shape. The first problem was how to find an unquestioned and acceptable centre of civil authority. The lawyers, like Whitelocke and Widdrington and St. John, were for something with a monarchical tinge, a mixed monarchy, and the Duke of Gloucester was suggested: soldiers like Disbrowe and Whalley stood out for a republic — there were successful republics elsewhere, said the former, then why not in England? Fleetwood thought the question very difficult: Oliver said little, except that a 'settlement of somewhat with monarchical power in it would be very effective.' Monarchy, it appeared, was coming again into popularity. The previous spring Thomas Hobbes had published his *Leviathan* approaching the question from a new angle, and providing one argument at least which must have weighed with those who

[1] *L. and S.*, II, 258.
[2] Letter of Bernardi, the Genoese *chargé d'affaires*, Sept. 29, 1651, in *Prayer Coll.*
[3] The report is in Whitelocke, 491–92.

both disliked the army and distrusted parliament. 'Where the public and private interests are most closely united, there is the public most advanced. Now in monarchy the private interest is the same with the public. The riches, power and honour of a monarch arise only from the riches, strength and reputation of his subjects; for no king can be rich, nor glorious, nor secure, whose subjects are either poor, or contemptible, or too weak through want or depression to maintain a war against their enemies.' Oliver was moving toward the notion of entrusting to some single person a large measure of executive power, combining this with a freer and juster system of representation. Clearly the present arrangement could not go on. He was beginning to think of it as what he called it six years later, 'the horridest arbitrariness that ever was exercised in the world.'[1] Hobbes called it an oligarchy,[2] some of its champions called it an aristocracy,[3] and Oliver was sufficiently in accord with John Lilburne to dislike both.

This, however, was a matter for three years ahead. Meantime something must be done at once in the way of reform. Parliament was induced in January 1652 to override its legal members, who cried out that every reform was the destruction of property, and to appoint twenty-one extra-parliamentary commissioners, with Matthew Hale as chairman, and including Hugh Peters and Disbrowe, 'to consider the inconveniences of the law, and the speediest way to remedy the same.' The commission drafted some excellent measures and began the work of codification. There was also an attempt to bring order into the religious life of England, which had become a cornfield full of tares and largely a jungle. John Owen, who had been Oliver's chaplain in Ireland and whom he had appointed dean of Christ Church, proposed a scheme of reconstruction which provided for a national church, with toleration for dissenting bodies. The scheme was submitted to a committee of the House of which Oliver was the chief member. A list of fifteen fundamental propositions was put up, the denial of which was not to be permitted, and at this Oliver took alarm. Not even from one whom he so respected as John Owen could he accept such a narrowing of Christian liberty. 'I had rather,' he declared, 'that Mahometism was permitted among us than that one of God's children should be persecuted.' He would prohibit popery

[1] *L. and S.*, III, 99. [2] In *Behemoth*.
[3] *Short Discourse between Monarchical and Aristocratical Governments*, etc., 1649 (Th.).

and prelacy because of their political dangers, but he would admit otherwise no limit to freedom of worship.

That was in the spring of 1652. Foreign events were now to divert the national mind from matters of domestic reform.

II

Oliver from his youth had had an interest in foreign affairs, as had every puritan, for the battles for the reformed faith were being fought out beyond the Channel. During his Irish and Scottish campaigns he had kept himself informed of what went on in Europe, since he realized that a foreign policy would be obligatory on the new republic. He had his own means of getting information, in addition to the intelligence department of the Council of State, and he turned especially to those argus-eyed emissaries of the Italian republics, who sat loose to the ordinary European groupings. The Cromwell family had Italian connections through having intermarried with the Genoese house of Pallavicino, and in the autumn of 1651 we find the Genoese Francis Bernardi dining alone at the Cockpit with Oliver, his wife and daughter. Dunbar and Worcester had wrought a change in foreign opinion, and Blake's doings on the seas had clinched the lesson. England could no longer be treated as a pariah; she must be enemy or ally.

When Oliver cast his eye over the world scene, he found that he could be easy in his mind about the British Isles. Ireland was firmly under the heel of England. Scotland was in process of subjugation, for Monk had sacked Dundee, the northern towns had yielded, by the summer of 1652 every fortress had surrendered, and Argyll, after sulking in his western fastnesses, had submitted to the English government. There was to be trouble in Scotland as long as Oliver lived, but never again a serious danger. The settlement in the north, which strictly embodied his policy, had indeed no hope of permanence, for it was in defiance of national feeling, but it was a most successful interim solution, and it removed the more glaring abuses of the former régime. George Monk, when he returned to the Scottish command in 1654, kept strict order in the land, and policed even the unruly Highlands. Free trade was established with England, and the act of 1707 was anticipated by a legislative union between the two countries. The power of the Kirk was crushed for ever, and in 1653 the General Assembly was suppressed. The country was miserably poor — 'I do think truly,' said Oliver, 'they are a very ruined nation' — and the taxation needed to support the army of occupation was a heavy burden: the incorporating union wounded the national spirit to the quick, for, said Mr. Robert Blair, 'it will be as when the poor bird is embodied in a hawk that hath eaten it up.' Yet those years of bondage had their compensations, for most of the old tyrannies were dead. Justice was even-handed, so that a Scot could write that 'the English were more merciful to the Scots than were the Scots to their own countrymen and neighbours, and their justice exceeded the Scots in many things'; [1] and Bishop Burnet, no friendly witness, considered 'the eight years of usurpation a time of great peace and prosperity.' [2] The spiritual life of the country, too, freed from the blight of political faction, had a new spring.[3] For the first time the middle-classes of Scotland could raise their heads.

Outside Europe there was little trouble. In New England and Newfoundland the colonists gladly accepted the new régime, and the royalist sentiment elsewhere was easily crushed. In January 1652 Barbadoes and the other West Indies islands submitted to Sir George Ayscue's fleet, to be followed two months later by Virginia and Maryland. Oliver noted this with satisfaction, for he had never ceased to dream of a greater England overseas. He approved of the Navigation Act, passed in October 1651 and mainly the work of Vane and St. John. This measure was aimed at breaking down the Dutch monopoly of the carrying trade, and enacted that all goods entering England or English territory must be brought in English ships or in ships of the country to which the goods belonged.[4] The first trumpet had sounded in the wars of economic nationalism, and trouble with Holland was certain to follow. Attempts had been made to bring about a union of the two republics, but their commercial interests were too deeply at variance. The Dutch treaty with Denmark made it possible to close the Baltic to English trade, the Navigation Act aroused great bitterness in Holland, and the English claim that in war enemy goods could be seized in neutral ships increased the friction. This last in-

[1] Nicoll, *Diary*, 204.　　　[2] *Own Time*, I, 61.
[3] See Law, *Memorials*, 7; *Life of Robert Blair*, 120; Livingstone, *Life*, 54, etc.
[4] It should be remembered that the Cromwellian Navigation Act only applied to imports; it was the Act of Charles II that extended the principle to exports, and made the system complete.

deed made war an immediate likelihood, and parliament with its strong mercantile interests was not willing to speak smooth things to England's secular trade rival.

For the rest, parliament was inclined to friendship with Spain, which had been the first to recognize the republic, while Oliver, on this point a belated Elizabethan, had an invincible distrust of that Power. He was more eager for an understanding with France, now distracted by the Fronde, for that would enable England to use her influence to protect the Huguenots. He sent his own emissaries both to De Retz and to Mazarin, and for a time negotiated with the latter for the cession of Dunkirk. So far he had scarcely a policy, only dreams, and the dreams were tending to move west of the Atlantic. 'The idea rooted itself gradually in his mind that England had most to gain in allying herself with France. Such an alliance would make it impossible for the French Government to permit persecution of Protestants in the King's dominions, whilst England would benefit by the seizure of Spanish colonies and Spanish treasure-fleets.'[1]

The expected war with Holland came in May 1652. Its details need not concern us, for Oliver disliked it, as did the army, but since England's prestige was involved, he did not go openly into opposition. The English admirals were his old soldiers, Blake who had only gone to sea two years before and Monk who had never been to sea at all. At first England was successful, but Tromp defeated Blake off Dungeness in November, and the year closed with the Channel in Dutch hands. Things changed with the success of Blake and Monk off Portland in February 1653, and the subsequent victories of the summer. The actions were bloody and desperate, and the war was popular nowhere except among the merchant fraternity, who soon lost their zeal for it when their trading vessels were captured, and when the cost of it mounted daily. To Oliver and the soldiers it seemed a crazy thing that England should be fighting fellow-protestants. It meant only an increase in popular destitution, and the postponement of the most urgent of all matters, the settlement of England.

III

A foreign war and domestic reforms are usually incompatible, but the apathy of parliament towards the latter was due to

[1] Gardiner, *Cromwell's Place in History*, 75.

something more than the pressure of other business. Its whole mood had changed. It found itself with a powerful fleet and an incomparable army, which in the then condition of Europe made it feared among the nations, and able to threaten and dictate. The puritan spirit in it, which set religion first among human concerns, had almost gone. Its vision now was of mundane glory and tangible material gains; things like the Navigation Act seemed of greater importance than a pure religion and a moral community. As for its own reform it saw no reason for haste. Its baser members, who had their hands in the public purse, were unwilling to withdraw them, and the honest men dreaded any appeal to the people, knowing well that it would mean a royalist majority. It had acquired that belief in its own indispensability which is common to representative bodies that have been long in power. It was already tinctured with the worldly-wise materialism which was the spirit of the Restoration.

But the old dreams were alive in the army which was parliament's only support. In August 1652 the soldiers, who disliked the Dutch war and had grown weary of waiting for reforms that never came, found their patience running low. They presented a petition to parliament pressing for a number of measures, some concerned with religion and public morals, some with the corrupt conduct of government. The original draft included a demand for an immediate dissolution, but Oliver, who approved of the petition in general, had this changed to a request for a consideration of the constitution of future parliaments which 'might secure the election only of such as are pious and faithful to the interests of the Commonwealth.' The chief mover in the matter was Lambert, who, when Oliver laid down his lord-lieutenancy of Ireland, was aggrieved that he was not chosen as his successor. Lambert was a fine soldier and the ablest after Monk of the Cromwellian captains; he was liked by the rank-and-file who were overawed by Oliver; and, having had no hand in the king's death, he was more tolerable to the royalists. But he was consumed by personal greeds and jealousies, and there were few forms of intrigue to which he would not stoop. Lucy Hutchinson understood his character when she wrote of him that his ambition had this difference from Oliver's, 'the one was gallant and great, the other had nothing but an unworthy pride, most insolent in prosperity and as abject and base in adversity.' [1] 'Bottomless Lambert,' Oliver was to call

[1] Hutchinson, II, 205.

him, and unfathomable he was to his contemporaries, not be
cause of his depth but because of his murkiness. Events were so
shaping themselves that he had ample scope for his talents.

Parliament received the petition civilly, but did nothing
beyond referring it to a committee. During the autumn Oliver,
who feared above all things a violent dissolution compelled by
the army, did his best to bring the soldiers and the House together by private conferences. But he was faced with the *vis
inertiae* of vested interests, and every day he found it harder
to keep the army in hand. In November he had a talk with
Whitelocke,[1] and poured forth to that shrewd lawyer his fears
for the commonwealth. Whitelocke said that the chief trouble
lay in the dictatorial attitude of the army. Not so, Oliver replied; it lay in the misdeeds of the civilians and the self-seeking
of the parliament men. Such a condition of affairs must end in
anarchy and revolution. 'Unless there be some authority and
power so full and so high as to restrain and keep things in better
order, and that may be a check to these exorbitances, it will be
impossible in human reason to prevent our ruin.' Whitelocke
replied by asking what could be done. 'We ourselves have
acknowledged them the supreme power, and taken our commissions and authority in the highest concernments from them,
and how to restrain and curb them after this it will be hard to
find out a way for it.' Suddenly Oliver broke out: 'What if a
man should take upon him to be king?' The scared lawyer
stammered that the remedy would be worse than the disease,
and then set out various weighty objections, of which Oliver
admitted the force. But as a practical solution of the immediate
problem he had nothing better to suggest than that they should
come to terms with the young Charles.

The outbreak is a flashlight upon Oliver's mind. He thought,
as he told Whitelocke, that the monarchical title meant much
to England. He had been casting about for a monarch and
could find none. Again and again in his career he had been
forced to take up a task because no one else could be found for
it; might not this ultimate and fateful one be forced upon him?
It is likely that the notion only entered his mind to be rejected,
for he set himself more industriously than ever to effect an
accommodation with parliament. But there were many in
England who had the same thought and did not reject it, and
many, too, who were not converts to monarchy, saw in Oliver a

[1] Whitelocke, 523–26.

king in all but name. That year a pamphleteer contrasted the attitude of the nobility towards him with their attitude towards Buckingham. 'It is a wonder to me to see how nice they are now of their honours, and what a scruple they make of submitting to this power — when I remember how basely I have seen them or their fathers lying at the feet of the court minion; scrambling for his dirty nieces, not leaving inns, shops, and (if not belied) worse places, unsought, to find some of his female kindred for their heirs.... Look upon our General in his cradle, and you shall find him as good a gentleman as most of them. But consider him in his saddle, and you shall find such low spirits unworthy to be his footmen.' [1]

By January 1653 the patience of the army had gone. The leaders canvassed the regiments, and presently the agitation was so great that parliament took alarm. The soldiers' demands were modest — reform of the law, greater liberty of conscience, more activity in the provision of gospel preaching, and a new House. Behind the formal requests there was much variety of opinion, from Lambert's policy of a parliament as freely elected as was compatible with the public safety, to Harrison and the Fifth Monarchy men with their plan for an exclusive convocation of saints. But all sections were pressing for a forcible dissolution, and Oliver found it hard to mediate, especially as the House, after some spasms of energy, had relapsed by March upon its old apathy. 'I am pushed on by two factions,' he complained to a friend, 'to do that the consideration of the issue whereof makes my hair to stand on end.' [2]

The bill for the new form of representation slowly dragged on, and in the middle of April it was through committee. Oliver had got his way in making overtures for a peace with the Dutch, and the majority in parliament liked him little for this work. They talked of finding a new general, and were busy with intrigues against him. He stayed away from the House for a month, till his discovery of the contents of the new bill, as amended in committee, brought him back to it on April 15th. The bill was a curious hotch-potch, largely the work of Vane, whose old scheme of partial elections it revived. The present members were to keep their seats without re-election, and they were to have power to exclude any member elected

[1] *A Persuasive for a Mutual Compliance*, etc., 1652 (Th.).
[2] Ludlow, I, 346.

for a vacancy of whom they did not approve. Apparently the system was to continue indefinitely, which meant that, for the future, parliament would have the right to reject all popularly elected members whom it did not favour. Moreover, parliament was to adjourn as soon as the bill was passed, so that no pressure could be put upon it to repeal or amend it.

As an emergency measure there was something to be said for the scheme, for it kept the guidance of the still infant commonwealth in the hands of those who had brought it to birth. The misfortune was that these men had lost the confidence, not of the army only, but of the great majority of English men. The army had many objections to raise; — the franchise was too loose and might let in royalists and neutrals; the existing members would go on however weary their constituents might be of them, which was a mere mockery of popular government. But the objection which most weighed with Oliver was that this was to erect an irremovable oligarchy which possessed both legislative and executive power. 'We should have had fine work then,' he said later. 'A Parliament of four hundred men, executing arbitrary government without intermission, except some change of a part of them; one Parliament stepping into the seat of another, just left warm for them.... I thought, as I think still, that this was a pitiful remedy.'

Yet alone among the soldiers he still stood for a compromise. He shrank from any form of violence, and he longed to preserve every shred of legal continuity that remained. He had no very clear alternative to propose, but he had an idea of something definitely provisional, something like an emergency council to be appointed by parliament till a better system could be elaborated. He forced upon his colleagues a final conference, which met at his Whitehall office on the 19th. Lawyers were there like Whitelocke and Widdrington and St. John, as well as Vane and Scot and Haselrig, and Oliver's scheme for a provisional government was set forth by the soldiers, and supported by St. John. It was furiously opposed by Haselrig and criticized by Vane, the author of the new bill. Vane had in the last four months been gradually moving away from his old friend. He seems to have disliked the proposal for a national church; at any rate he was the idol of those who, like John Milton, were opposed to any form of establishment. He was a stiff republican and did not share Oliver's belief in the monarchical principle. He appears to have had an inclination for an alliance with

Spain, which Oliver repudiated.[1] He feared desperately the army as the chief foe to his ideal republic, and he had done his best to counterbalance it by strengthening the fleet. He clung to the existing parliament, for he dreaded lest the alternative should be some wild conclave of visionaries like Harrison. Nevertheless he seems to have been impressed by the debate at this conference. He and his friends, before it broke up, pledged themselves to suspend proceedings on the bill in the House next morning, and to meet the soldiers again in the course of the afternoon.

But when parliament met on the 20th, it was in no mood to accept the private bargains of its leaders. As soon as prayers were over, it proceeded with the bill, Haselrig being the leader in the business. Vane, who no doubt honestly desired to keep his promise of the night before, found himself powerless in face of the temper of the House. The rank and file, who knew that if once parliament were dissolved they would never return to it, and who had, many of them, bad consciences about their past doings, were playing desperately for safety. Harrison warned them that they were at a dangerous game, but no one listened to him.

Meantime Oliver, in his room at Whitehall, had a private meeting with some of those who had attended the conference. He trusted Vane and did not mean to go to the House that day, so he had put on old clothes — a plain black suit and grey worsted stockings. The meeting was short, for presently the parliament men left it to go to St. Stephen's. Then came a message from Harrison telling what was happening there, and then a second and a third. Oliver, half incredulous, half indignant, set off for Westminster; but first he ordered a party of musketeers from his own regiment under Lieutenant-Colonel Worsley to follow him.

He entered the House and took his usual seat. There was a small attendance, not more than fifty or sixty. For a little he listened to the debate, and, as he saw whither matters were tending, a slow fury took possession of him. He beckoned to Harrison, who was sitting on the other side, and whispered that the time had come and that this mischief must be scotched. Harrison, stout heart as he was, shrank from the purpose which he read in his leader's eye. 'The work is very great and danger-

<hr>

[1] The Genoese Bernardi believed that Vane and Henry Marten were Spanish pensioners. Letter of May 5, 1653, in *Prayer Coll.*

ous,' he said; 'therefore I desire you seriously to consider it before you engage in it.' Oliver nodded, and for another quarter of an hour listened quietly to the speeches.

Then the Speaker rose to put the third reading of the bill, and Oliver rose with him. 'This is the time,' he muttered to Harrison. 'I must do it.' He removed his hat, and addressed the House. He began in vast rambling sentences by recalling the great work which the Long Parliament had done in its early days, its 'pains and care of the public good.' This part of his speech he had no doubt considered before, and it seemed as if he meant to make a reasoned appeal to the House not to be unfaithful to its high traditions. And then, as he looked round at the members, his mood changed. He saw the furtive faces of the profiteers, the prim lips of the lawyers, the gross mouths of the evil livers, the unquiet eyes of Vane averted so as not to meet his own. Suddenly a great nausea filled him at the whole business. He was like a man climbing a tall church tower who inadvertently seizes the bell-rope instead of the guide-rope and rings a tocsin which he has not intended.[1]

In wild words that tumbled over each other he poured forth his inmost soul. He told the members what was the truth, if not the whole truth. He spoke of their injustice, their corruption, their petty jealousies; he spoke of their private sins, drunkenness, embezzlement, uncleanness, and as he spoke he looked hard at this and that embarrassed member. Then he clapped his hat on his head, to show that his respect for the House had gone, and as he spoke he strode up and down the floor, now and then stamping his foot. 'It is not fit,' he shouted, 'that you should sit as a Parliament any longer. You have sat long enough unless you had done more good.' Up rose Sir Peter Wentworth from Oxfordshire to complain of this unparliamentary language, the more scandalous, he said, since it came from 'their servant whom they had so highly trusted and obliged.' This was the last straw, for it brought back to Oliver's mind a personal grievance; these men proposed to degrade him from the lord-generalship and put in Fairfax in his stead, as the Roman Senate would have prevented Cæsar's second consulship that they might have him at their mercy. 'I will put an end to your prating,' he cried. 'You are no Parliament. I say you are no Parliament. I will put an end to your sitting.' He turned to Harrison: 'Call them in! Call them in!'

[1] I have borrowed the metaphor from Karl Barth.

Worsley with his thirty musketeers filed into the chamber. At last Vane found his tongue. 'This is not honest,' he cried. 'It is against morality and common honesty.' Oliver turned on him, and his harsh voice had sadness in it as well as wrath. 'O Sir Henry Vane! Sir Henry Vane! The Lord deliver me from Sir Henry Vane!' He signed to Harrison to deal with the Speaker. Lenthall declined to move, so he was pulled from his chair. Algernon Sidney, sitting on his right hand, refused to go till he was forced. Then Oliver's eyes fell on the mace. 'What are we to do with this bauble?' he asked the leader of the musketeers, using the word applied to a jester's staff with its cap and bells. 'Take it away!' As the members hustled out like driven cattle, Oliver gave them his parting words. He told Marten that he was a whore-master, which was undoubtedly true, and Wentworth that he was an adulterer, and a certain alderman that he was a thief, and Challoner that he was a drunkard; even Whitelocke he accused of injustice. Vane he called a juggler without common honesty, and reproached him with being the cause of the whole trouble. 'It's you,' he shouted to the whole body, 'that have forced me to this, for I have sought the Lord night and day that he would rather slay me than put me upon the doing of this work.' From the clerk at the table he snatched the bill, and no man knew what became of it. He saw that the door was locked and went home.[1]

The Council of State, against which he had not the same rancour as against parliament, was in session that afternoon. Oliver, with Lambert and Harrison, attended, and the proceedings were brief. 'If you are met here as private persons,' he told the members, 'you shall not be disturbed, but if as a Council of State, this is no place for you; and since you cannot but know what was done at the House in the morning, so take notice that the Parliament is dissolved.' Bradshawe replied with a famous sentence: 'Sir, we have heard what you did at the House in the morning, and before many hours all England will hear it. But, sir, you are mistaken to think that the Parliament is dissolved, for no power under heaven can dissolve them but themselves. Therefore take you notice of that.'

[1] The chief authorities for the dissolution of parliament are Lord Leicester, who as Lord Lisle was an eye-witness (Blencowe, *Sidney Papers*, 139, etc.), and Ludlow (I, 352, etc.), who must have got the details from Harrison. See also Whitelocke, 529 and Bernardi's letter of May 5, in *Prayer Coll.*

There was now not any government in the land except the man who the year before had been made commander-in-chief of the armies in the three nations of Britain.

The Long Parliament perished unlamented by the English people of the time; the regrets for it came at a later date from those who had not suffered from its incubus. 'There was not so much as the barking of a dog,' said Oliver, 'or any general and visible repining at it.' Only the ejected members complained, and the simple devotees of republicanism, like Ludlow in Ireland and Blake at sea. Oliver was right when he declared that any man like himself, who went much up and down in the land, knew that the Rump was loathed by the nation at large. On the night of April 20th some cockney wit scribbled on the door of St. Stephen's, 'This House to be let unfurnished.' The most popular ballad sung in the streets had the refrain, 'Twelve Parliament men shall be sold for a penny.' Foreign envoys wrote to their governments that Oliver's last deed had brought him more glory than all his victories. Royalists, both at home and in exile, rejoiced at the fate of their original and most inveterate foe.

But the emotion of a moment was not the considered judgment of the nation. By the impulsive act of that April morning Oliver made the second great blunder of his career. Bradshawe's appeal to constitutional law was, indeed, of little substance, for every vestige of law had long vanished from the mutilated relic which Oliver destroyed. Parliament had secured from Charles I the right not to be dissolved except by its own consent, but it had ceased to be, except in name, the body which had won that privilege. It had become the remnant of a remnant; the justification which Pym had claimed for its authority had gone, for it represented no one but itself; in its dozen years of life it had ridden roughshod over every accepted principle of the law and the constitution. It had resisted first the king, and then the army, and then the people, and its final act had been an attempt to perpetuate itself as an oligarchy.[1] It was simply not the body that a decade before had done the great work of liberation. It stood wholly outside the current of popular desires and interests. But it is not less clear that Oliver

---

[1] Attempts have been made (e.g. in Ireland, *Life of Vane*, 347, etc.) to deny this purpose and credit parliament with an earnest intention to dissolve; but the after-thoughts of ejected members cannot rank as evidence against the weight of contemporary opinion. See the authorities cited by Gardiner, *Comm. and Prot.*, II, 252, etc.

CROMWELL EXPELLING THE PARLIAMENT, 1653

From a satirical Dutch print, in the British Museum. Cromwell, Lambert, Cooper and Strickland are bidding the members 'begone'; Harrison 'lends' the Speaker 'a hand to come down'; near the Chair Cromwell again appears, having seized the mace, and in the act of driving out a goose with a peacock's tail. In the foreground are two dogs, one of them being evidently a caricature of the British Lion. The owl with spectacles, and carrying a lighted candle fixed on a collar round its neck, is a detail frequently introduced in Dutch satirical prints of this period. It occurs in a picture by Jan Steen, now in the Rijks-Museum at Amsterdam, where the painter has added the motto, in minute characters, as follows:

'Wat baeten Kaers of Bril
Als den Uil niet sien wil.'

i.e. 'Of what use are candle or spectacles when the owl will not see?'

From Green's *Short History of the English People*, Vol. III, Macmillan and Co., London, 1893.

was the last to be converted to the need for its dissolution. The suspicions of his enemies like Ludlow and the Hutchinsons are unjustifiable on any reasonable interpretation of human nature; no mortal man could have sustained so long and so earnestly a course of dissimulation. He laboured up to the last moment to save it, and, when he struck, it was less in consequence of a reasoned judgment than in a fit of temper.

No doubt he had potent forces behind him to drive him to violence. The army at the time had in it some of the best brains of the nation, it had done all the heavy work of revolution, it alone preserved something of the old religious fire of puritanism, and it had many grievances. Could any man have prevented it from rising against the claims of a handful of corrupt and incompetent civilians?... Oliver could. He knew that it was wisdom for him and for England to let parliament blunder and bluster, and to guide it firmly towards self-dissolution. He had nothing to fear from it in the long run, if he were only patient. In the end it was his temper that snapped, not his convictions that changed. He recognized what Lambert and Harrison and the rest never understood, the stubborn legality of the English people. They could not break with the past; some link they must have, even if they criticized it bitterly, some overt proof of continuity. With the Rump went the last of the old things, and when the nation came to its senses it would realize this — realize that it was wandering in an uncharted wilderness of first principles with nothing to rule it but the sword.

Oliver's motive, behind his momentary ill temper, was an honourable passion to integrate England once more, to establish in a polity the ideals for which he had fought, to make his country a power for truth and righteousness in a chaotic world. He was conscious as never before of supreme gifts for the government of men, and he believed that he was the chosen vessel of the Lord. He was maddened by the delays which human perversity interposed to so urgent and glorious a duty. But on that wild April day he sinned, as he had sinned at Charles's death, against his better judgment. He went too far; his only safety lay in going further.

Now, as after Worcester, he could have made himself king. The glamour of his victories was still about him; for eighteen months he had lived quietly, making no enemies, but many new friends; he had been free from the unpopularity of the Dutch war; what was known of his policy commended him to the plain man; he had the army docile to his will, over-awed even when it was not convinced; his marshals still retained much of the personal loyalty of the campaigns; and, since men may temporarily benefit by their errors, the dissolution of the Rump had enhanced his prestige with every class. If, having abolished one traditional thing, he had restored another older and more sacrosanct, he would have drawn to him the good will of the bulk of the people. The country, as is clear from the contemporary press, was prepared for the step. It would have been an earnest that anarchy was ended and a settled life restored. England would have had again that mystic and indivisible centre of national unity which in all her history she has demanded. The majesty of the thing restored would have ennobled the restorer.

Oliver did not take this further step — there is no evidence that at this time he even contemplated it — and in consequence he was condemned for the remainder of his days to sterile compromises. Henceforth he is like a hero of tragedy, immeshed in the toils of fate. He was to be a prince, but a prince who must remain standing, since he had no throne.

Book Five
THE PRINCE

Chapter I

THE QUEST FOR A CONSTITUTION
(1653 – 1655)

His old instructor officiously sought opportunities of conference, which the
prince, having long considered him as one whose intellects were exhausted, was
not very willing to afford.

RASSELAS.

A numerous host of dreaming saints succeed
Of the true old enthusiastic breed.

DRYDEN.

I

THE improvised republic had fallen because it had no roots
either in tradition or in the confidence of the people; as has
been well said, a republic cannot be made merely by decapi-
tating a monarchy. No single one of the former sanctions
remained, for Crown, Church, Commons, Lords, even the Law
had gone, and the government of Britain lay with the Lord
General and his marshals. The slate had been cleaned, and it
was left to weary and confused men to write on it something
new. The land was a noisy laboratory of constitutional theorists,
a laboratory full of strange and bewildering gases. Oliver's
first step was to issue a declaration [1] on April 22, recapitulat-
ing recent events, justifying them on the ground of 'necessity
and Providence,' and enjoining all public officials to continue
in their duties. Then he turned to the task which could not
wait, the provision of a civil authority supplementary to the
sword.

There were three schools of thought in the omnipotent army.
First came that of Lambert and the *politiques*. His supple,
self-centered mind was immensely confident, and was not
cumbered with any uncomfortable idealisms. He sought a
settlement which would leave the government in the hands of
men like himself, and provide both a career for his ambitions
and opportunity to enjoy their fruits. He wanted therefore the
executive power entrusted to a small council of a dozen or so.
To this he would apparently have added an elected parliament,
the candidates being carefully winnowed, and, in order to

[1] Gardiner, *Const. Docs.*, 400–04.

prevent future parliamentary encroachment, he would have had the powers of both council and parliament defined by some kind of written constitution. He and most other officers had always in mind the old 'Agreement of the People.' He had probably on his side the principal army leaders, and a considerable weight of civil opinion, chiefly among the lawyers.

In fierce opposition to such a view stood the political Levellers, of whom John Lilburne was the voice. These men were sworn to a republicanism as unyielding as that of Helvidius Priscus. They stood for what they called government by the people, parliaments based on manhood suffrage. They were for reform in law and society, for freedom of conscience, and for the end of the military hegemony, but their root principles were a trust in popular elections and the supremacy of a parliament so formed. They were the high Tories of parliamentaryism, men like Ludlow, who would not abate one jot of their principles on prudential grounds, to whom even the farcical Rump was an object of veneration, and who were wholly unmoved by the plea that a free appeal to the English people would mean the loss of everything for which the war had been fought. They would be faithful to their creed though the heavens fell.

Equally opposed to Lambert, but on different grounds, was the growing party of the Fifth Monarchy, whose ideals were wilder and less mundane. A man like Thomas Harrison may be taken as the type. A more gallant soldier never fought, and an honester man never meddled with politics. He had little education except a knowledge of the apocalyptic parts of the Bible, his mind worked on no known principles of logic, and he glanced at facts only to reject them. He was a dreamer whose business it was to shape an unwilling world to his dreams, to establish on earth a kingdom of the saints, and to command a corps in the ultimate Armageddon. Drunk with prophecies and visions, and ignorant of the meaning of doubt or fear, he was the most dangerous explosive force in the land. He cared nothing for parliaments, and would have had England ruled by a nominated council of godly men, seventy in number as was the Jewish Sanhedrin. He had a large following in the army and in the sects, and he kept alive the spirit of furious zeal which had won the battles against the king but which was now fast dying. The seventh chapter of Daniel was the gospel of his party, and by diligent arithmetic they discovered that the prophecies were on the eve of fulfilment, that the conversion of the Jews was imminent, and that then Christ would come a second time and the Millennium begin. The year 1660 was given by the best authorities as the date of the Fifth Monarchy. Such men were to the last degree bellicose, rejoicing in every foreign war as ordained by the prophets. 'Thou gavest a cup into the hand of England, and we drank of it,' said one preacher. 'Then thou carried'st it to Scotland and Ireland, and they drank of it. Now thou art carrying it to Holland, and they are drinking of it. Lord, carry it also to France, to Spain and to Rome.' [1] They welcomed the dissolution of the Rump, holding it a sign that the Ancient of Days had now set up his throne in England. The Lord General was the divinely appointed agent to begin the reign of the saints. Soon they were to change their minds and regard him as the Little Horn in the head of the Fourth Beast of Daniel, replacing in that dignity William the Norman and the Pope.

Oliver's first act was to provide for current business. He appointed on April 29 a decemvirate of seven soldiers and three civilians to carry on the government. He would fain have summoned all parties to the shaping of a new constitution, and he offered Fairfax a seat on the Council which Fairfax declined. To the views of the Levellers he was utterly hostile. He believed as little as Milton in the plenary inspiration of numerical majorities, and he was no idol-worshipper to revere a discredited relic like the late parliament. Also, as a practical man he was not willing out of pedantry to run the risk of losing everything gained by the war. He agreed with Lambert that any council should be small, but, profound as his contempt was for the Fifth Monarchy whimsies, he had some sympathy with Harrison's dream of the rule of the saints. Some kind of parliament must be found, for he was determined to make an end of military dictatorship; why should that parliament not be a nominated one, composed of wise and godly men who would honestly devote themselves to the task of re-making a shattered England? Members thus chosen would be helpmates and not obstructionists. This definite emergency work demanded a selected parliament whose single-heartedness and competence could be guaranteed beforehand. After all, he told himself, what the country longs for is good government, not self-government.... And then he may have started, for these had been Charles's last words on the scaffold.

So in each shire the independent churches were asked to

[1] Canne, *A Voice from the Temple to the Higher Powers*, 1653 (Th.).

nominate suitable candidates, 'persons fearing God and of approved fidelity and honesty.' From the lists sent in, which included Scotland and Ireland, one hundred and fifty names were selected. Having carried his point against Lambert, Oliver left the choice largely to his officers.[1] On June 6 writs were issued to these nominees in the name of the Lord General. Fairfax and Vane (the latter at Oliver's request) were offered seats, but declined.

II

On July 4 the members of the new parliament (called variously the Little and the Barebone Parliament) assembled in the Council chamber at Whitehall. It was a curious body, with a considerable proportion of unpractical fanatics in it, but the majority, contrary to the usual belief, were moderate men. Fairfax and Vane were absent, but some of the old figures were there, and there were new members who were to be loyal colleagues of Oliver — his second son, Henry, and George Monk, and among the Scottish members William Lockhart of the Lee. There were baptists, like Henry Lawrence, later president of the Council of State, and Samuel Richardson, who were staunch supporters; there were able business men, too, with high reputations in the city, like William Kiffin and Hanserd Knollys and Samuel Moyer.[2] Of the hundred and fifty members at least eighty were moderates, and of the remainder only Harrison's group of twenty or so were irreconcilable and spoke the language of the Millennium.

It was a novel experiment, of which Oliver was to declare later that the 'issue was not answerable to the honesty and simplicity of the design.' But for a moment he saw it in the golden light of his dreams. In the Council chamber, standing by the window in the middle of the room, he welcomed the members in a high rapture of spirit. For hours, while his hearers sweltered in the July noon, he unburdened his soul, speaking not only to his audience but to the people at large, and to foreign nations whose representatives were in dire bewilderment. At moments his strident voice seemed to be charged with the thunders of Sinai; at other times he faltered and stammered. It was a revelation of Oliver not as the iron-handed man of affairs but as the perplexed dreamer, and for a brief space, as

[1] 'Not an officer of the degree of a captain but named more than he did,' Oliver to the army deputation, Feb. 27, 1657, *Lans MSS.*, 821.   [2] Glass, *Barebone Parliament*, 77.

in his letters, a corner of the curtain is lifted from his inner life. There was no logical sequence, he was in turn explanatory, expostulatory, denunciatory, dithyrambic and wistful.[1] Much of it was probably delivered extempore, as was his habit, for he could remember little of a speech a few days after he had delivered it.

He defended all he had done in the past, he pled for a wider toleration in a famous passage which I have already quoted,[2] but above all he enlarged on the mysterious leading of Providence and the great work to which they had been divinely called. 'I confess I never looked to have seen such a day.... And why should we be afraid to say or think that this may be the door to usher in the things that God has promised, which have been prophesied of, which He has set the hearts of His people to wait for and expect? We know who they are that shall war with the Lamb against his enemies: they shall be a people called and chosen and faithful.... Indeed I do think somewhat is at the door. We are at the threshold; and therefore it becomes us to lift up our heads, and encourage ourselves in the Lord. ... You are at the edge of the promises and prophecies.' He concluded with a rhapsody based upon the noble rhythms of the 68th Psalm. His audience shared his mood. On July 12 the members issued a declaration in the same tone; as before the birth of Christ, God's people were aware of the coming of a new world: let England be the instrument to complete the divine work, by breaking the yoke and removing the burden of sin![3]

On the opening day Oliver informed the new body of the nature of its tenure; it was to last till November 3, 1654, and three months before its dissolution to choose its successors. Next day it began its sittings in the chapel of St. Stephen. It arrogated to itself the name of parliament, elected as an executive a new Council of State, and appointed twelve committees to examine grievances. It chose as Speaker Francis Rous, who had been Provost of Eton, and was the author of the Scottish metrical version of the Psalms. Oliver had a seat in both parliament and Council, and in November he had the latter reconstructed, thereby securing a working moderate majority. Things were less comfortable in the House itself, for

[1] There are several versions — one in Nickolls, *Letters and Papers of State*, from Milton's papers, which was used by Carlyle (*L. and S.*, II, 272, etc.); one in *O. P. H.*; and one, which purports to be a true copy, in a pamphlet of 1654 (Th.).

[2] See p. 44.   [3] *Cal. S. P. Dom*, 1653-54, 21.

the moderates, who had the greater numbers, were lax in their attendance, and the day-by-day conduct of business was in the hands of the diligent extremists.

While the new House debated at Westminster Oliver had much heavy business of detail on his hands. The Dutch war dragged on, in spite of Monk's victories of the summer, and at first he could not persuade parliament to abate its extravagant terms; it was not till he got his new Council in November that he could even begin to consider the preliminaries of peace. He had no trouble with the fleet, for Blake had laid down its creed: 'It is not the business of a seaman to mind the state affairs, but to hinder foreigners from fooling us.' The army on the whole was in good heart, which was as well, for there was a new rising in Scotland, and many threatened royalist plots, while John Lilburne, who had returned to England and was being tried for contumacy, was exercising his old power over unstable souls. In the first month of the Little Parliament Oliver's mind was mainly on foreign affairs, which, as we have seen, had always a special fascination for him. He was learning the manners and the language of diplomacy. He addressed Mazarin at first as his 'very affectionate friend'; but presently the puritan soldier was informing the French cardinal that he was surprised that his eminence should remember a person so inconsiderable as himself.[1]

The honeymoon attitude of parliament did not last long. At once the House set about domestic reforms, and made a wild business of them. Not a single lawyer had a seat in it, but nevertheless it proceeded light-heartedly to abolish the court of Chancery after a single day's debate, and to attempt a codification of the law. It established civil marriage, and provided for the registration of deaths, marriages and births — a useful step; but it alarmed every owner of property in England by abolishing church patronage, by all but abolishing tithes, and by threatening university endowments. Harrison's party had got the upper hand, and Oliver saw all his pet reforms in Church and State endangered by these hot-heads. He tried his old method of private conference, but no agreement could be reached, and in September he was complaining to a friend that he was more troubled now with the fool than with the knave. 'Fain would I have my service accepted of the saints,' he told Fleetwood, 'if the Lord will, but it is not so. Being of different judgments, and those of each sort seeking most to

[1] L. and S., III, 288, 290.

propagate their own, that spirit of kindness that is to all, is hardly accepted of any.'[1] The Fifth Monarchy preachers were more extravagant than ever, demanding the abolition of the common law and the substitution of the code of Moses. Lunacy was rampant, and Oliver was appalled at the malign genie he had raised. Every substantial element in the nation was outraged by the antics at Westminster, and not least the army. The Lord General drew away from Harrison, and came nearer to Lambert.

Lambert still held by his old plan. He wanted a parliament elected under strict supervision, and a written constitution, and to these he now added a king. Oliver was coming round to the first point, though he did not like the second as involving bondage to a lifeless written word, and he had no wish for a throne. This last was not a new proposal, for the army had made it after the dissolution of the Rump.[2] Lambert, who was later to be its chief opponent, was now its abettor; he had not yet become jealous of his leader, and believed that his own ambition would best be served by the aggrandizement of Oliver's power. Moreover parliament showed signs of interfering with the army pay, and the army, multiform as its views were, would on such a threat draw solidly behind the only man who could at once control it and protect it. A throne for Oliver at an early date was the universal expectation at home and abroad. 'I believe he resolves to be king,' Queen Christina of Sweden told Whitelocke. The royalists thought that the only way to prevent it was by Charles marrying his daughter and making his father-in-law a duke and perpetual governor of Ireland.[3] Henry Cromwell was hailed in Spring Gardens with shouts of 'Room for the Prince.' In May Oliver's portrait had been set up in the Exchange, with three crowns above it and the lines:

> Ascend three thrones, great Captain and Divine,
> By the will of God, old Lion, they are thine.

Moreover by his conduct he had encouraged the rumour, for, when he walked abroad in St. James's Park, he insisted on all men unbonneting.

---

[1] *L. and S.*, II, 307. [2] See Oliver's own words, *Lans MSS.*, 821.

[3] See the curious pamphlet, *The Euroclydon Wind*, by Arise Evans (Th.), in which the writer saw in a vision Oliver accept the crown only to hand it to Charles. Some mystics saw an immediate millennium, in which both Oliver and Charles should be caught up into heaven and never die. Cf. *Charles Stuart and Oliver Cromwell United*, 1655 (Th.). There were some royalists who fell under Oliver's spell and would rather have had him as sovereign than 'any other in the three nations.' Cf. *The True Cavalier*, 1656 (Th.).

He refused Lambert's scheme — partly because he would not have the title of king, and partly because he did not wish another violent dissolution of parliament — and its author retired to Wimbledon, to sulk among his flowers and tambour-frames. But parliament was resolved to make itself impossible. The crisis came on the question of tithes, for by a majority of two the House refused the report of its own committee, and so pledged itself to the rejection of tithes and of a state-endowed church. This meant that the provision of regular ordinances of worship throughout the land, on which Oliver had set his heart, was now impossible. Lambert and his group saw a chance of forcing his hand. Unknown to him they assembled the moderate members of the House on Sunday, December 11, and, having won the assent of the Speaker, concerted a plan. On the 12th the moderate majority was early in the chamber and caught their opponents napping. It was moved that 'the sitting of this Parliament any longer as now constituted will not be for the good of the Commonwealth'; the Speaker did not put the question, but left the chair, followed by some fifty or sixty members,[1] made his way to Whitehall, and put his resignation in Oliver's hands. Oliver seems to have accepted it unwillingly, declaring that it was a heavy burden they were laying on him. But parliament had dissolved itself and so removed his chief scruple. A remnant of about thirty remained in the chamber, and proceeded to draw up a protest declaring that they were 'called of God to that place.' Two colonels, acting on Lambert's instructions, appeared and bade them withdraw. They refused on the ground that, having been brought there by the Lord General, they would only leave on an order from him, so the colonels, having no such order, could only call in a file of soldiers and evict them. It is said that one of the colonels asked what they were doing and was told that they were seeking the Lord. 'Come out of this place, then,' was his answer, 'for to my knowledge the Lord has not been here these twelve years past.'

The rule of the saints had come to an untimely end. Oliver, said John Carew, one of the Fifth Monarchy members, 'took the crown off from the head of Christ and put it upon his own.'[2]

[1] Eventually some eighty members, a clear majority, signed the act of abdication.

[2] The bitterness of the extreme puritans is well shown in the pamphlet *The Protector, So-called, in Part Unveiled, by a late member of the Army*, 1655 (Th.).

III

The supreme authority returned like a boomerang to the man who had tried to renounce it. 'My own power,' he declared later, 'was again by this resignation as boundless and unlimited as before; all things being subjected to arbitrariness, and myself the only constituted authority that was left, a person having power over the three nations without bound or limit set.' [1] Once again he had a blank page to write upon. His resolution was as fixed as ever; he could not remain merely the army's nominee and rule by force; he must find some means of regularizing his position (he had never the slightest intention of relinquishing his real authority) and through some kind of parliament get the 'back and breast of steel' which Oxenstierna had recommended on his behalf to Whitelocke. But the failure of the Little Parliament had wrought a certain change of mind. Some of his dreams had gone for ever. Saints were no doubt sure of their portion in the next world, but they were often a feeble and uncomfortable folk in the present one. For him the ebb had already begun, and he was thinking more of earthly prudence than of heavenly imaginings. He had to face that bitterest of human experiences, the narrowing of wide horizons. Harrison he dismissed from his command; his colleagues now must be the worldly-wisemen, Lambert and the like, whom he neither loved nor trusted. If England was to be saved he must walk narrower and humbler roads. In Mr. Gardiner's words, 'his work of striking down the opponents of Puritanism had for the most part come to an end. His work of striking down those who exaggerated Puritanism was now beginning.' [2] The visionary and the practical man in him had been at strife, and the latter had triumphed, but the triumph left an uneasy conscience behind it. From this date Oliver is more deeply immersed in material things; he is aware that his spiritual life is stunted, and now and then there comes from him a sharp cry of regret.

He accepted Lambert's scheme at once, for there was no alternative. A written constitution was prepared, the 'Instrument of Government,' [3] which placed the legislative power in a parliament elected on a new franchise and with a sweeping redistribution of seats, a plan borrowed from the old 'Agree-

[1] *L. and S.*, II, 373.
[2] *Cromwell's Place in History*, 85.
[3] Gardiner, *Const. Docs.*, 405, etc.

ment of the People.' Such a parliament was to meet once in
three years and to sit for not less than five months. The executive power was vested in a Lord Protector [1] and a Council, the
members of which were to be appointed for life. Any bill passed
by parliament was to be delayed for twenty days for the Protector's consideration; but he had no ultimate right of veto and
it could be made law without his consent. Yet in spite of this
power parliament had only a shadowy authority. It had no say
in the choice of the executive, except the right, in the case of a
vacancy in the Council, to propose six names out of which the
Council and the Protector made their own selection. In finance
a huge sum, in the old Tudor fashion, was set aside for civil,
military and naval expenses, and over this parliament had no
control.

Again, the ordering of the armed forces had to be done with
the consent of parliament when it was sitting, but when it
was not in session the power of the Council was absolute. The
Protector was fairly well under the control of the Council, but
very little under the control of parliament. The best that could
be said for the latter was that it was more representative of the
nation than any previous body, though the broadening of the
franchise was wholly confined to the counties. A national
church was established, but there was to be toleration outside
it for all except papists and prelatists. The constitution provided no machinery for its own amendment, since the soldiers,
who were its authors, did not envisage any amendment. The
essence of the plan was the sovereignty of the executive, for
Protector and Council had a lifelong tenure and parliament
could exercise no real control of day-to-day government. As an
elected body it might be in some small degree the voice of the
nation, but it was a voice and nothing more, and it was a voice
chiefly of the middle classes.

Yet after the vagaries of the Little Parliament the nation
accepted the new régime with a certain hope. The Fifth Monarchy men were in raging opposition, and Oliver was now firmly
enshrined in their cosmogony as the fulfilment of the darkest
images of the prophets — the 'Old Dragon,' the 'Little Horn,'
the 'Man of Sin,' the 'Vile Person' of Daniel xi. and 21.[2] To

[1] Drummond of Hawthornden, writing in 1639, forecast the very title: 'During these
miseries, of which the troublers of the State shall make their profit, there will arise
presently one who will make himself Protector, etc.' *Works* (1711), vii.

[2] An anthology of this apocalyptic abuse will be found in L. F. Brown, *Baptists and
Fifth Monarchy Men*. (American Hist. Ass., 1912.)

Richard Baxter he was the far-sighted intriguer who had invented bogeys to frighten the timid, and then win their gratitude as their saviour. To Ludlow he was now revealed in all his treachery and corruption of heart. But to the plain man, craving only security and peace, he seemed to bring into affairs a refreshing spirit of good sense, and Edmund Waller's panegyric was not very remote from the mood of the substantial part of the nation:

> Still, as you rise, the State exalted too
> Finds no distemper while 'tis changed by you,
> Changed like the world's great scene where without noise
> The rising sun night's vulgar lights destroys.

No time was lost in setting the new system to work. On December 16 Oliver, in a plain black suit, took the oath as Lord Protector in Westminster hall. He was then ceremoniously conducted to Whitehall, which was made his official residence. On February 8, 1654, he was banqueted in the city in Grocers' hall, and drove there in a splendid procession with all his colonels around him, himself in a musk-coloured suit embroidered with gold. The recorder made him a speech at Temple Bar, the Tower guns saluted him, and poets of an exquisite badness hymned his praise. He was given a rich gift of plate, and after knighting the lord mayor drove home by torchlight.[1] But it was observed that there was little or no applause in the streets. London was subdued, puzzled, and vaguely alarmed. There had been a succession of portents — the river flowing and ebbing hours before its time, part of St. Paul's tumbling down, a comet in the heavens, and the ghost of Charles walking in Whitehall. The satisfaction of the bourgeoisie was not shared by the mob.

Since parliament would not meet for eight months, Oliver began by governing through ordinances. His Council included notable men. Lambert of course sat on it, and soldiers like Fleetwood, Disbrowe, Skippon and Edward Montague; among the civilians were Algernon Sidney's brother, Lord Lisle, Henry Lawrence, Richard Mayor of Hursley, Walter Strickland, Gilbert Pickering, and a wise youth out of Dorset, Sir Anthony Ashley Cooper, who had once been a royalist soldier, had taken Corfe Castle for parliament, and ten years later was to be a power in English statecraft. Of the eighty-two ordinances passed between December 1653 and September 1654 most were police

[1] There is a full account in *The Weekly Intelligencer*, Feb. 7-14, 1654 (Th.).

measures and minor matters of administrative reform, but certain larger questions were dealt with which show the direction in which Oliver's thoughts were moving. At the Restoration all the ordinances were expunged from the statute book, but the single volume of them has more than an antiquarian interest, for it is a revelation of a slow mind struggling towards that clarity which a legislative act demands.

The incorporating union of Scotland and Ireland was completed, and the oath of allegiance to the original commonwealth was repealed — a public confession that that experiment had failed. But the main legislative effort lay in three directions, legal, ecclesiastical, and social reform. Under the first came the re-casting of the court of Chancery, and an attempt to abolish delays and needless expense. The purpose was good, but such a body as the Council, even with the help of Matthew Hale, was not best fitted for a complicated task like legal reform, and it is not to be wondered at that lawyers like Lenthall and Whitelocke declared the new procedure unworkable. Modern critics have found its weakness in the fact that it was too rigid, substituting 'hard-and-fast rules for the flexibility necessary to a due administration of equity'; [1] but it should be remembered that the court of Chancery at the time could scarcely have been worse, and that equity law as a system was still in its cradle.

No easier was the business of church reform. Its basis was toleration and liberty of conscience. The church established was of course non-episcopalian, but, apart from this embargo, its foundation was broad, for Oliver cared nothing for dogmatic niceties. Some provision must be made for the universal preaching of the Word and the maintenance of the clergy. For the latter tithes must remain, and the income of poor livings was to be supplemented out of a central fund drawn from royalist fines and the sale of episcopal lands. More important was the character of the clergy thus established. A presentee to a living must have a certificate of godliness from three persons of established repute, and commissioners known as 'triers' were to vouch that he was 'a person for the grace of God in him, his holy and unblamable conversation, as also for his knowledge and utterance, able and fit to preach the gospel.' Such clergy were to be a spiritual aristocracy, and they might adopt any non-episcopalian system they chose, presbyterian,

[1] Inderwick, *The Interregnum*, 224-29.

independent or baptist; but a minister was liable to expulsion by a local body called 'ejectors' for immorality, blasphemy, or atheism. Outside this state system there was liberty for dissenters to form congregations of their own, the so-called 'gathered churches.' Quakers were ruled out as blasphemous, but there was little heresy-hunting, episcopal congregations which met quietly were not disturbed, and even catholics were not molested provided they gave no public cause of offence. In June Oliver tried to save the life of a condemned priest, and two years later he could tell Mazarin — 'I have plucked many out of the fire, the raging fire of persecution, which did tyrannize over their consciences, and encroach by arbitrariness of power over their estates.' [1]

This religious settlement was the most tolerant yet seen in England, the most tolerant to be seen for many a day. Beyond doubt it was far in advance of public opinion, since it offended alike the rigid voluntaries and the rigid presbyterians. It could not endure, for its exclusion of episcopacy limited the state church to a section of the nation, but it was an honourable effort to raise the spiritual level of the people. Richard Baxter, an unsparing critic of Oliver's 'treason and rebellion, aggravated by perfidiousness and hypocrisy,' was yet constrained to admit that 'it was his design to do good in the main, and to promote the gospel and the interest of godliness, more than any had done before him.' [2]

Most characteristic of all were the social reforms. Some were an attempt to amend public morals, by abolishing duels and punishing swearing and drunkenness. These experiments were not harsh as compared with the views of the ordinary puritan, and often their purpose was political. The most important measures concerned education. Milton in his famous pamphlet of 1644 had dealt only with 'noble and gentle youth'; but Oliver had a dream of education for all, since he regarded it as the ally of true religion. In Scotland he carried on the work of John Knox. In England he provided for the ejection of incompetent schoolmasters, and for a licensing of the duly qualified; he appointed commissions to visit the universities and the public schools; he stood by Oxford in defending her endowments; he presented manuscripts to the Bodleian, and he continued to press the scheme which he had fathered in 1651 for a new college at Durham. Oxford under him, said Clarendon,

[1] *L. and S.*, III, 6.   [2] *Rel. Baxt.*, 71.

'yielded a harvest of extraordinary good and sound knowledge in all parts of learning.' He was more interested in higher than in elementary education, and he would have had it free to all.

Foreign affairs occupied a large part of the Council's time, for the whole of the Protectorate was to be a season of war or of preparation for war. In April peace was made at last with the Dutch, who admitted the supremacy of the British flag in the Narrow Seas. Oliver had never liked that particular war, but he did not regard the treaty of April as the basis of a general peace, but rather as clearing his feet for other and more ambitious campaigns. The army which had made him Protector was to be used to further the Protector's policy of colonization and conquest. Presently he settled other preliminaries — a treaty with Sweden negotiated by Whitelocke; another with Denmark, which brought the protestant Powers of Europe into line; one with Portugal, which freed British trade with the Portuguese colonies in Asia, Africa and America. All the time, too, he was working at greater matters, busied with intricate negotiations with France and Spain; leaning now to one and now to the other, for his mind was not yet made up. Both nations were bidding for his support, Spain offering subsidies and the recovery of Calais, France Dunkirk and the abandonment of Charles II. The religious issue to him was the major one. An alliance with France would enable him to protect the Huguenots, an understanding with Spain to abate the horrors of the Inquisition. But the latter government was scandalized by his demand that English merchants in Spanish ports should be permitted the free exercise of their religion. That, said the Spanish ambassador, was 'to ask for his master's two eyes.' By August in Oliver's mind the balance had declined against Spain.

The first eight months of the Protectorate were a quiet season in England, but to an observer there were ugly movements in the air.[1] An ordinance early in the year had made it treason to conspire against, or to speak evil of, Oliver's person and government, and the law was strictly enforced. Men went to gaol for its breach, and since a trial would have meant their condemna-

[1] The letters to Sir Dudley North during these months from his brother John (*North MSS.*) show that the chief popular interest was in the rumours of plots and in foreign and Scottish affairs. The election and the first meeting of Parliament excited people, but in October John could write 'there is little speech of Parliamentary affairs, and people are not so curious or inquisitive as at the first thereof.' The ordinary Englishman, then as ever, was apathetic about constitutional questions.

tion and death, Oliver kept them untried in confinement — a piece of humanity which did him no good with the people: he would have consulted his own interests better if he had permitted batches of Fifth Monarchists and Levellers to be hanged. England loved neither group, but she loved still less arbitrary imprisonment. Oliver's life was frequently threatened, which was no great matter for wonder, and royalist plots sprang up like mushrooms. The army as a whole was still loyal to him, but there had been a sad falling away of old comrades-in-arms like Harrison and Okey, Overton and Sexby, and even in the army there were mutterings. 'I'll tell you a common proverb that we had among us of the General, that in the field he was the graciousest and most gallant man in the world, but out of the field, and when he came home again to government, the worst.' [1] Oliver knew that everywhere he had bitter and passionate enemies, many of them of his own household of faith. Edmund Calamy, it is said, told him that out of every ten men in England nine were against him, and he replied, 'What if I disarm the nine and put a sword in the tenth man's hand?' If he spoke the words, they represented not his ultimate ideal but his temporary expedient. He must keep the sword by his side till he converted his ill-wishers. For he was beginning to dream high imperial dreams, of a world-wide protestant confederacy under England's leadership, an England sublimated and exalted beyond faction, her loins girt and her soul fired for the last and greatest of the Crusades. Well might a foreign ambassador write to his masters: 'If the Catholic princes knew what is being planned, they would cease fighting and destroying one another, and would think of themselves and their religion.' [2]

IV

The first parliament of the Protectorate, which met on September 3, showed, in spite of electoral manipulations, a clear verdict of the English people. The whimsies of the Little Parliament were repudiated, and only four were returned out of the fifty-six members who had given the vote which led to its dissolution. A few republicans like Bradshawe, Scot and Haselrig were elected, and in the west even one or two ineligible royalists; Wildman the Leveller was there, and some of the old puritan guard like Lenthall and Skippon and Francis Rous; Fairfax, too,

[1] *Cal. S. P. Dom*, 1653–54, 306.   [2] Sagredo in *Prayer Coll.*

and Anthony Ashley Cooper, and the elder Vane; Lambert and Fleetwood, and Oliver's son-in-law Claypole, and his sons Richard and Henry, and from Ireland Broghill and Reynolds. Godliness was not the qualification for this parliament; it was a gathering largely of propertied men, conservatives and presbyterians.

On Sunday the 3rd, the day of Dunbar and Worcester, Oliver welcomed the members in the Painted Chamber. Next day in royal state he drove from Whitehall to the abbey church of Westminster. Whitelocke has described the great coach in which he rode with Lambert and Henry Cromwell beside him, the richly dressed lackeys and pages, the jingling life-guards, the dignified procession of members of Council, and the company of officers and gentlemen with uncovered heads. It was an ill spectacle for Bradshawe and Haselrig. Thomas Goodwin preached the sermon, which was an exhortation to submit to the powers established by God. Thereafter, in the Painted Chamber, Oliver, set high in a canopied chair, addressed the new House. His speech [1] was very different from the fervent outpouring of the year before. He knew the audience he was addressing, and he emphasized those views which he shared with them, views which meant a defection from his former idealism forced upon him by the constraint of facts. In his new philosophy there were echoes of Charles and Laud and Strafford; it was the case for discipline and sobriety of thought, for realism as against day-dreams, order against anarchy.

He began by reminding his hearers of the ordeal through which England had passed. That was now over; their business was 'healing and settling.' He proceeded to deal faithfully with the obstacles to recovery. First the Levellers, in speaking of whom he adroitly but not very honestly lumped together the communist and political wings. What was the constitution of society which England had known for hundreds of years? 'A nobleman, a gentleman, a yeoman; the distinction of these; that is a good interest of the nation, and a great one. The natural magistracy of the nation was it not almost trampled under foot, under despite and contempt, by men of Levelling principles?' A strange plea from one who had himself helped to destroy a throne! He turned to the Fifth Monarchists, with words of which Laud had often spoken the substance. 'Such considerations and pretensions of liberty of conscience, what are they

[1] *L. and S.*, II, 339–59.

leading us towards? Liberty of conscience and liberty of the subjects, two as glorious things to be contended for as any God has given us; yet both these also abused for the patronizing of villainies.' He went on to defend his domestic and foreign policy — law reform; an established church 'to put a stop to that heady way of every man making himself a minister and a preacher'; the calling of a free parliament. 'I say, a free Parliament.... It's that which as I have desired above my life, so I shall desire to keep it so above my life.' Abroad they had now peace with the Danes, the Dutch and the Portuguese, but there were still clouds in the sky and a great work on hand; let them not imitate the children of Israel, 'who rather desired to eat the onions of Egypt than to pursue their journey.' It was a speech directed with extraordinary skill to the audience he was addressing, but its whole spirit was at startling variance not only with certain of his former utterances but with current puritan feeling. One critic quoted the verse of Proverbs, 'There be three things too wonderful for me, yea four that I know not,' and added: 'If it were honest and lawful to add to Scripture, one might put in a fifth way, viz., The way of a Protector in his speeches and between them and his actions, for no man that follows him there is able to find him out.' [1]

If we may believe the Dutch envoys, Oliver concluded with an invitation to the House (not in the printed text) to consider and ratify the 'Instrument of Government.' The reception of his speech may have convinced him that the majority had the same desire as himself to establish order at all costs. Parliament, if it was to have any meaning, must act as a constituent assembly, and formally accept the new scheme: otherwise there was no parliamentary government. 'They sat there by the authority of the good people of England, and how could it be contended that their authority did not include the right of judging the system on which the good people of England were henceforth to be governed?' [2] When the House met on September 5 it was a member of Council who proposed that the Instrument should be at once considered. [3] But parliament proved too ardent in this work, and threatened to throw the whole new constitution into the melting-pot. The formula most acceptable to it was that government should be 'in a Parliament and single person, limited and restrained as Parliament should think fit.'

[1] *The Protector, So-called, in Part Unveiled*, 1655 (Th.).
[2] Morley, *Cromwell*, 392.   [3] See Gardiner, *Comm. and Prot.*, III, 182 *n*.

This was to cripple seriously the authority of the Protector and his co-ordinate power, and to give parliament a sovereignty easily open to abuse. Oliver was prepared to modify the Instrument, but there were three points on which he could not yield; it must be impossible for a parliament to perpetuate itself, there must be liberty of conscience, and the control of the armed forces must not lie solely with parliament, but be shared with himself.

A little more constitutional wrangling and the situation would get out of hand. On September 22 when members arrived at the House they found the doors locked and were told that the Protector awaited them in the Painted Chamber. There he delivered to them one of the best of his homilies [1] — compact, coherent, without hesitations, for he now knew his own mind, and he delivered it with the ringing clarity of a battle-order. He began with a sentence which might have been spoken by Charles: 'I said you were a free Parliament, and truly so you are, while you own the Government and authority that called you hither.' He then explained the nature of his own position. 'I called not myself to this place. I say again, I called not myself to this place. Of that God is witness.' But, having been constrained to the duty of government, he had acquired unlimited authority which of his own will he desired to reduce: by the Instrument he was not assuming power, but was laying it down. He was willing that parliament should revise the Instrument, provided certain essentials remained; they might do as they pleased with 'circumstantials' but they must not touch the 'fundamentals.' 'The things which shall be necessary to deliver over to posterity, these should be unalterable.' These fundamentals were four in number: liberty of conscience, government by parliament and a single person, a limitation of parliament's sittings, and a joint control of the armed forces. On these there could be no compromise, for on them orderly government depended. 'The wilful throwing away of this Government, such as it is, so ordered by God, so approved by men... is a thing which, and that in relation not to my good, but to the good of these nations and of posterity, I can sooner be willing to be rolled into my grave and buried with infamy than I can give my consent unto.' He therefore demanded an oath from the members to be faithful to the commonwealth and the Protector, and not to alter the government as settled in one

[1] *L. and S.*, II, 364–91.

person and a parliament — which was indeed no more than the
terms on which they had been elected. The extreme republicans
like Bradshawe, Haselrig and Wildman, refused — about a
hundred in all — but within a few days the remainder had
subscribed the test.

Yet parliament, as soon as it resumed its sittings, began to
debate the Instrument and to trench upon the fundamentals.
Such a course was inevitable, for no body of able men can
work together without an inclination to assert and to aggrandize
their authority. It is needless here to enter into the details of
those constitutional debates. The House whittled down the
proviso as to religious liberty, and claimed the right to deal
with heresy and ecclesiastical discipline over the head of the
Protector. It made the office of Protector elective and not
hereditary, and claimed greater control over the Council. That
might pass, but in its attitude towards the army it struck a
final rock of offence. The Instrument placed the standing army
at 30,000 men, but it had swollen to 57,000 which involved an
annual deficit to the exchequer of nearly half a million pounds.
The House proposed the restoration of the smaller figure, and
a reduction of the soldiers' pay; any further troops that might
be necessary should be militia, under the influence of its own
class, the country gentry. Moreover, it desired to limit its
grant of supply to five years, thus reserving to itself the ultimate financial control — in effect the ultimate sovereignty.
This set the army by the ears. In October three colonels,
Alured, Okey and Saunders, had petitioned in favour of a free
constituent parliament, and against the autocracy of the
Protector, but now the ranks closed up in loyalty to the full
terms of the Instrument. Yet the House in this matter had on
its side many moderates who longed to reduce the army influence, and it is likely that the proposal in December to give the
Protector the name of king, supported by Ashley Cooper and
Henry Cromwell, was designed to help Oliver, with the prestige
of the old title, to stand out against his marshals. The same
desire was widespread in the land, and the lunatic Thomas
Taney, who lit a bonfire in Lambeth into which he threw a
Bible, a saddle, a sword, and a pistol, declaring that these were
now the gods of England, spoke the thoughts of many wiser
men.

All that autumn and early winter the land was full of perilous
stuff. Everywhere royalist plots were hatching below the

surface, and the Levellers were joining hands with the cavaliers. The fanatics were in revolt. One or two, like Anna Trapnell, might fast under Oliver's windows in Whitehall and sing hymns in his honour, but most were his enemies, declaring like John Rogers that he had 'violently taken away the house he builded not,' and that he should 'feel no quietness in his belly.' The latter prophecy was fulfilled, for Oliver's health, which had been good since Worcester, became once again uncertain. He seems to have suffered, apart from his recurring ague, from some form of stone, and his condition was not improved by an accident which befell him in September. The Duke of Oldenburg had sent him a present of six horses, and he had them put to a coach and took Thurloe for a drive in Hyde Park. Loving horse-flesh and knowing how to handle it, he took the box-seat, driving apparently four in hand, with a postilion in charge of the two leaders. The animals were fresh, he used the whip too freely, the postilion lost control of the leaders, and the team bolted. Thurloe, inside the coach, jumped out and sprained his ankle. Oliver was pitched from the box on to the pole, and then fell on the ground with his feet caught in the traces. He was dragged some way, and a pistol went off in his pocket. When the runaways were stopped he was found to be badly shaken and to have damaged a leg, so that for some days he had to keep his room.[1] His escape was celebrated in verse by George Wither and Andrew Marvell, while from the royalist side a young lawyer, who was afterwards to be Chief Justice Scroggs, expressed the hope that the Protector's next drop might not be from a coach but from the hangman's cart.[2] On November 16 Oliver gave some sharp words to a committee of the House on the matter of toleration, for he was full of family cares. His mother was ill, and that night in her ninetieth year she died. She had been one of the main formative influences in his life, and, while his wife confined herself to household matters, his mother had been his confidante and counsellor from the old simple days of Huntingdon and Ely up to the splendours of Whitehall. Thurloe has recorded her last words. 'The Lord cause His face to shine upon you, and comfort you in all your adversities, and enable you to do great things for the glory of the Most High God, and to be a relief unto His people. My dear son, I leave my heart with thee. A good night.'

The inevitable break with parliament could not be long de-

[1] Thurloe, I, 652.   [2] *A Jolt on Michaelmas Day.*

layed. On the question of army control there was no room for compromise; parliament saw little hope of a settled government unless on this point it had the ultimate say, and Oliver saw only anarchy if it had; in both views there was a certain element of reason, but the reason in each could not be harmonized, since neither disputant could submit his case to the judgment of the nation. On January 22 the five months which the Instrument had fixed for the duration of parliament had elapsed, if these months were taken as lunar. Once again Oliver summoned the members to the Painted Chamber, and made them a speech.[1] It was long and confused, and the tone was that of extreme irritation. 'There be some trees that choose to thrive under the shadow of other trees. I will tell you what hath thriven... under your shadow. Instead of peace and settlement, instead of mercy and truth being brought together, righteousness and peace kissing each other, by settling the honest people of these nations... weeds and nettles, briars and thorns have thriven under your shadow.' But in the end, after much rambling, he managed to put the point at issue — the control of the army. 'If it should not be equally placed in him (the Protector) and the Parliament, but yielded up at any time, it determines his power either for doing the good he ought, or hindering Parliament from perpetuating themselves, or from imposing what religions they please on the consciences of men, or what government they please upon the nation, thereby subjecting it to dissettlement in every Parliament, and to the desperate consequences thereof.' He did not trust parliament; it was still too risky to trust the people; therefore he must trust himself. There could be only one conclusion: 'I think it my duty to tell you that it is not for the profits of these nations, not fit for the common and public good, for you to continue here any longer. And therefore I do declare unto you that I do dissolve this Parliament.'

For the third time Oliver had sent a House of Commons about its business; and now he had come to an *impasse* where it was imperative for him to revise all his constitutional notions. Circumstances had forced him to assert a divine right to rule as stiff as any claim of Charles, and to dismiss the wishes of the governed in government with all the arrogance of Strafford. The face of 'Black Tom Tyrant,' as he remembered him at his

[1] *L. and S.*, II, 404-30.

trial in Westminster hall, must have often haunted his mind. The imperfections of the Instrument need not concern us; it was a hastily improvised measure put together by amateurs, and it lacked that essential of all written constitutions, some authority, like American Supreme Court, for its interpretation. The trouble lay far deeper than any defects of machinery. The condition of the land did not yet permit of the relegation of the army to a subordinate place, and without some such relegation there could be no true parliamentary government. To adopt Cicero's words of Cæsar, England was a slave to Oliver, and he himself was a slave to the times. He had more power than any English king since William the Conqueror, but he had it only as a master of legions. No man was more conscious of this than the master himself. There is every reason to believe that his hand was forced by the army and that he would have been prepared to continue patiently the parliamentary experiment. He had no belief in government by a junto of colonels. What his son Henry wrote to Thurloe two years later was always in his mind: 'I wish his Highness would consider how casual the motions of a parliament are, and how many of them are called before one can be found to answer the ends thereof; and that it is the natural genius of such great assemblies to be various, inconsistent, and for the most part froward with their superiors; and therefore that he would not wholly reject so much of what they offer as is necessary to the public welfare. And the Lord give him to see how much safer it is to rely upon persons of estate, interest, integrity, and wisdom, than upon such as have so amply discovered their envy and ambition, and whose faculty it is by continuing of confusion to support themselves.' [1] In these words lay the whole philosophy of parliamentary government, and Oliver would have admitted their wisdom.

But the danger of parliamentary encroachment remained — recent history could not be forgotten — and to check that there were only two methods, the appeal to the nation and the appeal to the sword. From the first he was estopped by the knowledge that the nation, if given a choice, would destroy much that he held dear, so he was driven back upon the second. There was a further difficulty. He had no belief in what is often assumed to be a cardinal point in democratic government, the rule of a numerical majority, and he had all Selden's contempt for the creed that identified the odd man with the Holy

[1] Thurloe, VI, 93.

Ghost.[1] It was the business of the government to put quality into the nation, to educate the people into a nobler life, and not merely to bow to and interpret the brutish commonplaces of the average man. His purpose now, nebulous at first, but slowly crystallizing into shape, was to devise some form of parliament which would give counsel but would not dictate; to keep a firm hand upon the army and steadily bring it under subjection to the civil power; and meantime to press on with that policy of his own which he believed would build up a new England, a new Europe, and a new world. Not since Cæsar after Munda set about the re-ordering of the globe, had a mortal will bent itself to so bold an enterprise.

[1] See Selden, *Table Talk*, 'Council.'

Chapter II

THE CONSTABLE OF ENGLAND
(1655–1658)

Truly I have as before God often thought that I could not tell what my business was, nor what was the place I stood in, save comparing myself to a good constable set to keep the peace of the parish.

OLIVER CROMWELL.

I

IF OLIVER was again a dictator, he was determined to set strict limits to his arbitrariness. He would rule in accordance with the spirit of the Instrument, which was all the constitution there was. He levied the assessment at the reduced rate which the late parliament had imposed, and he avoided at first the promulgation of ordinances, which would have meant the assumption of the legislative power. But it was obvious that such self-denial could not continue, new monies would be needed if a reforming policy were to be pursued, and a law-giver must be found. So from the beginning of 1655 the question of his status as Protector was a burning topic in the Council. The preparation of the great seal of the Protectorate was delayed till it was clear what title it should bear. Many officers would have called him emperor, a name which to them had no ugly memories and under which he could assume what powers he pleased. The civilians would have made him a king.

Since his Council was his medium of government his success largely depended upon his colleagues. He was beginning to know his irreconcilable foes — the Levellers, purists of a republic; the mountebank-martyrs of the Fifth Monarchy; the royalists, plotting in ruined manor-houses and tramping the backstairs of foreign courts. These were open enemies with whom he could deal: more dangerous were the brittle friends, and the restless careerists like Lambert. Among his marshals he could count with confidence on the ablest, George Monk, whose sole interest was his profession, and who, when others dabbled in theory, only turned the tobacco quid in his gross cheeks. Blake, too, did his work and asked no questions, and, stout commonwealth man as he was, had written to Thurloe approving of the dissolution of parliament.[1] Lambert Oliver had discounted; Harrison he had dismissed; his kinsman Disbrowe would give little trouble; nor would men like Whalley and Goffe and Sydenham and Hewson, though they might need humouring. He could reckon on the heart and head of his son Henry. Of his son-in-law Fleetwood he had no high opinion — 'milksop,' he was to call him later;[2] the man was a fair soldier, and undeniably pious, but weak and unstable, though some of the stupider of the army officers saw in him 'the living image of our Lord Jesus Christ.' Edward Montague was a different person, a good soldier and soon to be a better admiral, and unfalteringly loyal to the greatest son of his own shire. Among the civilians there was Bulstrode Whitelocke, a lawyer who was not scared by novelties, but who had a stiff knuckle of principle and candour. There was Nathaniel Fiennes, unluckiest of military commanders, but a plodding and faithful servant. There were able men, too, in the secretariat, like John Milton and Andrew Marvell. And above all there was their chief, John Thurloe.

Thurloe was the linch-pin of the whole régime. As secretary of state he combined in his own hands nearly every portfolio of a modern cabinet, but he was also the chief of police and the head of the secret service. He was the greatest intelligence officer that ever served an English ruler, a greater even than Walsingham. Oliver allowed a large sum for his intelligence service, an annual £70,000, and Thurloe expended it so well that, in the words of a speaker in a Restoration parliament, he 'carried the secrets of all the princes of Europe at his girdle.' His agents were everywhere, and some of them were high in the confidence of the exiled Charles: no plot was hatched in the back streets of Brussels or the Hague but Thurloe knew of it at its inception: the cabinets of Paris and Madrid might meet behind guarded doors, but Thurloe in a few days had the record of their decisions. 'There is no government on earth,' the Venetian ambassador Sagredo wrote, 'which divulges its affairs less than England, or is more punctually informed of those of the others.' Whether he was tracking a plot against Oliver's life or following the movements of a Spanish plate-fleet, Thurloe had the same subtlety and precision and success. Penniless royalists, broken Highland chiefs, simple-minded fanatics, young rakes on the windy side of the law, condemned men reprieved for the purpose — he had them all on his working

[1] Thurloe, III, 232.　　[2] *Ibid.*, VI, 811; Ludlow, II, 33.

lists, and many of them never knew that they were in his service. He intercepted letters with such regularity that the royalist post-bag might as well have been delivered to his office. Poor Hyde in France, with not a farthing to spend on anything, did not know that the quiet little Essex lawyer read him like a large-print book, and had a note on his files of his most secret plans almost before they were completed.

There was need of such a watch-dog, for Oliver's life was threatened from a dozen quarters. Physically he was not the man he had been; every few weeks he had a bout of ill-health, his penmanship had become feeble, and that year foreign ambassadors noticed how, when he greeted them, it was with a shaking hand. But his prestige had never been higher, for he was beginning to seem like a great portent of nature, something above and beyond the common race of men. Awe was mingled with the hate of his enemies and the love of his friends. The sense was going abroad that the whole man and his works partook of the miraculous, the feeling that inspired Hyde's verdict: 'To reduce three nations, which perfectly hated him, to an entire obedience to all his dictates; to awe and govern those nations by an army that was indevoted to him and wished his ruin; was an instance of a very prodigious address.'[1] This growth of his fame stirred up his opponents to desperate efforts, which he met with a firm hand. The army rebels like Overton and Harrison and Wildman were easily suppressed. The machinations of the Sealed Knot, the group of royalist conspirators, were closely watched, and when in March Penruddock rose in Wiltshire it was easy to scatter his little band. The same fate befell the abortive risings in the midlands and the north. There was no vindictive aftermath; only nine of the rebels suffered death, though a number were shipped to the plantations, and to 'barbadoes' a man became a verb in the language. Oliver had at first ordered out the militia, but the order was countermanded when it was clear how feeble was the opposition. Instead he set himself to reduce the army, as his late parliament had requested, disbanded over ten thousand men, and lowered the pay of those left on the rolls. Penruddock's business had convinced him of the loyalty of the forces under his command.

It had also led him to a more dangerous deduction. The mischief was not dead, it had only gone underground, and to

[1] Clarendon, *Hist.*, VI, 94.

check it there was need of a new police — the militia which
parliament had proposed, but a militia not locally controlled
but under the charge of army officers. He followed the apparently inevitable fashion of revolutions, and appointed commis-
sars. England was divided into eleven areas, over each of which
he set an officer with the local rank of major-general. These
officers had under them the local militia, supplemented by
special troops of horse. The funds needed he regarded as
emergency payments outside the regular army budget, and
raised them by a 'decimation,' an extra tax of ten per cent
upon the incomes of the impoverished royalist gentry.

As a police measure it was successful, but as statesmanship
it was disastrous. The brief régime of the major-generals was
the most intolerable experience that England had ever known.
It was an era of petty tyranny and petty espionage. Some of
them were reasonable men, some like Boteler in the midlands
were heavy-handed fools, but the instructions of all were an
outrage upon liberty and decency. Not only had they to curb
disorder, but they were enjoined to suppress vice and encourage
virtue — and these latter instructions must have been due to
Oliver himself. Punishments were arbitrary and capricious.
'For the community at large the danger lay in the growing
habit of the executive, strong in the force of military support,
to deal out penalties at its own will and pleasure, without
definite rules laid down beforehand, and without adequate
security for the release of the innocent. Even Charles had better
preserved the forms of legal justice.'[1] Swearing, tippling
and gaming were put down; horse-races, cock-fights and bear-
baiting were prohibited, and Major-General Barkstead slew
the bears, while Colonel Pride wrung the necks of the game-
cocks.[2] Merry England became a silent and melancholy place,
where no man could trust his neighbour; vagabondage disappeared from the highways, because all the gaols were over-
flowing.

No class had a good word for the experiment. 'A company of
silly, mean fellows called major-generals,' the puritan Colonel
Hutchinson wrote. 'These ruled according to their wills, by
no law but what seemed good in their own eyes, imprisoning
men, obstructing the cause of justice between man and man.'
But it was on the unfortunate royalists that the brunt fell. The

[1] Gardiner, *Comm. and Prot.*, III, 339.
[2] Carte, *Original Letters*, II, 83; *Rump Songs*, I, 299.

Verney Memoirs show to what an intolerable new persecution country squires were subjected who only desired to live peaceably, the very men whose cause Oliver had pled in his speech to his first Protectorate parliament.[1] Not only were their lives made a burden to them by insane restrictions, but many of them, who after a voluntary composition had been promised freedom for the future, now found the particulars of their estates, which they had furnished in all good faith, used for the purpose of the new decimation. A minor grievance was the mean extraction of the tyrants. 'Colonel Philip Jones, who has now £7000 per annum, was born to £8 or £10 a year. Sir John Barkstead was a thimblemaker; Kelsey sold leather points; Major-General Bridge was a common dragoneer in Yorkshire.'[2]

Conjointly with the appointment of the major-generals there was a general tightening up of public discipline. An edict was issued ordering that no ejected clergyman should keep school or be a tutor in a gentleman's house or use the prayer-book — an edict which, perhaps because of the plea of the old Archbishop Ussher, was not enforced. The press was put under a strict censorship, and the previous medley of journals was cut down to a single paper appearing twice a week. Quakers were sternly dealt with, though Oliver did his best on their behalf, while he also strove to legalize the return of the Jews to England. There can be no question that the doings in 1655 did more than any other event to disgust the land with puritan habits of thought, and that they lost to Oliver many moderate royalists whom he had almost won over. Undoubtedly that year saw a long-needed reform in the policing of the land, which was becoming notorious for highway robbery and other outrages: but one kind of security was won at the expense of another. No nation could be at ease when an old Devon squire of seventy-six could be transported to the plantations without a trial, and a major-general could send Jeremy Taylor arbitrarily to prison.

This government by edict of Council was not palatable even to the most liberal legal minds. Two judges, Thorpe and Newdigate, on the commission for the trial of the northern rebels, made difficulties and were summarily dismissed. A London merchant named Cony refused to pay a tax, and his counsel questioned the validity of the ordinance imposing it. The

[1] See *L. and S.*, II, 370. [2] Burton, *Diary*, I, 331.

chief justice, Rolle, was so much of the same view that he resigned his post. To question the ordinance was to question the
Instrument, and therefore to undermine the whole foundation
of the Protectorate. Cony's counsel were sent to the Tower,
but they presently apologized; Cony submitted, and the matter
was dropped. But the situation was bad among men of the
long robe, for both Whitelocke and Widdrington, commissioners of the Great Seal, had resigned on another point. Lenthall,
now Master of the Rolls, was developing scruples, and the
judges generally were talking about Magna Charta. Oliver
summoned them before him, and gave them a trouncing. To
their plea of Magna Charta he is said to have replied with a
farm-yard jape.[1] This thing touched the heart of his authority,
and he could permit no weakening, but Clarendon, who tells
the story, adds that 'in all other matters which did not concern the life of his jurisdiction, he seemed to have great reverence for the law, and rarely interposed between party and
party.'

Oliver for the moment was in a truculent mood, convinced
that all he did was justified by necessity and Providence.
'If nothing should ever be done but what is according to law,
the throat of the nation may be cut while we send for someone
to make a law.'[2] His temper is illustrated by a letter written
in July to Thurloe about an admission to the Charterhouse.
'I have not the particular shining bauble or feather in my cap
for crowds to gaze at or kneel to, but I have power and resolution for foes to tremble at. To be short, I know how to deny
petitions; and whatever I think proper, for outward form, to
refer to any officer or office, I expect that such my compliance
with custom shall be also looked upon as an indication of my
will and pleasure *to have the thing done.*'[3]

II

Under the Instrument the next parliament was not due till
1657, but, since money was needed for the war with Spain,
and the major-generals promised the election of only docile
members, Oliver issued writs for a new House in July 1656.
But the major-generals had miscalculated, for some hundred
of the members returned, men like Scot and Haselrig, were in

[1] It will be found in Clarendon, *Hist.*, VI, 93.
[2] *L. and S.*, II, 543.   [3] *Ibid.*, II, 454.

bitter opposition. Bradshawe, indeed, was not there, nor Ludlow; and Vane, having tried for a seat, had now been sent into confinement at Carisbrooke. Vane had just published his pamphlet *A Healing Question*,[1] in which, after an impassioned plea for religious liberty, he confessed himself prepared for any change, however drastic, provided it were ratified by parliament. But his parliament was not to be elected by the nation at large, but by the adherents of his own creed, and Oliver was entitled to ask whether such a limitation was superior to other forms of forcible control. 'The nation must be governed by its own consent,' Ludlow had harped at their last meeting, but Ludlow meant at bottom the consent of those of his own way of thinking, not the will of the majority. 'Where shall we find this consent?' Oliver pertinently asked. 'Amongst the Protestant, Presbyterian, Independent, Anabaptist or Levelling parties?' He was getting very weary of this parrot-cry of free parliaments, to whose freedom every demagogue set his own special limits, and, having been given the right of selection by the Instrument, he did not hesitate to use it. The clerk in the lobby dealt out certificates of admission, and no member without a certificate could enter the House. What remained was a meek company of presbyterians and independents, all moderate men. The cry at the polls had been 'no courtiers, decimators or swordsmen,' but of the 352 members left most were soldiers, place-holders, or Oliver's own kin.

On September 17 in the Painted Chamber the Protector addressed the new parliament in a speech [2] (it lasted three hours of a blazing noon) which contained much fustian and rhetoric, but also some of the most memorable words he ever spoke. It was a defence of the major-generals, a summary of the troubles of the past year, and a defiance of Spain. He made no apology for his efforts to raise the morals of the land.

> I say, if it be in the general hearts of the nation, it is a thing I am confident our liberty and prosperity depends upon — Reformation. Make it a shame to see men to be bold in sin and profaneness, and God will bless you. You will be a blessing to the nation, and by this will be more repairers of breaches than by anything in the world. Truly these things do respect the souls of men and the spirits — which are the men. The mind is the man. If that be kept pure, a man signifies somewhat; if not, I would fain see what difference there is betwixt him and a beast.

[1] It is reprinted in *Somers Tracts*.   [2] *L. and S.*, II, 508-53.

At the close he was whirled into a rhapsody on the 46th Psalm:

> I beseech you, in the name of God, set your hearts to this work. And if you set your hearts to it, you will sing Luther's psalm. That is a rare psalm for a Christian.... If Pope and Spaniard and Devil all set themselves against us, though they should compass us about like bees, yet in the name of the Lord we should destroy them. And as it is in this Psalm of Luther's, 'We will not fear though the earth be removed, and though the mountains be carried into the middle of the sea, though the waters thereof roar and be troubled, though the mountains shake with the swelling thereof. There is a river the streams whereof shall make glad the City of God. God is in the midst of her, she shall not be moved.'

The House, with Widdrington as Speaker, proved at first sufficiently complaisant. The success of the war with Spain and the capture of Spanish treasure induced the members to vote readily the necessary supplies. They passed bills annulling the title of the Stuarts to the throne, and making it high treason to plot against the Protector's government. But the delicacy of the whole position was revealed by the case of James Naylor. Naylor, who had served as a quartermaster in Lambert's regiment, had become a Quaker, and had thence wandered into a strange world of vision. In appearance he was like the traditional portraits of Christ, and he made an entry into Bristol which was a blasphemous parody of Christ's entry into Jerusalem. He was arrested and sent to London for trial, and in October his case came before parliament, when he was given a savage sentence of branding, scourging, and imprisonment. Now the Instrument conferred no judicial powers on the House, and the claim to them could only be defended by overriding the Instrument and harking back to the rights of the old parliaments. 'We have all the power,' said one member, 'there was in the House of Lords, now in this Parliament.' This was a challenge which Oliver could not refuse, for it outraged not only his clemency but also his reading of the new constitution. As he had interfered the year before to save John Biddle the Socinian, so now he intervened on behalf of Naylor. On December 25 he wrote to the Speaker: 'We detest and abhor the giving or occasioning the least countenance to persons of such opinions and practices.... Yet we, being entrusted in the present government on behalf of the people of these nations, and not knowing how far such proceedings (wholly without us) may extend in the consequence of it, do desire that the House will let us know the grounds and reasons whereupon they have proceeded.'[1] The House made no reply, but it persisted with the sentence, and the most that Oliver could do was to try to alleviate the prisoner's sufferings.[2] The position was grave, for the authority of the Instrument had been flouted, and Oliver under the Instrument had no power of restraint. He began to realize the need of an upper chamber to review the doings of the lower. 'Here is your power asserted on the one hand,' said a member; 'the supreme magistrate on the other hand desiring an account of your judgment. Where shall there be *tertius arbiter*? It is a hard case. No judge upon earth.'[3]

The majority of the soldiers were with Oliver in Naylor's case, for they saw in parliament's behaviour a tendency to add to its powers and an attack upon toleration. The fate of the major-generals widened the breach with the civilians. A bill was introduced to continue the system of decimation, which the lawyers strongly opposed, and which was rejected on January 29, 1657, by a majority of thirty-six. The soldiers supported it, as did Thurloe; Oliver remained neutral, but the fact that his son-in-law John Claypole moved the rejection, and that Broghill, who was very close to him, voted on the same side, suggested that the Protector had in fact thrown over his new system of police.... A shrewd blow had been struck in the fight of the civilians against army domination.

The year 1657 therefore opened with ominous questions banking like clouds on the political horizon. Moreover it became clear that Oliver's life was in constant peril. Thurloe's spies revealed a nest of murderous intrigues in many quarters. The Fifth Monarchy fanatics were at their old business, led by one Venner, a cooper, who was afterwards to swing for plotting against Charles II. To them Oliver was now the Bastard of Ashdod, but their conspiracies moved slowly, for 'the ancient wise Christians' like Harrison and John Carew stood aside, and there were chronological doubts as to whether the reign of the Beast had yet fulfilled the period laid down by the Book of Revelation. The royalist plotting was a more dangerous affair. The renegade Sexby was busy, for it was believed that Oliver's life alone averted a new chaos which would assist a Stuart restoration. In 1654 Charles had issued a proclamation offering a knighthood and £500 a year to the slayer of 'a cer-

[1] *L. and S.*, III, 20.   [2] Firth, *Last Years*, I, 104.
[3] Burton, I, 249.

tain base mechanic fellow called Oliver Cromwell.'[1] The most decorous cavaliers approved of the business. They welcomed the doctrine of the pamphlet, *Killing no Murder*, published a few months later. Ormonde and Hyde were privy to all the assassination plots. 'No man,' wrote the respectable Nicholas, 'that should effect so glorious a work can possibly fail of an ample and very honourable reward for it as well on earth as in heaven.'[2]

An instrument was found in one Miles Sindercombe, a Leveller and an old Ironside, but Sindercombe was too cautious a bravo. He hoped to kill the Protector at the opening of parliament, but was deterred by the number of people present. Thereafter he dogged his man with a pistol in his pocket, on his journeys to Hampton Court and on his rides in Hyde Park, but found no opportunity. So he resolved to smoke out his quarry's earth and fire Whitehall: 'It was the fittest hole for a tyrant to live in, and if that were burned there is never another place in England where he could hide and secure himself.' The plan was betrayed and Sindercombe was arrested. When parliament on January 19 moved an address to the Protector congratulating him on his escape, John Ashe, member for Somerset, proposed a startling rider. 'I would have something else added,' he said, 'which in my opinion would tend very much to the preservation of himself and us and to the quieting of all the designs of our enemies; that His Highness would be pleased to take upon himself the government according to the ancient constitution, so that the hopes of our enemies in plots would be at an end.'[3]

The question of a crown had been raised and could not be dropped, for though Ashe was an obscure figure he spoke the mind of the majority of the House and of many powerful groups outside its walls. The civilians in parliament knew that Oliver's death would mean the downfall of the government and their own ruin, and desired to protect him with the ancient sanctities. Moreover they realized that only by a revival of monarchy could they effectually prevent the army from dictating policy. The crown was the symbol of civilian as opposed to military government. On the other hand a section of the soldiers feared the tyranny of parliament, especially its interference with religious liberty, and believed that if Oliver were king there would be an end to its encroachments. The ordinary man in the coun-

[1] Thurloe, II, 248.   [2] *Nicholas Papers*, III, 265.   [3] Burton, I, 362.

try had no illusions about the government of the swordsmen, for he had had more than enough of the recent experiment. 'They are so highly incensed against the arbitrary actings of the major-generals that they are greedy of any power that will be ruled and limited by law.'[1] Moreover Oliver's victories abroad had given him the aura of a conqueror, and in the English memory the conquerors had been kings. Edmund Waller, whose ear was close to the ground, spoke for many besides himself when he urged in his verses that the captured Spanish gold should be used to make a crown and a sceptre for the victor. Early in February London citizens were wagering that a few weeks would see a notable change in the form of government.[2]

On Monday, February 23, Sir Christopher Packe, a London member whom Oliver had knighted, was given permission to introduce a 'remonstrance,' a bill to revise the constitution and permit the assumption by the Protector of the 'name, style, title and dignity of King.' The lines of cleavage were at once made clear. The measure was supported by the lawyers like Thurloe, Whitelocke and Glyn, by most of the civilian members of Council, by Oliver's intimates like Broghill and Edward Montague, by the Irish representatives generally, and by many country gentlemen like Sir Richard Onslow, the member for Surrey. Few high-placed soldiers were for it, except Skippon. The major-generals and most of the officers opposed it, Lambert and Sydenham violently, Disbrowe and Fleetwood more moderately as became Oliver's kin. Outside the House the city of London was generally in favour of the bill, especially the presbyterians. The Fifth Monarchy men were driven distracted by what they regarded as a blasphemous neglect of Scripture, and the Levellers and republicans and the sterner puritans were aghast at this rebuilding of the walls of Jericho. The rank-and-file of the army by a considerable majority were hostile. It was the army that moved first, and on February 27, four days after the introduction of Pack's bill, a deputation of one hundred officers waited upon the Protector.

Of this conference there are ample summaries,[3] but one would

[1] C. P., III, 91.

[2] The discussion between Colonel Bridges and Disbrowe (Lans MSS., 821) in the previous November shows how men's minds were working on the subject. The best account of the different strains of opinion will be found in Sir Charles Firth's articles on 'Cromwell and the Crown' (E. H. R., XVII, XVIII).

[3] The fullest is in a letter of Anthony Morgan to Henry Cromwell (Lans MSS., 821). Another is given by Burton (I, 382) and there are shorter versions in Thurloe, VI, 93 and C. P., III, 93. See also E. H. R. (1903), 60.

give much for a verbatim report, for Oliver liberated his soul, and must have used that blunt rustic freedom which was his custom with fighting men whom he had led and whose hearts he understood. He had not been privy, he told them, to the introduction of the Remonstrance, and had indeed only seen it the night before. He himself cared nothing for the title of king, but what ailed *them* at it? They had once not been averse to it, for they had pressed it upon him. He proceeded to give them a sketch of recent history. He had submitted to their wishes even when he thought them wrong, and all his constitutional experiments had been of their making. The Instrument clearly would not work, but the officers would not let parliament mend it; they would have mended it themselves, which he was sworn not to permit; otherwise he would have been a mere creature of their caprice. 'You might have given me a kick on the breech and turned me going.' Then came the present parliament; he had not been enthusiastic about it, but the officers had clamoured for it, since they thought that they could get a House after their own hearts. In this they had failed, and he had had the unpleasing task of excluding malcontents. 'When they were chosen you garbled them, kept out and put in whom you pleased... and I am sworn to make good all that you do, right or wrong.' And even now they were not satisfied, but complained of the doings of this body which they had themselves chosen and winnowed. The thing had become intolerable. Oliver's temper cracked, and he turned a hanging face upon the astonished delegates. 'I never courted you,' he thundered, 'nor never will. I have a sure refuge. If they (the House) do good things I must and will stand by them. They are honest men and have done good things. I know not what you can blame them for unless because they love me too well.' They were offended at the proposed House of Lords, but did they not see that it was only by some such balancing power that they could defend their cherished religious liberty? Had not Naylor's case taught them that?... Enough for the present. Let them choose six or seven of their number, and he would talk with them again. He curtly bade them good night, and they went meekly away, their self-sufficiency as shrunken as a pricked bladder.

That interview for a little quieted the soldiers. Lambert, Sydenham, Hewson and Disbrowe were as sullen as ever, and Fleetwood as plaintive, but men like Whalley, Boteler and

Goffe had come to heel. On March 5 an army deputation assured the Protector 'of their satisfaction in his Highness, and of their resolution to acquiesce in what he should think to be for the good of these nations.' Meantime in parliament the discussion on the Remonstrance continued. The first paragraph dealing with the kingship was postponed, but one by one the others were carried, including the House of Lords article, which passed without a division. On March 24 consideration of the first paragraph was resumed, Broghill, Lisle and Whitelocke being the chief advocates of the kingly title, with Lambert and Disbrowe in violent opposition, while Fleetwood delivered an invective against monarchy watered by copious tears. Next day by 123 votes to 62 the fateful resolution was carried — 'That your Highness will be pleased to assume the name, style, title, dignity and office of King of England, Scotland and Ireland, and the respective dominions and territories thereunto belonging, and to exercise the same according to the laws of these nations.' On the 31st of March in the Banqueting House in Whitehall under the name of 'The Humble Petition and Advice' the scheme was presented to Oliver. He replied briefly, and with obvious emotion.[1] He had lived the latter part of his life 'in the fire, in the midst of trouble,' but nothing had ever befallen him which so much moved his heart 'with that fear and reverence of God that became a Christian' as this proposal But there were many weighty things to consider: he was an old man, and he might perhaps be 'at the end of his work'; he must have a little space for reflection.

The world at large believed that he would accept, but when the answer came on April 3rd it was a refusal. Parliament had made the offer indivisible; all the articles must be accepted or none — probably with the idea of making it easier for Oliver to go back on his former rejection of the crown, since a crown was the price of a general settlement. 'You do necessitate my answer to be categorical; and you have left me without a liberty of choice save as to all.... I am not able for such a trust and charge.... I have not been able to find it my duty to God and you to undertake this charge under that title.'[2] He could assent to everything in the petition except the name of king.

There were rejoicings in Lambert's faction and consternation among the majority in parliament, for to them the royal name

[1] *Lans MSS.*, 822. The speech is in *L. and S.*, III, 25–29.
[2] *L. and S.*, III, 31–32.

was the foundation of any settlement. 'It is better,' said Colonel Bridges, 'to settle upon the old bottom.' 'The title is not the question,' Thurloe wrote to Henry Cromwell, 'but it's the office which is known to the laws and this people. They know their duty to a king and his to them. Whatever else there is will be wholly new, and be nothing else but a probationer, and upon the next occasion will be changed again. Besides, they say, the name Protector came in by the sword out of parliament and will never be the ground of any settlement; nor will there be a free parliament so long as that continues, and as it savours of the sword now, so it will at last bring all things to the military.' [1] Oliver had not seemed to bolt the door. 'The truth is, his carriage in this debate was such that it gave great hopes to men that he would at last comply with the parliament. But that time must show; for the present we can but guess. It's certain the body of this nation doth desire it.'

So for five weeks the House laboured to alter the Protector's resolution. Oliver was making up his slow mind, and as usual he was torn with doubts. Sir Francis Russell, Henry Cromwell's father-in-law, found him at Whitehall 'in a notable powerful spirit, tramples this world and the outward majesty of it under his feet; he tells me, and I do believe so much, that he is in great peace and quiet, this work being over.' But a fortnight later it would appear that his mood had changed, for Sir Francis wrote to Henry that he would soon be addressing him as Duke of York, since the Protector had come out of his clouds and was likely to take the kingly name. 'I cannot think there will be the least combustion about it. This day I have had some discourse with your father about this great business, and he is very cheerful, and his troubled thoughts seem to be over.' [2]

Up till the early days of May Oliver appears to have leaned to the side of the civilians. The title of king was the one question at issue, for with the rest of the Humble Petition he was more or less in agreement. The parliamentary committees who interviewed him had to put up with frequent adjourn-ments and mysterious answers; he had another of his fits of ill-health, and would receive them, 'coming out of his chamber, half unready, in his gown, with a black scarf round his neck.' [3]

---

[1] Thurloe, VI, 219.   [2] Lans MSS., 822.

[3] Hist. MSS. Comm., 3rd Rep. (Sutherland MSS.), 163. The discussion will be found in Somers Tracts, VI, 346, etc.

Now and then he was closeted with his special counsellors like Broghill and Thurloe, who found him in a strange mood. 'He would sometimes be very cheerful with us, and laying aside his greatness he would sometimes be very familiar with us, and by way of diversion would make verses with us, and everyone must try his fancy: he commonly called for tobacco pipes and a candle, and would now and then take tobacco himself; and then he would fall again to his serious and great business.'

By Wednesday, May 6, the rumour was strong that he would accept the crown; indeed he had said as much to some of his intimate friends.[1] A day or two before he had taken Fleetwood with him to dine with Disbrowe, in an attempt to win over the marshals, and had 'drolled with them about monarchy, and, speaking slightly of it, said it was but a feather in a man's cap, and therefore wondered that men would not please the children and permit them to enjoy their rattle.'[2] He was answered by grim faces and downcast eyes. On the 6th he met Disbrowe in St. James's park, and told him of his decision; to which Disbrowe replied that, while he would never act against him, he could act with him no more but must withdraw from all public employment, and that Lambert and Fleetwood were of the same view. The officers made one last attempt to change his mind. Pride got Dr. John Owen to draw up a petition, and Mason, his lieutenant-colonel, collected signatures. On the morning of Friday, May 8, Mason presented the petition at the bar of the House, protesting against kingship and begging that the Protector should not be further pressed. The members repaired, according to the arrangement, to the Banqueting House, where to their amazement Oliver revealed himself as in agreement with the soldiers. He spoke for only a few minutes. After apologizing for his troublesome delays, he said: 'I cannot undertake this government with this title of king. And that is mine answer to this great and weighty business.'[3]

He had made the *gran rifiuto* but not *per viltate*. What had been the arguments which presented themselves to him during those anxious weeks? 'All the disputes,' Clarendon wrote, 'were now within his own chamber, and there is no question that the man was in great agony, and in his own mind he did heartily desire to be king, and thought it the only way to be safe.' Clarendon, like Swift after him, set his refusal down to a failure of nerve. That explanation at any rate may be rejected. The army did not terrorize him, for he presently took order with the army, and Lambert joined Harrison in disgrace. But this much may be admitted — that the petition of the officers on May 8 was the proximate cause of his refusal. A soldier is a member of a clan islanded amid great seas of peril and death, and he acquires a loyalty to his colleagues closer than the ties of kinship. To break finally with that which had made him and to which he had given the best work of his life was a hard thing for a man of Oliver's fierce affections. For the protests of the arid republicans and the constitutional pedants like Prynne [1] he cared not at all; nor was he greatly moved by the rage of the sectaries and the anabaptists. [2] The royalist argument that now the quarrel would be not between republic and monarchy but between the ancient house of Stuart and the upstart house of Cromwell left him cold, for he was confident that he could make as good a king as any. But the appeal of his old soldiers — or at least half of them — against the title could not easily be dismissed. On April 13 he had told a parliamentary deputation: 'If I know as I do that very generally good men do not swallow the title... it is my duty to beg of you that there may be no hard things put upon me; things, I mean, hard to them which they cannot swallow.... I would not have you lose them. I would not that you should lose any servant or friend who may help in this work, or that they should be offended by that that signifies no more to me than I told you. That is, I do not think the thing necessary.'

It was not the vapourings of Lambert or the tears of Fleetwood that moved him, but the bewilderment of the plain soldiers, such an one as Captain William Bradford who wrote that he was of the number that loved him, having gone along with him from Edgehill to Dunbar. 'Those that are for a crown, I fear you have little experience of them; the others, most of them, have attended your greatest hazards.... Good my lord, remember you are but a man, and must die and come to judgment; men of high degree are vanity... my freedom proceeds from a large proportion of love and no bye-ends.' [3] Could he cause these humble folk to stumble? Had a crown seemed to

---

[1] See Prynne, *King Richard the Third Revived.* (Th.).

[2] For this see Firth, *Last Years,* I, 154, etc.; and Brown, *Baptists and Fifth Monarchy Men,* 122, etc.

[3] Nickolls, *Original Letters,* 141.

him a necessity for England he would have done violence to his natural feelings and dared the hazard. But it was only a convenience, not a necessity.

That it was a convenience he had no doubt. He was wholly convinced by the arguments of Thurloe and the lawyers. He had travelled far since the days when he had accepted Pym's parliamentaryism as the last word in wisdom. He had had his fill of high-flying whimsies and the worship of formulas and names, and his creed was now that opportunism which was being preached by his chief journalistic supporter: 'That all forms of government are but practical expedients, to be taken on trial as necessity and right reason of state enjoins, in order to the public's safety; and that as 'tis a madness to contend for any form when the reason of it is gone, so 'tis neither dishonour nor scandal, by following right reason, to shift through every form, and after all other experiments made in vain, when the ends of government cannot otherwise be concerned, to revert upon the old bottom and foundation.'[1] He saw the value of the kingly title, but it was a circumstantial and not a fundamental. The scheme of the Humble Petition gave him the kind of stable and constitutional government which he desired, and as Protector he had all the power of a monarch — as much at any rate as a new world would permit. We may judge the view of the father from that of the like-minded son. In April Henry Cromwell wrote to Thurloe: 'As I believe... that it is but peevishness in some to oppose the title desired by the remonstrance, so I cannot well satisfy myself that these are altogether blameless who, for not being honoured in a title and a very word, should suddenly withhold what would make themselves and others happy. I would not have the sober and judicious party so much justify the weakness of the other as to contend over earnestly for a name.'[2]

These were weighty reasons of state, but Oliver was slow to convince, for he was looking below the surface of things to the foundations. His new Protectorate was a mighty power, under which he might rule England till his death, but could he hand it on, in spite of the provision made by parliament? For it was a new thing, with no inherent or accumulated majesty. Its strength lay in the man who held the office, and not in the office itself, and without the latter sanction there was no guarantee

---

[1] Marchamont Needham in *Mercurius Politicus*, March 26–April 2, 1657 (Th.).
[2] Thurloe, VI, 182.

of endurance. Oliver understood as well as any man the in-grained reverence in English hearts for the crown, however contemptible its wearer might be. The Throne was not only higher than any other human estate, it was of a different kind from any other, and there was an impassable gulf between its occupant and his loftiest subject. Such a majesty would never inhere in any parliament-made Protectorate. Could he revive it as king, and to the houses of Plantagenet and Tudor and Stuart add that of Cromwell, greater because more English than any? He looked round his family; his eldest son had reverted to the easy-going country gentleman, but Henry had courage and brains, and his daughters would make as good princesses as any in Europe.

This thought must have been often with him during his weeks of indecision, and at one time he dallied with it. But his strong good sense convinced him of its impracticability, and the petition of the officers was only the last ounce which tipped the balance against it. For he realized that he had missed his chance. After Worcester, with the glamour of a national saviour about him, he might have carried with him to a throne the goodwill of the great mass of the English people, and have forced the remnant of the Long Parliament into compliance, winning thus the title by both law and conquest. There was another opportunity when he dismissed the Rump — less certain, but possible — for he would have had the nation's profound satiety with talk and its deep craving for security to aid him. On both occasions he could have carried the army, and as king he could soon have reduced that army to its proper place in the state. But now he had lost the goodwill of the plain man, the moderate royalist, the unashamed neutral, for the rule of the major-generals had made his name to stink in the land. He had the lawyers and the solid merchants behind him, many of the country gentry, and perhaps half the soldiers, but not England. He was too late for the only kind of kingship which could endure.

Two other reflections were present to decide him. To set his house firmly on the throne, he needed some assurance that for a reasonable time he would hold in his own hands the reins of power. His assurance was far otherwise, for he knew now that length of days would be denied him. He was already an old man with a failing body. And there was another and deeper reason, which he had stammered out when the Humble Petition was being presented; he might not only be near the end of his work; he might be a person in whom God took no pleasure. He was conscious that in late years he had become a different man from the simple soldier of Christ who had lived happily in the field with the certainty that he was doing the commands of his master. The world had been too much with him, and in the throng of earthly cares he had been apt to forget the things of the spirit. He no longer had his cherished communion with the unseen. Mundane wisdom had had the upper hand, and the whirl of affairs had distracted him from divine contemplations. Half the devout, many of them his ancient friends, looked on him now as a renegade and a backslider. In secular affairs he knew them to be fools, but might they not be God's witnesses against him? The awful doubt returned always to torture him — could a man who had been once in grace ever fall from it?

III

Parliament, much disheartened, did what was permitted to it. On May 25 it presented again the Humble Petition with Oliver's emendations and without the title of king, and Oliver duly accepted it. The Protectorate in this revised form was virtually a restoration of monarchical and parliamentary government. The Protector had the right to nominate his successor with parliament's approval. He had the right to nominate the members of the new House of Lords. He was granted a permanent revenue of £1,300,000 for normal expenses, and an additional revenue of £600,000 for the next three years for the purposes of war. The House of Commons, with a second chamber to check it, was to be freed now from the risk of arbitrary exclusions. The Council, irremovable without the consent of parliament, took the oath of allegiance to the person of the Lord Protector and his successors. It was a form of constitution which had been reached by the method of trial and error, and the general belief was that any further amendment would be in the direction of kingship. 'I confess I like gradual proceedings best,' Henry Cromwell wrote, 'and this the better because it seems such; for I take the late Instrument and way of government to have been a real relief against the wild courses of the Little Parliament, and am glad no alteration in that Instrument was effected, till time and experience have taught us both its faults and remedies. Wherefore I am contented that the finishing of our settlement be also deferred, till a competent trial has been made of the present way.'[1] He spoke the thought of most reasonable men.

Oliver, as always happened after a great decision, improved in both health and spirits. 'The truth is,' Sir Francis Russell wrote to Henry Cromwell, 'your father hath of late made more wise men fools than ever. He laughs and is merry, but they hang down their heads and are pitifully out of countenance. All the lawyers are turned Quakers, who before boasted they would make penknives of the soldiers' swords.'[2] With his recovered cheerfulness he made a grand occasion of his instalment as Protector for the second time. He had never the foolish pride which apes humility; he was the first man in the state and must carry the appurtenances of that dignity; he had issued writs, to the scandal of the precise, summoning members to a parliament which he called 'his,' as King Charles had never done; his wife and children bore the courtesy titles of the highest nobility; his infrequent entertainments were always on a princely scale. Accordingly on June 26 London witnessed a splendid pageant. At the upper end of Westminster hall had been prepared a platform under a rich canopy, where stood the chair brought from Westminster abbey which contained the Stone of Destiny, the ancient coronation seat of the kings of Scotland. The Protector was robed by the Speaker in ermine and purple velvet, and girt with the sword of state, while on the table before him lay a nobly bound Bible. The Speaker administered the oath, and one Mr. Manton prayed; the people huzzaed, the trumpets sounded, and Oliver took his seat, a massive gold sceptre in his right hand, with beside him the ambassadors of France and the United Provinces, and around him the lords of the Council with drawn swords.[3] The greatest of English monarchs had that one hour of royal ceremonial.

The new régime at once got to work. Lambert was dismissed, to the general satisfaction of the lieges, including most of the army, but otherwise the Council remained the same, the only new members being Thurloe and Richard Cromwell. Then came the task of choosing the second chamber. It was a thorny business, for its members must be men of property and influence, they must represent all three countries, and they must be loyal to the Protector and his cause. The chamber must be strong, but not so strong as to overweight the elected House. Oliver had to face all the difficulties which had confronted later consti-

---

[1] Thurloe, VI, 330.   [2] *Lans MSS.*, 822.   [3] Whitelocke, 661.

tution-makers in the creation of a second chamber, and the task
occupied him till almost the end of the year, for he recognized
the importance of his selection. 'A mistake here,' said Thurloe,
'will be like that of war and marriage; it admits of no repentance.' In the end he produced a list of sixty-three persons —
seven peers of England, one of Scotland, and one of Ireland; his
two sons, three sons-in-law, and two brothers-in-law; the rest
colonels of regiments, country squires, some judges, and a number of high officials. There was no intention of creating a
hereditary peerage, for the appointment was only for life.[1] Of
the English peers summoned none but Fauconberg and Eure
obeyed the writ; even Warwick and Wharton refused, apparently on the ground that acceptance would mean the surrender
of the inherited rights of their order. Nevertheless the new
House of Lords was to the popular mind a dignified and representative body, and it showed as high an average of talent as
any second chamber known to history. But it was small, only
forty-two.

That winter there were many conspiracies, for the revised
Protectorate made the royalists desperate. The Levellers were
busy with their bungled plots, though the better sort of republicans scrupled to do murder. Sexby was caught and committed to the Tower, where he presently died, after confessing
everything. Men with pistols were apprehended in Whitehall,
and Thurloe was advised to let the Protector read no foreign
letter lest it might be poisoned.[2] It was bitter cold weather; in
England the crows were frozen in the fields; at Bruges Charles
and Hyde had scarcely means to pay for food and firing. Rumour had it that Oliver, since he refused the crown, went in terror
of his life, trembled at the sight of a stranger, and drove about
with doubled guards.[3] But rumour lied, for Oliver's iron nerves
were never affected by any concern for his personal safety. He
dismissed the assassination threats as 'little fiddling things.'
At home and abroad his mind was filled with urgent problems,
and such absorption is the best prophylactic against fear.

On January 20, 1658, parliament met again after its six
months' vacation — in substance a new parliament, for the

---

[1] A proof is that Oliver created Charles Howard Viscount Howard of Morpeth some
months before he summoned him. See Firth, *H. of L.*, 249. He also made Edmund
Dunch Baron Burnell, and offered Whitelocke a viscounty, which was declined.

[2] *Clarendon S. P.*, III, 385; Thurloe, VI, 713.

[3] Heath, *Chronicle*, 80, 731; Clarendon, *Hist.*, VI, 88.

places had not been filled of those members who had been called to the Lords, and the ninety members excluded from the former session were now admitted. Oliver opened the proceedings in a speech in the upper House, in which for the first time he addressed his hearers as 'My lords and gentlemen.' Leaving to Nathaniel Fiennes, who followed him, the task of defending the recent changes, he summoned his parliament to confidence and hope. They had been passing through the furnace, and had emerged purified. They had won peace and liberty for true religion; let them build on this firm foundation. He was ill and could only speak briefly, so he concluded with a passionate exhortation: 'If God shall bless you in this work, and make this meeting happy on this account, you shall be called the Blessed of the Lord. The generations to come will bless you. You shall be the 'repairer of breaches and the restorers of paths to dwell in.' And if there be any higher work that mortals can attain to in the world beyond this, I acknowledge my ignorance of it.' [1]

His hopes were speedily dashed. On the benches sat the old guard of the republicans, veterans of the Long Parliament, men like Arthur Haselrig and Thomas Scot, John Weaver, and Luke Robinson. They were the skilled parliamentary hands, who well understood the technique of obstruction. No practical needs could bend their stubborn pedantry; they could not see that to upset the new régime meant the restoration of the old, with the Tower and the gallows waiting for themselves. On January 22 they opened the fight with an attack upon the new House of Lords. The group was a mutual-admiration society working closely together, and, since the best parliamentarians among Oliver's friends had gone to the upper chamber, they easily dominated the debate. They would not hear the name of 'Lords,' since it meant a restoration of an old infamy; at the best it was 'the other House.' They would have no second chamber which was a clog upon the Commons, and therefore upon the people of England. With the snobbery of their type they attacked its composition, on the ground that it did not represent the landed interest as the old peers had done. 'They have not the reason or the quality of lords,' said Scot; 'they have not interest, not the forty-thousandth part of England'; to which Boteler replied that they had better qualifications, 'religion, piety and faithfulness to the commonwealth.' [2] Another added, too truly, that they had the power which lay in the

[1] *L. and S.*, III, 157–58.   [2] Burton, II, 320, 409.

command of many regiments. A year later a third member was to offer a more picturesque defence: 'The Lord Protector did not think fit to make every lump of gilded earth a lord.'

On January 25 Oliver, seeing a breach between the two Houses imminent, summoned them to his presence and spoke to them gravely.[1] He pointed to the uneasy posture of affairs abroad. He warned them that the royalists were projecting an invasion and had honeycombed the land with their plots. England stood alone, and could only save herself by unity, boldness, and a constant vigilance. 'You have accounted yourselves happy in being environed with a great ditch from all the world beside. Truly you will not be able to keep your ditch, nor your shipping, unless you turn your ships and shipping into troops of horse and companies of foot, and fight to defend yourselves on *terra firma*.' Domestic concord was a prime need. In vivid phrases he pointed out the various elements of disunion, the wretched bickering about circumstantials. That way lay ruin, final and irrevocable. 'If you run into another flood of blood and war, the sinews of this nation being wasted by the last, it must sink and perish utterly.... It will be said of this poor nation, *Actum est de Anglia*.'

These weighty words had no effect on his opponents. For the next ten days the debate on the second chamber continued with the same strenuous futility. Meantime the opposition leaders entered upon more dangerous roads. They organized the Fifth Monarchy men and the sectaries in the city, and prepared a petition demanding the restoration of something like the Long Parliament, a single chamber with absolute authority, unlimited by any Protector's veto. A curtailment, too, was demanded of parliament's power over the army, as a bid for the support of the army malcontents, and it was proposed to make Fairfax commander-in-chief. When Thurloe, who held every thread of the plot, told Oliver of it, the latter realized at once how grave was the menace. This was to undo all that had been done, and to plunge the land into the wildest anarchy. He issued warrants for the arrest of certain anabaptist leaders, who had been tampering with the soldiery, and changed the guards at certain points so as to prevent collusion. At ten o'clock on the morning of February 4, telling no man of his intention, not even Thurloe, he set out for Westminster, leaving Whitehall by a back door and intending to take a boat. The ice on the river

[1] *L. and S.* III., 162, etc.

prevented this, so he picked up a common hackney-coach. He reached the House about eleven, and refreshed himself with toast and ale. Then he summoned the judges from Westminster hall and the Commons from St. Stephen's to the Lords' chamber.[1] Fleetwood met him and would have dissuaded him. 'By the living God,' said Oliver, 'I will dissolve the House.'

In his speeches he was apt to pour forth all that had been in his mind for many days, garnished with scriptural memories, so that the rivulet of argument trickled thinly through a jungle of superfluities. But now his thoughts came with the force of a pent-up torrent. He had had 'very comfortable expectations' of this parliament. He was Protector not of his own will but at the call of the Humble Petition. 'There is ne'er a man within these walls that can say, sir, you sought it, nay, never a man nor woman treading upon English ground.... I cannot but say it in the presence of God, in comparison of which all we that are here are like poor creeping ants upon the earth, that I would have been glad as to my own conscience and spirit to have been living under a wood side, to have kept a flock of sheep, rather than to have undertaken such a place as this... but upon such terms as I did — that I undertook it for the safety of the nation.' He had made conditions which they had granted, and one was a second chamber to 'prevent a popular and tumultuary spirit.' He had chosen that chamber honestly, as he was empowered to do, and yet they were not satisfied. Another condition had been that there should be 'a just reciprocation between the government and the governed,' that parliament should play its willing part in the settlement, as he had played his. Instead they had tried to overturn it by faction within the House and intrigue outside it. What was this but 'the playing of the King of Scots his game?' If this was their mood and this the purpose of their session, the sooner it ended the better. 'I declare to you here that I do dissolve this Parliament. Let God judge between you and me.'[2]

Once again, and for the last time, the man who would fain have built was compelled to destroy. Of all his dissolutions this one was the most abundantly justified. He was faced with mutiny and treason which no patient tolerance could have rid

---

[1] Thurloe, VI, 281, etc.; Ludlow, II, 33; Burton, II, 462; *E. H. R.* (1890), 106.

[2] *L. and S.*, III, 187–92. There is a better version from the *Pell MSS.* printed *ibid.*, 503–08. Descriptions of the scene are in Thurloe, VI, 778, etc.; *Lans MSS.*, 754; and *E. H. R.* (1892), 102.

him of, and with his infallible instinct for action he struck at the
right moment. When he summoned God to judge between him
and his opponents the republicans cried 'Amen.' They were
confident in their faith, but between them and Oliver history
has no difficulty in deciding. Whatever England needed and
desired it was not the sterile formulas of Scot and Haselrig, a
creed without pride of ancestry or hope of posterity.

These last weeks had made the Protector very weary. He
had kept his chamber and had seen few people. His steward
reported that his anxieties 'drank up his spirits, of which his
natural constitution yielded a vast stock.' He was sickening for
the illness which overtook him before the end of the month,
when he had to take to his bed with a dangerous abscess in his
back. But the call to action was for the moment a tonic to
body and mind. In a few weeks he had scattered the plotters,
royalist, Leveller, anabaptist, and army mutineer, and brought
himself to the zenith of his power. But it was a power dependent upon his own spirit, and the last hope had gone of a constitution which should be its lasting repository.

Chapter III

THE CONSTABLE ABROAD
(1654–1658)

> God's interest in the world is more extensive than all the people of these three nations. God has brought us hither to consider the work we may do in the world as well as at home.
> OLIVER CROMWELL.

> The greatest honour that ever belonged to the greatest monarchs was the inlarging their dominions, and erecting Commonweals.
> CAPTAIN JOHN SMITH.

I

AMONG the manuscripts at Hinchingbrooke there is a note [1] in the writing of Edward Montague, the first Lord Sandwich, of a discussion in the Council of State in the summer of 1654, when peace with the Dutch had left '160 sail of brave ships well appointed swimming at sea, and store of land forces.' Oliver is revealed as eager for war with Spain, and the reasons he gives are a clue to his whole foreign policy. The ships should be used, he said, and not laid up, because 'God has not brought us hither where we are but to consider the work we may do in the world as well as at home.' The first duty was to advance the protestant cause, and of that Spain was the arch-enemy. Lambert demurred; they had sufficient to do at home; far-off adventures would be but a slender aid to protestantism, and they would be very costly. Not so, was the reply, for it would cost little more to employ the ships than to lay them up. Indeed it would be a profitable business, for there were Spain's rich possessions in the New World very open to attack, and there were her plate-fleets upon the sea. Lambert was unconvinced; war, he argued, could not be waged on the principle of limited liability; the conquest alone of the West Indies would be of little use, for settlers would not go there unless the conquest was fully maintained, and that would mean a prodigious outlay. Besides there would be the loss of the lucrative Spanish trade. To this Oliver made an answer based on Elizabethan practice — that war with Spain in the Indies need not involve a breach with her in Europe. Lambert stuck to his guns; the cost would be enor-

[1] It has been printed in *C. P.*, III. App. B.

mous, and the exchequer balances were lean. The reply was in the manner of Drake and Raleigh. 'The design will quit cost. Six nimble frigates shall range up and down the bay of Mexico to get prey.' Lambert repeated the mercantile objection; the Dutch would absorb the Spanish trade which England lost, and 'increasing in their riches may be invited to a revenge.' '*Deus providebit*,' said Oliver.

This instructive debate reveals the Protector at the meeting-place of two worlds with a foot in each. He is a crusader of the Middle Ages, who would plant the flag of his religion by force of arms throughout the globe, and he is also the economic national-ist with a quick eye to the material fortunes of his people. In his first aspect he is more than an Elizabethan, for the Eliza-bethans fought the battle of protestantism when it was in deadly peril. That danger had almost gone; the tides of the Counter-Reformation had ebbed; there would be no reconquest of the world by catholicism — indeed, when the English guns sounded in the Mediterranean, it was the Pope who had most cause for fear. To Oliver his faith was to be a conquering thing, like the creed of Islam. He sought to form an alliance of pro-testant states which would be far more than a mere league of defence, and in his proposal to the Dutch in 1653 he had a scheme for sending protestant missionaries abroad among all nations. On this side he is more mediæval than Elizabethan, and has in him more of Peter the Hermit than of Gustavus.

Of the reality of his belated crusading fervour no one can doubt, and it was the profoundest of his motives. But there were others of a very different kind. Through his diplomacy he intended to prevent any Stuart restoration by foreign help. More important, he desired to expand the commerce of Eng-land, and no arguments were more carefully weighed by him than those which dealt with mercantile prospects. He was re-solved that his policy should show a good balance-sheet. On this material side there was a stiff determination that England, which too long had been a cypher in world affairs, should play a masterful part again. Like Richelieu he would be the leader of an international brotherhood, and the ambassadors of the nations should wait humbly in his ante-room. This desire was not based on any petty *folie des grandeurs*, but on a passionate belief in the quality of his race and the greatness of its destiny. At the back of it, too, was his sense of an immense broadening world in which England must have her share. London was full of merchants who traded to the ends of the earth, he had himself in earlier days dabbled in overseas ventures, and he was daily meeting sea-captains with their tales of opportunities waiting for bold men. He was as ready as his secretary, who with dimming eyes wrote the Council's Latin dispatches, to kindle to the magic of strange names like

> Cambalu, seat of Cathaian Can,
> And Samarchand of Oxus,

or of strange merchandise like that listed by the East India Company in 1650, 'dragons' blood, elephant's teeth, tamarind, frankincense, taffeties of Persia.'

These various impulses all played their part in determining Oliver's foreign policy, but, when it came to action, the decisive motive was the practical needs of the case. If he had to choose between two forms of papistry, he would lean to that which was the more useful ally. This opportunism was revealed in the ingenuity with which he distinguished between the catholicisms of France and Spain, and his disregard of the religious question altogether in his treaty with Portugal. It was revealed still more notably in his attitude towards the readmission of the Jews to England. He was in favour of the step because of his views on toleration in general, but its strongest supporters were the millenarians with whom he had no sympathy. At the discussion in the Council in 1655 he could use the language of the latter — 'Since there was a promise of their conversion, means must be used to that end, which was the preaching of the Gospel, and that could not be done unless they were permitted to dwell where the Gospel was preached.' But it is clear that his main motive, as the Dutch emissaries saw, was commercial. The admission of the Jews was part of the policy of the Navigation Act. They controlled the Spanish, Portuguese, and much of the Levant trade; they were deeply interested in the maritime adventures of the East and West Indies; they commanded the flow of bullion; they could help him in the difficult finances of his government and in the making of his new colonial empire. Therefore he would encourage them to transfer their counting-houses from Amsterdam to London, but — lest the city should be scared — he would let the main motive be obscured by high speech about religious freedom and the fulfilment of the prophecies.[1]

[1] For this interesting subject see Wolf, *Manasseh Ben Israel's Mission*, Introduction, and the papers in *Trans. Jew. Hist. Soc.*, Vols. I. and II. There were Jews who believed that Oliver was the Messiah and who had his pedigree investigated in the hope of discovering his descent from David. Tovey, *Anglia Judaica* (1738), 275.

II

The foreign policy of Oliver falls naturally under two heads. There was the problem at England's door, her relations with the Dutch and with the northern states that commanded the Baltic. In the second place there were her relations with the two major Powers of Europe, France and Spain, which involved the questions of the Mediterranean and the New World.

The Dutch war had been none of his making, and when he became Protector he forced a peace in spite of the London merchants. The peace gave him two of his cherished objects; the Navigation Act was accepted by its principal critics and English commercial rights were secured by treaty, while royalist exiles could no longer find asylum or help on Dutch soil. At first he seems to have honestly believed in an enduring friendship between the two maritime Powers. The world, he told the Dutch envoys, was wide enough for both; and, when after the signing of the treaty he entertained them at Whitehall, he made them join with him in singing the 133rd Psalm, 'Behold how good and pleasant it is for brethren to dwell together in unity.' But soon it appeared that there was no goodwill attending this formal peace. The sleepless commercial jealousy between the two states kept them watching each other like angry dogs. The Dutch were the main obstacle to his scheme of a protestant alliance, and they laboured, with a side glance at England, to stir up strife between the Baltic Powers. Above all they goaded on the quarrel between Denmark and Sweden. 'This war is of great consequence,' wrote Henry Cromwell in 1657, 'especially because it's fomented by the Dutch, who favour the Danes, hoping by this means to get the trade and commerce of the East Sea.'[1] In every stage of his diplomacy Oliver found the Dutch obstructive and suspicious — with good reason indeed, for the forward policy of England threatened the foundations of their prosperity.

With Denmark, as we have seen, he made a treaty in 1654, which gave English merchant vessels the right to pass the Sound into the Baltic. Thereafter the only difficulties with Denmark sprang from her secular quarrel with Sweden. The latter was the nation which was then chiefly endeared to England because of the great Gustavus, and the treaty which Whitelocke negotiated in 1654 was attended on both sides with

[1] Thurloe, VI. 425.

warm popular goodwill. In Sweden Oliver believed that he had found the true basis of his protestant league. But dynastic changes moved Swedish interests into a different orbit. Queen Christina abdicated in the year of the treaty, and her cousin Charles X succeeded to an empty treasury and a fine army. In 1655 he used the latter in a campaign against Poland, and in two months he had occupied Warsaw and Cracow. But it was easier to conquer Poland than to hold it, and presently Charles's difficulties made him seek the support of England in men and money. Oliver, seeing in him a re-birth of Gustavus, was at first eager to help, dreaming of a grand assault not only against catholic Poland but against catholic Austria. But his Council advised caution, and he was reluctantly compelled to stand back. England's interests must come before any dream of a protestant crusade, and it was not her interest that the Baltic should become a Swedish lake. Moreover Charles's successes would combine against him the Elector of Brandenburg, the Danes and the Dutch, so a protestant alliance would be hopeless from the start. A commercial treaty in 1656 was the only fruit of the negotiations. Plain people in England saw another reason for discretion. Though the Poles were a popish nation, were they not a bulwark against something worse? 'They were a good bar for that side,' Mr. Robert Baillie wrote, 'against the Turks' and Tartars' encroachments, and if they be ruined a great gap will be opened for these Scythian barbarians to fall on us all.' [1] For once a Scottish Covenanter took the long view.

In 1657 a powerful coalition was forming against Charles of Sweden. He had been forced out of Poland, and a hostile Dutch squadron was in the Baltic. Again he turned to England, but Oliver made the cession of Bremen a condition of his assistance. England would demand some security for money lent, and if she was to send troops to the Continent she must have a military base from which to operate. Charles refused, and before the end of the year was in desperate straits. Holland, Brandenburg and Denmark were in arms against him, and behind them was the great house of Hapsburg. Oliver took alarm, for this seemed to him the Counter-Reformation panoplied and marching, a return of the black days of the Thirty Years War. He did his best by diplomacy to mediate between the Danes and the Dutch, but he came round to the view that at

[1] *Baillie*, III. 293.

all costs he must prevent Charles from being crushed, and must intervene, if necessary, with both fleet and army. To his parliament in January 1658 he expounded the peril. Spain and Austria and the Pope, aided by deluded protestant states, were warring against the cause of true religion.[1] 'Who is there that holdeth up his head to oppose this great design? A poor Prince; — indeed poor, but a man in his person as gallant, and truly I think I may say, as good, as any these later ages have brought forth.... He is now reduced into a corner.' After his fashion he added a practical appeal: 'It is a danger against your very being.... If they can shut us out of the Baltic Sea and make themselves masters of that, where is your trade? Where are your materials to preserve your shipping? Or where will you be able to challenge any right by sea, or justify yourselves against a foreign invasion in your own soil? Think upon it. This is in design. I do believe, if you will go to ask the poor mariner in his red cap and coat as he passeth from ship to ship, you will hardly find in any ship but they will tell you this is designed against you.'

England was not called upon to land troops on the Baltic littoral. Within a fortnight of Oliver's speech Charles had moved twenty thousand men over the frozen Belt and brought Denmark to her knees. The grandson of Gustavus and the grandfather of Charles XII had wrought his own salvation. It was the English ambassador, Meadows, who negotiated the treaty of Roeskilde, and Sweden showed her gratitude by resolving in April to send help to Oliver if he were troubled either by his parliament or by the house of Stuart. But the protestant league was no further forward, and the disputes about the election of an Emperor that summer and Mazarin's new league of the Rhine dissipated its last hope. Each protestant Power preferred 'gain to godliness,' for a new world had dawned in which religion took second place to nationalist ambitions and nationalist economics. As Oliver lay dying the Baltic states were once again at each other's throats.

III

The year 1654, which saw pacts made with the northern states, passed without any settlement with France and Spain. Clearly England could not be at war at the same moment with

[1] *L. and S.*, II. 167, etc.

the two greatest of European Powers, but it took Oliver long to make up his mind which should have the honour of his friendship. With both there had been for years a steady private war at sea. Against both he had grievances — against France for her treatment of the Huguenots, and against Spain for the intolerant catholicism which embarrassed English traders in every part of her empire. From war with Spain England had much to gain, for her unwieldy possessions overseas invited dismemberment. As an ally she could be of little use and she could not pay the subsidies she promised. France, on the other hand, in spite of her domestic troubles, was growing in power, and she was ruled by a minister who had an eye to realities. Mazarin had courted Oliver ever since Worcester. He took from him plain speaking which would have wrecked most negotiations, and for four years the two men stood to each other in an attitude of confidence, almost of friendship. It is probable that the French cardinal understood what was understandable in the Protector as well as any man in Europe.

Oliver at first would have preferred to ally himself with neither, though his sympathies leaned strongly towards France. But his Hispaniola expedition and Blake's doings in the Mediterranean made a choice imperative. On October 24, 1655, the treaty of Westminster was signed with France, and a few days later war was decided upon with Spain. In form the French treaty was only a commercial agreement, but a secret clause provided for the expulsion of English royalists from France, and there was a private promise from Mazarin to protect the Huguenots in their rights under the Edict of Nantes. Meanwhile in that year an event had befallen which had set Oliver on a pinnacle in the eyes of his countrymen, and which had brought Mazarin into closer relations with him and into better odour with England. The Waldenses or Vaudois, whose protestantism dated from the Middle Ages, had been extending from the Alpine valleys west of Turin into the lower plains. In January the Duchess of Savoy ordered that they should be forced back to the bare mountain glens, and in April Savoyard troops executed the order with every circumstance of barbarity. Many were slain, many were driven to the high snows, and many were compelled to renounce their ancestral faith. The news of these atrocities stirred England to her depths. Milton turned from his secretarial tasks to indite a sonnet like a trumpet-call. Oliver appointed a day of humiliation, and opened a collection for the sufferers, contributing himself £2000. He sent a special envoy to Turin, summoned the pro- testant Powers of Europe to intervene, threatened to hire the Swiss for a campaign against Savoy, and told Mazarin roundly that there would be no treaty between England and France unless the latter used his influence to have the wrong righted. Mazarin obeyed, Paris put pressure upon Turin, the massacres ceased, and the Vaudois were reinstated, though no vengeance was taken upon the malefactors. The incident brought Oliver and England to the forefront of the European stage.

To Europe, too, the doings of England at sea seemed so swift and triumphant that her disasters in the west were soon for- gotten. Spain, now nearing the end of the first century of her slow decline, found an enemy that chased her from the element where she had been so long the mistress. Blake, who had much of Oliver's crusading fervour, had already carried the English flag into the Mediterranean and made himself the constable of that sea. He had frightened alike the Grand Duke of Tuscany and the Pope; he had taken order with the Moslem sovereigns of north Africa, redeeming the English captives at Algiers and making a treaty with the Dey, and bringing the Dey of Tunis to reason by bombarding his forts and burning his ships. The war with Spain, when it opened that autumn, was not a Med- iterranean but a high seas campaign. Blake's business was to intercept the plate-fleets, and watch the Spanish harbours so that no reinforcements could be sent to the West Indies. Dur- ing these months of blockade Oliver came to realize the impor- tance of Gibraltar and suggested to Blake its seizure. 'If pos- sessed and made tenable by us, would it not be both an ad- vantage to our trade and an annoyance to the Spaniard; and enable us, without keeping so great a fleet on that coast, with six nimble frigates lodged there to do the Spaniard more harm than by a fleet, and ease our own charge?' [1] Seldom can the man on the spot have received more sagacious counsel from the man at home, and small wonder that the Council of State were compelled to buy a new atlas, and keep a globe always at hand in their chamber.

Blake could not take Gibraltar without a land force and that was not forthcoming, so the long waiting continued. The re- ward came in September 1656, when Captain Stayner, with a cruiser squadron from Blake's command, fell in with the plate-

[1] *L. and S.*, II. 489.

fleet off Cadiz, destroyed four ships with a treasure of two millions, and captured one laden with silver worth £600,000. Next spring Blake himself fought his Trafalgar. He had kept his place on the Spanish coasts during the winter, a thing unprecedented in naval warfare.

> Others may use the ocean as their road,
> Only the English make it their abode,
> Whose ready sails with every wind can fly,
> And make a covenant with th' inconstant sky;
> Our oaks secure as if they there took root,
> We tread on billows with a steady foot.[1]

On April 20, 1657, came his opportunity. He found the Spanish plate-fleet in the bay of Santa Cruz in Teneriffe; sailed into the harbour, fought and silenced the batteries, and sank or burnt all of the sixteen ships. 'It was the hardest action that ever was,' reported one of his captains, but no English ship was lost. 'Truly your great enemy is the Spaniard,' Oliver had told parliament. 'He is naturally so, by reason of that enmity that is in him against whatsoever is of God.' [2] England had dealt that enemy a blow from which he never recovered either as a continental or a maritime Power. Blake, who for a year had been a sick man living on broths and jellies, died on August 7th, as his ship entered Plymouth Sound. Patient, hardy, masterful, merciful and chivalrous, there is no nobler figure in the sea story of England. The best epitaph was that spoken by one of his captains: 'As he had lived so he continued to the end, faithful.' [3]

During 1656 Philip IV of Spain had made terms with Charles II, had promised him a pension and funds for an invasion, and was subsidizing the plots in England against the Protector's life. By the spring of 1657 it had become clear to Oliver that Spain must be fought on land as well as at sea. The events in the Low Countries in 1656 had convinced Mazarin that he needed the help of England. Oliver's price was Dunkirk. Spain had offered him Calais, and two years before Mazarin had talked to him of Dunkirk; he desired it not only as a bridgehead on the Continent, but to enable him the better to control the Channel and to destroy the nest of pirates in that port. 'A bridle to the Dutch,' wrote Thurloe, 'and a door into the continent.' On March 23, 1657, the treaty of Paris was signed which brought England into the centre of European politics.

[1] Waller, 'Of a War with Spain and a Fight at Sea.'
[2] *L. and S.*, ll. 511.   [3] *Cal. S. P. Dom*, 1657–58, 57.

She was to receive Mardyck and Dunkirk, and in return to supply a fleet and 6000 men.

Turenne commanded the army of France, and he pronounced the English contingent, when it arrived under Sir John Reynolds, to be the finest troops in the world. At first the French employed Reynolds on minor sieges in the interior, till Oliver ordered Sir William Lockhart, his ambassador, to use plain words. These had their effect, and in October Mardyck was taken and handed over to an English garrison. Then came the winter hiatus, and it was not till the beginning of May 1658 that the combined forces took the field, and the siege of Dunkirk began. On the 14th of June the two armies met on the sand-hills adjoining the town. The Battle of the Dunes was one of the most spectacular actions in history. It was witnessed by Mazarin and the young Louis XIV, then twenty years of age. The Spaniards were commanded by Don John of Austria, and had with them Condé and the Duke of York. The latter had five regiments under him, three of Irish loyalists, one of Scots, and one Charles's own regiment of guards. Under Turenne were Oliver's six red-coat regiments, who were given precedence over all the French units, except the Scots brigades. To these fell the *beau rôle*. Reynolds being dead, Lockhart was in command — one of the few warrior-ambassadors in modern times — and under him the English pikes stormed through the musketry salvos and swept the enemy from the key position on the sandhills. That charge decided the day, and ally and foe paid tribute to its desperate gallantry. It was the supreme moment of the New Model — and the last.[1]

Oliver's foreign policy had one immediate result; it raised the prestige of England to a dazzling height. He had made the name of Englishman as formidable as had once been the name of Roman. The panegyrics of Waller and Dryden and Marvell were not poetic extravagances but sober statements of fact. It was he who in the words of the last-named

> Once more joined us to the continent,
> Who planted England on the Flanderic shore,
> And stretched our frontier to the Indian ore.

We have Clarendon's tribute: 'His greatness at home was but a shadow of the glory he had abroad. It was hard to discover

---

[1] The bulk of the English contingent were volunteers, but most of them must have been old soldiers. A quarter of the force was drafted from the standing army. See 'Royalist and Cromwellian Armies in Flanders.' *Trans. of R. H. S.*, 1902–03.

which feared him the most, France, Spain or the low Countries, where his friendship was current at the value he put upon it. And as they did all sacrifice their honour and their interest to his pleasure, so there is nothing he could have demanded that either of them would have denied him.'[1] When the dark days came and England was a suppliant instead of a master, Pepys could record 'how everybody do nowadays reflect upon Oliver and commend him, what brave things he did, and made all the neighbour princes fear him.'[2]

But the glamour of his triumphs must not blind us to the fact that most of them were transient and unsubstantial. They rested on no secure foundation. He was attempting to put forth the strength of England at the same time by land and sea, a task to which, a hundred years later, France with her far greater resources proved unequal. His pressing need was a settlement at home, but with such a settlement foreign adventures were inconsistent, for they involved the maintenance at full strength of that army which formed his most difficult constitutional problem. They meant, too, a crushing burden of taxation, which daily increased the unpopularity of his government. Before his death it was plain that the burden was becoming too heavy for the land to bear, and the efficiency of the fleet and the condition of the seamen were deteriorating through sheer lack of money.[3] Had Oliver lived longer he could not have surmounted these difficulties, for they were insuperable; indeed he died at a fortunate moment for this aspect of his fame.

He was no conqueror in the vulgar sense of being inspired by a lust for conquest. But the purpose behind his work, though honourable, was impracticable. His vision of a protestant ascendency in Europe was a dream born out of due season. Protestantism, as we have seen, was no longer in serious danger, since the era of religious wars had gone for ever. Such a criticism, it may be argued, is wisdom after the event, for Oliver could not know that; on the other hand he ought to have realized that protestant ascendency meant English ascendency, and that such a maladjustment of power would lead sooner or later to a league against England, the kind of league that was afterwards formed against Louis XIV. Had he lived, and had he been able to adjust his finances, he might indeed have re-

[1] *Hist.*, XV. 152.   [2] *Diary*, July 12, 1667.
[3] See Oppenheim, *Administration of the Royal Navy...from* 1509 *to* 1660.

strained the French king from his more dangerous blunders, but in time the spirit of Europe would have revolted against the dictation of the two Powers, as much as against the dictation of one of them. The acquisition of Dunkirk was a step away from the true interests of England. Nor did the other side of his policy, the practical, commercial side, prove in fact good business. He lost the support of all monied men by the weight of his taxes, and he forfeited the confidence of the new commercial class, already one of the strongest things in the land, by the particular orientation of his aims. To them the real enemy was Holland. The war with Spain lost them a valuable form of trade which passed into the hands of neutrals. Spanish frigates made every venture uncertain on the western seas. Isolated captures of plate-ships and the acquisition of remote islands were no compensation, since the mechanism of business had now become far more complex than in Elizabeth's day. At a time when English finance needed peace and leisure to adjust itself to new conditions he provided a fresh irritant.

Much of Oliver's foreign policy perished with him, but his work was not all fruitless. Apart from raising the pride and quickening the spirit of his country, he left it certain indubitable assets and certain enduring principles. The navy, fostered under difficulties by Charles I, was made by him the first in the world. The long spells of continuous employment made it a true profession, with its own institutions and traditions, for the fleet was for the first time in our history a fleet of war-ships, wholly independent of merchant auxiliaries. More, he not only provided the instrument, but he adumbrated the true lines on which it should be used; for he summoned England to the Mediterranean and to a vision of empire.

Of the Mediterranean and England's vital interest therein he was in fact the discoverer. The purpose of Blake's first expedition there in 1654 was to frustrate a French plan, the proposed expedition of the Duke of Guise for the conquest of Naples; its secondary aims were to show the British flag in the Mediterranean ports and to protect the Levant trade against corsairs. Incidentally new methods of naval warfare were discovered, for the attack on the Dey of Tunis was the first case of shore batteries being silenced from the sea without any landing of troops. More important, the expedition opened up new principles of naval strategy. Merchantmen being relegated to their proper place as occasional auxiliaries, their protection became the chief duty of the navy; the main lines of trade became also the main lines of naval policy, and their intersection the strategical key-points. Hence the extreme importance of Gibraltar. Oliver learned much from the big globe in the Council chamber. The occupation of Dunkirk was an aberration; Gibraltar was his true inspiration. He saw English commerce as a world-wide thing, ramifying to east and west, but with a bottle-neck between its two working-grounds. Its great rivals, France and Spain, had the same defile of the Straits between their two spheres of activity, and whoever held Gibraltar and that defile must dominate the Mediterranean and have the initiative in any naval war. Blake laid bare the secret, but Oliver saw its full significance, and, though he went astray into continental side-shows, he left the doctrine as a legacy to his successors. To it Britain owed her final dominion of the sea. 'The visionary aim of the zealot died with him, and the master current he had found resumed its flow. In this way, at least, if in no other, his imprint remained and still remains sharp and undefaced upon British polity.'[1]

There was one other sphere in which his work did not perish with him — the new world in the west, and his dream of empire.

IV

We have seen that from his youth Oliver had been interested in colonization schemes beyond the Atlantic. Among the puritans there was always a double line of policy; to form free communities dedicated to a pure religion, and in the rich lands claimed by Spain to extend by settlement, and if necessary by conquest, the commerce and the greatness of England. The second line was that of his chief friends, Pym, Warwick, Saye, Brooke and St. John, who in 1630 founded the Providence Company. The English pirates at Tortuga, in New England, and elsewhere — one of them was a Captain Cromwell — acted as the illicit advance-guard of this enterprise. For three years, between 1642 and 1645, a certain Captain William Jackson conducted a bold expedition of picory among the Spanish possessions. Starting from Barbadoes, he attacked Margarita, ravaged the coasts of the Main, and took, and for a short time held, Jamaica.[2] The exploit roused the interest of England, and,

[1] Julian Corbett, *England in the Mediterranean*, II. 2.
[2] The narrative of his doings has been edited by Mr. T. V. Harlow, *Camden Miscellany*, XIII.

since Jackson became an officer in the Cromwellian navy,[1] he must have been available for consultations with the Protector. Early in 1654 the mind of Oliver was turning resolutely to the West. Thurloe was collecting Dutch books on navigation, and drumming up experts — Captain Shelley who knew the American coast, and Captain Powel who could speak for the Gulf of Mexico.[2] In those days there were odd visitors at Whitehall. One was Monk's cousin, Colonel Thomas Modiford, a member of the Barbadoes council, who submitted a plan for the annexation of Cuba and Trinidad, to be followed by a comprehensive conquest of the Spanish Main.[3] Another was the renegade Dominican, Thomas Gage, now a protestant minister, who had published a book on the West Indies, and who advised an attack upon Hispaniola.[4] New England, too, was pressing for the enterprise, and John Cotton, rapt into prophecy, declared that it would lead to the drying up of the Euphrates foretold in the Book of Revelation.[5]

Oliver's motives were as usual mixed. He disliked the religious bigotry of Spain and revolted against her assumption of exclusive sovereignty in the West; he had in his bones the Elizabethan tradition, not very defensible on any ground of public morals, that the West was still a no-man's-land where England might raid and annex Spanish territory and plunder Spanish ships without fighting Spain in Europe; he had his commercial notions, derived from his old Providence Company days. But above all there was growing up in his mind a vision of a great overseas England, settled by English stock and faithful to English traditions. In his own lifetime he had seen the birth and the growth of a colonial empire both on the American mainland and in the islands — Virginia, New England, Barbadoes, Bermuda, Guiana. He had supported the Navigation Act which inaugurated a trade policy for the mother and daughter countries. He believed that the national spirit had been strongly quickened and must have space for expansion. The substance of Harrington's sentence was always in his mind: 'You cannot plant an oak in a flower-pot; she must have earth for her roots, and heaven for her branches.'

His active policy had two sides — an attack upon the Spanish islands, and a paternal care for the interests of New England. The first began with the Hispaniola expedition in De-

[1] *Cal. S. P. Dom*, 1653-64.   [2] Thurloe, II. 250.   [3] *Ibid.*, III. 62.
[4] *Ibid.*, III. 59-61.   [5] *Amer. Hist. Review* (1899), IV. 2.

cember 1654 — thirty-eight ships commanded by Penn and 2500 troops under Venables, these latter being largely augmented by volunteers from the West Indian islands. There were civil commissioners with the expedition, one of them the New Englander Edward Winslow. Disbrowe, upon whom the duty of equipment fell, was not notably efficient, and in any case it was no small task to arrange for the transport of several thousand men over three thousand miles of sea. The blunder was made of sending new units made up of drafts and recruits instead of formed regiments under their own officers. Things went ill almost from the start. Oliver had embarked on the venture with something of the thoughtlessness of Buckingham; he had underrated the difficulties, forgotten to take account of the climate, and overlooked the dangers of a divided command. Moreover, instead of the kind of army with which he had won at Dunbar and Worcester, he had sent a rabble, for not a thousand of the men were disciplined soldiers. In April Venables landed in Hispaniola and marched through the forests to San Domingo, the capital. Three times he failed, beaten by ambuscades, fatigue, indiscipline and tropic rains. On May 4 what remained of the raw, diseased and ill-victualled army embarked for Jamaica. That island, which contained only a few hundred Spaniards, soon capitulated. If England was to settle new lands it was desirable that there should be no large catholic population to control and absorb, for the Cromwellian troops who pelted the statues of the Virgin with oranges would not have been conciliatory masters.

Oliver was bitterly disappointed with the meagre result, and took it so much to heart that he fell ill. But he was all the more resolved to cling to Jamaica, for it would be his starting ground 'to strive with the Spaniard for the mastery of all those seas.' [1] The thing moved slowly. The soldiers of the garrison made poor colonists, and died like flies from the climate, the first item in England's terrible bill of mortality in the West Indies, which was to extend over nearly two centuries. Oliver tried in vain to get settlers of the right sort from elsewhere; from Scotland and Ireland, which proved too risky, and from New England the inhabitants of which bluntly refused. There was always fighting going on. Buccaneering raids were the order of the day, and many Spanish ships were taken and many towns on the Main sacked and plundered. But none of the Spanish attempts at reconquest from Santiago or Havana came near

[1] *L. and S.*, II. 477.

success. Jamaica remained securely English, and the flag of Spain had to remain at half mast in the Caribbean.

To New England Oliver was at once a protector and a counsellor. He mediated in the local quarrels of the different colonies, and he would suffer no cause of bickering between them and the home government. They were his own people, his advanced post in that wilderness which should some day be a garden. To New England he never dictated, only suggested and invited. The Dutch war made difficulties; Massachusetts would not attack the Dutch possessions in America for conscientious reasons, though they fatally cramped the natural development of the English colonies. Oliver in February 1654 sent three ships to capture the Dutch settlement which was to become New York, but peace came before the thing could be attempted, and the Dutch were not ousted till after the Restoration. But this same little fleet took all the land from Penobscot to the mouth of the St. Lawrence, and it remained English territory till Charles II relinquished it.

Oliver, thinking of the far future, strained every nerve not only to annex new lands but to settle them. Spain claimed her overseas empire under the judgment of Pope Alexander VI; Oliver, like Sir Walter Raleigh, based the English title on effective occupation. He had wanted New Englanders to come to Ireland as far back as 1650, and now he desired them to be the backbone of Jamaica. But his colonizing ideas stretched far further than the mere establishment of hard-working and God-fearing English nuclei in his new possessions. He regarded settlement as a kind of strategy, and would have moved human beings about the globe as freely as he moved troops before Worcester. Late in 1655, for example, we find him discussing with Simon de Caceres, Spinoza's cousin, a plan for colonizing Surinam, those five years a British possession, with Jewish fugitives from Brazil.[1] The Navigation Act was exclusive and protectionist in purpose, but Oliver's colonizing schemes were notable for their liberality. He dreamed of an empire which should be wisely and methodically planned, but which at the same time should have the freedom of a natural growth — an ideal which Britain has not yet reached, but towards which in the last century of her imperial history she had been slowly moving. He borrowed much from his predecessors, but he gave his borrowings his own impress, and what he built has endured, since it was based upon the abiding instincts of his people.

[1] *Trans. Jew. Hist. Soc.*, III. 82–86.

Chapter IV

THE LAST STAGE
(1658)

Pax erit omnibus unica, sed quibus? —
Immaculatis,
Pectore mitibus, ordine stantibus,
ore sacratis.
BERNARD OF MARLAIX.

I

OLIVER's dissolution of his last parliament was a surprise to his friends, and at first a cause of rejoicing to his enemies. The republicans saw in it an act of despair, and the royalists a proof of panic and confusion. But one of Hyde's shrewder agents had his doubts. 'Any other in his condition,' he wrote, 'would be deemed irrecoverable, but as the dice of the gods never throw out, so is there something in the fortune of this villain that often renders ten to one no odds.'[1] In the seven months of life remaining to him Oliver withdrew himself into a profound isolation, sharing his inner thoughts with none,[2] but his hand in action had never been more sure. Opposition crumbled before him. 'All things seemed to succeed at home and abroad to his wish,' Clarendon wrote, 'and his power and greatness to be better established than ever it had been.'[3] The land lay quiet under his will, till men came to take it for a thing that had ever been and must ever be. A proof is the current pamphleteering; the abuse of him is as acrid as ever, but it is not contemptuous; it is shrill and desperate, as if the writers struggled against awe.

His first business was to deal with the unrest in the army. On February 6 he called together the officers in the London district and made them a speech. They shouted that they would live and die with him, and his health was drunk in many bottles. Then he sent for Major Packer and the malcontents in his own regiment of horse, and, after talking to them sternly, cashiered the six ringleaders. The army was cowed, and the

[1] *Clarendon S. P.*, III, 387.

[2] 'His Highness, finding he can have no advice from those he most expected it from, saith he will take his own resolutions.' Thurloe to Henry Cromwell, July 13, 1658.

[3] Clarendon, *Hist.*, XV, 143.

Fifth Monarchy agitators in it found their market gone. Monk and his troops, the most efficient of all since they had been continuously on active service, sent in assurances of fidelity, and the English regiments followed suit. The Irish army was especially cordial. 'We did not,' so ran their address, 'take up war as a trade, esteeming it the worst remedy of the worst evils; wherefore to prevent the same for the future, and to deter such as would again embroil us therein, we do heartily and unanimously declare in the presence of the Lord that we will stand by your Highness, as well against the particular animosities of turbulent spirits as other our professed enemies.'[1] From the city of London he received similar assurances, and the city militia was remodelled. The total of the armed forces had been substantially reduced, for in spite of the contingents serving in Flanders and Jamaica it was 10,000 less than it had been four years before, and the cost was down by nearly £400,000. This meant lowered taxation, and the ordinary man, beginning to see the return of normal conditions, breathed more freely than for many years.

Oliver handled with equal firmness the sudden outburst of civil unrest. The Fifth Monarchy fire-brands were extinguished by gaol, and the more dangerous royalist agitation, far graver than the 1655 affair, was sternly suppressed. A rising had been planned in the home counties, at the back of which was a London episcopal clergyman, Dr. John Hewitt, who had been chaplain to Charles I. Ormonde came over from Holland to keep an eye on it, but made little of the business; his disguise was penetrated, and he was given a hint that he would do well to get back across the Channel. In March Oliver struck, the leaders were arrested, and a special commission was appointed under the Great Seal for their trial. The evidence was overwhelming, and the two chief offenders, Hewitt and Sir Henry Slingsby, a Yorkshire squire, were beheaded in June on Tower Hill, while a number of lesser culprits were hanged. Lord Fauconberg, who had married Mary Cromwell, did his best to save the life of his kinsman Slingsby, Mazarin was appealed to, and some even of the Protector's chief friends thought that, in Ludlow's words, 'he had had very hard measure.' But Oliver was adamant. Slingsby had proposed to betray the vital port of Hull to Charles and Spain, and for such treason there could be no forgiveness.

[1] *Mercurius Politicus*, June 17-24, 1658 (Th.).

By midsummer the government had settled all its difficulties except the eternal one of finance. The Long Parliament had left the exchequer in chaos, and, though under the Protectorate the financial administration had been thrifty and efficient, the deficit had been increased by the wars abroad and the need to keep armies of occupation in Scotland and Ireland. Oliver was no financial genius; he always complained that he knew as little about arithmetic as about law, and unhappily he did not number a Sully or a Colbert among his counsellors. Thurloe's letters are one long wail about poverty, but his mind, so fruitful in other things, seemed to suffer paralysis when confronted by figures. In 1658 there was a deficit of something over £400,000 in the national budget; moreover the pay of the army was badly in arrears, and certain taxes were already approaching the point when any increase must mean a decline in their yield. The remedy of funding the old debt and meeting the war deficits by loans, of doing in short what was done in 1692, did not occur to the statesmen of 1658, when the principles of public credit were ill understood.[1] But somehow or other fresh revenue must be raised, and that meant another parliament.

During the summer England was full of rumours of this new parliament, which, said some, was to be on the old pattern of Lords and Commons 'called and constituted according to the ancient rights of the nation in the late king's time.' There is no doubt about Oliver's general decision, but how the parliament would have been constituted we shall never know. It seems certain that it would have involved a further decline in the army's power. Henry Cromwell would have had its meeting preceded by a purging of the army, 'for that being full of its humours makes the honest party timorous and the others insolent in their respective proposals';[2] and there is reason to think that something of the sort was in Oliver's mind. It was also intended to set the position of royalists on a proper basis. All men believed that the new parliament would insist on Oliver's accepting the crown, and London tradesmen were making plans for a coronation. The army was coming round to this view,[3] and, if we may judge from the letters of Fauconberg and Henry Cromwell, Oliver himself was not averse. Public opinion, even

---

[1] On the question of the Protectorate finances see Firth, *Last Years*, II, ch, XVII. and Dr. Shaw's chapter in *Cambridge Modern History*, IV.

[2] Thurloe, VI, 858.   [3] *Hist. MSS. Com.*, 6th Report, 443.

puritan opinion, in London and the provinces was overwhelmingly for a return to monarchy.

As the summer advanced Oliver's power seemed to move to its meridian. Whatever parliament was called would assuredly give constitutional sanction to that power. The army was tractable and no more a suspicious independent body. Even the stubborn republicans, like Vane and Ludlow, were abating their rigidity and were speaking respectfully of England's ruler. Abroad the fame of the Protector had become a legend. His emissary Fauconberg was received with honours which would have been denied to an envoy of the Emperor. The news that reached English shores was all of glory. In April had come word that the Spanish invasion of Jamaica had been repelled, and the fiasco of Hispaniola was forgotten. There followed in June the great tale of the Battle of the Dunes and the winning of Dunkirk. Then came an embassy from France, which would have contained the young king Louis himself but for his inopportune small-pox, a splendid group of young nobles bearing a jewelled sword of honour to 'the most invincible of Sovereigns.' The dullest English heart could not but thrill at this homage to the greatness of a nation which ten years before had been the most disconsidered in Europe.

'Does not your peace depend upon His Highness's life?'[1] Henry Cromwell's question must have been on the lips of many as they saw Oliver's bowed shoulders and heavily preoccupied face among the life-guards when he drove from Whitehall to Hampton Court. As the sands sink in the glass, let us look more closely at this man whose shadow lay across the world.

II

The basic stuff of Oliver's character was the same as that of the ordinary English countryman, of more delicate texture than most, and interwoven with finer strands, but essentially the same tough workaday fabric. He had none of the leaden arrogance of the superman who seeks a pedestal apart from humanity. Though pinnacled high enough by fate, he was never out of hearing of the common voices of life. Nature had made him all for peace, Marvell said, anticipating Wordsworth's picture of the happy warrior. The leaning of his master-bias was always 'to homefelt pleasures and to gentle scenes.'

[1] Thurloe, VII, 218.

He was greatly dependent upon family affection, giving much and receiving much. He could not bear to be long out of the household circle, and dined and supped with it even in the thick of his heaviest cares. Only one member can be said to have really influenced him, his mother, whom, till she died at a great age, he visited every night before he went to bed. She had done much to form him, but she was a little awed at her handiwork, and her pride in him was tempered by a constant anxiety about his safety. His wife Elizabeth was also a careful mortal, who struggled hard with honours to which she had not been born, and tried to forget the great lady in the prudent housewife. She did her best to live up to his state, but as a ceremonial figure she may have lacked something, for Lucy Hutchinson says that grandeur sat as ill on her as scarlet on an ape. But she acquired unexpected tastes, one of which was a little picture gallery of her own, for we find her asking foreign ambassadors for portraits of their countries' notables.[1]

Six grown-up children made up the Protector's household; two boys had died long ago, and he never forgot them. Richard, the eldest surviving son, had thrown back to the Huntingdon squires — Lucy Hutchinson will have it to the Huntingdon peasants. He was a plain country gentleman, not without brains and breeding, but sluggish except in sport, careless about his affairs, and wholly wanting in ambition. Henry was of another stamp, for his work in Ireland showed that he could handle men, and his letters to Thurloe prove that he had no small share of political wisdom. Oliver's attitude towards his sons was characteristic. He was deeply concerned about their spiritual state, and was always in fear lest indulgence on his part should mar their characters. His letters to them, for all their tenderness, are a little school-masterish in tone. He did not quite realize that they had grown up, even when Henry had given proof of his competence.

A masterful father is often happiest with his daughters, and certainly the Cromwell girls were not unworthy of him. Their portraits show them as comely young women, their faces a little heavy in the lower part, but redeemed by fine brows and compelling eyes. The carriage of their heads has a notable dignity. All talked and wrote the language of Zion, like dutiful children, but cheerfulness often broke into their piety, not wholly to their father's displeasure. Bridget the eldest, wife first of Ireton and

[1] Gardiner, *Comm. and Prot.*, IV, 149.

then of Fleetwood, was likest her mother, an anxious pilgrim whose spirit had often to be fortified. 'Bid her be cheerful,' wrote Oliver, 'and rejoice in the Lord' — but 'poor Biddy' had also her worldly moods and had a taste for splendid petticoats of yellow silk. The second daughter Elizabeth was her father's pride, and also his chief anxiety. Her portrait shows her different from the rest, for her curls, her vivacious eyes, and the tilt of her chin give her a most un-puritan air of *espièglerie*. She feared nothing, not even her father, and she had a naughty wit. She was not very worthily married, for her husband John Claypole was something of the clod spiced with the rake — a 'debauched ungodly cavalier,' Lucy Hutchinson calls him — and this may have caused her to lean upon her father. But she demanded her own way, and generally got it. She befriended in difficulties Harrington, the author of *Oceana*, and often pled with Oliver for royalist prisoners.[1] Her doings were an offence to the strait-laced. She chaffed the solemn Whitelocke; she drove abroad with her sisters in a wonderful costume of green, at which the crowd gaped; and once at a wedding, when someone asked where the wives of the major-generals were, she said wickedly, 'I'll warrant you washing their dishes at home as they use to do.'[2] The younger daughters were both married in November 1657, Mary to Lord Fauconberg, a royalist peer, and Frances to Lord Warwick's grandson, and the wedding festivities caused much scandal, for there was mixed dancing all night in Whitehall to the strains of forty-eight violins.[3] 'Insolent fools,' Lucy Hutchinson calls the Cromwell ladies, but the rest of the world did not find them so, and foreign ambassadors willingly jogged down to Hampton Court to enjoy their society. To Oliver they were a perpetual delight, and in his letters he speaks of them with a lyrical affection. Old men, who remembered the young Elizabeth of Bohemia, saw something of her grace and daring in Elizabeth Claypole.

Having become ruler of England and prince in all but name, Oliver's sturdy good sense made him resolved to keep up a state worthy of his dignity. He succeeded in combining the intimacies of family life with the splendour of a court — 'a court of sin and vanity,' its critic croaks, 'and the more abominable because they had not yet quite cast away the name of God, but pro-

[1] Ludlow, II, 41; *Hist. MSS. Comm.*, 5th Report, 143; but see Thurloe, VII, 171.
[2] *Clarendon S. P.*, III, 327.
[3] *Hist. MSS. Comm.*, 5th Report, App. 177.

THE PALACE OF WHITEHALL
Residence of Cromwell as Lord Protector

faned it by taking it in vain among them.'[1] It was indeed a curious mixture of pageantry and piety, but the blend was impressive, the velvet glove with the hardness of steel behind it, the silken mantle over armour. There were interminable sermons — three hours when John Howe preached — and multitudinous lengthy prayers, and there was always a psalm at the supper parties. There were fast days when a sabbath calm filled the palace. But the ceremonial occasions were managed high and disposedly, for, as his bitterest critics confessed, Oliver 'had much natural greatness and well became the place he had usurped.'[2] He had one hundred thousand pounds to spend annually on his household, and, though he gave away at least a third of this in charity, he used the remainder well. He had his scarlet-coated life-guards, and, apart from lackeys, some fifty gentlemen about his person clad in uniforms of black and grey with silver trimmings. He kept a good table, and his guests could taste the first pineapples ever brought to England. His own diet was plain English fare with no foreign kickshaws, and his drink was a light wine or a very small ale.

His one indoor hobby was music. At Hampton Court he had two organs, and at Whitehall a variety of instruments. Whenever he gave a dinner, whether to foreign ambassadors or parliament men or members of Council, he had music played throughout the evening. He loved the human voice and had a taste for glees and part-songs, in which he took a share. For art he had respect, and he saved the Raphael cartoons for England, but he had little knowledge of it; his inclination seems to have been towards realism, for he bade Lely in painting his portrait reproduce all the roughnesses of his face. There is no evidence that he read much, or indeed anything, beyond the Bible, but he had a kindness for men of letters and protected even those who opposed him, and he was a painstaking chancellor of Oxford.

To the end of his life he remained the countryman, and his happiest hours were spent in the long week-ends at Hampton Court, where he had constructed fish-ponds and inclosed a warren.[3] That was the sole relaxation permitted him, for the times were too critical to go far from London. The only game he played was bowls, but in field sports he had a most catholic taste. Hawking had been the amusement of his earlier days and

[1] Hutchinson, II, 203.   [2] *Ibid.*, II, 202.
[3] *The Picture of a New Courtier*, 1656 (Th.).

he never lost his zest for it. Old, out-at-elbows, cavalier falcon-
ers won his favour, and he did his best to entice away Whitelocke's servant who had good skill in hawks. But hawking demanded a freedom of movement and a leisure which he did not
possess, and as Protector he had few opportunities for it beyond
an occasional day on Hounslow Heath. So also with hunting,
another pastime of his youth. Marvell speaks of

> his delight
> In horses fierce, wild deer, or armour bright.

His love of the dun deer was famous, and Queen Christina of
Sweden collected as a present for him a small herd of reindeer,
which was unfortunately destroyed by wolves before it could be
dispatched to England. As Protector he had to confine his indulgence in the chase to the park at Hampton Court, where
after dinner he would sometimes course a buck, and amaze the
foreign ambassadors by his bold jumping.

Horses were his abiding passion. He suppressed bear-baiting
and cock-fighting because of their cruelty, but his prohibition
of horse-racing was only local and temporary, and due solely to
its political danger as an excuse for royalist meetings. The old
cavalry leader was the best judge of a horse in England. There
is no evidence that he raced himself,[1] but his stud was his delight, and he laboured to improve the breed. We hear of his
well-matched coach-teams — reddish-grey and snow-white —
better, said rumour, than any king of England had ever possessed. The Godolphin Barb and the Darley Arabian had their
predecessors in his stables, and every English agent on the Mediterranean shores held a roving commission from the Protector.
He bought barbs in Tripoli and arabs in Aleppo, for he had had
enough of the heavy Flanders brand and knew that what the
English stock wanted was the fineness of the East. At one crisis
of his life, when a deputation from parliament visited him on
the matter of the crown, he kept it waiting for two hours while
he inspected a barb in the garden.[2] This constant touch with
the natural world was one of his rare founts of refreshment.
It was a link with the old simple country life for which he always hankered, and it kept him in tune with his fellow-men.
A spirit, which otherwise might have lost itself in aerial flights,
had this wholesome tether to English soil.

---

[1] Weylen (*House of Cromwell*, 322) gives no authority for the story that Oliver raced
in Hyde Park and had Dick Pace as his trainer, and it is intrinsically unlikely.

[2] Thurloe, III, 526; *Cal. S. P. Dom*, 1657-58, 96.

Of his manner and bearing we have many accounts, which in substance agree. He had a quick temper and from his boyhood had been liable to bursts of wrath. He was a hero to his steward John Maidston, who wrote candidly of him that his 'temper was exceeding fiery, as I have known, but the flame of it kept down for the most part, or soon allayed, with those moral endowments he had.' Now and then, as we have seen, passion got the upper hand to his own undoing, but of such bouts he always repented. A temper held in curb is a useful possession for a ruler, for it is no bad thing for the world to realize that somewhere there are banked fires. This high spirit well-bitted gave him a fine stateliness on the proper occasions, for all observers are agreed on what Sir Philip Warwick called his 'great and majestic deportment.' But this majesty was not habitual, for pride was no part of his philosophy; rather he held it a sin. He was the most accessible of men, labouring to be conciliatory and to understand another's point of view.

> For he no duty by his height excused,
> Nor, though a prince, to be a man refused.

He had no egotism, and would readily take advice and allow himself to be persuaded. He would even permit opponents to enlarge on his faults and point out his spiritual defects, than which there can be no greater proof of humility.

Yet his brooding power and the sense of slumbering flames would, in spite of his patient courtesy, have repelled most men but for another endowment which impressed all who came into his company. He radiated an infinite kindliness. Here was one who hated harshness and cruelty, and who loved, and would fain be loved by, his fellows. 'He was naturally compassionate towards objects in distress,' says Maidston, 'even to an effeminate measure.' In war he had been notably merciful; in peace he had a heart that felt for all suffering and squandered almost too readily its affection. Marvell is the best witness, Marvell who had a poet's insight, and who had watched him often in the Council chamber and in the privacy of his family. The keynote of Marvell's memorial verses is the 'wondrous softness of his heart.'

> His tenderness extended unto all.
> And that deep soul through every channel flows
> Where kindly Nature loves itself to lose.
> **More strong affections never reason served.**

They did not always serve reason; that was their peculiar charm; they often defied logic and good sense and prudence, being no bridled and calculated things but the overflow of a deep loving-kindness. There is one illuminating phrase of the poet's, when he looks at the dead Protector and laments that those eyes are closed which once shed 'a piercing sweetness.' Here, more than in his moments of Sinaitic awe, lay the secret of Oliver's power over men. The doubter, who had not been persuaded by his wordy and halting arguments, saw suddenly the stern face, roughened by weather and lined by care, transformed into a strange beauty. A great mercy, a wistful tenderness looked out of the eyes. The critic went away a disciple, for he had had a glimpse of something divine.

III

Oliver's mind was like a powerful mill which avidly took in grist but which ground slowly and fitfully. He had no deft logical mechanism always at his command. One talent he possessed in the highest degree, the perceptive, the power of recognizing and appreciating facts. Unlike many religious men of his day he did not rely upon divine admonitions, having a wholesome contempt for those who construed their own private whims as the voice of God. God worked through events, providences, facts, and it was in them that men should read His will. But the puzzle lay in interpreting these concrete celestial messages, for it was not enough to recognize their urgency, since from them a rule of action must be drawn and a philosophy of conduct. He generalized, as we have seen, with extreme difficulty. Texts of Scripture assisted him. Ireton had been a wonderful clarifier of his mind, and now and then he got help from divines like Howe and Sterry and from wise laymen like Whitelocke and Thurloe. But for the most part he did his own theorizing, and his cloudy trophies were hardly won. There was nothing in him of the doctrinaire, for his experience and reflection did not easily shape themselves into dogmas, and never into formulas. But painfully over long tracts of time a policy would distil itself, which was no more than a working rule, for a change of circumstances might compel him to revise it. In these processes there was little formal reasoning, though when it was necessary he could argue acutely. Unconscious instinct played a larger part than ratiocination. He was made in the traditional

mould of Englishmen, and had behind him all the centuries of
England — the dreams of Langland, the ripe wisdom of Chaucer,
the radicalism of Wycliffe, the conservatism of the lawyers, the
peasant's kinship with the earth, the Elizabethan adventurers'
open eyes and insurgent hearts. Much that was hoar-ancient
crept into the substance of his thought.

Few minds have had a more invincible candour. 'A soldier
disciplined to perfection in the knowledge of himself,' Milton
called him,[1] and he was altogether free from the lie in the soul.
Such candour involves inconsistency, for consistency is usually
the product of either obtuseness or vanity. No man was ever
more extravagantly inconsistent. Between 1653 and 1658 he
tried five systems of government — a military dictatorship; a
dictatorship with a picked parliament; a dictatorship with a
written instrument; a military dictatorship again; a quasi-
constitutional monarchy. His inconsistency extended into those
matters where politics and morals meet. He did everything —
and more — that the men he had broken had done, and repeated the very offences for which he had opposed them. He
taxed the people more highly and disregarded parliament more
shamelessly than Charles; he treated the Irish more harshly
than Strafford; he interfered with personal liberty more tyran-
nously than Laud.[2] It was easy for his enemies, both of his own

[1] *Defensio Secunda.*

[2] Cowley has a famous passage on this subject:
'What can be more extraordinary than that a person of mean birth, no fortune, no
eminent qualities of body, which have sometimes, or of mind, which have often, raised
men to the highest dignities, should have the courage to attempt, and the happiness to
succeed in, so improbable a design as the destruction of one of the most ancient and
most solid founded monarchies upon the earth? That he should have the power and
boldness to put his prince and master to an open and infamous death? To banish that
numerous and strongly allied family? To do all this under the name and wages of a
Parliament? To trample upon them, too, as he pleased, and spurn them out of doors
when he grew weary of them? To raise up a new and unheard-of monster out of their
ashes? To stifle that in its very infancy, and set up himself above all things that ever
were called sovereign in England? To oppress all his enemies by arms, and also his
friends afterwards by artifice? To serve all parties patiently for a while, and to command them victoriously at last? To overrun each corner of the three nations, and overcome with equal facility both the riches of the south and the poverty of the north? To
be feared and courted by all foreign princes, and adopted as brother to the gods of the
earth? To call together parliaments with a word of his pen and scatter them with the
breath of his mouth? To be humbly and daily petitioned that he would please to be
hired, at the rate of two millions a year, to be the master of those who had hired him
before to be their servant? To have the estates and lives of three kingdoms as much at
his disposal as was the little inheritance of his father, and to be as noble and liberal in
the spending of them? And lastly (for there is no end of all the particulars of his glory)
to bequeath all this with one word to his posterity? To die with peace at home and
triumph abroad? To be buried among kings, and with more than regal solemnity?'[3]

[3] *Works*, II, 585.

and later ages, to present him as a man of a cool and insatiable ambition, who had calculated every step and allowed no moralities to stand in his way. Such an explanation is too simple, and it is incompatible both with a great body of evidence, and with the structure of human nature; but superficially it was not without its warrant. As we have seen, he always desired to persuade rather than to compel, and his persuasion was often not far from cajolery, for to different people he would use different and contradictory pleas. If he did not lie, he sometimes acted a lie, and the charge of duplicity was not always unfounded. 'If a man is not a good, sound, honest, capable liar,' Samuel Butler has written, 'there is no truth in him,' and assuredly the truth that was in Oliver was not a pedantic fidelity to the letter.

To understand him we must remember that he was first and foremost a man of a crisis, struggling to put together again that which fate had broken. For such a task opportunism is the most necessary virtue, an eye for changing facts and a readiness to change with them. The oddest charge ever levelled against him is that of fanaticism; on the contrary he was the hammer of fanatics, one who turned unhesitatingly to the instant need of things. If the poet is right and

> to know all naked truths,
> And to envisage circumstance, all calm,
> That is the top of sovereignty —

then he was born to rule. His success in war had been largely due to the fact that he never worked by a preconceived plan, but let events shape his course for him, and he carried the same principle into statecraft. 'He could vary the methods with which he combated each evil of the day as it arose. Those who attached themselves to him in his struggle against the King, or against the different Parliaments of his time, or against the military power, were as incapable as he was capable of facing round to confront each danger as it arose. From the moment that each partial victory was won, the old friends had to be reasoned with, then discarded, and at last restrained from doing mischief.'[1] His working rule was that of Marchamont Needham; government was 'an art or artifice found out by man's wisdom and occasioned by necessity,' and not a deduction from 'principles of natural right and freedom.'[2] He had as deep a

[1] Gardiner, *Oliver Cromwell*, 283.
[2] *Mercurius Politicus*, March 28–April 2, 1657 (Th.).

contempt for the compact and riveted logic of the republican and the Leveller as for the fantasies of the Fifth Monarchy men. His mind was wholly unspeculative, and he never felt the compulsion which others have felt to weave his views into a harmonious system of thought.

It was impossible for him, being the man he was, to leave any permanent construction behind him, any more than he could leave a code of principles. He was the creature of emergencies, and he died while he was still feeling his way. England, let it be remembered, blundered and sidled into modern parliamentarism. Oliver more than any other of her historic rulers had the hard bourgeois sense of reality, and he decided that Pym's notions simply would not work. In that he was right. The spirit of the Restoration was largely negative; certain old things disappeared for ever, but it took several generations, and many false starts, to frame a system which combined expert administration with a measure of popular control. Something in the nature of a permanent civil service had first to be created.[1]

But if Oliver left nothing that endured, no more did the Vanes and Ludlows who opposed him. It may be argued that democracy, in the sense of government by the whole people, is not a system for a fallible world; in England at all events it was not achieved, and it was not seriously desired. The land had had too much of being governed, and the ordinary man wished as little as possible of the attentions of the State. In normal times whiggism, *laissez faire*, is the temper of England. In Macaulay's words, she looks for success not to 'the intermeddling of an omniscient and omnipotent State, but to the prudence and energy of the people.' So long as in the last resort she has the right of interference she will be apathetic about most of the business of government. The two centuries after Oliver's death saw a marvellous advance in her fortunes. The nation marched forward to undreamed-of wealth, to a humaner and freer social life, to triumphant heights in letters and science and thought. But this was due to the untrammelled vigour of the individual, and very little to any corporate or State-directed effort. There were governing classes but no government. The merit of successive administrations was that they left the people alone, or at the most removed obstacles. The system is best described as oligarchy or aristocracy — with a popular sanction. Burke, its prophet, goes no further in democratic principle than to admit

[1] On this point see G. M. Trevelyan, *England under Queen Anne*, II, 163, etc.

that the whole people, in any matter which deeply stirs them, is wiser than any group or individual, and that a free constitution requires that they may have some power of making their wishes felt; and his doctrine of the true character of the representative is æons removed from the kind of theory which Oliver combated. During the past century Burke's creed has been relinquished and the mechanism of politics has steadily become more plebiscitary, but it is still far from the democratic ideal of a whole people organically enlisted in the work of governing themselves. It remains in substance a fluid oligarchy, which has the task, daily becoming more difficult, of pacifying its uninstructed masters.

Oliver stands out in history as the great improviser, desperately trying expedient after expedient, and finding every tool cracking in his hand. He dies, the experiments cease, and there is a fatigued return to the old ways. But it is possible to discover in that cloudy mind an ideal of the State which he was not fated to realize, but which he did not cease to cherish. Dryden had a glimmering of this when he wrote in his memorial verses,

Poor mechanic arts in public move,
Whilst the deep secrets beyond practice go.

Like Cæsar, another man of a crisis, we must judge him not only by his actual work but by his ultimate purpose, the substance of things hoped for.

His profoundest conviction, which on occasion could make him tender even towards the zealots of the Fifth Monarchy, was that government should be in the hands of the good and wise, of those whom he thought of as the people of God. For the fundamental tenet of plebiscitary democracy, the virtue of a majority of counted heads, he had only contempt. The justification of such a method on the ground of practical convenience — its only serious justification — would have seemed to him a sin against the divine purpose. The mechanism of the ballot-box was no more to him than a child's toy. He believed in government by the general will, but he did not define that as the will of all. The essence of common democracy is quantity, and he desired quality. The mind was the man, he told parliament; with an impure mind man was no better than a beast, and a beast could not rule: the State must be controlled by the seeing eyes and the single hearts.

But to this conviction he added another, which made him a democrat of an extreme type in his ultimate ideals. His religion taught him the transcendent value of every immortal soul, even though dwelling in the humblest body. He dreamed of an aristocracy of quality where the best would govern, but all would be the best. The State he thought of as, in Kant's words, 'a kingdom of ends, where all are sovereign because all are subjects.' His zeal for education and for the faithful preaching of the Word is the practical proof of a belief which appears in broken gleams everywhere in his speeches and letters. He was no leveller to seek a monotonous, unfeatured community. He believed in diversity of station — noble, squire, yeoman, merchant and peasant — as congenial to human nature and as giving stability to society, but he would have made each class a partner in the duties and a sharer in the rights of the English polity. His toleration was based on the same principle, that variety of emphasis in faith tended to strengthen the spiritual life of a nation. Tolerance ultimately triumphed, though the cynics and sceptics taught that such differences were trivial, and therefore negligible; Oliver with a brave optimism stood for them because of their value. His one exception proved his rule, for he was chary about popery because it was of its nature to press 'from an equality to a superiority.' Liberty was his ultimate goal, the liberty of God's people, where all were free because all were servants of the same high purpose, and Milton was not wrongly inspired when he hailed him as *patriae liberator, libertatis creator, custosque idem et conservator*. But liberty to him meant not a mechanic thing measured out in statutory doses, still less a disordered license, but the joyous collaboration of those whom the truth had made free, 'a partnership,' in Burke's great words, 'in every virtue and in all perfection.'

He summoned his country to an *ascesis* which was beyond its power, and certainly beyond its desires. England turned to another creed — a minimum of government and that government a thing of judicious checks and balances. It was the doctrine of Montrose, the other great idealist of the age, that won the day. The satiety with high communal, as with high spiritual, dreams permitted men to devote themselves to their own concerns, and in the next two hundred years to build up a national life founded upon a rich and strenuous individualism, with the State guarding the ring and charging a modest entrance fee. In the quasi-democratic creed of these centuries Oliver had no part, for it was based upon quantity not quality, enumeration not evaluation, arithmetic not philosophy. He did not fail to establish democracy, as some have said. He failed in a far greater task, to create a spiritualized and dedicated nation.

But if his faith after his death went out of public view, indeed almost out of the memories of men, it did not therefore perish, for it was born of an age when the nation was emptied from vessel to vessel, and it was certain of a re-birth should time bring some new great loosening of the foundations. In a sense the seventeenth century plumed depths of human experience which later centuries have neglected.... The mind of the world changes, and it can be argued that the quality of a work of art alters with the change in the mood of the mind which appreciates it. This is even truer of political creeds. They may have been justly discarded for generations when circumstances made them meaningless, but the day comes when they cease to seem futile or irrelevant and have again a compelling power. Today the world has suffered that *discordia demens* which England knew three hundred years ago, and nations are prepared for the sheer sake of existence to sacrifice the easy freedom of more comfortable times. A corporate discipline, of which quality is the watchword, seems to many the only way of salvation. Minds surfeited with a sleek liberalism are turning to a sterner code, and across the centuries Oliver speaks to us strangely in the accents of today.

But his bequest to the world was not institutions, for his could not last, or a political faith, for his was more instinct and divination than coherent thought. It was the man himself, in his good and ill, his frailty and his strength, typical in almost every quality of his own English people, but with these qualities so magnified as to become epic and universal. He belongs to the small circle of great kings, though he never sat on a throne; like Milton's Adam.

> in himself was all his state
> More solemn than the tedious pomp that waits
> On princes.

His figure still radiates an immortal energy. 'Their distinction,' Burke has written of him and his kind, 'was not so much like men usurping power as asserting their natural place in society. Their rising was to illuminate and beautify the world. Their conquest over their competitors was by outshining them.

The hand that like a destroying angel smote the country communicated to it the force and energy under which it suffered.' [1] Though he wrought in a narrower field and influenced far less profoundly the destinies of mankind, and though in sheer intellect he was manifestly their inferior, he had the same power as Cæsar and Napoleon, the gift of forcing facts to serve him, of compelling multitudes of men into devotion or acquiescence.

But it is on that point alone that he is kin to those cyclopean architects and roadmakers, the world's conquerors. Almost without exception they were spirits of an extreme ambition, egotism and pride, holding aloof from the kindly race of men. Oliver remained humble, homely, with a ready sympathy and goodwill. For, while he was winning battles and dissolving parliaments and carrying the burdens of a people, he was living an inner life so intense that compared with it the outer world was the phantasmagoria of a dream. There is no parallel in history to this iron man of action whose consuming purpose was at all times the making of his soul.

IV

We can only see Oliver's spiritual struggles through a glass darkly. No one can enter into the secret world of another who has not himself been through the same experience, suffered the same agonies, and exulted in the same release. For a modern man that is impossible. The narrow anthropomorphic cosmogony of the seventeenth century has gone. The phrases, having become the language of technical theology, have been largely drained of meaning, and, 'pawed and fingered by unctuous hands for now two hundred years,' [2] have lost their fresh appeal. Counters have been worn and blurred by use which to Oliver were new-minted and sharply superscribed.

His creed was the Christian fundamentals — a belief in God, and in His revelation through the Scriptures, in man's fall, in Christ's death and atonement for sin, in a new life on earth made possible by grace, in the resurrection of the dead and the life everlasting — coloured by the Calvinistic interpretation. The entry into this new life, and the steadfast walking in it, were not to be achieved by any sacramental method, but by grace working in the heart of the believer. The Christian had there-

[1] *Reflections on the Revolution in France.*   [2] Froude, *Bunyan,* 34.

fore before him a pilgrimage where with God's help he and he only must find the road and brave the perils. When Oliver as a young man at Huntingdon was converted he entered upon a continuous struggle, a fight which must be fought out in the recesses of the soul by him alone.

Certain aids were provided. He had like-minded friends; divines, too, such as Owen and Goodwin and Hugh Peters,[1] and notably Sterry, who was a disciple of Whichcote, and had something of the liberality and gentleness of the Cambridge Platonists. Throughout his life he was always seeking help, and he repelled none who might give it him. In 1655 George Fox the Quaker was brought as a prisoner to Whitehall and after a long talk Oliver released him. 'Come again to my house,' he said, 'for if thou and I were but an hour a day together we should be nearer one to the other.'[2] There was above all the Bible, which in its English form was great poetry as well as divine truth, for the translators by the beauty of their rhythms had done something to moralize even the crudest tribal legends of the Old Testament. Oliver held with Calvin that 'we do not seek God anywhere else than in His Word, we do not think of Him save with His Word, we speak nothing of Him save through His Word.' But that Word was not a bare letter, but a living thing from which the meaning had to be wrested, as Jacob wrested a blessing from the angel. We see continually Bible texts fermenting and clarifying in his capacious memory.

Two other points may be noted in his approach to religion. The Renaissance exalted man, and Oliver rejected that exaltation. To him the Creator was everything, the creature nothing. He had none of Milton's humanistic, free-thinking, intellectual audacities. He could never have written as Milton did in *Tetrachordon*, that 'no ordinance, human or from heaven, can bind against the good of man,' or have assented to the view of an inward light given in *De Doctrina*. He had nothing of the proud Renaissance individualism, which indeed the doctrine of predestination made impossible. On one point only he agreed with Milton, though he might have hesitated to formulate his view; he had the belief, or rather the instinct, that there was some essential goodness in matter, some innocency in the natural

---

[1] There was more in Peters than the roystering fanatic of the royalist pamphleteers. He could be sober and impressive in his homespun way. Cf. his letter to Henry Cromwell of April 20, 1656: *Lans MSS.*, 821.

[2] Fox, *Journal* (ed. 1901), 210, 332, 333.

world, and he looked joyfully upon much from which the narrow puritan averted his eyes.

More important, this man, who faced the world with utter fearlessness, was always humble in the dust before his God. His crushing sense of sin made him abase himself before the awful purity of the sinless. The northern stock to which he belonged had an inclination to defy its deities and to try a fall with fate. The Northman worshipped Odin, but was prepared to contend with Odin. The temper of most fighting men is perhaps that of Hector's speech to Polydamas, 'We spurn augury.'

> If neither Christ nor Odin help, why then
> Still at the worst we are the sons of men.

Reverence with such in the last resort wears thin. The abbot of Clugni in the tale of Huon of Bordeaux vows that if any ill befalls Huon he will take it out of St. Peter himself. In the Sagas this pride reaches its height. 'Thorgils said: "They are all three bold men to the full; yet two of them, I think, may tell what fear is like. It is not in the same way with both; for Thormod fears God, and Grettir is so afraid of the dark that after dark he would never stir, if he had his own way; but I do not know that Thorgeir, my kinsman, is afraid of anything."' [1] Oliver had no touch of this northern bravado any more than he had the complacency of a certain type of piety which is at ease in Zion. He approached the presence of God with a manly fear.

His theology was simple, like all theologies of a crisis. He accepted the Calvinist's unbending fatalism, which instead of making its votaries apathetic moved them to a girded energy. But his unspeculative mind was careless about niceties of dogma; probably he would have come off badly in any doctrinal examination; and he never assented to the view that intellectual error was a sin to be implacably punished in this world and the next. The foundation was a personal experience, a revelation which he might have described in Luther's words — 'I do not know it and I do not understand it, but, sounding from above and ringing in my ears, I hear what is beyond the thought of man.' This revelation demanded the assent of the mind, but, above all, the submission of the will. God manifested Himself as creator, reconciler and redeemer, and while the horror of sin was intensified its burden was removed. Against the darkness of sin shone the light of grace, and it is upon grace that he dwells

[1] *Grettis Saga*, c. 51.

most often, grace the only link between the worlds of God and of man. The state of salvation into which the soul entered was not a continuation of the old life on a higher plane, but a wholly different life. The kingdom of God was an *ingressio*, the advent of a new thing. The soul was washed and transformed through the mystery of the atonement, and thereafter breathed a different air. The legalism — that hardy English growth — which so narrowed puritan theology, meant nothing to Oliver. He talks often of 'covenants,' but he means promises, not bargains. No fear of future punishment was the reason of his conversion, but a passion for purity and a horror of evil. Like Dante's Farinata degli Uberti he 'entertained great scorn of Hell.'

The majesty and transcendence of God is the rock of his faith, a majesty so awful that without grace man must be shrivelled like a leaf in its burning light. Oliver is what Novalis called Spinoza, a *Gott-betrunkener Mann*. He is stupefied by the wonders of the Almighty, and is lost in an abasement of worship. It is a mood which is strange to the bustling religiosity of later times and the Mr. Brisks and Mr. Talkatives of our casual creeds, but it is a mood which must always appear in a time of crisis. The single purpose of those who share it is to bring the will into subjection to the divine will; to attain, in the words of Clerk Maxwell, 'an abandonment of wilfulness without extinction of will, but rather by means of a great development of will, whereby, instead of being consciously free and really in subjection to unknown laws, it becomes consciously acting by law, and really free from the interference of unrecognized laws.'

In front of this background of eternal Omnipotence stood the figure of Christ, the revelation of the love and the fatherhood of God, the God-man, the world's redeemer. In his contemplation of Christ awe is mingled with a personal devotion such as is revealed in Pascal's fragment, the *Mystère de Jésus*. Through Christ his relation to God became that of a son, and sometimes he writes of the mysteries of faith as he writes to his children, with a familiar human affection:

> Love argueth in this wise: What a Christ have I; what a Father in and through Him! What a name hath my Father; merciful, gracious, long-suffering, abundant in goodness and truth; forgiving iniquity, transgression and sin! What a nature hath my Father! He is Love — free in it, unchangeable, infinite. What a Covenant between Him and Christ, for all the seed, for everyone, wherein He undertakes all, and the poor soul nothing.[1]

[1] *L. and S.*, II, 258-59.

Had he had the poet's gift he might have written something akin to Henry Vaughan's celestial nursery rhymes.

Such a faith must make its possessor a mystic, like St. Paul, however firm his hold may be on concrete realities. For Oliver there was a secret world of the soul compared to which the world of sense was only a shadow. His overt seasons of worship, to borrow an image of Newman's, were like little islands in a sea which were really the peaks of a vast submarine range of mountains. He was always in a listening attitude, waiting for the divine whisper. Long hours of meditation and prayer were essential for his spirit lest the *mystica catena* should snap. They were necessary to help him to read the will of God in the events which God ordained, the judgments and the providences, for he did not forget Christ's words about the Tower of Siloam. They gave him illumination and assurance, but at many periods of his life they tortured him, when he was conscious of being over-weighted with worldly cares or remorseful for some backsliding in conduct. For the visions of the mystic are sublimations of his current thoughts, conditioned by his nature and sensuous experience. Sometimes the divine communion was clouded and he turned with dull eyes to the tasks of life; but at other times he seemed to descend from the mount of vision, 'armed with no less than the terrors and decrees of the Almighty Himself.' [1]

From his agonies and his exaltations he emerged with a great charity towards men, and something nobler than humanism. The world with all its suffering and sinning mortals was God's world, which He had created and redeemed, and he looked upon it with a patient kindness. Of such a creed as his, and of such a temperament, quietism could not be the fruit. He must be up and doing, for he was called upon to assist in the building of the City of God. There was no security, no hope of laying aside the task. A man all his days must be busy making his soul, and forcing the world to conform to the heavenly will. Oliver had long thoughts of a little ease at last, of an old age like a Lapland

---

[1] It is an error, I think, to regard this inner life, as some have done, as involving a schism in his nature, the condition which is known to psychologists as dissociated personalities. In him there was no fissure between the religious consciousness and his sense of the realities of the outer world. His power over the latter was most manifest, when the former was most alert. The seasons when his spiritual life was deadened were the occasions when he fumbled in practical ways; conversely, there were times when his bewilderment as to his next step parched the springs of inner consolation. There was no strife or sedition between the two domains of his soul, for they were organically one.

night, when he could return to a simple life of family joys and
country peace.[1] But he resolutely put them aside, for he knew
that he had entered upon a war in which there was no dis-
charge, and that ease was not for him on this side the grave.
He must be content with an occasional vision, such as the shep-
herds of the Delectable Mountains gave to the pilgrims from
the high hill called Clear. 'Our rest we expect elsewhere; that
will be durable.'

[1] This longing for rest was shared by many in that age. Cf. Sir Francis Russell to
Henry Cromwell: 'When you are weary of this world do but send to me and we will
turn monks together, for I profess I do hope for nothing more than a retirement; the
very thought of such a kind of life puts off all my melancholy. Sir John Reynolds will
bear us company, I suppose, for he talks to me of such a kind of thing.' *Lans MSS.*, 821.

Chapter V

THE END
(1658)

As on a voyage, when your ship has moored off shore, if you go on land to get fresh water, you may pick up as an extra on your way a small mussel or a little fish. But you have to keep your attention fixed on the ship, and turn round frequently for fear that the captain should call; and if he calls, you must give up all these.... So it is also in life. If there be given you, instead of a little fish or a small mussel, a little wife or a small child, there will be no objection. But if the captain calls, give up all that and run to the ship, without even turning to look back. And if you are an old man, never even get far away from the ship, for fear that when He calls you may be missing.

EPICTETUS, *Enchiridion.*

The possession of the earth to its last limits, the kingdoms of the world can serve me for nothing. Better it is for me to die in sight of Jesus Christ than to reign over the confines of earth.... The hour of my birth is drawing near.

IGNATIUS, *Epistle to the Romans.*

THE summer of 1658 was a cruel season in England. The spring had been backward, and for the first six months of the year the wind blew steadily from the north. In June came hail-storms as icy as winter. In the previous year a malignant form of influenza had raged through the land in spite of days of prayer and fasting, and in April it returned, and again in August. The news of foreign victories cheered the nation, but only for a moment; the popular mind was depressed and expectant of calamity. Portents were not lacking. In June a great whale came up the Thames and was killed at Greenwich 'after a horrid groan.' [1]

In July Oliver left Whitehall for Hampton Court, where his daughter Elizabeth Claypole lay gravely ill. It had been a melancholy year for his household. 'We have been a family of much sorrow all this summer,' Henry wrote from Ireland, 'and therefore we deserve not the envy of the world.' [2] In February Frances lost her husband, Robert Rich, after three months of marriage, and in May Warwick followed his grandson. Oliver's own health had been slowly worsening. His old trouble, the stone, had returned, and an attack of gout prevented him from taking the exercise necessary for one of his habit of body. The

[1] It is described by Evelyn, *Diary*, June 3, 1658, and referred to in Dryden's memorial verses on Cromwell. See also Audrey, *Miscellanies*, 41.

[2] *Lans MSS.*, 823.

doctors, in their endeavour to cure the gout, seem to have used remedies which were hurtful to his constitution.[1] A month earlier he had had another carriage accident, when Richard's coach, in which he was riding, was knocked to pieces.[2] At the back of all, too, was his predisposition to fits of ague, increased by weariness of body, family anxieties, and the inclement weather.

Elizabeth Claypole had made a plan that summer to visit her brother Henry in Ireland,[3] but troubles came thick upon her and the loss of her youngest son was followed by the revival of an old internal malady. Oliver never left her, the meetings of Council were held at Hampton Court, and there he received foreign ambassadors. The whole family, except Henry and Bridget Fleetwood, was gathered round the sick-bed, the girl Frances in her new widow's weeds, Richard summoned from Bath, and the Fauconbergs from a semi-royal progress in Yorkshire. In the first days of August she rallied a little, and her father slept the first time for many days; but at three o'clock in the morning of August 6 she died.

Oliver, distracted with grief, became himself very ill, and for five days lay abed with a malady which puzzled his physicians, a sickness perhaps as much of the mind as of the body.[4] He withdrew into the shadowy places of the spirit, and that inner world, which the press of terrestrial cares had lately occluded from him, now became the one reality. The intricate round of duties, the glory of his victories, the glittering embassies from the kings of the earth, the cabals of his enemies and the doubts of his friends, his dreams for England and Europe, all fell away to an infinite distance, and he was left face to face with his soul. He had lost the dearest thing in life. 'Poor Bettie' now knew the Lord's mercies which he had so often besought for her, but they were far from him. In those tortured days he found comfort at last in the fourth chapter of the Epistle to the Philippians, the scripture which he said had saved his life when his eldest son died long ago at school. 'Reading on to the thirteenth verse where Paul saith, "I can do all things through Christ that

[1] Bate, who made a post-mortem examination, found most of the organs in a diseased condition. *Elenchus Motuum Nuperorum*, Pt. II, 236. Oliver had been treated in 1655 for vesical calculus by the royalist physician Moleyns.

[2] Vaughan, *Protectorate*, II, 468.   [3] Thurloe, VII, 94.

[4] The authorities for Oliver's last days are Thurloe, VII, 320, etc.; Bate, *Elenchus Motuum Nuperorum* (1663); *A Collection of Passages concerning... Cromwell in the Time of his Sickness, by a Groom of the Bedchamber* (Harvey) 1659 (Th.); Ludlow, II, 42, etc.; *C. P.*, III, 161; *Cromwelliana*, 174; Baillie, III, 425; Fox, *Journal* (ed. 1901), 440.

strengtheneth me," then faith began to work, and his heart to feel support and comfort, saying thus to himself, "He that was Paul's Christ is my Christ too," and so drew water out of the well of salvation.'

By August 17 he had mended a little, and that day he was permitted to be out of doors for an hour, but the doctors were still uneasy, especially Bate, who had been with him in Scotland, and remembered his illness there. The weather in mid-August was tempestuous, and on the 18th came that storm from the south-west which destroyed John Evelyn's orchards. Oliver insisted on taking the air abroad, a grey and haggard ghost in the midst of his escort. On the 20th George Fox arrived with a petition. It was their third meeting, but on the last occasion Oliver had been in the mood to chaff the solemn Quaker on his spiritual complacency, and Fox had withdrawn offended and perplexed. Now his plea was heard and he was bidden come again on the morrow. 'Before I came to him,' he wrote, 'as he rode at the head of his life-guards, I saw and felt a waft of death go forth against him; and when I came to him he looked like a dead man.'

Next day, Saturday the 21st, when Fox appeared he was not admitted, for Oliver was sick again. The low fever of the past week had increased to what the medical science of the day called a bastard tertian ague, accompanied by fainting fits and cold sweats. His five physicians [1] had a consultation, and prescribed a few days quiet and then a change of air. Having for the moment won spiritual peace he was in a happier mood, and confident of his recovery. 'I shall not die this bout,' he told his wife; 'I am sure on't.' He bade his doctors not look so melancholy, but deal with him as they would with a serving man. His confidence communicated itself to his chaplains, and Thomas Goodwin prayed not for his life but for speed in his convalescence.

On Tuesday the 24th he was taken to Whitehall, partly for the change of air and partly for the greater ease in treatment which residence in the capital afforded. It was intended to remove him to St. James's as soon as it was made ready, for that palace, with a green hill behind it and a deer park in front, was at once rural and metropolitan. In Whitehall the alternate heats and chills grew more violent, and it was clear that he was desperately ill.

[1] For Oliver's doctors see a paper in the *Proceedings of the Royal Society of Medicine*, May, 1931.

With the decline of his vital power came a dreadful confusion of spirit. All over England men were on their knees for him; in an adjoining chamber Owen and Goodwin and Sterry made continuous supplication; but in the sick-room, superheated and airless, Oliver found no comfort in prayer. He was a naked soul, shivering on the brink of eternity, and fighting again the spiritual battles of his youth. His sins brooded over him like birds of night — his passion and injustice, his duplicities, his hours of pride, his absorption in the things of time, his forgetfulness of God. Every twinge of conscience in his past life returned as an agony. The dualism which is inevitable in the practical mystic, the desire both to be unspotted by the world and to overcome and order the world, and which at normal times he construed as the will of God, seemed now to have been deadly sin. He had forgotten his assurance of recovery, for recovery meant nothing to him; what he clutched at, and lost, and clutched at again was the promise of redemption and eternal life. He babbled much in his fever, repeating mechanically the formulas of his creed, but without conviction, almost without hope. Thrice he was heard to murmur, 'It is a fearful thing to fall into the hands of the living God.' Once he demanded of a chaplain, 'Tell me, is it possible to fall from grace?' 'It is not possible,' was the answer. 'Then I am safe,' he cried, 'for I know that I was once in grace.'

On Friday the 27th Thurloe wrote to Henry that his fears were more than his hopes. During the Saturday and Sunday the sick man was often unconscious. But by the Monday his mind was clearer, and from some profound deeps of the spirit he had received peace. 'The Lord hath filled me,' he murmured, 'with as much assurance of His pardon and His love as my soul can hold.' And again, 'I am the poorest wretch that lives, but I love God, or rather am beloved of God.... I am more than a conqueror through Christ that strengtheneth me.' He had escaped from Doubting Castle to the Land of Beulah.

On Monday the 30th came the greatest storm that England had known for a hundred years. The wind mowed swathes through forests and wrecked many a noble avenue, swept the sheaves from the harvest fields, sank a multitude of ships, stripped dwellings of roofs and chimneys, and tumbled down church steeples. Ludlow, coming up that morning from Essex, could not start because of the gale, and in the afternoon only got as far as Epping. The fury of the hurricane did not stir the stagnant air in the sick-room, but its rumour filled Whitehall with strange voices. Thurloe, quick to detect signs of returning clearness in his master, seized the occasion to get the business of the succession settled. The revised constitution permitted the Protector to name his successor, and this Oliver had done before his second installation, in a letter addressed to the secretary, which he had kept secret. When he first fell ill at Hampton Court a messenger had been dispatched to London to fetch the letter, but it had gone astray. That Monday night Thurloe raised the question, and Oliver named his eldest son. But he was feeble and dazed, and there was no witness but the secretary. Thurloe could only wait his chance for a more formal nomination.

Next day, the 31st, the fever had ebbed and Oliver for a moment came back to the world. Once again he could concern himself with the things of sense and time. He was told that Ludlow was in town and sent Fleetwood to see what mischief he was after; the old republican replied that he had come to visit his mother-in-law, and sent a kindly message to Oliver that he wished him a good recovery. That night the Protector's introverted mood had passed, for his prayer was not for himself, but for his country and for the people of God. One present recorded this last testament:

> Lord, though I am a miserable and wretched creature, I am in covenant with Thee through grace, and I may, I will, come to Thee for Thy people. Thou hast made me, though very unworthy, a mean instrument to do them some good and Thee service; and many of them have set too high a value upon me, though others wish and would be glad of my death. Lord, however Thou dost dispose of me, continue and go on to do good for them. Give them consistency of judgment, one heart, and mutual love, and go on to deliver them, and with the work of reformation, and make the name of Christ glorious in the world. Teach those who look too much on Thy instruments to depend more upon Thyself. Pardon such as desire to trample upon the dust of a poor worm, for they are Thy people too. And pardon the folly of this short prayer, even for Jesus Christ's sake, and give me a good night if it be Thy pleasure.

On the Wednesday the improvement continued. He was very weak, but the fever had gone, and Monk's correspondent wrote that he was out of danger. But on Thursday it was plain that he was dying, dying in peace and with full clearness of mind. Now, if ever, he must formally appoint his successor, and that evening in the presence of Thurloe and Goodwin and several members of Council he nominated Richard. It was his last dealings with the world. All night he was restless and in pain, while his great bodily strength disintegrated, but his soul was at rest. He was heard to mutter often, 'God is good, indeed He is,' with a thrill of joy in his voice. Once he said, 'I would be willing to live to be further serviceable to God and His people.... But my work is done.... God will be with His people.' He was offered a sleeping-draught, but declined it. 'It is not my design to drink or to sleep, but my design is to make what haste I can to be gone.' Towards morning he spoke 'some exceeding self-debasing words annihilating and judging himself,' but he murmured also broken texts 'implying much consolation and peace.'

About dawn on Friday, September 3, he fell into a coma, and did not speak again. It was the anniversary of the day when he had arrived at Drogheda, the day when he had opened his first parliament as Protector. On that day he had seen the Scots break on the hillside at Dunbar, and the hopes of Charles shattered among the Severn cornfields. There was a concourse of people at the palace gate, no very large gathering, for the news of his condition had not gone abroad, and the watchers were mainly humble well-wishers who prayed for him.... Between three and four in the afternoon a whisper ran from the sick-room to the ante-chamber, and thence to the waiting crowd and the London streets, and the world knew that Oliver was dead.

For a little there fell a stillness like that which follows a landslip. The Council accepted Richard as his father's successor, and army and city docilely concurred. Next day the heralds proclaimed the new Lord Protector at the customary places amid the acclamations of the populace and the volleys of the troops. England went into ceremonial mourning, as did the principal courts of Europe. Couriers spurred north and west, and George Monk had the news on the 8th and Henry Cromwell on the 10th. 'There is not a dog that wags his tongue,' Thurloe wrote to the latter, 'so great a calm are we in.' But beneath the surface there was soon a furious activity. Before many days had passed the army chiefs had begun their cabals, the old malcontents of the Long Parliament were flocking to town, and the Fifth Monarchy men were whipping up their followers. Charles at Hoogstraaten, busy courting the young Henrietta of Orange, received the breathless Stephen Fox with the news that it had 'pleased God out of His infinite goodness to do that which He would not allow any man the honour of doing.' Amsterdam made high holiday to celebrate the death of Holland's master, and the children danced in the streets. Everywhere what Oliver had exiled, or suppressed, or curbed raised its head and drew breath in hope.

For his family and his intimates the sun had gone out of the sky, and they could only grope and stumble. The little household in Whitehall, still a royal family in name, huddled together, like bewildered children who had been led to a mountaintop and left alone. Humble and pious men throughout the land, many of whom had been long estranged from Oliver, now remembered with a pang 'those ejaculatory breathings of his soul for the blessing of love and union among the servants of God, particularly praying for those that were angry with him.' Those who had been close to him and had shared in his dreams knew that the light had departed from their lives. Sterry consoled his weeping congregation with the thought that 'that blessed holy spirit was with Christ at the right hand of the Father, there to intercede for us and to be mindful of us.' Thurloe, worn to a shadow with toil and care, was a stricken man. 'I am not able to speak or write, this stroke is so sore.... I can do nothing but put my mouth in the dust and say It is the Lord.'

But to most men after the first shock came a half-ashamed sense of relief. They had lost their protector, but also their mentor. They had been dragged up to unfamiliar heights, and they were weary of the rarefied air. Sensible folk like Broghill's sister, Lady Ranelagh, reflected that 'we shall learn to value him more by missing him than we did when we enjoyed him,' but there was a hint of relief in their moralizings. The bow must relax, for it had been strung too tight. The satiety with high endeavour which led to the Restoration was now manifest. Already a new realism was being born, a prosaic and critical spirit —

> Thy Wars brought nothing about,
> Thy Lovers were all untrue.
> 'Tis well an Old Age is out,
> And time to begin a New.

Yet even the dullest understood that a great thing had gone from the world. Men according to their natures mourned or rejoiced, feared or hoped, but with a strange sense of dislocation and with something like awe. The poets abounded in panegyrics, of which the motive can scarcely have been mercenary — Edmund Waller, the dead man's cousin; young Thomas Sprat who was one day to be a bishop; John Dryden, kinsman and secretary to the chamberlain, Sir Gilbert Pickering; Andrew Marvell, who brought to the task a warm and judicious affection. But it was reserved for an impenitent royalist to write the most fitting epitaph. Abraham Cowley, studying physic in Kent and preparing for a flight to France, was rumoured to have followed the fashion and composed memorial verses now lost to us. But he was also setting down, in prose finer than his rhymed conceits, his thoughts of this man who had outraged all his sanctities. Though he puts the words into the mouth of a dark angel and leaves Oliver no single rag of virtue, he is poet enough to realize how great a thing had overshadowed his age. A name, he wrote, 'not to be extinguished but with the whole world, which, as it is now too little for his praise, so might have been too little for his conquests, if the short time of his human life could have been stretched out to the extent of his immortal designs.'

INDEX

INDEX

Sterry, Peter, 424, 432, 440, 443
Steward, Sir Thomas, 36, 41, 64
Steward, William, 35
Stewart, Lady, of Allenton, 317
Stirling, 322, 397
Stonyhurst, 225
Stow-in-the-Wold, 175, 181
Strachan, Colonel Archibald, 295, 298, 300, 303, 312, 313
Strafford, Thomas Wentworth, first Earl of, 22, 23, 49, 52–54, 57–62, 65, 68, 70, 74–81, 86, 91, 95, 289
Strickland, Walter, 361
Strode, William, 56, 71, 86
Stuart, Lord Bernard, 116
Suarez, 37
Suckling, Sir John, 85
Sulby Hedges, 170
Sussex, Lady, 91
Swallow, Robert, 126
Sweden, relations with, 364, 402–404
Swift, Jonathan, 388
Sydenham, Colonel William, 375, 384, 385

Tadcaster, 141, 147
Taney, Thomas, 369
Tate, Zouch, 158, 159, 160
Tattershall, 30
Taunton, 164
Taylor, Jeremy, 210, 378
Temple, Sir Purbeck, 247
Tenby, 217
Thornhaugh, Colonel, 226
Thorpe, Francis, 378
Thurloe, John, 370, 374, 375, 379, 382, 384, 387, 388, 390, 393, 394, 396, 407, 412, 417, 419, 424, 440–43
Tilly, 46, 68, 170, 286
Tippermuir, battle of, 165
Tockwith, 145
Tomlinson, Colonel, 253
Torrington, 175
Traherne, Thomas, 19, 28
Trapnell, Anna, 370
Trent, river, 133–35
Trim, 282
Tromp, Admiral van, 388
Tunis, 406, 410
Turenne, 408
Turin, 405, 406
Turner, Sir James, 223, 226

Turnham Green, 121
Tuscany, Grand Duke of, 406
Tusser, Thomas, 330
Tweed, river, 136

Urry (or Hurry), Sir John, 142, 145
Ussher, Archbishop, 38, 78, 288, 378
Uxbridge, negotiations of, 161, 207

Valentine, Benjamin, 50, 56
Van Dyck, Sir Anthony, 71
Vane, Sir Henry, the elder, 70
Vane, Sir Henry, the younger, 64, 72, 75, 77, 94, 95, 130, 151, 157, 182, 189, 190, 212, 213, 233–35, 243, 249, 262, 302, 337, 341–45, 354, 380, 418
Vaudois. See Waldenses
Vaughan, Henry, 28
Venables, Colonel, 413
Venner, Thomas, 382
Vermuyden, Cornelius, 65
Verney, Sir Edmund, 102, 106 n., 118
Verney, Sir Edmund, the younger, 278, 280
Virginia, 337, 412

Wakefield, 133
Waldenses, the, 405, 406
Walker, Clement, 277
Walker, Sir Edward, 307
Wall, Colonel, 278
Wallenstein, 48, 56, 99
Waller, Edmund, 71, 73, 82, 361, 384, 408, 444
Waller, Sir William, 64, 71, 93, 102, 103, 110, 111, 123, 129, 130, 136, 137, 139, 140, 153, 154, 155, 161, 162, 163, 182, 193, 194
Wallingford, 121
Walsingham, Sir Francis, 375
Ward, Samuel, 38
Warren, Colonel, 278
Warwick, 113, 116
Warwick, Sir Philip, 41, 42, 71, 73, 79, 83, 84, 107, 116, 122, 255, 423
Warwick, Robert Rich, second Earl of, 64, 76, 102, 113, 394, 411, 437
Washington, Colonel, 117
Waterford, 283, 284, 286, 287
Wauton (or Walton), Colonel Valentine, 73, 96, 126, 149